# Lecture Notes in Business Information Processing

529

Series Editors

Wil van der Aalst, *RWTH Aachen University, Aachen, Germany*
Sudha Ram, *University of Arizona, Tucson, AZ, USA*
Michael Rosemann, *Queensland University of Technology, Brisbane, QLD, Australia*
Clemens Szyperski, *Microsoft Research, Redmond, WA, USA*
Giancarlo Guizzardi, *University of Twente, Enschede, The Netherlands*

LNBIP reports state-of-the-art results in areas related to business information systems and industrial application software development – timely, at a high level, and in both printed and electronic form.

The type of material published includes

- Proceedings (published in time for the respective event)
- Postproceedings (consisting of thoroughly revised and/or extended final papers)
- Other edited monographs (such as, for example, project reports or invited volumes)
- Tutorials (coherently integrated collections of lectures given at advanced courses, seminars, schools, etc.)
- Award-winning or exceptional theses

LNBIP is abstracted/indexed in DBLP, EI and Scopus. LNBIP volumes are also submitted for the inclusion in ISI Proceedings.

Václav Řepa · Raimundas Matulevičius ·
Emanuele Laurenzi
Editors

# Perspectives in Business Informatics Research

23rd International Conference
on Business Informatics Research, BIR 2024
Prague, Czech Republic, September 11–13, 2024
Proceedings

*Editors*
Václav Řepa
Prague University of Economics and Business
Prague, Czech Republic

Raimundas Matulevičius
University of Tartu
Tartu, Estonia

Emanuele Laurenzi
FHNW University of Applied Sciences
and Arts Northwestern Switzerland
Olten, Switzerland

ISSN 1865-1348　　　　　ISSN 1865-1356 (electronic)
Lecture Notes in Business Information Processing
ISBN 978-3-031-71332-3　　ISBN 978-3-031-71333-0 (eBook)
https://doi.org/10.1007/978-3-031-71333-0

© The Editor(s) (if applicable) and The Author(s), under exclusive license
to Springer Nature Switzerland AG 2024

This work is subject to copyright. All rights are solely and exclusively licensed by the Publisher, whether the whole or part of the material is concerned, specifically the rights of translation, reprinting, reuse of illustrations, recitation, broadcasting, reproduction on microfilms or in any other physical way, and transmission or information storage and retrieval, electronic adaptation, computer software, or by similar or dissimilar methodology now known or hereafter developed.
The use of general descriptive names, registered names, trademarks, service marks, etc. in this publication does not imply, even in the absence of a specific statement, that such names are exempt from the relevant protective laws and regulations and therefore free for general use.
The publisher, the authors and the editors are safe to assume that the advice and information in this book are believed to be true and accurate at the date of publication. Neither the publisher nor the authors or the editors give a warranty, expressed or implied, with respect to the material contained herein or for any errors or omissions that may have been made. The publisher remains neutral with regard to jurisdictional claims in published maps and institutional affiliations.

This Springer imprint is published by the registered company Springer Nature Switzerland AG
The registered company address is: Gewerbestrasse 11, 6330 Cham, Switzerland

If disposing of this product, please recycle the paper.

# Preface

Business Informatics is concerned with using digital solutions and technologies to support and improve the efficiency and effectiveness of complex organisations. In a way, Business Informatics stands at the intersection of many disciplines, including computer science, social sciences, data science, business administration, and many more. Over the years, the International Conference on Perspectives in Business Informatics Research (BIR) has established itself as a prominent venue for researchers from these disciplines to meet.

The 23rd edition of the conference (BIR 2024) was organised by the Prague University of Economics and Business and was held from September 11–13, 2024, in Prague, Czech Republic. This was the second edition to be held in Prague: eight years earlier, BIR 2016 was the first BIR conference outside the Baltic Sea region. The founder of the BIR conference series, Stanislaw Wrycza, argued for this exception because of the deep cultural and historical ties between the Bohemian (Czech) region and the Baltic countries, so Prague could also be considered a Baltic city.

The central theme of BIR 2024 was "Artificial Intelligence (AI) in Business Informatics: Opportunities and Challenges". The conference received 43 submissions from 12 countries. A rigorous single-blind reviewing process was adopted as usual for any BIR edition. The 2024 Program Committee had 52 reviewers coming from 17 countries. At least three reviewers reviewed each paper. Out of the 43 papers, the Program Committee accepted 15 papers as full papers and one as a short paper. All the accepted papers were then presented at the conference. The acceptance rate was 37%. The papers in these proceedings cover different aspects of the discipline, focusing mainly on subdomains such as AI opportunities and challenges, AI applications and use cases in business, Business intelligence, Business and information systems development, and Knowledge and traceability management.

The conference invited two keynote presenters. Jan Romportl, an independent AI researcher, delivered the first one. The speech, titled "Democratization of AI Tools: Bridging the Gap between Business Informatics and Accessible AI Innovation", provided valuable insights for academics and practitioners interested in the intersection of AI and business informatics, offering a comprehensive overview of the current state and future directions of AI tools in business innovation.

Giancarlo Guizzardi, a Professor at the University of Twente, the Netherlands, delivered the second keynote speech. The talk, entitled "A Meaningful Road to Explanation", discussed the strong relationship between semantics, ontology, and explanation under specific interpretations and presented a concept of explanation called Ontological Unpacking, which aims to explain symbolic domain descriptions such as conceptual models, knowledge graphs, and logical specifications. The relationship between ontological unpacking and other forms of explanation in philosophy, science, and artificial intelligence was also discussed.

Following the conference tradition, the first day was dedicated to satellite events: workshops and the doctoral consortium. The Doctoral Symposium, chaired by Filip Vencovský from the Prague University of Economics and Business and Björn Johansson from Linköping University, allowed young researchers to discuss their ideas with the BIR community. Anne Gutschmidt from the University of Rostock and Ana-Maria Ghiran from the University of Cluj-Napoca were the chairs for this year's workshops. Three workshops were organised: the 9th Workshop on Managed Complexity (ManComp 2024), the 2nd Workshop on Domain-specific Modeling Methods and Tools - OMiLAB Nodes Experience & Knowledge Exchange (OMiLAB-KNOW 2024), and the 14th Workshop on Business and IT Alignment (BITA 2024).

We want to thank Marite Kirikova and the BIR Steering Committee members for their continued support and guidance during the conference organisation. We want to thank all the authors who submitted their papers and the Program Committee members who provided timely reviews. We also thank the Springer team for the prompt support in producing these BIR 2024 proceedings. We are grateful for their continued partnership with BIR, an important factor in the conference's longevity.

Last but not least, the Prague University of Economics and Business local team, led by Oleg Svatoš, Veronika Kostrouchová, and Dana Malcová, deserves sincere thanks for organising the event and supporting all conference participants.

July 2024

Václav Řepa
Raimundas Matulevičius
Emanuele Laurenzi

# Organization

## General Chair

Václav Řepa                     Prague University of Economics and Business, Czech Republic

## Program Committee Chairs

Raimundas Matulevičius          University of Tartu, Estonia
Emanuele Laurenzi               FHNW, Switzerland

## Steering Committee

Mārīte Kirikova (Chair)         Riga Technical University, Latvia
Björn Johansson (Co-chair)      Linkoping University, Sweden
Kurt Sandkuhl                   University of Rostock, Germany
Robert Buchmann                 University of Cluj-Napoca, Romania
Rimantas Butleris               Kaunas Technical University, Lithuania
Sven Carlsson                   Lund University, Sweden
Peter Forbrig                   University of Rostock, Germany
Dimitris Karagiannis            University of Vienna, Austria
Andrzej Kobyliński              Warsaw School of Economics, Poland
Raimundas Matulevičius          University of Tartu, Estonia
Lina Nemuraitė                  Kaunas Technical University, Lithuania
Jyrki Nummenmaa                 University of Tampere, Finland
Malgorzata Pańkowska            University of Economics, Katowice, Poland
Andrea Polini                   University of Camerino, Italy
Václav Řepa                     Prague University of Economics and Business, Czech Republic
Janis Stirna                    Stockholm University, Sweden
Benkt Wangler                   University of Skövde, Sweden

## Program Committee

| | |
|---|---|
| Gundars Alksnis | Riga Technical University, Latvia |
| Said Assar | Institut Mines-Télécom Business School, France |
| Per Backlund | University of Skövde, Sweden |
| Peter Bellström | Karlstad University, Sweden |
| Catalin Boja | Bucharest Academy of Economic Studies, Romania |
| Dominik Bork | TU Wien, Austria |
| Tomáš Bruckner | Prague University of Economics and Business, Czech Republic |
| Robert Andrei Buchmann | Babeș-Bolyai University of Cluj Napoca, Romania |
| Chiara Di Francescomarino | University of Trento, Italy |
| Antinisca Di Marco | University of L'Aquila, Italy |
| Peter Forbrig | University of Rostock, Germany |
| Ana-Maria Ghiran | Babeș-Bolyai University of Cluj-Napoca, Romania |
| Jānis Grabis | Riga Technical University, Latvia |
| Anne Gutschmidt | University of Rostock, Germany |
| Knut Hinkelmann | FHNW University of Applied Sciences and Arts Northwestern Switzerland, Switzerland |
| Mubashar Iqbal | University of Tartu, Estonia |
| Amin Jalali | Stockholm University, Sweden |
| Dimitris Karagiannis | University of Vienna, Austria |
| Michael Alexander Kaufmann | Lucerne University of Applied Sciences and Arts, Switzerland |
| Marite Kirikova | Riga Technical University, Latvia |
| Emanuele Laurenzi | University of Applied Sciences and Arts Northwestern Switzerland, Switzerland |
| Michael Le Duc | Mälardalen University, Sweden |
| Moonkun Lee | Chonbuk National University, South Korea |
| Francisco J. Lopez-Pellicer | University of Zaragoza, Spain |
| Ginta Majore | Vidzeme University of Applied Sciences, Latvia |
| Andreas Martin | FHNW University of Applied Sciences Northwestern Switzerland, Switzerland |
| Raimundas Matulevičius | University of Tartu, Estonia |
| Andrea Morichetta | University of Camerino, Italy |
| Anastasija Nikiforova | University of Tartu, Estonia |
| Jacob Nørbjerg | Copenhagen Business School, Denmark |
| Jyrki Nummenmaa | Tampere University, Finland |
| Victoria Paulsson | Linköping University, Sweden |

| | |
|---|---|
| Jens Myrup Pedersen | Aalborg University, Denmark |
| Pierluigi Plebani | Politecnico di Milano, Italy |
| Paul Pocatilu | Bucharest University of Economic Studies, Romania |
| Andrea Polini | University of Camerino, Italy |
| Barbara Re | University of Camerino, Italy |
| Ben Roelens | Open Universiteit, Netherlands |
| Christian Sacarea | Babeș-Bolyai University, Romania |
| Kurt Sandkuhl | University of Rostock, Germany |
| Hanlie Smuts | University of Pretoria, South Africa |
| Oleg Svatoš | Prague University of Economics and Business, Czech Republic |
| Ann Svensson | University West, Sweden |
| Torben Tambo | Aarhus University, Denmark |
| Pedro Valderas | Universitat Politècnica de València, Spain |
| Filip Vencovský | Prague University of Economics and Business, Czech Republic |
| Gianluigi Viscusi | Linköping University, Sweden |
| Anna Wingkvist | Linnaeus University, Sweden |
| Hans-Frieder Witschel | FHNW University of Applied Sciences and Arts Northwestern Switzerland, Switzerland |
| Endri Xhina | University of Tirana, Albania |
| Jelena Zdravkovic | Stockholm University, Sweden |
| Alfred Zimmermann | Reutlingen University, Germany |

## Workshops Co-chairs

| | |
|---|---|
| Anne Gutschmidt | University of Rostock, Germany |
| Ana-Maria Ghiran | University of Cluj-Napoca, Romania |

## Doctoral Consortium Co-chairs

| | |
|---|---|
| Bjorn Johansson | Linköping University, Sweden |
| Filip Vencovský | Prague University of Economic and Business, Czech Republic |

## Organization Chair

Oleg Svatoš                     Prague University of Economics and Business, Czech Republic

## Organization Committee

Veronika Kostrouchová          Prague University of Economics and Business, Czech Republic
Dana Malcová                    Prague University of Economics and Business, Czech Republic

# Keynotes

# Democratization of AI Tools: Bridging the Gap between Business Informatics and Accessible AI Innovation

Jan Romportl

Elin.ai

In recent years, the landscape of business informatics and artificial intelligence (AI) has undergone a significant transformation, particularly in the context of democratizing advanced AI tools for businesses. This keynote presentation delves into the evolution of AI integration within business processes, highlighting the pivotal shift from the necessity of in-house expert data science teams to the accessible, cost-effective implementation of Foundation Models, including Large Language Models (LLMs) and diffusion models. The talk underscores the profound impact of the rapid development of the AI ecosystem, cloud tools, ML/LLM libraries, and no-code/low-code platforms on lowering the entry barriers for companies aiming to innovate within the realms of business intelligence (BI), data science, and machine learning (ML).

The presentation explores the paradigm shift in software engineering, propelled by AI-driven tools like GitHub Copilot, which poses both a challenge and an opportunity for the software development profession. This technological evolution not only necessitates a transformation in the skill set and roles of software engineers but also significantly impacts the cost dynamics and availability of skilled professionals. The democratization of AI tools, as discussed, is not merely a technological advancement but a catalyst for organizational innovation, enabling companies to swiftly develop and deploy AI-driven products and services by leveraging existing AI technologies and benefiting from reduced human capital expenses. In line with the main theme of BIR 2024, "Artificial Intelligence in Business Informatics: Opportunities and Challenges," this talk aims to bridge the theoretical and practical aspects of business informatics research with the latest trends in AI development. It emphasizes the importance of adaptability, interoperability, and the need for a human-oriented approach in designing high-quality, trustworthy AI systems that cater to the evolving needs of businesses and consumers alike. The session will provide valuable insights for academics, practitioners, and doctoral scholars interested in the intersection of AI and business informatics, offering a comprehensive overview of the current state and future directions of AI tools in business innovation. Attendees will gain a deeper understanding of the opportunities and challenges posed by AI in business informatics, fostering an intellectually stimulating environment conducive to the exchange of ideas and advancements in the field.

# A Meaningful Road to Explanation

Giancarlo Guizzardi

University of Twente, The Netherlands

Cyber-human systems are systems formed by the coordinated interaction of human and computational components. The latter can only be justified in these systems to the extent that they are meaningful to humans – in both senses of 'meaning', i.e., in the sense of semantics as well as in the sense of purpose or significance. On one hand, the data these components manipulate only acquire meaning when mapped to shared human conceptualizations of the world. On the other hand, they can only be justified if ethically designed. Ultimately, we can only build trustworthy cyber-human systems if the interoperation of their components is meaning preserving, i.e., if we are able to: semantically interoperate these components; transparently demonstrate (i.e., explain) how their interoperation positively contributes to human values and goals. To meet these requirements, we must be able to explicitly reveal and safely relate the different theories of the world (i.e., ontologies) embedded in these components. In this talk, I discuss the strong relation between the notions of semantics, ontology, and explanation under certain interpretations. Specifically, I will present a notion of explanation termed Ontological Unpacking, which aims at explaining symbolic domain descriptions (conceptual models, knowledge graphs, logical specifications). I show that the models produced by Ontological Unpacking differ from their traditional counterparts not only in their expressivity but also in their nature: while the latter typically merely have a descriptive nature, the former have an explanatory one. Moreover, I show that it is exactly this explanatory nature that is required for semantic interoperability and, hence, trustworthiness. Finally, I discuss the relation between Ontological Unpacking and other forms of explanation in philosophy and science, as well as in Artificial Intelligence. I will argue that the current trend in XAI (Explainable AI) in which "to explain is to produce a symbolic artifact" (e.g., a decision tree or a counterfactual description) is an incomplete project resting on a false assumption, that these artifacts are not "inherently interpretable", and that they should be taken as the beginning of the road to explanation, not the end.

# Contents

## AI Opportunities and Challenges

Business, Data and Analytics: Specifying AI Use Cases with the Help of Modeling Techniques .................................................. 3
    Matthias Brunnbauer

Generative AI for BPMN Process Analysis: Experiments with Multi-modal Process Representations .................................................. 19
    Damaris Naomi Dolha and Robert Andrei Buchmann

LLM-Assistance for Quality Control of LLM Output ...................... 36
    Kurt Sandkuhl

## AI Applications and Use Cases in Business

Unlocking Viewer Insights in Linear Television: A Machine Learning Approach .................................................. 53
    Javier Carreno, Khuong An Nguyen, Zhiyuan Luo, and Andrew Fish

Comparison of AI-Based Document Classification Platforms ................ 68
    Leon Görgen, Leon Griesch, and Kurt Sandkuhl

Towards Model-driven Enhancement of Safety in Healthcare Robot Interactions .................................................. 85
    Georgios Koutsopoulos, Penelope Ioannidou, George K. Matsopoulos, and Dimitrios D. Koutsouris

## Business Intelligence

Modelling of Organisational Rules in Complex Adaptive Systems: a Systematic Mapping Study .................................................. 103
    Jöran Lindeberg, Martin Henkel, and Eric-Oluf Svee

Towards Method Support for Variability Modelling in Enterprise Architecture Management .................................................. 119
    Ahmed Dehne and Kurt Sandkuhl

Cross-section of Business Intelligence Projects: Information Systems
Success Perspective .................................................... 135
   *Dace Kvalberga and Jānis Grabis*

**Business and Information Systems Development**

Incorporating Ethical Aspects in Information Systems Requirements
Engineering ........................................................... 153
   *Olga Levina*

Suitability of Business Process Modeling Methods for Requirements
Elicitation ............................................................ 162
   *Liene Ieva Kraupša and Marite Kirikova*

Software Architectures and the Use of Knowledge Graphs to Support
Their Design .......................................................... 176
   *Ana-Maria Ghiran and Sven-Alexander Gal*

Technical Debt – Insights Into a Manufacturing SME Case Study ............. 191
   *Katharina Greger and Michael Möhring*

**Knowledge and Traceability Management**

Discovery Rules for Depicting Tacit Knowledge Usage and Management
in Fractal Enterprise Models ........................................... 209
   *Ilia Bider and Erik Perjons*

DDIs-Graph: an Approach to Identify Drug-Drug Interactions
and Recommend Alternative Drugs ........................................ 225
   *Amin Jalali, Paul Johannesson, and Erik Perjons*

Exploring the Information Flow and the Grounding of Digital Product
Passports Using the Work-Oriented Approach, an Industrial Case Study ....... 242
   *Anders W. Tell*

**Author Index** ........................................................ 259

# AI Opportunities and Challenges

# Business, Data and Analytics: Specifying AI Use Cases with the Help of Modeling Techniques

Matthias Brunnbauer[✉]

University of Applied Sciences Mainz, 55128 Mainz, Germany
`matthias.brunnbauer@hs-mainz.de`

**Abstract.** While artificial intelligence promises a wide range of potential for businesses, its adoption poses major problems for some organizations. This paper presents a modeling framework that aims to specify AI use cases. It models three views: Business, data and analytics, that are adopted for the requirements of AI. The framework was applied in a real-world case study leading to several AI use cases and two proof of concepts. While the business view is a useful tool to derive ideas for AI use cases in general, the data and analytics views are very specific to each use case. The framework serves as a means to an end to communicate the project goals, deliver practical guidance and to capture the main results. As its application is time consuming and challenging, this paper closes with guidelines for its efficient use in practice.

**Keywords:** Conceptual Modeling Framework · Artificial Intelligence · Case Study · Use Case Identification

## 1 Introduction

Artificial intelligence (AI) recently received huge public attention due to the performance of large language models such as Open AI's GPT models. In general, AI systems take over tasks that are considered to require some level of human intelligence, e.g., perceiving, deciding, creating, automating or innovating [1]. AI covers a variety of technologies from, e.g., robotic process automation, robots, expert systems, natural language processing, computer vision to deep learning and machine learning (ML) techniques. The latter is the most important subfield of AI and is divided into supervised, unsupervised, semi-supervised and reinforcement learning [2]. Supervised ML systems account for most AI systems. They require a labeled dataset, i.e., the target variable is known within the training and test dataset. The algorithm learns the connections between input and target variables and can use them for upcoming data inputs. AI systems can thus only be as good as the data they are fed with. They may improve their performance over time with increasing available data. Other important AI characteristics deal with its black box character, i.e., the outputs can't be fully comprehended, and AI's experimental character, i.e., being non-deterministic but rather probabilistic [3]. Despite the huge potentials, e.g., AI has been named the top game changer technology by CIOs in 2019 [4], by far not all organizations that experiment with AI have gained any business value.

Several AI initiatives entirely fail or do not meet their goals [5]. One risk factor is an inaccurate definition of the underlying AI use case [6]. Thus, supporting organizations to find and evaluate purposeful AI use cases is an important step in the early stage of AI adoption.

The typical AI use case leading to a success story is the improvement of existing business processes, e.g., by automating a process step or supporting decision making [7, 8]. Often, there are certain data-driven decisions, tasks or process steps that are not yet supported by AI techniques or not even automated or digitalized at all. These could be aided, e.g., by automating or providing superior algorithms, through the wide range of AI's technological capabilities. As such, modeling and analyzing existing business processes is a potential starting point to identify AI use cases. For example, a bank found that its process for granting a loan to a customer was either too slow, long or complicated [9]. Thus, it aimed to improve the process and hired an external AI provider to train a ML system to automatically decide whether to grant a loan. Besides process automation, AI can also emulate humans' tasks or decisions by learning from human performances [10]. This may eventually also lead to more efficient processes. For example, analyzing lawyers' manual workflow for litigation analytics enabled a startup to specify an AI use case aiming for a more automated analysis of judgment files [11]. Therefore, a user-centric approach that analyzes customers' or employees' behavior, challenges, working systems or interactions could also be used to identify ideas for AI use cases.

Both the analysis of existing business processes as well as human performances applying user-centric approaches can be supported by modeling techniques. Our research opportunity allowed us to conduct a real-world case study to identify AI use cases. This paper reports on the case study requirements, the modeling techniques we used as well as the results and lessons learned. We discuss the usefulness of the modeling framework and practical advice for its use. As such, this paper addresses the following questions:

1. Which modeling techniques are useful to identify and evaluate AI use cases and how are they adjusted to meet the requirements of AI?
2. How effective are these modeling techniques in a practical setting and how to apply them in an efficient manner?

## 2 Case Study Setting and Related Requirements

### 2.1 Case Study Setting

The project partner is a public organization that specializes on construction projects and real estate management. They aim to introduce advanced analytical solutions, e.g., utilizing AI techniques, to support processes, decisions, and products on the mid- to long-term. They don't employ data scientists or AI experts yet. As an AI explorer [12], they haven't identified AI use cases before and searched for external consulting to design use cases from scratch until the proof of concept (PoC) stage. The organization consists of a headquarters of about 200 + employees and eight independent subsidiaries. Several customer groups commission dozens of construction projects each year. The headquarters coordinates the incoming projects and transfers them to one of the eight subsidiaries. These are responsible for detailed design and construction planning. They use both internal and external workforce, although the share of external service providers continuously grew over the last years. We collaborated with nine business user groups each consisting of 2–3 practitioners from distinct business units. They were supported by the project sponsor's person in charge and the research team, i.e., one project lead, an AI expert and two data scientists.

## 2.2 Case Study Requirements

For the case study, we need a structured approach that leads to the aspired results: AI use cases until the PoC phase. Such an approach typically requires three overarching stages [10, 13]: Identify a business case first, then collect, analyze and prepare the required data and eventually design the AI model for the PoC. This is also in line with CRISP-DM [14], the most used procedural model to guide data science projects. The basic concept is to identify a set of use case ideas first. They are specified step by step and continuously evaluated for their expected business impact and feasibility [15] as well as further AI specific criteria. Infeasible or insignificant use cases are dropped. For each stage, we specified the constituents of the AI use case as shown in Fig. 1.

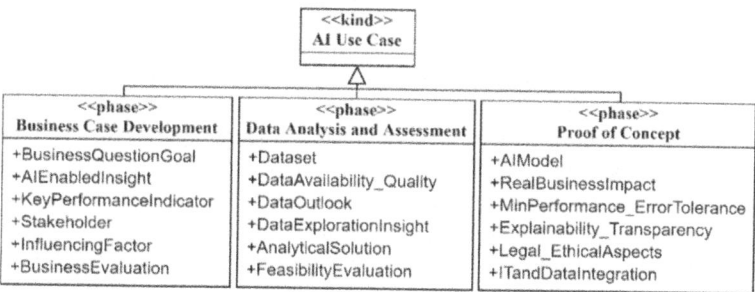

**Fig. 1.** Development of an AI use case until the proof of concept

AI use cases aim to alter a business-related aspect by utilizing AI techniques. They are mainly motivated by business needs [16], so the first phase specifies the underlying business case. The addressed business question goal must be formulated together with potential AI enabled insights to solve it. To make improvements measurable, key performance indicators (KPI) related to the business question goal should be used. The business case should outline the relevant stakeholders and influencing factors. It should be evaluated for its potential business impact, i.e., for its expected business improvement, alignment with business and newness.

AI solutions can only be as good as the underlying data allows, so the second phase builds a data view. This requires an idea of the aspired analytical solutions that relevant datasets should be identified and collected for. The availability and quality of such data must be evaluated and is the key aspect to assess the use case's feasibility. An outlook whether more and better data will be provided in future is also useful as AI solutions can be improved over time with more and better data. Furthermore, data exploration insights allow for a more qualified statement on the expected business impact. The latter must be compared with the feasibility. For the feasibility, the alignment of the analytical solution with existing processes can also be evaluated as well as the project definition.

In the third phase, the PoC outlines the impact and feasibility aspects in more detail. An AI model must be designed and fed with the currently available data to measure the real business impact. This must be compared with the minimum required performance [17] respectively an error tolerance. The PoC must consider further AI aspects [18] such as explainability and transparency [19] to confront AI's black box character. Legal and ethical aspects must also be taken into account, especially if the AI use case concerns the people or sensitive topics [20]. In addition, AI solutions are usually embedded within existing workflows [21], wherefore the process fit can be assessed beforehand. For the PoC, requirements for IT and data integration should be formulated as well as the integration into existing working processes of employees and/or customers.

## 3 Related Work and Choice of the Conceptual Model

Our first phase aims to develop the business case. Conceptual modeling techniques can thereby help to elicit relevant business goals [22, 23] that may lead to business cases. By modeling business goals and their relations top-down, one can identify goals that may be improved by applying new technologies. Such a business view is also used by the Conceptual Modeling Framework for Business Analytics (CMFBA) [24]. It supports the identification, specification and requirements analysis of data analytics systems in particular [25]. The CMFBA also proposes an analytics design view that helps to choose the required analytical solution. It is closely related to a data preparation view that models the required data preparation steps for the aspired analytical solution. This is well in line with our second and third phase to specify the data view and the PoC.

Thus, we apply an extended approach that is adjusted for the requirements of AI and matches the elements within Fig. 1. We add a continuous evaluation throughout the views and the emerging use cases in line with previous research [26]. We specify the evaluation criteria as explained when outlying the constituents of an AI use case. While the business view focuses on the business impact criteria, the data view additionally delivers feasibility criteria. These criteria can be quantified, e.g., using a 3 point Likert scale. The use cases can then be mapped within an impact-feasibility-matrix for comparison [15]. For the PoC criteria, the requirements are analyzed in more detail as explained before. Figure 2 presents the overall process model.

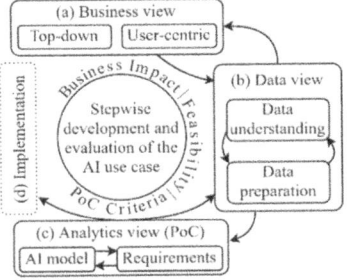

**Fig. 2.** Overall process model

Besides related modeling techniques, related work also provides procedural guidance to manage AI projects in a real-world setting [26–29]. They provide useful instructions to perform an AI project and can be combined with modeling techniques.

### 3.1 Business View

We specify the business view as shown in Fig. 3 by adding two strategies to identify business question goals and associated AI enabled insights.

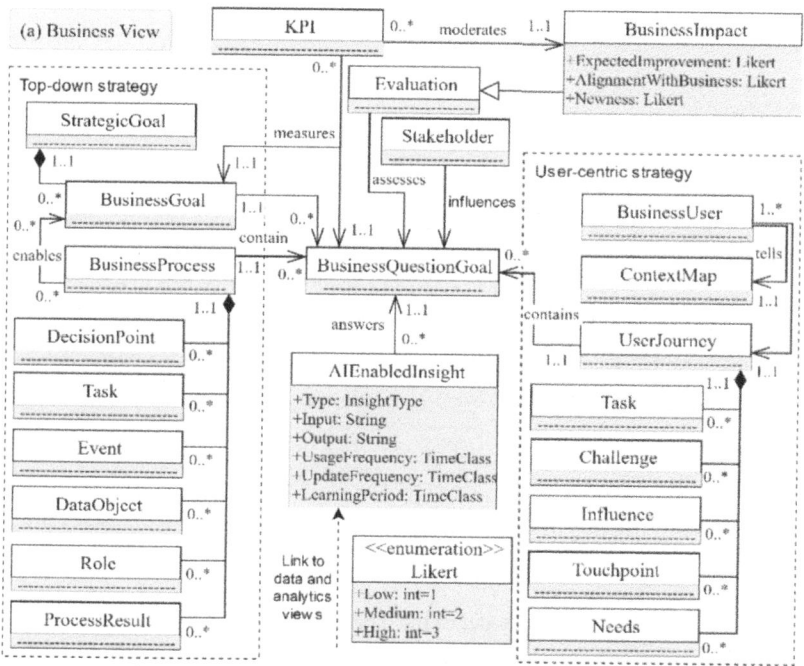

**Fig. 3.** Meta model of the business view

The top-down strategy initially models a business unit as proposed by the CMFBA, i.e., analyzing hierarchically aligned business goals [24, 30, 31]. As successful AI use cases often improve existing business processes, we include their analysis, e.g., using BPMN models [32]. The aim is to identify business question goals related to tasks, decision points, events, process results or business goals that might be improved by AI. The process models should explicitly contain incoming and generated data and information.

The user-centric strategy focuses on the business users. To learn about their business environment, user-centric approaches are useful, e.g., design thinking principles [33–35]. We apply two models: first, a context map to gain a general understanding of relevant influencing factors of the business users' working environment. Second, user journeys that include different aspects a business user faces [36, 37]. We model relevant user tasks, related challenges, needs, touchpoints and relate them to influences from the context map. When then match the former with AI's technological possibilities, so the business question goals and aspired AI enabled insights can be derived.

### 3.2 Data and Analytics View

We then use data understanding and data preparation tasks for the data view, see Fig. 4 which also covers the analytics view.

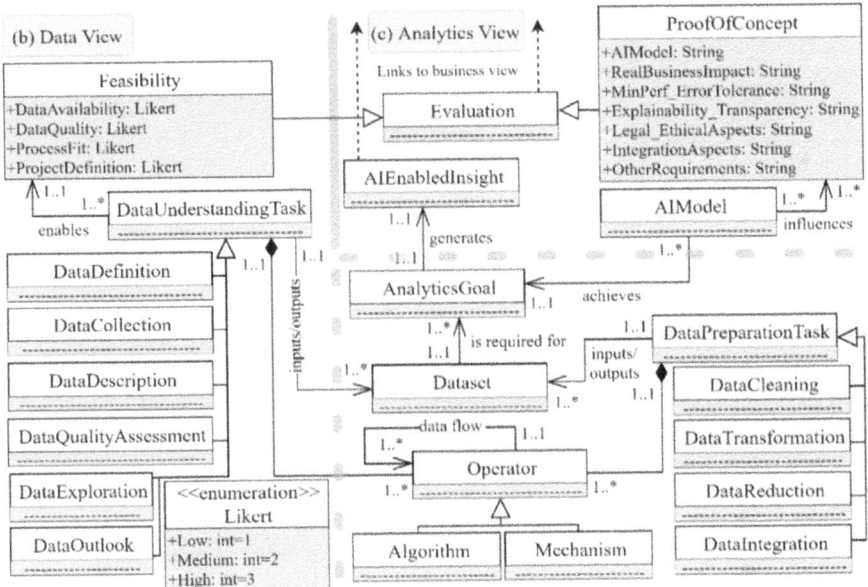

**Fig. 4.** Meta model of the data and analytics views

The CMFBA data preparation view doesn't cover data understanding tasks. We add them, i.e., the definition, collection, description, assessment and exploration of required data. Relevant data can be identified via currently used data within related processes and tasks as well as the influencing factors identified in the business view. In most cases high quality data is scarce. Checking for external data, e.g., purchased data, is useful. Afterwards, the available data is collected while the missing data is noted. The data should be described, i.e., its source, owner, type, scope, update frequency, its values as well as its practical meaning. The data quality assessment then evaluates its completeness, validity, interpretability and accessibility [38]. The data exploration follows to assess the usefulness of the data for the aspired AI enabled insight. For such an exploration, data processing tasks are required, i.e., operators which perform single data processing tasks using certain mechanisms [39], e.g., join or filter, and potentially necessary algorithms [25]. The data understanding tasks lead to the required datasets. These (raw) datasets are then processed to datasets required for the analytics goal [25].

The analytics view helps to choose and design the required AI models. These are iteratively fed with the prepared datasets and evaluated. Data preparation and modeling tasks are thus highly iterative, so they are shared among the data view and the analytics view in Fig. 4. The results of the AI model allow for a realistic estimation of the current business impact. To support the choice of suitable algorithms, the CMFBA provides an algorithm catalogue [25]. For AI specific technologies and exemplary algorithms, an overview can be found, e.g., in [40].

## 4 Application in a Real-World Case Study

### 4.1 Business View by Top-Down Strategy

A part of the business view is presented in Fig. 5 for a headquarters division.

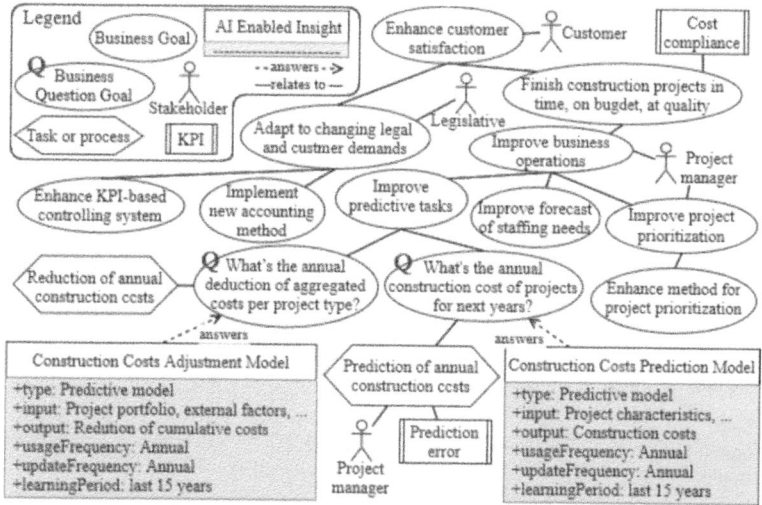

**Fig. 5.** Excerpt of the business view for a headquarters division

They aim to enhance customer satisfaction who wish to get the construction projects finished in time and on budget. Customers demand precise forecasts of construction costs, so the organization aims to improve their predictive tasks. The business question goal that asks for the volume of project specific annual construction costs was formulated by three different groups proving its business relevance. The related process is modeled in Fig. 6. Thanks to the process model, another business question goal could be derived. When the headquarters aggregate individual values to the project portfolio value, they must reduce the sum. This is due to unpredictable events that cannot be linked to single projects, e.g., project cancellations. However, there is little knowledge on the required reductions concerning different project types and so forth. Hence, the business question goal 'What's the annual deduction of aggregated costs per project type?' emerged.

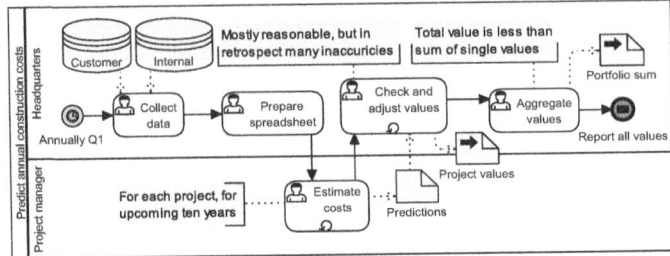

**Fig. 6.** Process model for the prediction of annual construction costs

### 4.2 Business View by User-Centric Strategy

In Fig. 7, the context map shows a part of the important influencing factors for a project manager. Construction projects are affected by their inherent characteristics and internal and external organizational factors. For the latter, mainly factors related to external architects and engineers, customers and the legislative are relevant.

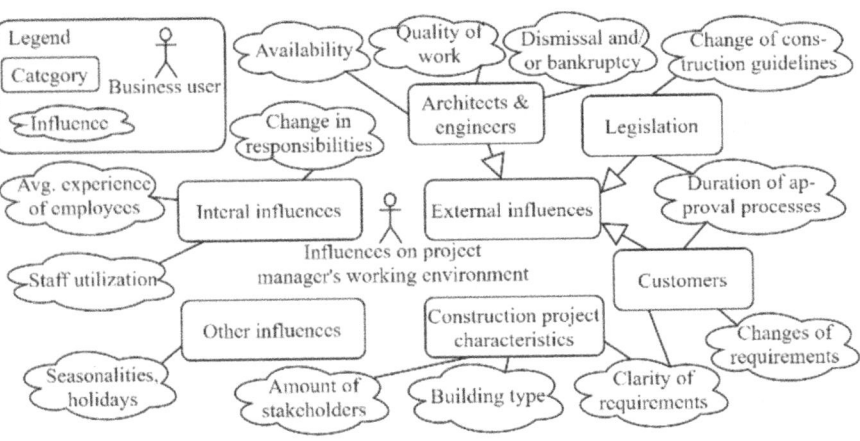

**Fig. 7.** Excerpt of a project manager's context map

In Fig. 8, a greatly shortened version of the user journey of a project manager is presented. The user journey concerns the typical lifecycle of a construction project from assignment until completion. Projects are assigned by the headquarters. Project managers then check the project's requirements, the available resources and set up the project constellation. As soon as the project is set up, they control and communicate its progress until the project is delivered to the customer. There are several related challenges, influences, and associated needs. Project managers especially seek assistance for their daily routines, i.e., planning and allocating resources as well as managing risks. This led to the definition of several ideas for AI use cases.

Two exemplary business question goals are shown. Project managers need to know the most suited project setup, e.g., concerning the team setup, for an upcoming construction project. This requires insights such as a project setup recommendation that accounts

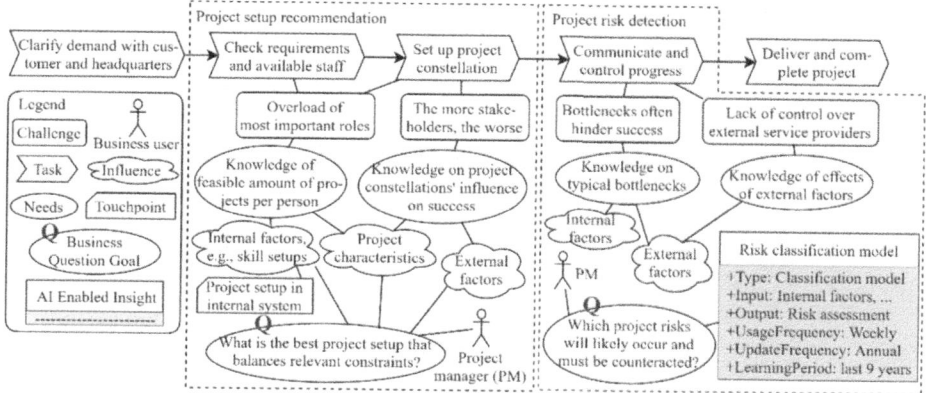

**Fig. 8.** Excerpt of a project manager's user journey

for, e.g., the project's expected staff demand compared with current staff resources and employees' experience and skill setup for certain project types. Another business question goal asks when countermeasures must be initiated to tackle project risks such as typical bottlenecks. To do so, an insight on the severity and likelihood of such risks is required. Both question goals could potentially be supported by AI enabled solutions. For example, unsupervised ML algorithms could detect typical bottlenecks and project risk patterns in past projects. These could be utilized to recognize and assess similar risks for current projects earlier on.

### 4.3 Data View for the Prediction of Annual Construction Costs

In this section, we present the data view for one selected AI use case: the prediction of annual construction costs as shown in both Figs. 5 and 6. For this use case, we first defined relevant data which is mainly informed by the data and information from the process models. We then identified required datasets for past and current projects, e.g., regarding projects' master data, previous construction costs back to 2005, internal and external incidental building costs as well as project progress data. These are briefly sketched in Fig. 9 together with the most basic data processing steps and additional information, e.g., a brief data description for one dataset.

The data quality assessment revealed tremendous issues for several projects, especially small ones. At times, no construction costs were stored, e.g., entirely for the years 2007 and 2008. The project progress data at times didn't match the cost related data, e.g., if no incidental building costs are recorded although a project already passed several milestones. For the data exploration, project data was matched on the level of an individual construction project. Interestingly, although large amounts of data were available in the beginning, i.e., data on more than 1.000 projects, only few correlations between the target variable and assumed input variables occurred. The expected business improvement was thus adjusted to a lower level. With the current data quality and availability, an ML based solution may not lead to an improved prediction. However, the organization implements enhanced data standards, so the data outlook is positive. The

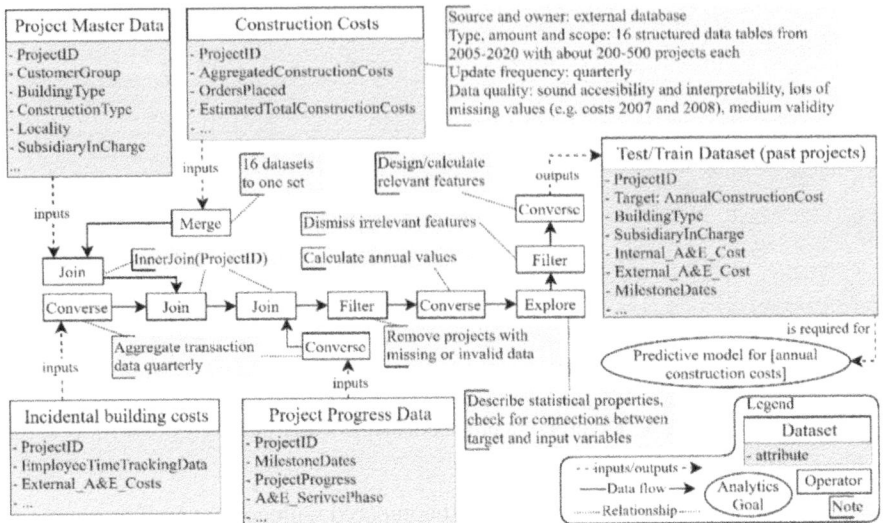

**Fig. 9.** Excerpt of the data view for the prediction of annual construction costs

project partner thus aimed for the PoC wherefore we prepared datasets to test different analytical solutions. For a random forest regressor for example, 380 projects were used to train and test the AI model.

### 4.4 Analytics View for the Prediction of Annual Construction Costs

In this section, we present the analytics view for the same use case, see Fig. 10.

We tested different supervised machine learning regression models to predict project's annual construction cost values. We mainly evaluated the performance of a random forest regressor and a multiple linear regressor. However, as the data exploration already revealed, they couldn't yet beat the current human-based estimations and therefore not yet provide the minimum expected performance. In the upcoming years, data related issues are however expected to be reduced, thus the solutions can be improved step by step. We also tested simpler models that follow a different analytical strategy but are not considered actual AI models. The preferred model learns the typical quarterly distributions of construction costs from past construction projects for different project types at first. It is provided with several input variables including human-based estimations and rules. It then estimates the expected distribution of upcoming construction costs. This model proved to be superior for the moment. It achieved similar performance as the current estimations and, if unrealistic estimations are adjusted, it can even beat it. However, this still requires notable human inputs, so this is an interim solution which integrates a data-driven analysis into the existing workflow. On this basis, the share of data-driven predictions should be enhanced and equipped with advanced ML techniques. We provided our project partner with two software prototypes: one that is integrated via Tableau and the other one is integrated into an Excel spreadsheet via VBA coding. Each

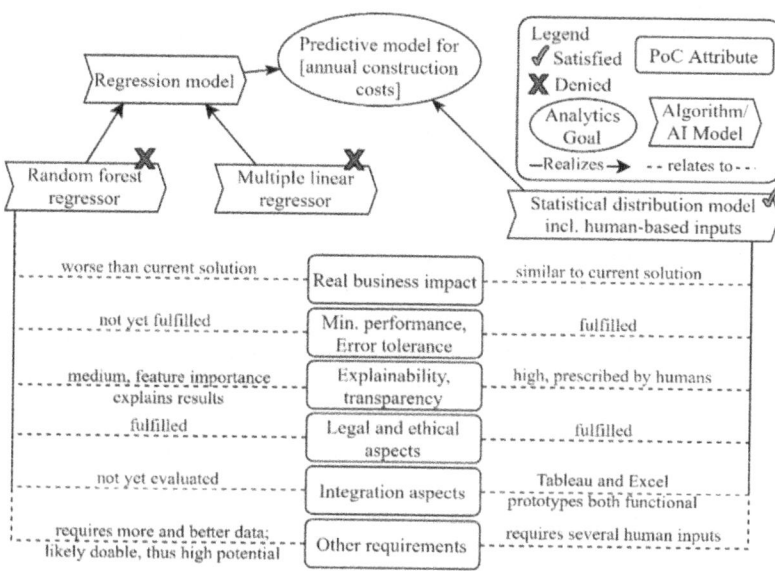

**Fig. 10.** Summary of the analytics view for the prediction of annual construction costs

software is currently in use, so our prototypes show two paths for a practical integration into existing data workflow and working procedures.

## 5 Usefulness and Practical Application Tips

### 5.1 Usefulness of the Conceptual Models

The business view differs the top-down and user-centric strategies. In the practical setting, the business users grasped the strategies in a short time and were able to formulate the required entities. The two strategies led to different results though. The top-down strategy is stricter by analyzing only business goals and associated processes. This leads to ideas for AI use cases affecting the internal business operations. As such AI use cases lead to the typical AI success story, the strategy fulfills its purpose. The top-down strategy is also very useful to assess the strategic alignment and the process fit of each idea.

The user-centric strategy in contrast captured detailed everyday issues that the business users face. The context map is useful to gain a broader business understanding that includes influencing factors associated with employees' whole working environment. In combination with relevant tasks, challenges and additional information, the user journeys provide rich information to derive AI use case ideas. These were derived, e.g., from the mere challenges that business users face every day like an overload of projects they must supervise and thus the requirement for assistance. However, the broader spectrum of ideas and their disentanglement from current processes meant that these use case ideas are less aligned with existing business and consequently with available data.

The data view provides guidance to perform data understanding and data preparation tasks. However, the data processing details are elaborate to grasp with the meta models.

In Fig. 9, the data processing steps are still a great simplification. For example, the datasets for project master data and construction costs are managed by the customer and inherent a different logic for the ProjectID. Another issue accounts for projects with addendums as each receives an additional ProjectID. Their construction costs had to be added to the parent project. The target variable, i.e., annual construction costs per project, also had to be calculated for all projects at first as the data tables only included the aggregated total construction costs spent. Hence, while Fig. 9 only says 'merge' for the construction costs and then 'join' for the two datasets, the reality covers about a dozen steps. For the analytics view, a similar observation is true. It is highly iterative with the data preparation tasks and emerges step by step, so that not every single step should be modeled. It is useful to map and compare the performance of different AI algorithms regarding the different PoC criteria. The data and the analytics view serve to communicate the project progress and the main procedural steps to capture the relevant results in more detail ex-post.

### 5.2 Efficient Use of the Conceptual Model

The design of the models requests a lot of effort, so they must be used efficiently. One consideration asks whether all elements should directly be modeled and in which level of detail. The business view is where the initial ideas for AI use case are generated together with the business users. It is the base for all upcoming steps and will decide whether promising use cases are found or not. Thus, a thorough identification and evaluation is key. The meta models should be applied with detail to allow for a broad spectrum of relevant information and subsequent use case ideas. For the top-down strategy, the collection of existing processes in the strategy map should be emphasized. When analyzing the business processes, an emphasis on required and generated data is recommended. For the user-centric strategy, the user journeys should emphasize the user tasks and associated information. The data and analytics views in contrast are required to assess which use case ideas are feasible but not to generate new business cases. As such, the models should be used as efficiently as possible, i.e., as a guideline which overarching activities to perform and to capture the relevant results ex-post. The latter comprises only the main data processing steps, e.g., which datasets were joined by which key attributes. Details can be left for a separate data processing report.

An important efficiency consideration is to follow the most impactful and feasible use case ideas only. To do so, we introduced evaluation steps and criteria for each view. These proved very valuable as the number of AI use case ideas has been large in the beginning. The project groups identified 47 ideas for AI use cases. Eventually, we ended up designing two complete PoCs, although one served three groups. Lots of ideas faced the issue of not being equipped with sufficient data, so especially consider the process fit, data availability and data exploration insights for evaluation.

Another aspect deals with termination conditions. There is no guidance when to stop collecting business question goals. We used time restrictions to set a limit and followed the assumption that the most relevant business question goals will likely be formulated early on which was indeed the case. For the data view, we analyzed the use cases according to their business prioritization. Lots of use cases ideas also required similar data understanding, preparation and analytical tasks. Identifying interdependencies between different use cases early on is strongly recommended.

## 6 Conclusion

This paper asks how to support the identification and evaluation of AI use cases with modeling techniques. To do so, we extend a framework for the requirements of AI and a real-world case study. The proposed procedure is suitable to identify AI use cases especially for organizations from the non-tech sector that are yet unfamiliar with data-driven approaches such as AI. The procedure starts with a business view aiming for business question goals and associated AI enabled insights. Two strategies are proposed that lead to a variety of AI use case ideas. The business view is a universal approach to identify such ideas and is built upon well-established business concepts. We added distinct evaluation criteria that allow to estimate the expected business impact to follow the most promising use cases first. The second phase, data view, results in a qualified statement on the use case's feasibility as well as the required datasets for the AI solution. Data understanding tasks were added to the framework to achieve the former. In addition, data exploration insights help to assess the expected business impact in greater detail. However, the real-world complexities when choosing, collecting, and processing required data for a new use case pose wicked challenges. It is questionable whether one should model each required processing step in detail or model the main steps only but keep the details for a separate data preparation report. The third phase, analytics view, is highly iterative with the data preparation steps of the data view. It provides guidance to build and evaluate an AI model that is fed with currently available data. Only this way, the true business impact can be stated. For such a proof of concept, we added additional AI specific criteria that must be outlined, e.g., explainability, transparency and legal aspects. These must be specified with the end users and other relevant stakeholders. The analytics view is useful to provide guidance and present the main results.

It is of great importance to apply the meta models in an efficient manner. We discuss several aspects to achieve that, e.g., evaluation criteria, ending conditions and when to use the models in detail. Regarding the latter, the meta models should be viewed as a means to an end to achieve the practical goals. They can support a project aiming for AI use cases by providing the entities which should be identified and modeled. It also prescribes the potential design of the results, thus serving as an auxiliary tool to communicate the results and the progress. Still, intermediate results may need to be adjusted several times to meet the ever-changing discoveries and constraints when designing new AI solutions from scratch. Hence, the real-world situation demands a trade-off between a rigorous application of the meta models and the actual practical benefits.

## References

1. Benbya, H., Davenport, T.H., Pachidi, S.: Artificial intelligence in organizations: current state and future opportunities. MIS Q. Exec. (2020). https://doi.org/10.2139/ssrn.3741983
2. Enholm, I.M., Papagiannidis, E., Mikalef, P., Krogstie, J.: Artificial intelligence and business value: a literature review. Inf. Syst. Front. (2022). https://doi.org/10.1007/s10796-021-10186-w

3. Engel, C., Ebel, P., van Giffen, B.: Empirically exploring the cause-effect relationships of AI characteristics, project management challenges, and organizational change. In: Ahlemann, F., Schütte, R., Stieglitz, S. (eds.) Innovation Through Information Systems. WI 2021. Lecture Notes in Information Systems and Organisation, vol. 47. Springer, Cham (2021). https://doi.org/10.1007/978-3-030-86797-3_12
4. Howard, C., Rowsell-Jones, A.: 2019 CIO Survey: CIOs Have Awoken to the Importance of AI. Gartner (2019)
5. Ransbotham, S., Khodabandeh, S., Fehling, R., LaFountain, B., Kiron, D.: Winning with AI. MIT Sloan Management Review and Boston Consulting Group (2019)
6. Westenberger, J., Schuler, K., Schlegel, D.: Failure of AI projects: understanding the critical factors. Procedia Comput. Sci. (2022). https://doi.org/10.1016/j.procs.2021.11.074
7. Davenport, T.H., Ronanki, R.: Artificial intelligence for the real world. Don't start with moon shots. Harvard Bus. Rev. **96**, 108–116 (2018)
8. Collins, C., Dennehy, D., Conboy, K., Mikalef, P.: Artificial intelligence in information systems research: a systematic literature review and research agenda. Int. J. Inf. Manage. **60**, 102383 (2021). https://doi.org/10.1016/j.ijinfomgt.2021.102383
9. Mayer, A.-S., Strich, F., Fiedler, M.: Unintended consequences of introducing AI systems for decision making. MIS Q. Exec. **19**, 239–257 (2020). https://doi.org/10.17705/2msqe.00036
10. Andrews, W.: Build the AI business case. A CIO's guide to building the strategy and business case to implement AI in the enterprise. Gartner (2018)
11. Zhang, Z., Nandhakumar, J., Hummel, J.T., Waardenburg, L.: Addressing the key challenges of developing machine learning AI systems for knowledge-intensive work. MIS Q. Exec. **19**, 221–238 (2020). https://doi.org/10.17705/2msqe.00035
12. Uba, C., Lewandowski, T., Böhmann, T.: The AI-based transformation of organizations: the 3D-model for guiding enterprise-wide AI change. In: 56th Hawaii International Conference on System Sciences (2023). 102456
13. Maass, W., Storey, V.C.: Pairing conceptual modeling with machine learning. Data Knowl. Eng. **134**, 101909 (2021). https://doi.org/10.1016/j.datak.2021.101909
14. Martinez-Plumed, F., et al.: CRISP-DM twenty years later: from data mining processes to data science trajectories. IEEE Trans. Knowl. Data Eng. **33**, 3048–3061 (2019). https://doi.org/10.1109/TKDE.2019.2962680
15. Brethenoux, E., Karamouzis, F.: 5 Steps to Practically Implement AI Techniques. Gartner (2019). https://emtemp.gcom.cloud/ngw/globalassets/en/doc/documents/383797-5-steps-to-practically-implement-ai-techniques.pdf. Accessed 23 Feb 2022
16. Borges, A.F., Laurindo, F.J., Spínola, M.M., Gonçalves, R.F., Mattos, C.A.: The strategic use of artificial intelligence in the digital era: systematic literature review and future research directions. Int. J. Inf. Manage. **57**, 102225 (2021). https://doi.org/10.1016/j.ijinfomgt.2020.102225
17. Davenport, T.H., Seseri, R.: What Is a Minimum Viable AI Product? MIT Sloan Management Review (2020)
18. Engel, C., Elshan, E., Ebel, P.: Deploying a model for assessing cognitive automation use cases: Insights from action research with a leading European manufacturing company. In: 54th Hawaii International Conference on System Sciences, pp. 6253–6262 (2021)
19. Haresamudram, K., Larsson, S., Heintz, F.: Three levels of AI transparency. Computer **56**, 93–100 (2023). https://doi.org/10.1109/MC.2022.3213181
20. Felzmann, H., Villaronga, E.F., Lutz, C., Tamò-Larrieux, A.: Transparency you can trust: transparency requirements for artificial intelligence between legal norms and contextual concerns. Big Data Soc. **6**, 2053951719860542 (2019). https://doi.org/10.1177/2053951719860542

21. Salwei, M.E., Carayon, P.: A sociotechnical systems framework for the application of artificial intelligence in health care delivery. J. Cogn. Eng. Decis. Making **16**, 194–206 (2022). https://doi.org/10.1177/15553434221097357
22. Amyot, D., Ghanavati, S., Horkoff, J., Mussbacher, G., Peyton, L., Yu, E.: Evaluating goal models within the goal-oriented requirement language. Int. J. Intell. Syst. **25**, 841–877 (2010). https://doi.org/10.1002/int.20433
23. Jiang, L., Barone, D., Amyot, D., Mylopoulos, J.: Strategic models for business intelligence. In: Jeusfeld, M., Delcambre, L., Ling, T.-W. (eds.) ER 2011. LNCS, vol. 6998, pp. 429–439. Springer, Heidelberg (2011). https://doi.org/10.1007/978-3-642-24606-7_33
24. Nalchigar, S., Eric, Yu., Ramani, R.: A conceptual modeling framework for business analytics. In: Comyn-Wattiau, I., Tanaka, K., Song, I.-Y., Yamamoto, S., Saeki, M. (eds.) ER 2016. LNCS, vol. 9974, pp. 35–49. Springer, Cham (2016). https://doi.org/10.1007/978-3-319-46397-1_3
25. Nalchigar, S., Yu, E.: Business-driven data analytics: a conceptual modeling framework. Data Knowl. Eng. **117**, 359–372 (2018). https://doi.org/10.1016/j.datak.2018.04.006
26. Brunnbauer, M., Piller, G., Rothlauf, F.: Top-down or explorative? A case study on the identification of AI use cases. In: PACIS 2022 Proceedings (2022)
27. Brunnbauer, M., Piller, G., Rothlauf, F.: idea-AI: developing a method for the systematic identification of AI use cases. In: AMCIS 2021 Proceedings (2021)
28. Studer, S., et al.: Towards CRISP-ML(Q): a machine learning process model with quality assurance methodology. Mach. Learn. Knowl. Extr. **3**, 392–413 (2021). https://doi.org/10.3390/make3020020
29. Hofmann, P., Jöhnk, J., Protschky, D., Urbach, N.: Developing purposeful AI use cases - a structured method and its application in project management. In: 15th International Conference on Wirtschaftsinformatik (WI) (2020)
30. Barone, D., Topaloglou, T., Mylopoulos, J.: Business Intelligence Modeling in Action: A Hospital Case Study. In: Ralyté, J., Franch, X., Brinkkemper, S., Wrycza, S. (eds.) CAiSE 2012. LNCS, vol. 7328, pp. 502–517. Springer, Heidelberg (2012). https://doi.org/10.1007/978-3-642-31095-9_33
31. Barone, D., Eric, Yu., Won, J., Jiang, L., Mylopoulos, J.: Enterprise Modeling for Business Intelligence. In: Bommel, P., Hoppenbrouwers, S., Overbeek, S., Proper, E., Barjis, J. (eds.) PoEM 2010. LNBIP, vol. 68, pp. 31–45. Springer, Heidelberg (2010). https://doi.org/10.1007/978-3-642-16782-9_3
32. Chinosi, M., Trombetta, A.: BPMN: an introduction to the standard. Comput. Stan. Interfaces **34**, 124–134 (2012). https://doi.org/10.1016/j.csi.2011.06.002
33. Hehn, J., Mendez, D., Übernickel, F., Brenner, W., Broy, M.: On integrating design thinking for human-centered requirements engineering. IEEE Softw. **37**, 25–31 (2020). https://doi.org/10.1109/MS.2019.2957680
34. Micheli, P., Wilner, S.J.S., Bhatti, S.H., Mura, M., Beverland, M.B.: Doing design thinking: conceptual review, synthesis, and research agenda. J. Prod. Innov. Manag. **36**, 124–148 (2019). https://doi.org/10.1111/jpim.12466
35. Thoring, K., Müller, R.M.: Understanding design thinking: a process model based on method engineering. In: 13th International Conference on Engineering and Product Design Education, pp. 493–498 (2011)
36. Temkin, B.D.: Mapping the customer journey. Forrester Res. **3**, 20 (2010)
37. Ludwiczak, A.: Using customer journey mapping to improve public services: a critical analysis of the literature. Management **25**, 22–35 (2021). https://doi.org/10.2478/manment-2019-0071
38. Wang, R.Y., Strong, D.M.: Beyond accuracy: what data quality means to data consumers. J. Manag. Inf. Syst. **12**, 5–33 (1996). https://doi.org/10.1080/07421222.1996.11518099

39. Trujillo, J., Luján-Mora, S.: A UML based approach for modeling ETL processes in data warehouses. In: Song, I.Y., Liddle, S.W., Ling, T.W., Scheuermann, P. (eds.) Conceptual Modeling - ER 2003, 2813th edn., pp. 307–320. Springer, Berlin, Heidelberg (2003)
40. Mukhamediev, R.I., et al.: Review of artificial intelligence and machine learning technologies: classification, restrictions opportunities and challenges. Mathematics **10**, 2552 (2022). https://doi.org/10.3390/math10152552

# Generative AI for BPMN Process Analysis: Experiments with Multi-modal Process Representations

Damaris Naomi Dolha and Robert Andrei Buchmann[✉]

Faculty of Economics and Business Administration, Babeș-Bolyai University, Street T. Mihali 58-60, 400591 Cluj-Napoca, Romania
`robert.buchmann@econ.ubbcluj.ro`

**Abstract.** Advocating a convergence between generative AI and BPMN-based process analysis, this study reports on experiments with multi-modal business process representations. By leveraging the capabilities of the Bee-Up modeling tool for RDF serialization and the standard XML export of SAP Signavio, the report probes into the generative AI ability of BPMN interpretation according to these different serializations. In addition, the deployment of multi-modal AI – that directly processes image inputs – transcends traditional constraints of machine readability of BPMN diagrams. For prompt engineering, we employ a combined strategy utilizing semantic processing offered by Ontotext GraphDB integrated with LLM services from OpenAI, which, applied on RDF representations of BPMN, can push the boundaries of natural language interactions with visual process models. The investigation experiments with the interpretation of BPMN process models through such AI-based user interactions, highlighting possibilities of integrating conversational AI with the Business Process Management lifecycle. Assessments of outcomes are based on the RAGAs framework.

**Keywords:** BPMN · Generative AI · RDF · XML · Bee-Up · Signavio · RAGAs

## 1 Introduction

The paper reports on continuous experimentation with how selected LLM services interpret BPMN process models that are exposed to them multi-modally – as standard XML serializations, as non-standard tool-specific RDF graphs, as images. This work can inform future revisitations of the BPM (business process management) lifecycle through the lens of augmentations made possible by LLM services as a means of managing procedural knowledge.

As business environments become increasingly AI-driven, the demand for intelligent tools to manage, interpret and transform business processes has never been more critical. Within this context, BPMN (Business Process Model and Notation) remains the dominant standard for documenting processes, predominantly relying on XML for diagram serializations – e.g., XPDL, BPEL-WS, BPMN XML, ADOXML – with wide availability of process-aware systems or engines built on such process schemas, e.g.,

[1]. However, in a semantics-driven engineering context [2], the requirement of process understandability can become more important than process instantiation; or, the instantiation can be agilely tailored to a dynamic semantically rich context, possibly available in the form of knowledge graphs. Towards such needs, the introduction of RDF (Resource Description Framework) encoding of BPMN offers new semantic capabilities, as demonstrated by tools such as Bee-Up [3] and other demonstrators [4]. This format promises a transformation in Business Process Management (BPM), providing enhanced interpretative adaptability and a richer analytical landscape [5]. Building on this potential, our research explores the use of XML and RDF serializations of BPMN with generative Artificial Intelligence (GenAI), complemented by multi-modal capabilities of visually interpreting diagrams and also tapping into code generation capabilities for building diagrams by means of generative serialization. The experiments harness the Large Language Models (LLMs) provided by OpenAI. By means of targeted prompts that probe various aspects of the BPMN exemplars, we highlight nuanced superior semantic capabilities of RDF over XML despite it not providing a standard vocabulary such as those available in XML formats – revealing ways in which these serializations can facilitate more intricate interactions between humans and GenAI. Although the integration of RDF as BPMN knowledge structures is still in experimental stages [4, 6], the study highlights the capacity of RDF to facilitate context-aware dialogue with LLMs beyond the BPMN-as-data structure treatment imposed by the XML interchange formats.

This research aligns with a current stream of investigation into the capability of AI to engage with conceptual models [7]. It also furthers the investigation into how LLM services can understand and process serialized diagrammatic models, building upon the prompt strategies initially proposed in [8] and [9] - which were based on the more constrained functionalities of ChatGPT 3.5 and lacking a RAGAs-based introspection. Our comparative analysis also extends across a more diverse set of scenarios, thereby expanding the findings representativeness and insights.

We focus on serializations because most BPMS platforms and services rely on them as formats for process repositories and interchange; however, our experiments also transition towards visual BPMN interpretation by means of the recently launched multi-modal GPT capabilities. Certain stakeholders are expected to interact with LLMs on a visual level. The introduction of image recognition capabilities by the GPT-4 OpenAI model significantly enhances the multi-modal interaction possibilities [10], enabling a more holistic approach to understanding and interacting with BPMN models.

The paper is organized as follows: in Sect. 2, we establish the problem scope in the context of BPM. The evolution from traditional to contemporary strategies in process queries is traced in Sect. 3. Next, Sect. 4 summarizes the experimental setup, whereas the core findings of our experimental study are reported in Sect. 5, emphasizing some intricacies of RDF and XML and how visual data complements semantic processing. Concluding this paper, Sect. 6 summarizes the findings and maps out directions for future exploration.

## 2 Large Language Models and the BPM Lifecycle

Our investigation employs LLMs for both the semantic and visual analysis of procedural knowledge, which is quintessential to the BPM lifecycle. Process queries have traditionally depended on graph queries [4, 6], formal languages [11] and visual grammars [12]. Now, they must be revisited in relation to LLMs that radically depart from the conventions of pre-GPT process analysis tools. In [13], the authors draw attention to how these models can rewrite the phases of the BPM lifecycle. In the *process identification* phase, LLMs cut through the clutter of unstructured data: they do not just find information, they can gather workflow knowledge. Moving forward into *process discovery*, the influence of GenAI can enhance process mining frameworks. Traditionally tethered to XML event logs, RDF can push graph-based process mining [14]. When it comes to *querying processes*, XML frameworks and XPath are overhauled by multi-modal AI such as GPT-4 [15]. Yet, reliance on computer vision has its limits and must be complemented by a semantic serialization layer to capture non-visual aspects that remain semantically relevant – e.g., links between different models (e.g., RACI responsibilities on task level) or data attributes (e.g., task costs). In the *analytical* phase, the power of LLMs must distil vast amounts of data into actionable insights. Then, in the *redesign* phase, AI can advocate changes, using code generation on serializations to apply workflow updates. As those updates are *implemented*, LLMs enrich user interactions with detailed explanations, shifting emphasis from static workflow sequences to dynamic conversational choreographies. During the *monitoring phase*, LLMs are not confined to mere data display; they can interpret and analyze data.

The current report focusses on the process querying and interpretation, crucial stages within the *process discovery* phase, while also addressing innovative alternatives to traditional *process analysis*, with superficial comments on the other phases of the BPM lifecycle.

## 3 Related Works

As AI pushes the boundaries of Business Process Management, recent technological strides change the way processes can be analyzed. For instance, the BPMN2KG initiative [4] illustrates the conversion of BPMN 2.0 models into knowledge graphs and also marks a different view on the instantiation of process models. Similarly, a conversion tool reported in [6] allowed BPMN XML formats to morph into Neo4J labeled property graphs (LPG), providing another graph alternative to serializations that adhere to the BPMN 2.0 standards. The work of [12] has ventured into the application of LLMs for textual analyses within BPM. This study tests the effectiveness of LLMs, particularly GPT-4, in deriving both imperative and declarative process models from text, demonstrating a substantial advance regarding the role of AI in process querying, as further supported by findings in [16]. The urgency for semantic adaptability in Business Process Management Systems (BPMS) is also gaining attention [2]. The effectiveness of ChatGPT in generating and deciphering diverse conceptual models was analyzed in [7], suggesting operational nuances. An evaluation by Busch et al. [17] looked into prompt engineering for business process management. The integration of GPT-3.5 Turbo with

Lean Six Sigma 4.0 methodologies [18] unveils the potential for upgrading customer service and decision-making processes in real time. Moreover, the intersection of GPT technology with Robotic Process Automation (RPA) is scrutinized for potential risks and opportunities, especially concerning security and compliance issues [19]. Addressing the intrinsic challenges that come with LLMs, Yang et al. [20] propose forward-thinking strategies that involve merging LLMs with knowledge graphs. This innovative approach is particularly promising when these graphs are designed around diagrammatic procedural knowledge effectively serialized as semantic networks.

## 4 Experimental Setup

At the forefront of our study is Bee-Up 1.7 [3], component of the OMiLAB Digital Innovation environment [21], known for its role in enhancing both standard-based and domain-specific models with rich semantics, allowing the exploration of the inter-links and semantic bridges among a diversity of modeling languages – e.g., BPMN, UML, DMN, EPC and Petri Nets [22]. SAP Signavio [23] was used as a representative for tools supporting the standard BPMN 2.0 XML serialization. Both tools provide image exports as PNG and other image formats.

We focus our report on a model of a main process linked to a subprocess, as illustrated in Fig. 1.

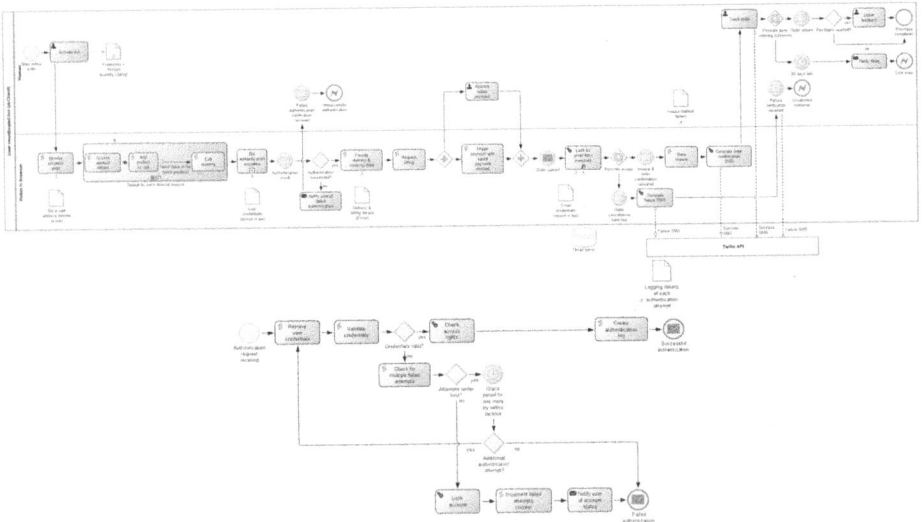

**Fig. 1.** BPMN diagrams from Bee-Up 1.7 depicting the main BPMN process and the "Bot authentication microflow" subprocess.

The process model depicts the logic of an RPA bot planned to mimic the human actions for on-line shopping, as well as the data requirements for the bot to accomplish such a task – including credentials needed to perform some authentication steps on behalf of the human. We only include the Bee-Up variants, having equivalent elements to the Signavio variants.

The key feature leveraged in Bee-Up is the RDF export, building on transformation patterns initially introduced in [24]. To manage and parse the RDF outputs as semantic graphs, we turned to Ontotext GraphDB 10.5 [25], after stripping away irrelevant attributes from RDF metadata. Ontotext GraphDB expands the standard SPARQL querying capabilities with OpenAI-oriented functions such as *gpt:ask()* [26] that engages directly with the GPT-4 model while exposing to it a convenient subgraph extracted from the RDF repository. The structure of the utilized query is shown below, targeting specific types of nodes and edges. To further refine results, we apply a *filter* to expose only specific graph edges that are relevant for the process description:

```
#prefixes removed for concision
# <...> are placeholders for relevant graph edges or node types, as well as the user prompt
SELECT ?answer WHERE {
SELECT (helper:rdf(helper:tuple(?x, ?prop, ?o)) AS ?rdf)
WHERE {
      ?x a <RDF_class_identifier>; ?prop ?o.
      FILTER (?prop IN (<property1>, <property2>, <property3>, <property4>, ...))
      }
BIND(helper:serializeRDF(?rdf, ?x, ?prop, ?o) as ?rdfSer)
?answer gpt:ask ("<user_prompt>" ?rdfSer)}
```

Another enabler of our analytical approach is *BPMN Analyst*, a custom GPT service using ChatGPT Plus [27], specifically engineered to dissect and interpret BPMN XML serializations from any BPMN imported files, through a series of trivial and non-trivial prompts. This strategic application of tailored AI tools enhances our capacity to analyze and understand BPMN content via Large Language Model (LLM) services. The examples provided in Fig. 1 were customized to include a range of both visual and non-visual patterns, covering control flows and inter-pool collaborations, event-based gateways, different events and a variety of element types.

The experimental setup was expanded to also incorporate the advanced image recognition and analysis features of GPT-4. This approach involves uploading BPMN diagrams in PNG format – upon uploading, the AI decodes the graphical elements and their interconnections within the BPMN models, in order to provide answers to user queries based on artificial vision.

## 5 Experimental Outcomes and Evaluation

We examine responses produced by GPT-4, during April 2024, to a variety of prompts probing its BPMN-based process analysis capabilities based on multi-modal content – the RDF representation, the XML standard serialization and exported images. In the first part, we refer by CASE I to the RDF variant and by CASE II to SAP Signavio exports. This approach is not intended to highlight limitations within any specific tool, but to explore the differences and potential insights that each format may reveal.

In the preliminary stages, the tools deployed in the aforementioned cases demonstrated adeptness in responding to straightforward inquiries, such as identifying participants within processes, elucidating the sequence of steps in the processes etc. These inquiries, predominantly aimed at recognizing basic BPMN elements established a baseline of competence. Given this proficiency in handling elementary symbol interpretations, our study shifted focus to more sophisticated queries.

We utilized the Retrieval Augmented Generation Assessment (RAGAs) framework [28] to compare the answers generated by the LLM across the formatted BPMN content, focusing on four key metrics: *faithfulness, answer relevancy, answer correctness* and *answer similarity* [29]. Starting with *Faithfulness*, this metric assesses the extent to which the claims made in a generated answer are supported by the information present in the BPMN model. An answer is considered faithful if it accurately reflects the processes and information modeled in the BPMN context without introducing inaccuracies or unsupported details. *Answer Relevance* measures how well the generated answer addresses the question posed, namely the prompt for each experiment. A high relevance score is awarded to answers that effectively reflect the specific requirements or queries related to the BPMN process, without adding irrelevant or redundant information. *Answer Correctness* evaluates the accuracy of the generated answer in relation to the ground truth, alias the process described in the BPMN model. This metric looks at both the semantic and factual similarity between the response and the ground truth. High correctness indicates that the answer not only addresses the question correctly, but also aligns closely with the details within the BPMN model. *Answer Semantic Similarity* focuses on how closely the meaning and context of the response align with what was expected in the ground truth.

## 5.1 RDF vs. XML Formats

The XML process serializations offer standard vocabularies, not only a standard structure (XML being traditionally a data interchange format). The RDF export of BPMN is only standard in the structural sense – as directed semantic graphs – and not as a process description vocabulary, for which intuitive tool-specific terms are generated by Bee-Up - derived from the concept labelling prescribed on metamodel level. Therefore, LLMs treat the RDF variant as a semantic network that happens to contain edges whose labels describe workflows, while the XML variant is recognized upfront as a standard interchange format widely available in training corpora and Web content.

The *contexts* array within our dataset is drawn from files provided either in TriG serialization format for RDF or BPMN format for XML, depending on the type of data representation needed. This distinction is crucial, as it ensures that our evaluations remain faithful to the actual context of our experiments, reflecting the true nature of the processes being analyzed. *Ground_truth* in this dataset is equally significant, because it serves as the gold standard against which the generated answers are compared. Our findings are presented in the tables below.

**Prompt 1:** Enumerate all activities after 'Add product to cart' action in the main process.

| CASE I | | CASE II | |
|---|---|---|---|
| Response generated by Ontotext GraphDB 10.5 using OpenAI gpt-4 model on RDF formatted data — 1. Edit quantity 2. Provide delivery & invoicing data 3. Request billing 4. Trigger payment with saved payment method 5. Approve online payment 6. Look for email from merchant 7. Save invoice 8. Generate order confirmation SMS 9. Notify delay 10. Track order 11. Leave feedback 12. Generate failure SMS 13. Notify user of failed authentication 14. Activate bot | | Response generated by *BPMN Analyst* on imported BPMN file — After the "Add product to cart" action in the main process, the next activity is "Edit quantity." If you need information on further activities or any other details from the process, feel free to ask! | |
| Ground truth | All the activities after "Add product to cart" action in the main process are: "Edit quantity", "Provide delivery & invoicing data" or "Notify user of failed authentication" (if applicable), "Request billing", "Trigger payment with saved payment method" and "Approve online payment", "Look for email from merchant", "Save invoice" or "Generate failure SMS" (if needed), "Generate order confirmation SMS", "Track order", "Leave feedback" or "Notify delay" (if applicable). | | |
| **RAGAs metrics** | | | |
| Faithfulness | 1.0 | Faithfulness | 0.926067 |
| Answer Relevancy | 0.778516 | Answer Relevancy | 0.339887 |
| Answer Correctness | 0.952734 | Answer Correctness | 0.5 |
| Answer Similarity | 0.90771 | Answer Similarity | 0.897952 |

The distinction between CASE I (RDF-formatted data) and CASE II (XML-formatted data) highlights significant differences in data handling and response generation. CASE I offers a rich, detailed response, leveraging the ability of RDF to use semantic relationships for a deep understanding of the process flow. This is evidenced by a perfect *faithfulness* score of 1.0, indicating that the generated answer can be accurately inferred from the provided BPMN process. However, its *answer relevancy* score of 0.778516, while lower than might be expected given the comprehensive response, suggests that the answer includes unnecessary and inaccurate details, such as the task "Activate bot", overshooting the needs of the prompt. Lastly, the high level of *answer correctness*, with a score of 0.952734, indicates a close alignment between the response and the ground truth. Conversely, CASE II presents a more streamlined response, focusing strictly on the immediate next step of the process. This approach, characteristic of the structured, tag-based processing of XML, captures data directly without the semantic depth of RDF. Although its *faithfulness* score is also high (at 0.926067), it indicates minor deviations from the complete process flow possibly expected in the response. The notably lower *answer relevancy* score of 0.339887 reflects a lack of comprehensive coverage of all subsequent activities, while the *answer correctness* of only 0.5 reveals that the response, while partially accurate, falls short in representing the depth and complexity of the BPMN process as required. The higher *similarity* score for CASE I (0.90771) suggests that it aligns more closely with the ground truth.

**Prompt 2.** What happens if the authentication is not successful?

| CASE I | CASE II |
|---|---|
| If the authentication is not successful, the user will be notified of the failed authentication. This is represented by the task "Notify user of failed authentication". This notification will likely prompt the user to attempt again, possibly resetting their password if they have forgotten it. The exact steps taken will depend on the specific protocols of the authentication system being used. | If the authentication is not successful, the process flows to a "sendTask" where the user is notified of the failed authentication. This task explicitly handles the communication of the unsuccessful authentication result to the user. |
| **Ground truth** | If the authentication is not successful, the user is notified of the failed authentication. |

| RAGAs metrics | | | |
|---|---|---|---|
| Faithfulness | 0.6 | Faithfulness | 0.0 |
| Answer Relevancy | 0.911374 | Answer Relevancy | 1.0 |
| Answer Correctness | 0.448622 | Answer Correctness | 0.529958 |
| Answer Similarity | 0.937347 | Answer Similarity | 0.919833 |

*Faithfulness* is a critical metric that measures the factual consistency of the response against the provided context. In the first case, the RDF-formatted data provided a structured context that aligns relatively well with the response, resulting in a *faithfulness* score of 0.6. This score indicates that while the response is largely aligned with the RDF context, it includes speculative steps like password reset, which are not part of the modeled process, thus reducing the score. For the second case, despite the correctness of the response, its *faithfulness* score was surprisingly low, at 0.0. The response might be correct in practical terms, but if it deviates in any way from the parsed context (e.g., due to incomplete or misinterpreted XML data), the faithfulness score would reflect this misalignment. In terms of *answer relevancy*, the response in CASE I is mostly relevant, with minor penalties for the additional, speculative details. Meanwhile, the perfect relevancy score in CASE II reflects the effectiveness of the response in addressing the core issue without introducing irrelevant details. Focusing on the next metric, namely *answer correctness*, the scores in both cases reflect responses that are nearly half correct. This is due to details that are not part of the modeled process. Concerning *answer similarity*, both CASE I and CASE II responses are semantically close to the ground truth, as indicated by their high answer similarity scores, although CASE I, with its detailed and contextual information, achieves a slightly higher score, demonstrating the benefits of RDF-formatted data in providing comprehensive responses.

**Prompt 3.** What are the costs within the current authentication subprocess?

| CASE I | CASE II |
|---|---|
| The costs within the current authentication subprocess are as follows: 1. Retrieve user credentials: $0.01 2. Validate credentials: $0.02 3. Check access rights: $0.03 4. Create authentication log: $0.01 5. Check for multiple failed attempts: $0.01 6. Lock account: $0.03 7. Increment failed attempts counter: $0.01 8. Notify user of account status: $0.02 9. Notify user of failed authentication: $0.02 Please note that these costs are likely representative of time, resources, and computational costs associated with each step in the subprocess. | The current authentication subprocess does not have any explicit cost-related metadata defined within the provided BPMN file. If you need detailed cost information, it might be necessary to check the process documentation or other relevant resources. If you have other specific queries about this subprocess or need to verify other elements, feel free to ask. |
| Ground truth | The costs within the current authentication subprocess are: Retrieve user credentials: $0.01, Validate credentials: $0.02, Check access rights: $0.03, Create authentication log: $0.01, Check for multiple failed attempts: $0.01, Lock account: $0.03, Increment failed attempts counter: $0.01, Notify user of account status: $0.02. |

| RAGAs metrics | | | |
|---|---|---|---|
| Faithfulness | 1.0 | Faithfulness | 0.0 |
| Answer Relevancy | 1.0 | Answer Relevancy | 0.0 |
| Answer Correctness | 0.749073 | Answer Correctness | 0.199727 |
| Answer Similarity | 0.996273 | Answer Similarity | 0.798452 |

This is based on costing attributes being annotated to the diagram elements. The RDF-based response (CASE I) has a perfect score in terms of *faithfulness* and provides an exhaustive breakdown of costs associated with each task in the evaluated subprocess, demonstrating explicit labeling and encoding of cost metadata alongside process elements. In comparison, the XML standard (CASE II), with a score of 0.0 with regard to this metric, adheres to a more semantically restricted, closed-world XML schema and does not connect it to attributes attached as arbitrary metadata or to Signavio dictionary assets (e.g., RACI links to organization roles) – although these can be exported separately and again linked by inter-tag key references or manually edited according to the generic metadata tags (with metaKey, metaValue attributes). *Answer relevancy* scores 0.0 in CASE II, proof that XML understanding seems to stick to generative content based on the standard XML schema, avoiding tool-specific extension; in contrast, even if the RDF export is tool-specific from the grounds up, it seems to be more organically navigated as a freely expandable network of labelled associations (with a perfect score for *answer relevancy*). This is somewhat ironical – as RDF has been often seen as a metadata standard rather than a graph database format – but for LLMs, it may be more semantically integrative than actual metadata based on intricate cross-references between keys. The relatively high *correctness* score of 0.749073 in CASE I indicates that while the response is mostly correct, it includes a minor assumption, namely the additional information on speculative nature of cost estimations, which affect the alignment between the generated answer and the ground truth. The lack of completeness and specificity in addressing the query results in a significantly lower *correctness* score (0.199727) for CASE II. The discrepancy between the scores related to the *answer similarity* RAGAs metric is not as drastic as it is regarding *answer correctness*; yet, CASE I stands out with a nearly perfect score of 0.996273, directly matching the ground truth.

## 5.2 RDF vs. Images (PNG)

Moving from serializations to computer vision, we assess how each conveys process information differently, particularly in how visual cues and structured data can variably influence the responses provided by the multi-modal capabilities of GPT-4. There is tendency of verbosity when interpreting an image compared to interpreting a data structure. Also, the visual interpretation will inherently miss any information not visually reflected – e.g., links between diagrams or attributes. The experiments within this category also benefit from incorporating RAGAs metrics. However, due to the constraints of the dataset which supports *contexts* as a list of strings, we could not apply the *faithfulness* and *answer relevance* metrics effectively. These metrics require external knowledge sources in the form of structured, text-based *contexts* to function correctly, which visual data inherently lacks. Despite these limitations, we utilized two other key metrics: *answer correctness* and *answer similarity*. These metrics do not require external data used to inform responses, allowing us to evaluate the semantic alignment and factual accuracy of the generated responses relative to the ground truth, providing valuable insights into how each format conveys BPMN process information differently.

**Prompt 4.** What are the distinct activities depicted in the main online ordering process, from the initiation of the order to the finalization of the purchase?

| CASE I | CASE II |
|---|---|
| Response generated by Ontotext GraphDB 10.5 using OpenAI gpt-4 model on RDF formatted data | Response provided by GPT-4 on imported images |
| Here are the distinct activities involved in the online ordering process: 1. Activation of online shopping site bot. 2. Browsing products page to select desired product. 3. Accessing product details to gain more information about selected products. 4. Adding selected products to the cart. 5. Editing product quantity within the cart. 6. Providing delivery and invoicing data for order processing. 7. Requesting billing details for payment purposes. 8. Triggering payment with saved payment method on the platform. 9. Approval of online payment by the customer. 10. Generation and receipt of order confirmation messages through Email or SMS. 11. Looking for an email from the merchant for other notifications such as invoice, delivery details etc. 12. Saving invoice for future references. 13. Tracking order status online. 14. Notification of delivery delay (if any). 15. Leaving feedback after receiving the product. 16. Generation of failure SMS if any step fails. 17. Notification of failed authentication if login details are incorrect. | The main online ordering process, as per the first BPMN diagram, can be dissected into the following distinct activities: 1. **Activation of Bot**: The process begins with the customer initiating an online order which activates the bot. 2. **Product Browsing and Selection**: The customer browses the product page. They access product details for items they are interested in. If the customer desires to purchase a product, it is added to the cart. The process allows for the repetition of the browsing and adding products to the cart as necessary. If more of the same product is needed, the quantity is edited in the cart. 3. **Authentication**: The bot then attempts to authenticate the customer using stored user credentials. If authentication fails, the customer is notified of the failed attempt. Successful authentication allows the process to proceed. 4. **Delivery and Billing**: Delivery and invoicing data are provided by the customer, likely in an Excel format. The customer then requests billing, which would include the generation of an invoice. 5. **Payment**: The customer approves the online payment. The payment method is triggered using the saved payment method details. 6. **Order Placement and Confirmation**: The order is officially placed. The bot searches for an email confirmation from the merchant, ensuring that the order has been acknowledged. An invoice is saved in the default folder once the order and payment are confirmed. If the system detects an order cancellation, a failure SMS is generated. If the order is successful, an order confirmation SMS is generated, likely through Twilio API. 7. **Post-Order Activities**: The customer has the option to track their order. If there is a delay beyond a set period (20 days late, as per the diagram), the customer is notified. Upon arrival of the order, the customer may be asked to provide feedback. If there is a failure in the delivery or other issues, the customer receives a failure notification. If the customer is unsatisfied, the process allows them to leave feedback. 8. **Finalization**: The process concludes with the successful completion of the purchase, assuming there are no issues with the order delivery or customer satisfaction. Each step in this sequence plays a pivotal role in the process, with the aim to ensure a seamless and secure customer experience, from the initial interest to the final post-purchase feedback. The BPMN diagram outlines not only the ideal flow but also the contingencies and feedback mechanisms in place to address any issues that may arise, thus covering the complete lifecycle of an online order. |
| Ground truth | The distinct activities depicted in the main online ordering process, from the initiation of the order to the finalization of the purchase are: 1. Activate bot, 2. Browse products page, 3. Access product details, 4. Add product to cart, 5. Edit quantity (if more of the same product is needed), 6. Bot authentication microflow, 7. Provide delivery & invoicing data (if authentication is successful), 8. Notify user of failed authentication (if authentication is unsuccessful), 9. Request billing, 10. Trigger payment with saved payment method and 11. Approve online payment, 12. Look for confirmation email from merchant, 13. Save invoice (if invoice and order confirmation are valid), 14. Generate order confirmation SMS, 15. Generate failure SMS (in case of order cancellation detected), 16. Track order, 17. Leave feedback (if needed), 18. Notify delay (if the order is 20 days late). |
| RAGAs metrics | | | |
| Answer Correctness | 0.241237 | Answer Correctness | 0.232882 |
| Answer Similarity | 0.964949 | Answer Similarity | 0.931607 |

The unexpected low *correctness* score of 0.241237 in CASE I is influenced by minor changes in the labeling of tasks (e.g., from "browse" – present tense, to "browsing" – present continuous), which, while still accurate, affects the exact match with the ground truth required for higher correctness. The only significant omission is the subprocess "Bot authentication microflow", which is essential for the BPMN process. CASE II, with a *correctness* score of 0.232882, maintains a high-level overview of the process, but also diverges in some details and structure from the ground truth. The high *similarity* scores in both cases (0.964949 for CASE I and 0.931607 for CASE II) indicate that both responses are semantically close to the ground truth. The structured and detailed mapping of CASE I results in a slightly higher *similarity* score compared to CASE II, which, while verbose, captures the essential elements of the process, but with more contextual information that diverges from the exact ground truth.

**Prompt 5.** In what specific cases is the user notified through SMS?

| CASE I | CASE II |
|---|---|
| Based on the provided information, the user is notified through SMS in the following scenarios: 1. When an order confirmation is generated. This is represented by the task "Generate order confirmation SMS". 2. When a failure occurs. This task is represented by "Generate failure SMS". Please note that the method of notification (i.e., whether it is through SMS, email, app notification, etc.) is not explicitly stated in the other tasks. | In the business process model you've provided, SMS notifications are sent to the user in the following specific scenarios: 1. **Order Confirmation SMS**: Once an order is successfully placed, an order confirmation SMS is generated. This notification informs the user that their order has been processed and is under way. 2. **Failure SMS**: In case of an order cancellation detected or if any other issue occurs that prevents the successful processing of the order, a failure SMS is sent to notify the user of the problem. 3. **Success SMS**: This might be part of the process that handles various successful transactions or acknowledgments not specifically detailed in the provided diagram. Typically, such an SMS could confirm successful payment processing or update on shipping status. These notifications are essential in keeping the user informed about critical events related to their order status and account activity, enhancing the user experience by providing timely and relevant information. |
| Ground truth | The user is notified through SMS in the following cases: when an order confirmation is generated, which is represented by the task "Generate order confirmation SMS", and when an order cancellation is detected, which is represented by the task "Generate failure SMS". |

| RAGAs metrics ||||
|---|---|---|---|
| **Answer Correctness** | 0.744594 | **Answer Correctness** | 0.481418 |
| **Answer Similarity** | 0.978424 | **Answer Similarity** | 0.925707 |

In CASE I, the *answer correctness* score of 0.744594 indicates that the response accurately captures the key scenarios where the user is notified through SMS. The response closely aligns with the ground truth, although it is slightly penalized for the redundant information at the end. In CASE II, the *correctness* score of 0.481418 is lower, because the response includes an additional scenario (Success SMS) that is not present in the ground truth. This inclusion diverges from the exact scenarios provided, reducing the *correctness* score. The additional context around the notifications, while informative, does not align strictly with the ground truth and thus, negatively affects the score. As for *answer similarity*, the structured and concise listing of SMS notification scenarios in CASE I results in a slightly higher *similarity* score compared to CASE II, which includes additional information that introduces a minor semantic divergence.

**Prompt 6.** What are the execution time and costs for notifying the user regarding their account status?

| CASE I | CASE II |
|---|---|
| The execution time for notifying the user regarding their account status is 2 seconds and the costs associated with it are 0.02 units. | The BPMN diagrams provided do not explicitly mention the execution time or costs associated with notifying the user regarding their account status. In a typical online ordering system, the execution time and costs for user notification would depend on several factors: 1. **Notification Medium: Email**: Usually free and nearly instantaneous, but can sometimes be delayed due to server issues or spam filters. **SMS**: Sending SMS messages via a service like Twilio would generally incur a cost per message sent, and delivery is usually within seconds. 2. **Service Provider**: Costs can vary significantly between different providers and are based on factors such as volume of notifications, destination, and service level agreements. 3. **Infrastructure**: On-premises solutions might have a higher initial setup cost but lower operational costs per notification compared to cloud-based services, which might be more expensive per notification but have lower setup costs. 4. **Automation Level**: Fully automated notifications through a bot would have different cost implications compared to a process that requires manual intervention. 5. **Geographical Factors**: International notifications may cost more and take longer than domestic ones. 6. **Volume**: High volumes of notifications can typically leverage bulk discounts. 7. **Urgency**: Notifications that require immediate delivery (such as those for real-time transactions) might have higher costs due to the need for more robust delivery guarantees. To determine the specific execution time and costs for notifying users about their account status within the given process, one would need additional information such as the service provider's pricing, the average number of notifications sent, and the geographical distribution of the users. Typically, these details would be defined in the operational parameters of the service level agreements with the providers and in the system's technical architecture documents. Without this information, it is not possible to provide precise timeframes or cost estimations. |
| Ground truth | The execution time for notifying the user regarding their account status is 2 seconds and the costs associated with it are 0.02 units. |
| **RAGAs metrics** ||

| Answer Correctness | 1.0 | Answer Correctness | 0.401071 |
|---|---|---|---|
| Answer Similarity | 1.0 | Answer Similarity | 0.854348 |

The specific and quantifiable data offered by CASE I enables superior analysis based on quantitative attributes, demonstrated by perfect scores regarding *answer correctness* and *similarity*. In contrast, CASE II utilizes visual diagrams exclusively, which inherently lack the capability to encapsulate certain metadata associated with process activities, obtaining significantly lower scores in terms of the evaluated metrics. While images are effective for outlining the overall flow and sequence of processes, they do not ensure granular means of visual annotation/attribute definition, whereas the RDF representation can expand with additional edges and nodes beyond the conceptualization established by the standard BPMN vocabulary and associated schemas. This hampers the utility of image recognition for detailed operational analysis therefore it should not be seen as a holy grail of interacting with BPM systems strictly by visual means – diagrammatic modeling should be seen as multi-modal encoding of knowledge (linear text, networked associations and visual abstractions) therefore coherent integration of these layers will be paramount for future AI-based Business Process Management Systems.

### 5.3 Future Work: Serialization Generation

The well-known LLM capabilities of generating code snippets can be repurposed for generating model serializations, which are of much more general use than having just a picture generated, often containing hallucinated visual artifacts, compared to the more deterministic nature of a serialization schema. However, just as with tailoring the right type of coding approach or coding style, adjustments are needed depending not as much on the serialization format, but on the targeted tool – where the generated model should be importable. Even for standards-compliant tools such as SAP Signavio, the expected XML input requires numerous trials to ensure interchange and layout. We noticed some carelessness in positioning on the visual canvas even for the simplest examples such as the one depicted in Fig. 2 – a tendency to place subsequent elements in some proximity of their preceding element, with no attention to connector routing or relative positioning. This is still subject to experimentation, to try to achieve some semblance of determinism in position generation without explicitly positioning every element.

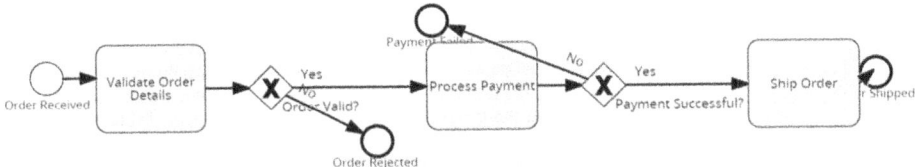

**Fig. 2.** SAP Signavio visualization of generated XML serialization.

We managed to generate correct diagrams by providing layout details for each particular element, but with a prescriptive effort much higher than simply drawing the diagram. Moreover, pointing to the BPMN XML standard and the need to import it in Signavio was insufficient, it had to be complemented with explicit requests to include BPMN-DI (diagram interchange) information, to ensure clear visual pathways, to include elements of the *signavio:* namespace and other details leading to highly complex prompts. The approach gets even more cumbersome when generating the tool-specific RDF serialization, which does not benefit from a standard vocabulary, thus requiring rich instructions for every edge and note type to appear in the graph. This line of experimentation is left out of the scope of this report, as it serves different phases of the BPM lifecycle and perhaps can be better served by more fine-tuned solutions.

### 6 Conclusions

Through the comparative use of RDF-encoded semantic graphs and XML-encoded diagrams, the experiments delineate nuanced treatments for BPMN models subjected to certain LLM services as procedural knowledge to be interpreted. Our findings, substantiated by the scores obtained using the RAGAs framework, indicate that RDF exports provide a more open-ended and context-aware approach to process interpretation, compared to the standard XML export which appears to be treated as a closed-world data structure, even though the RDF version employs a non-standard, tool-specific, process description vocabulary. The visual interpretation of BPMN images is apparently closer to the open-endedness of the RDF variant, but only in terms of verbose extrapolations to hypothetical contexts rather than as interpretation of explicitly networked information; moreover, visual scrutiny misses all linked information that is semantically relevant but not visually manifested. On managerial level the ability to relate elements that were visually recognized in different diagrams is critical. The benefits of visual intuitiveness and open-ended semantic enrichment must complement one another in a hybrid of sensory-reasoning interpretative capability.

The study has inherent limitations due to the fast evolution and stochastic nature of LLM services – not only variations between different versions, but also between work sessions are noticeable, thus posing challenges to reproducibility. Therefore this work is not intended to be an evaluation of capabilities of a certain LLM product, but more of a proposition of an interpretation and analysis protocol towards an augmented revisitation of the traditional BPM lifecycle as envisioned by [13].

Future work will be invested in further exploration of the possible synergies between the BPM lifecycle and LLM services, specifically on prompting strategies that can generate process serializations from narrative instructions in a way that balances visual clarity, expressive labelling, non-trivial complexity and granular serialization. We also need to revisit these experiments with a systematic focus on more granular workflow patterns, as the current study tackled end-to-end process interpretation to assess the LLM ability of contextualizing the business process descriptions.

**Acknowledgement.** This work was supported through the student research scholarship no. 36300/2024, granted to Damaris Dolha by Babeș-Bolyai University.

# References

1. Camunda: What is BPMN? business process model and notation. https://camunda.com/bpmn/. Accessed 16 Dec 2023
2. Cinpoeru, M., Ghiran, A.-M., Harkai, A., Buchmann, R.A., Karagiannis, D.: Model-driven context configuration in business process management systems: an approach based on knowledge graphs. In: Pańkowska, M., Sandkuhl, K. (eds.) Perspectives in Business Informatics Research: 18th International Conference, BIR 2019, Katowice, Poland, September 23–25, 2019, Proceedings, pp. 189–203. Springer International Publishing, Cham (2019). https://doi.org/10.1007/978-3-030-31143-8_14
3. OMILAB NPO: Bee-up for education. https://bee-up.omilab.org/activities/bee-up/. Accessed 30 Dec 2023
4. Bachhofner, S., Kiesling, E., Revoredo, K., Waibel, P., Polleres, A.: Automated process knowledge graph construction from BPMN models. In: Strauss, C., Cuzzocrea, A., Gabriele Kotsis, A., Tjoa, M., Khalil, I. (eds.) Database and Expert Systems Applications: 33rd International Conference, DEXA 2022, Vienna, Austria, August 22–24, 2022, Proceedings, Part I, pp. 32–47. Springer International Publishing, Cham (2022). https://doi.org/10.1007/978-3-031-12423-5_3

5. Buchmann, R.A., Ussenbayeva, M., Utz, W., Karagiannis, D: Leveraging RDF graphs, similarity metrics and network analysis for business process management. In: Martin A., et al. (eds.) Proceedings of the AAAI 2023 Spring Symposium on Challenges Requiring the Combination of Machine Learning and Knowledge Engineering (AAAI-MAKE 2023). Hyatt Regency, San Francisco Airport, California, USA (2023). https://ceur-ws.org/Vol-3433/paper14.pdf
6. Uifălean, Ș, Ghiran, A.-M., Buchmann, R.A.: Employing graph databases for business process management and representation. In: Silaghi, G.C., Buchmann, R.A., Niculescu, V., Czibula, G., Barry, C., Lang, M., Linger, H., Schneider, C. (eds.) Advances in Information Systems Development: AI for IS Development and Operations, pp. 73–92. Springer International Publishing, Cham (2023). https://doi.org/10.1007/978-3-031-32418-5_5
7. Fill, H., Fettke, P., Köpke, J.: Conceptual modeling and large language models: Impressions from first experiments with ChatGPT. EMISAJ **18**(3), 1–15 (2023). https://doi.org/10.18417/emisa.18.3
8. Dolha, D.N., Buchmann, R.A.: Comparative analysis of natural language query responses on BPMN model serializations: RDF graphs vs. BPMN XML. In: Presented at: The 23rd International Conference on Informatics in Economy. IE 2024. Timişoara (2024)
9. Dolha, D.N., Buchmann, R.A.: Experiments with natural language queries on RDF vs. XML-serialized BPMN diagrams. In: 28th International Conference on Knowledge-Based and Intelligent Information & Engineering Systems. KES (2024). In press
10. Guntur, B.H.: Automating data flow diagram generation from user stories using large language models. In: 7th Workshop on Natural Language Processing for Requirements Engineering, Winterthur, Switzerland (2024). https://hal.science/hal-04525925/
11. AQL query language: ADOxx documentation. https://www.adoxx.org/live/adoxx-query-language-aql/. Accessed 12 Jan 2024
12. Grohs, M., Abb, L., Elsayed, N., Rehse, JR.: Large language models can accomplish business process management tasks. In: De Weerdt, J., Pufahl, L. (eds.) Business Process Management Workshops. BPM 2023. Lecture Notes in Business Information Processing, vol. 492. Springer, Cham (2024). https://doi.org/10.48550/arXiv.2307.09923
13. Vidgof, M., Bachhofner, S., Mendling, J.: Large language models for business process management: opportunities and challenges. In: Di Francescomarino, C., Burattin, A., Janiesch, C., Sadiq, S. (eds.) Business Process Management Forum. BPM 2023. Lecture Notes in Business Information Processing, vol. 490. Springer, Cham (2023). https://doi.org/10.48550/arXiv.2304.04309
14. Jalali, A.: Graph-based process mining. In: Leemans, S., Leopold, H. (eds.) Process Mining Workshops: ICPM 2020 International Workshops, Padua, Italy, October 5–8, 2020, Revised Selected Papers, pp. 273–285. Springer International Publishing, Cham (2021). https://doi.org/10.1007/978-3-030-72693-5_21
15. OpenAI: GPT-4. https://openai.com/research/gpt-4. Accessed 15 Apr 2024
16. Polyvyanyy, A.: Process querying: methods, techniques, and applications. In: Polyvyanyy, A. (ed.) Process Querying Methods, pp. 511–524. Springer International Publishing, Cham (2022). https://doi.org/10.1007/978-3-030-92875-9_18
17. Busch, K., Rochlitzer, A., Sola, D., Leopold, H.: Just tell me: prompt engineering in business process management. In: van der Aa, H., Bork, D., Proper, H.A., Schmidt, R. (eds.) Enterprise, Business-Process and Information Systems Modeling. BPMDS EMMSAD 2023 2023. Lecture Notes in Business Information Processing, vol. 479. Springer, Cham (2023). https://doi.org/10.48550/arXiv.2304.07183
18. Shahin, M., Chen, F.F., Hosseinzadeh, A., Maghanaki, M., Eghbalian, A.: A novel approach to voice of customer extraction using GPT-3.5 turbo: linking advanced NLP and lean six sigma 4.0. Int. J. Adv. Manuf. Technol. **131**, 3615–3630 (2024). https://doi.org/10.21203/rs.3.rs-3246823/v1

19. Jasińska, K., Lewicz, M., Rostalski, M.: Digitization of the enterprise - prospects for process automation with using RPA and GPT integration. Procedia Comput. Sci. **225**, 3243–3254 (2023). https://doi.org/10.1016/j.procs.2023.10.318
20. Yang, L.F., Chen, H., Li, Z., Ding, X., Wu, X.: Give us the facts: enhancing large language models with knowledge graphs for fact-aware language modeling. IEEE Transactions on Knowledge and Data Engineering (2023). https://doi.org/10.48550/arXiv.2306.11489
21. Karagiannis, D., Buchmann, R.A., Utz, W.: The OMiLAB digital innovation environment: agile conceptual models to bridge business value with digital and physical twins for product-service systems development. Comput. Ind. **138**, 103631 (2022). https://doi.org/10.1016/j.compind.2022.103631
22. Buchmann, R. A., Burzynski, P., Utz, W: ER2023 tutorials: semantic enrichment & digital twins based on conceptual modeling: the bee-up tool. https://er2023.inesc-id.pt/program/tutorials/#tutorial3/. Accessed 30 Dec 2023
23. SAP Signavio: SAP signavio process transformation suite, academic edition. https://www.signavio.com/academic-and-research-alliances/. Accessed 15 Apr 2024
24. Buchmann, R.A., Karagiannis, D.: Pattern-based transformation of diagrammatic conceptual models for semantic enrichment in the web of data. Procedia Comput. Sci. **60**, 150–159 (2015). https://doi.org/10.1016/j.procs.2015.08.114
25. Ontotext, What is GraphDB? – GraphDB 10.5 documentation. https://graphdb.ontotext.com/documentation/10.5/. Accessed 15 Apr 2024
26. Ontotext: Querying OpenAI GPT Models. https://graphdb.ontotext.com/documentation/10.5/gpt-queries.html#configuring. Accessed 15 Apr 2024
27. OpenAI: Introducing ChatGPT Plus. https://openai.com/blog/chatgpt-plus. Accessed 15 Apr 2024
28. Es, S., James, J., Espinosa-Anke, L., Schockaert, S.: RAGAS: automated evaluation of retrieval augmented generation. In: Proceedings of the 18th Conference of the European Chapter of the Association for Computational Linguistics: System Demonstrations. Association for Computational Linguistics (2024). https://aclanthology.org/2024.eacl-demo.16
29. Ragas: Metrics. https://docs.ragas.io/en/v0.0.17/concepts/metrics/index.html. Accessed 15 Apr 2024

# LLM-Assistance for Quality Control of LLM Output

Kurt Sandkuhl[1,2]

[1] Institute of Computer Science, University of Rostock, Albert-Einstein-Street 22, 18057 Rostock, Germany
kurt.sandkuhl@uni-rostock.de, kurt.sandkuhl@ju.se
[2] School of Engineering, Jönköping University, Jönköping, Sweden

**Abstract.** Large language models (LLM) have been successfully applied in enterprise modelling (EM) for various tasks, such as supporting modellers and domain experts in modelling the current situation in enterprises. An important factor for the successful application of LLM is the quality of the LLM output. This paper's research investigates whether LLM can be used as a tool for the quality control of LLM output. Starting from an analysis of LLM evaluation approaches, the paper focuses on investigating scenarios for LLM use and relevant quality criteria. The main contributions of this paper are (1) an approach for using LLM as support for quality control of LLM output in enterprise modelling consisting of quality criteria for defined application scenarios and their operationalization and (2) quasi-experiments showing the applicability of the approach.

**Keywords:** Large Language Models · LLM · ChatGPT · Quality Control · Quality · Quality Assurance

## 1 Introduction

The recent progress in generative artificial intelligence (AI) has triggered a lot of research into potential application areas, new business models or entirely new products and services based on AI [1]. One branch of generative AI, the neural text generators or large language models (LLM), is considered in both industry and research as promising technology for automating routine tasks in various industries, with the perspective of substantial improvement of productivity (see, e.g., [2, 3]). AI technologies have the capability to perform cognitive functions in a way that resembles a human-like manner and the ability to learn and self-correct [4]. Initial experiences from applying LLM, such as OpenAI's ChatGPT, in engineering confirm this technology's potential for supporting development processes. Examples are the use of Co-Pilot in software engineering [5], ChatGPT in information system design for UML modelling [6] and in design and manufacturing [7].

An important factor for the successful application of LLM is the quality of the LLM output. Hallucinations in the output, prompts resulting in text not relevant to the task at hand, inconsistencies or incompleteness can turn LLM from a helpful tool into a burden, which is even more the case if the deficits remain undiscovered. In light of the increasing use of LLM for various purposes, tools supporting quality control of LLM output gain importance. In this context, the research presented in this paper investigates whether LLM can be used as a tool for the quality control of LLM output.

As the term quality has many different meanings, and the quality of a product or service can be perceived differently depending on the application context and different user groups in this context [8], an investigation into the quality of LLM output requires a more precise definition of what quality means. Due to our experience using LLM in enterprise modelling, we focus on the application of LLM to support the development of enterprise models. Results of our previous work indicate that LLM can serve in some enterprise modelling tasks as a proxy or support for domain experts, and prompt patterns are a suitable instrument to make the knowledge of how to use LLM reusable. Starting from this background, we attempt to define quality from a domain expert perspective and capture how to determine the quality level in reusable prompt patterns. This results in three research questions (RQ) for this paper:

- RQ1: What quality criteria should be applied to determine the quality of LLM output for EM from a domain expert perspective?
- RQ2: How can LLM assist in determining these criteria?
- RQ3: How can the approach to LLM-assisted quality control be made explicit?

The paper is structured as follows: Sect. 2 presents the theoretical background for our work from LLM and LLM in enterprise modelling. Section 3 discusses related work on quality control of LLM output. Section 4 develops an approach for using LLM as support for quality control of LLM output in enterprise modelling consisting of quality criteria for defined application scenarios and their operationalization. Section 5 documents quasi-experiments showing the applicability of the approach. Section 6 discusses the findings of our work and potential future activities.

## 2 Theoretical Background

### 2.1 Large Language Models

The release of ChatGPT by OpenAI in November 2022 marked a significant moment in integrating AI into mainstream applications, aiding in diverse problem-solving tasks. GPT-3, the model behind ChatGPT, operates with 175 billion parameters and utilizes datasets that include nearly a trillion words sourced from various corpora, such as the Common Crawl, WebText2, internet-based books, and the English version of Wikipedia [9]. Its training involves predicting the next sequence of tokens based on given contexts, which enables it to generate realistic and novel word sequences.

Large Language Models (LLMs) like GPT-3 are pre-trained in a task-agnostic manner [10], which allows for flexible customization through in-context learning during runtime via natural language prompts. This advancement facilitates experimentation and prototyping in AI without the need for initial model training. ChatGPT can perform tasks like summarization, translation, grammar correction, and more, providing accessible AI tools across various fields, including education, which raises opportunities and concerns regarding academic integrity.

Prompt engineering has emerged as a crucial discipline in LLM utilization, conceptualized by [11]. It involves formulating prompts that effectively "program" the AI to perform desired tasks. Research shows that prompt design lacks standardized methods, relying heavily on trial and error [12]. This has led to developing domain-specific languages like Impromptu to support consistent, platform-independent prompt creation [13], highlighting the need for more structured approaches in prompt engineering.

Significant discussions in the literature focus on the need for meta-models and software tools to support effective prompt design, allowing prompts to be reused in various contexts (see, e.g. prompt chainer [14]) and helping manage their complexity akin to traditional programming. However, there is still a notable gap in comprehensive methods for prompt design, calling for method-driven tools that integrate expert knowledge to enhance the validity and effectiveness of LLM interactions [15].

## 2.2 LLM Support for Enterprise Modelling

Enterprise modelling (EM) addresses the "systematic analysis and modelling of processes, organization structures, products structures, IT systems or any other perspective relevant for the modelling purpose" [16]. The role of EM is usually to provide methods, tools, and practices for capturing and visualizing the current ("as-is") situation and developing the future ("to-be") situation. In particular, a model of the current situation forms one of the fundamentals for supporting the future development of organizations. Without knowledge of the "as-is", a systematic design and development of future capabilities, products, or services are usually difficult. The variety and dynamics of methods, languages, and tools supporting EM are visible in work on research roadmaps and future directions, originating both from the information systems community (see, e.g., [17]) and from scholars in industrial organizations (e.g., [18]).

Given the complexity of enterprises, there is a need to understand, analyze, capture, and represent what is relevant for different stakeholders and/or modelling purposes. In this context, there seems to be an agreement in the academic literature related to enterprise modelling that a key feature of an enterprise model is that it includes various perspectives. Frank [19], e.g., states that "a perspective as a psychological construct constitutes a conception of reality, comparable to a particular viewpoint in spatial perception [...], which helps to reduce complexity [...]." Frequently used perspectives are the processes, organization structures, products and services or IT infrastructure.

Fill et al. [20] and our previous work [21] have investigated LLM use in enterprise modelling: Fill et al. conducted experiments to generate and interpret conceptual models. They used ChatGPT to produce ER, BPMN, UML, and Heraklit models from a textual description. Furthermore, they provided models in the same modelling languages as textual input to ChatGPT and asked to check the model's correctness or answer questions related to the model content. The core conclusion of their work is the "enormous potential of large language models such as ChatGPT for supporting modelling tasks if a textual problem description of the domain to be modelled exists".

Our own work focused on the potential of LLMs as a proxy for domain experts. We structured our work along the phases of a modelling project and the tasks of domain experts in these phases. [22] distinguishes the phases of scoping, modelling of the current situation, analysis of required changes and potential alternatives, and modelling of the future situation. [23] describe the tasks of domain experts in EM as "supplying domain knowledge, knowledge about organization units involved [...]; examining and evaluating the results of enterprise modelling, and integration of modelling results [...] into a consistent whole." Experiments with ChatGPT conclude that LLM can help in modelling the current situation by providing general information about the application domain and common business processes, which reduces the workload of domain experts in supplying domain knowledge. For identifying change alternatives, LLM proved as a source of inspiration for the domain expert for goals and business rules.

## 3 Related Work

### 3.1 Quality Evaluation of LLM Output

The quality evaluation of LLM in general and of LLM output or results, in particular, has attracted much research in the last few years. A comprehensive analysis of the state of research by Liang et al. [24] identifies the most relevant aspects of evaluation, structures the overall research field and identifies grand challenges in the field. In their "grand challenges", they conclude that "evaluation should be treated as an essential discipline to drive the success of LLMs and other AI models". The survey covers many different scenarios, but the use of AI to support modelling is not discussed. In the list of opportunities for future research, the paper concludes that "there are many other research areas of LLMs, and we need to develop evaluation systems that can support all kinds of tasks". We consider enterprise modelling to be one of these research areas.

Chang et al. [25] summarise the essential aspects of LLM evaluation in three questions: what to evaluate, how to evaluate and where to evaluate. What to evaluate addresses the aspect that LLM's strengths and weaknesses must be assessed for different tasks and application fields, such as natural language processing, social sciences, natural science and engineering, and medical applications. They propose establishing benchmarks and evaluation protocols to avoid failure cases of LLM use.

How to evaluate basically distinguishes between automatic evaluation and human expert evaluation. Automatic evaluation focuses on criteria and indicators that can be computed or measured by a technical system. Here, different groups of criteria are proposed, such as accuracy, calibration, fairness and robustness, which, to a large extent, are based on the comparison of LLM output with a predefined reference output. Human evaluation relies on manual evaluation by human experts and includes accuracy, but it also uses categories such as relevance, fluency, transparency, and safety.

Where to evaluate basically addresses the datasets, evaluation environments and tools to use, such as existing benchmarks or approaches such as AlpacaEval [26].

[24] in their work also cover the aspects of what, how and where but refine them into a more fine-granular structure including metrics. They also collect indicators and metrics which they call "desiderata". The list of desiderata is extensive and structured into a taxonomy that includes, e.g., accuracy, robustness, fairness, bias and stereotypes, toxicity, calibration and uncertainty, and efficiency. The exact definitions of the desiderata are available in [24].

Also, the use of LLM for LLM evaluation has been investigated in previous research. [27] present EvaluLLM, an application designed to help practitioners set up, run and review evaluations over sets of natural language generation (NLG) outputs, using an LLM as a custom evaluator. The core idea is to support the human expert in comparing blind reviews provided by humans with evaluation scores provided by computed indicators using pairwise comparison.

In conclusion, the literature about LLM evaluation provides a lot of approaches, recommendations, and inspiration for evaluating LLM output, but there are no specific scenarios, criteria, or metrics for evaluating LLM output for EM using LLM. For our paper, the "what" is LLM use in EM, the how still needs to be clarified by defining indicators and the "where" partly consists of LLM, which also needs further specification.

### 3.2 Literature Analysis on LLM for Quality Control in EM

The summary of related work in Sect. 3.1 is mostly based on the extensive survey article by [24]. As it did not reveal any work at the intersection of enterprise modelling, LLM and quality control, we also performed a structured literature review according to the method proposed by Kitchenham [28]. This approach recommends steps. Step 1 is to formulate the overall research question: **RQ-SLR:** What is the state of research on using LLM for quality control of LLM output in conceptual and enterprise modelling? Step 2, the process of paper identification, starts with defining the overall search space, which basically consists of determining the literature sources to consider in light of the research questions. Here, we decided to use Scopus, IEEE Xplore and AIS to include work from different disciplines. Paper identification continues with the population phase (step 3). In this step, the search string is developed and applied by searching the literature sources. For the search string, we started from the three areas included in the RQ-SLR and added synonyms (see Table 1).

**Table 1.** Search terms and synonyms for the SLR

| Enterprise Modelling | LLM | Quality |
|---|---|---|
| Enterprise Modelling | LLM | Quality |
| Conceptual Modelling | Large Language Model | |
| Enterprise Model | ChatGPT | |
| Conceptual Model | Neural Text | |

The final search string is: ( TITLE-ABS-KEY ( llm OR "neural text" OR "ChatGPT" OR "large language models") AND TITLE-ABS-KEY ( quality) AND TITLE-ABS-KEY ( "enterprise modelling" OR "conceptual modelling" OR "conceptual model" OR "enterprise model")). Table 2 shows the number of hits and relevant papers among the hits for the three selected literature databases for the above search string[1].

Afterwards, "paper selection" follows by defining inclusion and exclusion criteria and manually selecting relevant papers found in the population phase (step 4). In Scopus,

---
[1] The search was performed on May2, 2024.

there was no relevant paper among the five hits: three papers are conference proceedings mentioning the search terms in the conference call, one is a prototype description for the topic of business design, and one addresses scheduling in project management.

**Table 2.** Number of Hits in the SLR

| Literature Source | Hits | Relevant |
|---|---|---|
| Scopus | 5 | 0 |
| IEEE Xplore | 0 | 0 |
| AISeL | 0 | 0 |

The data collection phase (step 5) focuses on extracting relevant information to answer the research question from the set of identified relevant papers. The last step is the analysis of data and interpretation, i.e., to answer the research question defined in step 1 by using collected data of relevant papers. Both steps were not necessary as no relevant paper was identified.

## 4 Quality Criteria for LLM Output in EM

The analysis of related work in Sect. 3.1 showed that there is a recommendation to define the "what", "how" and "where" of LLM evaluation. For the "what", the definition of scenarios of LLM use is recommended as a suitable instrument. Furthermore, Sect. 2.2 discussed LLM use in EM and showed several usage scenarios, among them scenarios where LLM has already been successfully applied:

- Scenario 1: the generation of conceptual models from text,
- Scenario 2: the interpretation of conceptual models provided as text,
- Scenario 3: the support of domain experts in modelling parts of the current situation of an enterprise and
- Scenario 4: the identification of trends in the modelling domain to generate proposals for change opportunities in an enterprise.

As this paper focuses on quality control of LLM output and not on developing new application scenarios for LLM in EM, we use the above scenarios. The "how" is the focus of this section and requires the definition (Sect. 4.1) and operationalization (Sect. 4.2) of quality criteria. The "where" is discussed in Sect. 5 about experiments.

### 4.1 Definition of Quality Criteria

For RQ1, the criteria to use for evaluating the quality of LLM output, we argue that – as all scenarios selected (see above) have a strong connection to conceptual modelling - the quality criteria applicable for input to conceptual modelling also apply to the LLM output. We used a 3-step process to identify these criteria: We started from a quality model in conceptual modelling, extracted criteria, and compared and enhanced them with LLM quality criteria. This resulted in a combined list, which in the third step was presented to experts in EM and LLM, who were asked to evaluate and rank the criteria. The result of the expert ranking determined what we used in our experiments. The 3-step process is described in the following in more detail.

Our starting point for identifying the quality criteria was the Semiotic Model Quality Framework (SEQUAL) [22]. SEQUAL addresses quality on various semiotic levels, such as syntax, semantics, and pragmatics, and acknowledges that models are often created in collaboration between those involved in modelling. SEQUAL considers users and modellers as social actors and proposes to distinguish between different aspects of model quality:

- Physical Quality considers the externalization of the model, i.e., how it is accessible to the users.
- Syntactic Quality refers to the coherence between a model and the modelling language, for example, by comparing the model and its meta-model.
- Semantic Quality refers to the correspondence between a model and the modelling domain. The meaning of the concepts in a domain has to be equivalent to the corresponding concepts in the model. Closely related is Perceived Semantic Quality, which addresses whether actors from the domain think that the meaning of concepts in the model fits the meaning of the same concepts in the domain.
- Empirical Quality compares different models created by a modeller to express the same understanding.
- Social Pragmatic Quality refers to how well the model is understood by human actors, comparing the modeller's intended understanding of the model.
- Technical Pragmatic Quality defines to what extent tools can interpret the model.
- Social Quality addresses the question of whether actors agree on the interpretation of the model.
- Deontic Quality investigates if all model elements contribute to fulfilling the goals of modelling and if all goals of modelling are addressed through the model.

As LLM predominantly produces textual output and not visual conceptual models, we delegate representation-related aspects, such as physical quality, syntactic quality and technical pragmatic quality, to future work. For the remaining quality aspects, we identify criteria and compare them with LLM quality criteria originating from the analysis of related work in Sect. 3.1. The result is presented in Table 3.

We expected to find definitions of criteria in the literature on LLM evaluation that can be used for our purposes. However, a closer look showed that most definitions were not applicable, as they are based on comparing LLM output against predefined reference datasets or gold standards. This allows for calculating recall, precision, F-scores and other numeric indicators originating from information retrieval and data science. Accuracy, for example, can be defined using recall and precision. However, such datasets do not exist for enterprise modelling and are difficult to generate as the variety of tasks potentially in the scope of EM is huge. Thus, we decided to define criteria (see Table 3) based on the intentions of SEQUAL and inspired by LLM desiderata. For all criteria, we assume that the modelling task is from a defined "domain", "output" refers to the result of LLM for the given task in this domain, "user" is the recipient of the output and familiar with

**Table 3.** Proposed quality criteria

| SEQUAL quality aspect | Criteria to evaluate quality aspect | Related LLM quality criteria (from 3.1) |
| --- | --- | --- |
| Semantic quality | Understandability Correctness | Accuracy |
| Social pragmatic quality | Relevance Credibility | Accuracy Robustness |
| Social quality | Acceptance Soundness | Fairness, bias and stereotypes, Toxicity |
| Deontic quality | Relevance, Completeness | Accuracy |
| Empirical quality | All of the above criteria | Calibration and uncertainty Efficiency |

the domain. For each criterion, we envision a Boolean "scale", i.e., it can be determined if the criterion is given (true) or not (false):

- Understandability: all concepts used in the output are from the domain and familiar to the user
- Correctness: the output is free from factual errors and hallucinations
- Relevance: all information included in the output matters for the given task
- Credibility: There is a defined source or argumentative support for information in the output that is beyond the general knowledge in the domain. The output is correct and free from inappropriate or tendentious content.
- Completeness: everything published that matters for the given task is included in the output
- Acceptance: the users agree about the relevance, credibility and soundness of the output
- Soundness: the output is relevant and free from contradictions

The above list of criteria, including their definitions, was presented to three experts in enterprise modelling, two of whom also had experience in using LLM. The experts were asked to evaluate the definitions, check for missing criteria, and order them based on their importance. The three experts agreed that the defined criteria are useful and do not overlap substantially. For the definition's wording, there were ideas for improvement, but no urgent demands were formulated. Additional criteria were not proposed. Table 4 shows the ranking proposed by the three experts and the overall result.

The experts consider correctness, completeness and relevance to be the most important criteria. Thus, the remainder of this paper focuses on these criteria.

**Table 4.** Priorities of quality criteria from expert evaluation

| Criteria | Expert Evaluation | | | Final Rank (Average) |
|---|---|---|---|---|
| | Expert 1 | Expert 2 | Expert 3 | |
| Understandability | 4 | 5 | 4 | 4 (4.3) |
| Correctness | 1 | 2 | 1 | 1 (1.3) |
| Relevance | 2 | 1 | 2 | 2 (1.6) |
| Credibility | 7 | 4 | 6 | 5 (5.6) |
| Acceptance | 6 | 6 | 5 | 5 (5,6) |
| Soundness | 5 | 7 | 7 | 7 (6.3) |
| Completeness | 3 | 3 | 3 | 3 (3.0) |

### 4.2 Operationalization of the Defined Criteria

The intention of this research is to investigate the application of LLM to support the quality control of LLM output. Thus, operationalizing the quality criteria defined in Sect. 4.1 will primarily be based on LLM prompts and outputs. The basic ideas for implementing quality control investigated in this section are triangulation and inverse mappings.

**Triangulation**

As discussed in Sect. 2.2, EM is a multi-perspective modelling approach, i.e., different viewpoints in an enterprise have to be considered and modelled to fully describe the current situation in an enterprise or the desired future situation with all dependencies between processes, organization structures, products and IT-architecture. The mutual dependencies between different perspectives offer the possibility to use triangulation to check completeness and consistency. In many qualitative research methods, triangulation investigates the validity of research results. Triangulation basically combines at least two perceptions of the same phenomenon from different observation points to gather a richer set of information, increase the credibility of the observations and detect contradictions.

In enterprise modelling, we can exploit the dependencies mentioned above for triangulation. For example, the LLM could first be asked to describe the processes in a car rental company and the organizational roles responsible for them. The second task for the LLM could be to describe the information and documents required for a car rental company and the organizational roles using this information. The results of both tasks could be compared with a focus on the organizational roles. Differences or contradictions in the output of both tasks contribute to determining the correctness, completeness, credibility and soundness of LLM output describing the organizational roles.

In Table 5, when describing the operationalization, we use A and B as placeholders for the perspectives and Q as an abbreviation for query. If triangulation is suitable and sufficient or not is the subject of Sect. 5.

**Inverse Mappings**

The use of LLM in enterprise modelling only makes sense if the output we receive from

**Table 5.** Proposed operationalization of quality criteria

| Quality criteria | Operationalization |
|---|---|
| Correctness | *Triangulation:*<br>Q1: Describe A, B and their relationship<br>Q2: Describe B, C and their relationship<br>Q3: Find contradictions in results from Q1 and Q2 that describe B<br>If there are contradictions, the description of B cannot be considered as correct<br>*Inverse Mapping:*<br>Q1: Deliver output for task T<br>Q2: Define based on output for Q1 the task T<br>If the results of Q1 and Q2 match, the output can be considered consistent |
| Relevance | Not possible: LLM cannot replace domain expert when it comes to deciding on relevance |
| Completeness | *Triangulation:*<br>Q1: Describe A, B and their relationship<br>Q2: Describe B, C and their relationship<br>Q3: Find differences in results from Q1 and Q2 that describe B<br>If there are differences, the description was incomplete, but the combination of Q1 and Q2 might be<br>*Inverse Mapping:*<br>Q1: Deliver output for task T<br>Q2: Define based on output for Q1 the task T<br>If the results of Q1 and Q2 match, the output seems complete |

the LLM has a connection to the task we submit, i.e., we expect some kind of mapping between task and output. For example, a question put forward to the LLM should lead to a response to the question and a problem to be solved to a solution fitting the problem. If this mapping exists, we might use inverse mapping to reconstruct the task from the output, i.e., use the output as the task and expect the initial task as the output. If the correct task is delivered with this inverse mapping, this could indicate correctness or soundness.

## 5 Experiments into LLM for Quality Control of LLM in EM

Section 4 proposed an approach for LLM use to support quality control of LLM output in EM by defining scenarios, quality criteria and their operationalization. This section aims to evaluate this approach by conducting quasi-experiments. As the first two scenarios identified in Sect. 4 were already subject to experimentation in [20], the experiments in this section focus on scenarios 3 and 4. A controlled experiment in information systems development is "a randomized or quasi-experiment in which individuals or teams (the study units) conduct one or more [...] tasks for the sake of comparing different populations, processes, methods, techniques, languages or tools (the treatments)" [29]. In our work, we perform a quasi-experiment; the study units are ChatGPT and domain experts, and the treatments are different modelling tasks. A quasi-experiment is "an experiment in which units are not assigned to conditions randomly" [30]. The experiment does not aim to test a specific hypothesis but is exploratory research to answer the research questions. In each experiment, the prompt is from a different application domain, and the expert participating is a professional in this domain.

## 5.1 Experiments in Triangulation

**Table 6.** Outputs for Triangulation Prompt E1–1, E1–2 and E1–3

| Experiment 1, Q1<br>Role + Service; for triangulation | Experiment 1, Q2<br>Role + Business Proc., for triangulation |
|---|---|
| **Prompt E1-Q1**:<br>I am interested in companies offering repair and maintenance for heating, ventilation and air conditioning systems. Which services do such companies offer? Which organizational roles do they need for this? | **Prompt E1-Q2**:<br>I am interested in companies offering repair and maintenance for heating, ventilation and air conditioning systems. Can you describe the business processes such companies implement in customer service? Which organizational roles do they need for these processes? |
| **ChatGPT Output (excerpt):**<br>**HVAC Technicians**: They are the primary role and are responsible for the hands-on installation, maintenance, and repair of HVAC systems<br>**Customer Service Representatives**: Handle client interactions, schedule service appointments, and assist with customer inquiries and issues<br>**Service Managers**: Oversee the operations of the service department, including the work of HVAC technicians<br>**Sales Representatives**: Focus on selling HVAC systems and service contracts to both new and existing customers<br>**HVAC Engineers**: Involved in designing systems and solutions for more complex installations or in developing new technologies within the company<br>**Dispatchers**: Manage the logistics of sending technicians to job sites, ensuring efficient use of resources and timely response to service calls<br>**Inventory and Parts Managers**: Keep track of stock, manage orders for new parts, and handle logistics related to equipment and parts required for various jobs | **ChatGPT Output (excerpt):**<br>**Customer Service Representatives**: Handle initial customer inquiries and provide information about services and pricing<br>Service Technicians: Perform the actual repair and maintenance work on HVAC systems<br>**Dispatchers/Schedulers**: Coordinate the logistics of technician schedules and appointments to ensure efficient use of resources and timely service delivery<br>**Billing and Accounting Staff**: Manage invoicing, payment processing, and financial records<br>**Operations Manager**: Oversees the day-to-day operations of the service team and ensures that business processes are adhered to<br>**Quality Assurance and Feedback Specialist**: Monitor service quality and customer satisfaction |
| **Experiment 1, Q3** (find contradictions between output of Q1 and Q2) ||
| Prompt E1-Q3:<br>I have two texts describing organizational roles in companies offering repair and maintenance for heating, ventilation and air conditioning systems. Can you compare the descriptions if they include the same roles or have contradictions? ||
| **ChatGPT Output (excerpt):**<br>[…]<br>Conclusion<br>Both descriptions include essential service and operational roles without contradictions but focus on different aspects of the business structure, suggesting that they might come from companies with slightly different emphases in service delivery, customer engagement, and internal management ||

We conducted eight experiments using triangulation. All experiments consisted of instantiations of the three prompts shown for the criterion correctness in Table 5. The human expert was asked to work on the same task defined by the prompt. After each experiment, a researcher compared the results of the domain expert and the ChatGPT output to verify the relevance of the ChatGPT output. Furthermore, the domain expert was asked to compare the two outputs in each experiment produced for triangulation and the final output of ChatGPT. The comparison between domain expert and ChatGPT showed that in all experiments, there were overlaps but also differences, which motivated a more detailed quality control. The domain expert considered all outputs of the eight experiments free from hallucinations and factually correct but incomplete.

For brevity reasons, we only include one example in this paper. Table 6 shows the prompts used for triangulation in experiment 1, which had organizational roles in focus, including the output containing the role-related information and the prompt for comparing the outputs.

As visible in the above table, the output of the two prompts E1-Q1 and E1-Q2 are not identical, which is correctly pointed out in the output for E1-Q3. The domain expert considers the result of the triangulation as a valuable contribution to the quality criteria completeness. Other experiments focused on triangulation regarding required information in an organization, the needed IT infrastructure or an organization's products. The results were similar.

The experiments also showed that the operationalization of triangulation (see Table 5) is conceptually sound and detailed enough to be applicable, which is confirmed by the results shown in Table 6. However, it also became clear that some parts of the operationalization (e.g., identification of contradictions and differences) would be easier to execute if more detailed instructions existed.

## 5.2 Experiments in Inverse Mappings

We also performed eight experiments (numbers 9 to 16) using inverse mappings in the same setup described in Sect. 5.1. Again, the comparison between the domain expert and ChatGPT showed that in all experiments, there were overlaps but also differences, and the domain expert considered all outputs of the eight experiments as free from hallucinations and factually correct. For brevity reasons, we only include one example in this paper. Table 7 shows the prompt used for inverse mapping in experiment 9, including the output.

As visible in the above table, the output of E9-Q2 basically contains the input of E9-Q1, which shows the consistency of the outputs. The same observation was made in all eight experiments. The domain expert considered this result as a "good double check" but was not enthusiastic about the added value of the output. The experiments also showed that the operationalization of inverse mapping (see Table 5) is conceptually sound and detailed enough to be applicable.

**Table 7.** Outputs for Inverse Mapping Prompt E9–1 and E9–2

| |
|---|
| **Experiment 9** (Inverse Mapping) |
| Prompt E9-Q1:<br>What are the responsibilities of the chief information security officer in a public sector organization? |
| **ChatGPT Output (excerpt):**<br>The Chief Information Security Officer (CISO) in a public sector organization holds a pivotal role in ensuring the security and integrity of information and technology systems. The responsibilities of a CISO in the public sector can be broad and complex, reflecting the sensitivity and critical nature of government data. Here are some key responsibilities typically associated with this role:<br>[...] |
| Prompt E9-Q2:<br>Who would be responsible for following tasks in a public sector organization? Developing and implementing a comprehensive information security strategy that aligns with the organization's objectives and regulatory requirements; Creating, updating, and enforcing security policies and procedures that protect the organization's systems and data; Identifying, evaluating, and mitigating risks associated with the organization's information systems; Overseeing the development and implementation of incident response plans; Ensuring that the organization adheres to government regulations and standards related to information security; Leading efforts to educate and train employees in security best practices and awareness; Overseeing relationships with third-party vendors to ensure that their security practices meet the organization's standards; Managing the budget for information security, which includes allocating resources for security initiatives, technology investments, and staffing; Keeping abreast of security and technology trends to recommend and implement advanced security technologies; Collaborating with other senior leaders and departments to integrate security considerations into broader operational policies and IT projects |
| **ChatGPT Output (excerpt):**<br>All the tasks you've listed are typical responsibilities of the Chief Information Security Officer (CISO) in a public sector organization. The CISO is the key executive responsible for managing and overseeing all aspects of information security, including strategy, policy development, risk management, incident response, compliance, training, vendor relationships, budgeting, and technological updates |

## 6 Conclusion and Future Work

The aim of this paper was to investigate if LLM can be used to assist in the quality control of LLM-generated output in enterprise modelling. We identified quality criteria to evaluate the quality of LLM output for EM from a domain expert perspective (RQ1), we operationalized the criteria to show how LLM can assist in assessing the criteria (RQ2), and we provided initial prompt patterns (see Table 5) to make our approach explicit (RQ3).

Our work concludes as follows: LLM can support quality control of LLM output, but LLM cannot fully substitute quality control by human experts. We believe that an LLM should not judge the relevance of LLM output because the same algorithms and models that produced the output would form the fundament for checking the output. Triangulation can contribute to checking consistency and completeness, but if completeness is an essential quality criterion, the results of LLM-based triangulation should be complemented with additional quality checks, such as the assessment by human experts. However, the LLM-based completeness and consistency checking results proved useful and relevant, as they either enhanced initial results or showed inconsistencies. This can be interpreted as an additional indicator that using LLM to check LLM quality is not only possible but also a promising approach to reducing the workload of human experts.

An essential part of future work has to be to conduct more experiments to validate our initial findings. We investigated and showed the feasibility of LLM use within quality control of LLM output and got the first results regarding the potential and limits, but we have to gather more data to deepen the understanding. Future work is also required for all the last two research questions: we have to make the prompts more explicit and reusable (RQ3) and address the question of operationalizing the quality criteria identified in Sect. 4.1 but not tackled in Sect. 4.2 (RQ2).

## References

1. Mariani, M.M., Machado, I., Nambisan, S.: Types of innovation and artificial intelligence: a systematic quantitative literature review and research agenda. J. Bus. Res. **155**, 113364 (2023)
2. Makridakis, S.: The forthcoming artificial intelligence (AI) revolution: its impact on society and firms. Futures **90**, 46–60 (2017)
3. Eloundou, T., Manning, S., Mishkin, P., Rock, D.: GPTs are GPTs: an early look at the labor market impact potential of large language models. arXiv preprint arXiv:2303.10130 (2023)
4. Russell, S.J.: Artificial Intelligence a Modern Approach. Pearson Education, Inc. (2015)
5. Ziegler, A., et al.: Measuring GitHub copilot's impact on productivity. Commun. ACM **67**, 54–63 (2024)
6. Cámara, J., Troya, J., Burgueño, L., Vallecillo, A.: On the assessment of generative AI in modeling tasks: an experience report with ChatGPT and UML. Softw. Syst. Model. **22**, 781–793 (2023)
7. Wang, X., Anwer, N., Dai, Y., Liu, A.: ChatGPT for design, manufacturing, and education. Procedia CIRP **119**, 7–14 (2023)
8. Martin, J., Elg, M., Gremyr, I.: The many meanings of quality: towards a definition in support of sustainable operations. Total Qual. Manage. Bus. Excellence 1–14 (2020)
9. Brown, T.: Language models are few-shot learners. In: Larochelle, H., Ranzato, M., Hadsell, R., Balcan, M.F., Lin, H. (eds.) Advances in Neural Information Processing Systems, vol. 33, pp. 1877–1901. Curran Associates, Inc (2020)
10. Huang, W., Abbeel, P., Pathak, D., Mordatch, I.: Language models as zero-shot planners: extracting actionable knowledge for embodied agents. In: International Conference on Machine Learning, pp. 9118–9147 (2022)
11. Liu, P., Yuan, W., Fu, J., Jiang, Z., Hayashi, H., Neubig, G.: Pre-train, prompt, and predict: a systematic survey of prompting methods in natural language processing. ACM Comput. Surv. **55**, 1–35 (2023)
12. Oppenlaender, J.: Prompt engineering for text-based generative art. arXiv preprint arXiv:2204.13988 (2022)
13. White, J., et al.: A prompt pattern catalog to enhance prompt engineering with chatgpt. arXiv preprint arXiv:2302.11382 (2023)

14. Wu, T., et al.: Promptchainer: chaining large language model prompts through visual programming. In: CHI Conference on Human Factors in Computing Systems Extended Abstracts, pp. 1–10 (2022)
15. Du, R., et al.: Rapsai: accelerating machine learning prototyping of multimedia applications through visual programming. In: Proceedings of the 2023 CHI Conference on Human Factors in Computing Systems, pp. 1–23 (2023)
16. Vernadat, F.: Enterprise modelling and integration: from fact modelling to enterprise interoperability. In: International Conference on Enterprise Integration and Modeling Technology, pp. 25–33, Springer, Cham (2003). https://doi.org/10.1007/978-0-387-35621-1_4
17. Sandkuhl, K., et al.: From expert discipline to common practice: a vision and research agenda for extending the reach of enterprise modeling. Bus. Inf. Syst. Eng. **60**, 69–80 (2018)
18. Vernadat, F.: Enterprise modelling: research review and outlook. Comput. Ind. **122**, 103265 (2020)
19. Frank, U.: Multi-perspective enterprise modeling: foundational concepts, prospects and future research challenges. Softw. Syst. Model. **13**, 941–962 (2014)
20. Fill, H.-G., Fettke, P., Köpke, J.: Conceptual modeling and large language models: impressions from first experiments with ChatGPT. Enterp. Model. Inf. Syst. Architect. (EMISAJ) **18**, 1–15 (2023)
21. Sandkuhl, K., Barn, B., Barat, S.: Neural text generators in enterprise modeling: can ChatGPT be used as proxy domain expert? accepted for publication. In: Proceedings ISD 2023 Conference (2023)
22. Krogstie, J.: Quality in Business Process Modeling. Springer International Publishing, Cham (2016). https://doi.org/10.1007/978-3-319-42512-2
23. Stirna, J., Persson, A.: Enterprise modeling. Springer, Cham (2018). https://doi.org/10.1007/978-3-540-24744-9_14
24. Liang, P., et al.: Holistic evaluation of language models. arXiv preprint arXiv:2211.09110 (2022)
25. Chang, Y., et al.: A survey on evaluation of large language models. ACM Trans. Intell. Syst. Technol. **15**, 1–45 (2024)
26. Li, X., et al.: Alpacaeval: an automatic evaluator of instruction-following models. arXiv:2305.14387 (2023)
27. Desmond, M., Ashktorab, Z., Pan, Q., Dugan, C., Johnson, J.M.: EvaluLLM: LLM assisted evaluation of generative outputs. In: Companion Proceedings of the 29th International Conference on Intelligent User Interfaces, pp. 30–32 (2024)
28. Kitchenham, B., et al.: Guidelines for performing systematic literature reviews in software engineering. UK (2007)
29. Sjøberg, D.I.K., et al.: A survey of controlled experiments in software engineering. IEEE Trans. Softw. Eng. **31**, 733–753 (2005)
30. Cook, T.D., Campbell, D.T., Shadish, W.: Experimental and Quasi-Experimental Designs for Generalized Causal Inference. Houghton Mifflin Boston, MA (2002)

# AI Applications and Use Cases in Business

# Unlocking Viewer Insights in Linear Television: A Machine Learning Approach

Javier Carreno[1]([✉]), Khuong An Nguyen[1], Zhiyuan Luo[1], and Andrew Fish[2]

[1] Royal Holloway University of London, Surrey TW20 0EX, UK
Javier.Carreno.2023@live.rhul.ac.uk,
{Khuong.Nguyen,Zhiyuan.Luo}@rhul.ac.uk
[2] University of Liverpool, Liverpool L69 3BX, UK
Andrew.Fish@liverpool.ac.uk

**Abstract.** Amidst the digital transformation, traditional linear TV faces major challenges, including fragmented viewership, fixed schedule, and inaccurate targeting. Therefore, this paper proposes a novel Machine Learning framework to understand the audience's demographics from their viewing behaviour. By employing state-of-the-art classification models on an extensive TV first-party dataset, we achieved an average 88.6% accuracy in correctly identifying each household demographics. Our result offers promising outcomes for refining strategies within linear TV to improve viewer engagement, content programming, and market insights.

**Keywords:** Audience Insights · Machine Learning · Household Classification

## 1 Introduction

Linear television (TV) represents the traditional approach to broadcasting, where TV networks adhere to predetermined schedules, airing specific content at scheduled times for viewers [2]. Unlike modern on-demand or streaming services, linear TV restricts viewer control over content access, compelling them to tune in during scheduled broadcasts. While this model has historically been effective in reaching broad audiences, it presents challenges in gaining detailed insights into viewership demographics [5,7].

Understanding household demographics in linear TV goes beyond advertising effectiveness. With a nuanced understanding of their audience's demographics, broadcasters can curate content that resonates deeply with specific segments, fostering viewer satisfaction, loyalty, and engagement [3]. These are crucial for maintaining audience retention and competitiveness.

Integrating first-party data sourced from Freeview TV addresses limitations in traditional TV demographics. Acquired directly through viewers' connected TVs using the standard *Hybrid Broadcast Broadband TV* [10], this data offers valuable insights into viewers' habits and preferences.

Thus, this paper aims to utilise Machine Learning (ML) techniques to analyse first-party data and understand viewer profiles. In doing so, we aim to address the research question: **How accurately can ML be employed with just first-party TV data to classify household demographics?**

The contributions of our paper are:

- A **Machine Learning-ready dataset** with around 20,000 categorised devices from TV first-party data. It also includes a detailed household taxonomy and is available publicly at https://github.com/carrenyo/TV-Viewer-Demographics-Machine-Learning for further research.
- A **detailed pipeline** describing the entire process from initial *data collection* to the *final classification* of devices, for further improvements in the field.
- The **baseline results achieved** with state-of-the-art machine learning models to quantitatively demonstrate the feasibility of our approach.

The rest of the paper is organised as follows. Section 2 elaborates the *analytical pipeline* to collect the dataset and extract insights from it. Section 3 describes the dataset, and Sect. 4 details various ML algorithms and the baseline results on such dataset. Section 5 explains the related work. Finally, Sect. 6 summarises key insights and future research.

## 2 Pipeline

This section introduces a analytical pipeline involving 5 specific steps to extract valuable insights from TV first-party data (see Fig. 1).

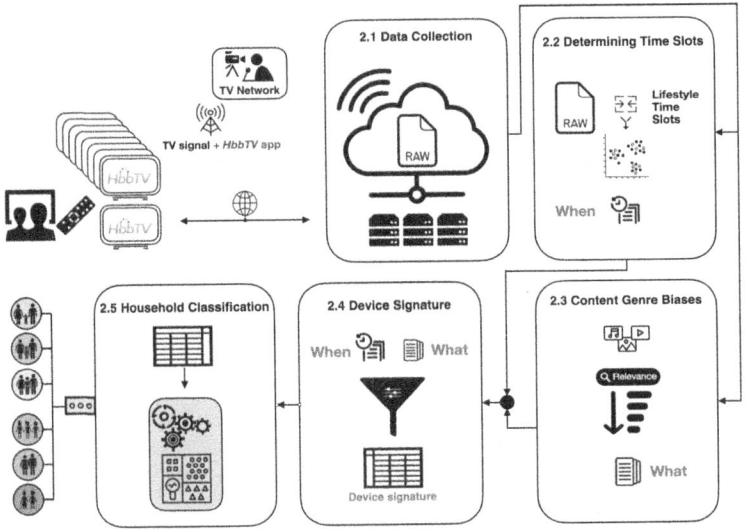

**Fig. 1.** Our proposed pipeline from data collection to device classification.

## 2.1 Data Collection

The first step involves collecting first-party data from Hybrid Broadcast Broadband TV (HbbTV), an open standard that integrates traditional broadcast TV (terrestrial, cable, or satellite) with internet connectivity, enhancing the TV experience to an interactive level [10]. With HbbTV, viewers using compatible devices can access additional content and interact with features using their remote controls [17]. The data collection from connected TVs involves an HbbTV application in the transport stream by TV networks. This embedded HbbTV app is unique as it does not need viewer installation. Viewer interactions while accessing TV network channels are systematically recorded and sent via the internet return channel to the cloud (see Fig. 2).

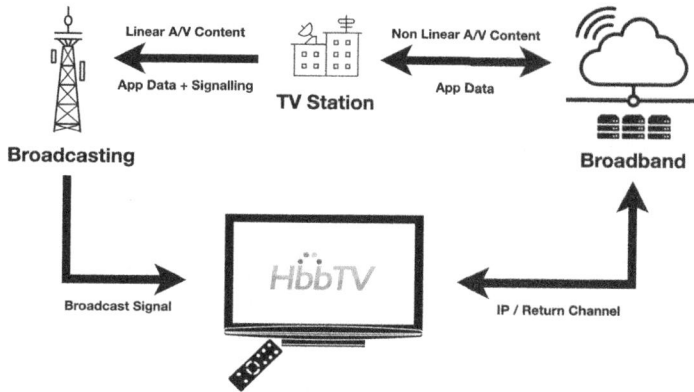

**Fig. 2.** HbbTV deployment diagram.

Our dataset includes essential details like *device ID*, *interaction timestamps*, *channel ID*, *IP Address*, and contextual information such as *device type* and *operating system version*. Most importantly, the data collection process includes a *consent management system* to comply with *GDPR regulations*. Viewers are explicitly asked for consent before their data is used for tasks beyond essential technical functions. Table 1 shows an excerpt of the raw data.

**Table 1.** A snapshot of first-party raw data.

| did | start | end | dur | active | userAgent | resolution | IP | chID |
|---|---|---|---|---|---|---|---|---|
| 0846... | 1693853858596 | 1693853958427 | 100 | true | Mozilla/5.0 (Web0... | 1920, 1080 | 91.11... | 4032 |
| 11ca... | 1693853413068 | 1693853690133 | 111 | true | Mozilla/5.0 (Web0... | 1280, 720 | 154.4... | 4032 |
| 1406... | 1693852329199 | 1693853956001 | 1501 | false | Mozilla/5.0 (Linu... | 1280, 720 | 95.2... | 4032 |
| 1a4a... | 1693852958450 | 1693853058459 | 100 | true | HbbTV/1.2.1 (+DRM... | 1920, 1080 | 83.49... | 4032 |
| 220d... | 1693853109400 | 1693853686558 | 550 | true | Mozilla/5.0 (Web0... | 1920, 1080 | 92.17... | 4032 |
| 257e... | 1693853428111 | 1693853528019 | 100 | true | HbbTV/1.4.1 (+DRM... | 1920, 1080 | 170.2... | 4032 |

## 2.2 Determining Viewer Time Slots

Using the raw first-party data above, this step aims to uncover the diverse TV viewership patterns, which are essential for effective audience understanding. A session starts when a device tunes in and ends when the viewer switches channels. Sessions lasting less than 300 s are labeled as *zapping* and are excluded from analysis, as they do not provide meaningful insights into viewer preferences, especially in linear TV where programmes typically have longer durations. Similarly, sessions lasting longer than 10,800 s are considered *extreme* and are also excluded (atypical behaviour).

The study then categorises devices based on their viewing consumption, considering *session frequency* and *total viewing time* on a weekly basis. Devices meeting specific criteria receive scores based on their weekly behaviour, with those having 20 or more sessions totaling at least 54,000 s getting a score of **3**, those with 5 or more lasting at least 7,200 a score of **2**, and those with 1 or more lasting at least 1,500 a score of **1**. These aggregated scores determine each device's viewership level over the sample period, as follows.

- **fan** if the cumulative score exceeds 2.5 times the study's duration in weeks.
- **regular** if the score surpasses 1.5 times.
- **occasional** if the score is more than 0.25 times.
- **no viewer** otherwise.

To capture the diverse viewer routines and lifestyles accurately, it is essential to establish cultural time slots linked to *meal times*, *work/school hours*, and *leisure periods*. Traditional 9am-5pm time slots are often too broad, making it difficult to discern specific viewing patterns like *lunchtime* or *mornings*. Hence, we divide each day into **seven time slots** for a more nuanced breakdown, effectively differentiating between *weekdays* and *weekend* (see Table 2).

**Table 2.** Our proposed finer-grained time slots for better distinction between weekdays and weekend for one specific Mediterranean European region.

| Time Slot | weekdays | weekend |
|---|---|---|
| breakfast | 07:00 - 08:30 | 07:00 - 10:00 |
| morning | 08:30 - 13:00 | 10:00 - 13:30 |
| lunchtime | 13:00 - 15:00 | 13:30 - 15:00 |
| afternoon | 15:00 - 17:00 | 15:00 - 17:00 |
| evening | 17:00 - 20:30 | 17:00 - 20:30 |
| dinner | 20:30 - 22:00 | 20:30 - 22:00 |
| afterdinner-night | 22:00 - 07:00 | 22:00 - 07:00 |

Once the time slots are established, each legitimate session is associated with one of them, and aggregated weekly per device. Our analysis involved two cluster analyses: *weekdays* and *weekend* [19]. We used the *Silhouette score* method to determine the optimal number of clusters, focusing on cohesion and separation within clusters [16]. The goal was to maintain high scores consistently across weeks. Only devices with **regular** viewership patterns were included to avoid skewed results, excluding *occasional* and *fan* viewers. Applying the bisecting k-means algorithm over four weeks consistently identified **6 clusters** as optimal for weekdays (see Fig. 3).

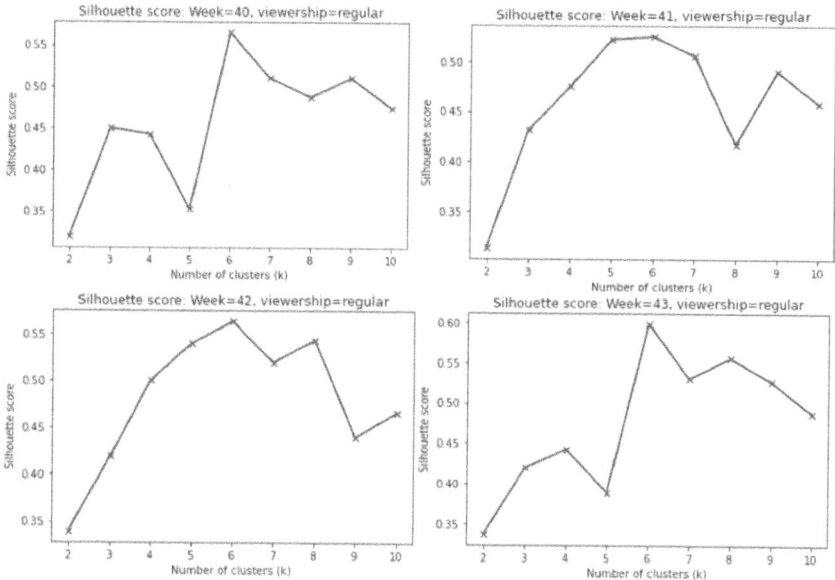

**Fig. 3.** Silhouette scores for weekdays cluster analysis, which indicated an optimal number of 6 clusters.

Then, we calculated **time slot ratios** for each cluster to highlight unique viewing behaviours.. The ratios were calculated by dividing the number of viewing sessions in each time slot by the total sessions for that cluster, showing what percentage of viewing occurs during different times of the day. Clusters with consistent viewing habits across the four-week period were merged into **prototypes**, while inconsistent patterns were excluded from further analysis. Ultimately, 5 *prototypes* emerged: **morning, lunchtime, afternoon, evening,** and **dinner**. Similar steps were taken for the second cluster analysis. Optimal results for *weekend* were also found with **k = 6**, yielding **five prototypes**: **morning, lunch, evening, dinner,** and **afterdinner-night**.

However, aligning weekly viewing behaviours with the identified clusters posed a challenge. The traditional k-means algorithm assigns all data points to centroids, which deviate from the primary objective of this analysis. Our goal was to label viewing patterns only when closely resembling the defined prototypes. To address this challenge, a customised threshold was created, incorporating *standard deviation* and *Euclidean distance* calculations. Data points within 2 times the standard deviation (Z-score) were labeled as **close**, while others were marked as **far**. This approach ensured that only data points closely matching the prototypes were assigned to clusters, guaranteeing accurate categorisation.

Once common consumption patterns are identified and matched with device usage on a weekly basis, it becomes possible to determine **when** the viewers watch TV. The next step is to establish **what** they watch.

## 2.3 Content Genre Biases: Unveiling Viewer Preferences

This step aimed to uncover biases towards content genres, crucial for categorising devices into household types, as genres heavily influence audience preferences [2]. Weekly analysis quantified viewing volume per genre per device, based on manual content classification in Table 3. Merging genres formed cohesive groups, enhancing identification of viewer engagement and reducing sparse viewing tracking.

Table 3. Content taxonomy used in this study.

| Category | Description |
|---|---|
| action & adventure | High-energy content with intense sequences and physical feats. |
| biography & historical events | Narratives about real-life individuals and historical occurrences. |
| children & family | Content suitable for family viewing, including kid-friendly themes. |
| comedy | Light-hearted, humorous content designed to entertain and amuse. |
| cooking & wellness | Programmes focused on culinary arts and general well-being. |
| crime & mystery & horror | Content centered on criminal investigations, mysteries, and horror. |
| current affairs & social issues | Programmes addressing contemporary events and societal concerns. |
| drama | Engaging emotional narratives delving into human experiences. |
| folk culture & heritage | Depictions of traditional customs, folklore, and cultural heritage. |
| game show & quizzes | Entertainment involving game formats and intellectual challenges. |
| magazines & talk shows | Shows featuring discussions, interviews, and topical segments. |
| media & popular culture | Exploration of media trends and elements shaping popular culture. |
| music & arts | Programmes dedicated to musical and artistic expressions. |
| news & politics | Informational content covering current news and political affairs. |
| romantic | Content centred around love stories and romantic relationships. |
| science & nature & animals | Exploration of scientific topics, nature, and wildlife. |
| sports | Coverage of various sports and related events. |
| thriller & suspense | Suspenseful and gripping narratives designed to captivate viewers. |
| travel & lifestyle | Programmes featuring travel destinations and diverse lifestyles. |

For a reliable assessment, substantial data covering multiple weeks is crucial to minimise the impact of seasonal fluctuations in traditional TV content. These fluctuations arise from factors such as holiday-themed programming, viewer shifts during major events, network schedule changes, and variations in viewer behaviour across seasons [2].

Determining viewer engagement with content genres often involves calculating the time ratio for each genre against total viewing time (*Relative Frequency Viewed*). However, unlike online platforms with *Video on Demand*, linear TV networks do not always offer all genres uniformly, curating their lineup for specific audiences throughout the day. Moreover, live events such as sports or award shows may also vary in availability, potentially biasing engagement metrics.

To address this challenge, we devised a genre '***Relevance***' metric. It compares the time spent watching each genre against the total viewing time and normalises it by the proportion of time each genre was broadcasted compared to the total broadcasted time within the week. This method helps assess the significance of content genres relative to their availability, refining our understanding of viewer engagement.

## 2.4 Device Signature: Capturing Essential Features

Constructing a *device signature* involves condensing all the activity and traits of each device into a single representative row. To address the variability in TV consumption, it is important to consider that a device may exhibit different behaviours from week to week.

In relation to viewer engagement, while the '*Relevance*' metric effectively gauges engagement with specific weekly genres, deriving '***Total Relevance***' by summing these scores across weeks has significant limitations, especially with infrequently broadcasted genres. For instance, if a genre like *adventure* is scarcely broadcasted, available only for 6 weeks, and a viewer engages with the genre only once during those weeks, displaying a high '*Relevance*' score in one week. When computing the '*Total Relevance*' by summing the weekly values, the resulting '*Total Relevance*' disproportionately impacts the analysis. To address this challenge, a new metric called the '***Relative Audience Engagement Index***' (**RAE Index**) was introduced. The '*RAE Index*' standardises the '*Total Relevance*', mitigating this distortion.

$$\text{RAE Index} = \frac{\text{Weeks Genre Viewed}}{\text{Total Weeks Viewed}} \bigg/ \frac{\text{Weeks Genre Broadcasted}}{\text{Total Weeks Broadcasted}} \quad (1)$$

By using the '*RAE Index*', the analysis ensures a more accurate representation of the viewer's genuine content preferences across all genres, regardless of variations in their broadcast availability. The '***Weighted Relative Audience Engagement***' (**WRAE**) was introduced to refine the relevance assessment, calculated by multiplying the '*Total Relevance*' by the '*Relative Audience Engagement Index*': WRAE = Total Relevance × RAE Index

Additionally, a '***Normalised Weighted Relative Audience Engagement***' (**nWRAE**) is computed for each genre by dividing it by the '***Total Weighted Relative Audience Engagement***'. This new metric is a valuable tool for assessing the level of audience engagement and contributes to refining the understanding of viewer preferences.

$$\text{nWRAE} = \frac{\text{Weighted RAE of Genre}}{\text{Total Weighted RAE of all Genres}} \qquad (2)$$

### 2.5 Household Categorisation: Timing and Content

The final step involves categorising devices based on their usage timing and preferred content genres, aligning with an established sociodemographic approach. This categorisation includes 'Couple with young kids (0–8 years)', 'Couple with teenagers (9–17 years)', 'Couple with adult children (18+ years)', 'Only young adults (18–35 years)', 'Only middle-aged adults (36+ years)', 'Seniors (elderly/retired adults)' [8,15]. Devices are classified based on their usage time and preferred content genres.

## 3 Data Analysis and Feature Selection

Our data came from the first-party data of an European regional Freeview linear TV channel, serving a population of over 5 million with a high internet penetration rate of over 80%. The one-year sample consists of approximately 700 classified TV programmes.

This study focused on the top 19,386 devices, with 994 labeled as **fan** and 18,392 as **regular**. Table 4 summarises key dataset details: sample size (devices), data source, served population, collection duration, recorded sessions, unique devices, TV programmes, genres, and classification features.

Table 4. Summary of the dataset.

| Number of Samples (Devices) | 19,386 |
|---|---|
| **Population Served** | Over 5 millions |
| **Duration of Data Collection** | 52 weeks |
| **Total Sessions Recorded** | 62,911,754 |
| **Unique Devices Connected via HbbTV** | 352,987 |
| **Number of TV Programmes** | Approximately 700 |
| **Number of Genres** | 19 |
| **Total Features** | 138 |
| **Subset of Features Used for Classification** | 31 |

The normalised weighted audience measurement ($nWRAE$) reveals varied audience preferences across genres. Genres such as *news & politics, cooking, drama*, and *science* showed higher mean engagement levels, indicating sustained audience interest. Conversely, genres like *action & adventure, children & family*, exhibited lower mean engagement levels, suggesting comparatively subdued viewer interest. Interesting patterns emerge in genres such as *crime & horror*, *game show*, and *romantic* genres. Despite lower mean engagement, these genres showed occasional high peaks in their maximum engagement values. These peaks suggest sporadic yet intensified audience interest in specific content within these genres (see Fig. 4).

## 3.1 Classification Results

Devices were categorised into household groups based on viewer behaviours and preferences using predetermined thresholds and business rules, complemented by insights from market research surveys and audience measurement panels [3, 7]. This heuristic approach facilitated the analysis of TV viewing patterns, providing practical insights for understanding viewer engagement. Table 5 illustrates the dataset's distribution across various household labels.

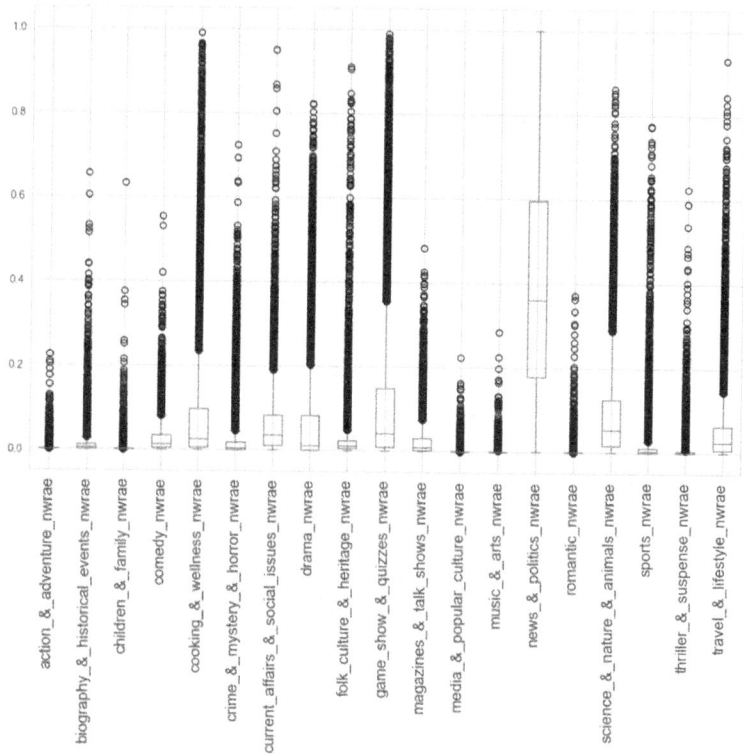

**Fig. 4.** Boxplots illustrating *nwrae* variation across genres. Only *news_&_politics* shows a distinct central tendency compared to other genres, with lower values and numerous outliers above.

Table 5. Household classification distribution.

| Household Classification | Num of Devices | Percentage |
| --- | --- | --- |
| Couple with young kids (0–8 years) | 143 | 0.74% |
| Couple with teenagers (9–17 years) | 1,514 | 7.81% |
| Couple with adult children (18+ years) | 3,567 | 18.39% |
| Only young adults (18–35 years) | 3,550 | 18.30% |
| Only middle-aged adults (36+ years) | 6,985 | 36.02% |
| Seniors (elderly/retired adults) | 3,627 | 18.74% |

## 3.2 Feature Significance

Feature significance is crucial in Machine Learning, revealing attributes driving predictions. Random Forest model's feature importance scores indicate each feature's contribution to predictive performance (see Fig. 5).

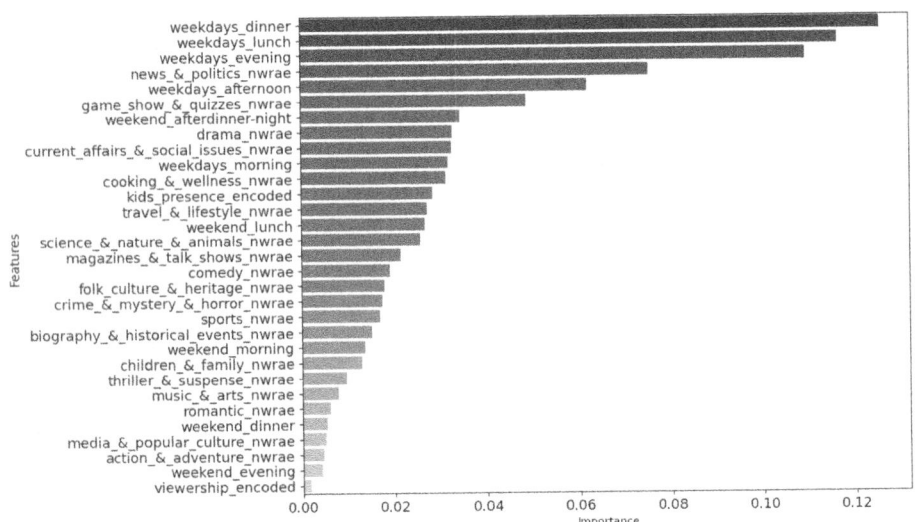

**Fig. 5.** Feature Importance for 31 ML features, highlighting their contribution to predictive accuracy and model performance.

Primarily, *weekdays_dinner* is the most influential factor, particularly during weekday dinner hours. Additionally, *news_&_politics_nwrae* and *weekdays_afternoon* also contribute significantly to the model's predictive capacity.

Features related to **various genres** like *drama, game shows, current affairs,* and *cooking, travel* also demonstrate notable importance in predicting household classifications. The presence of certain content themes like *crime, sports, biographies, comedy* and *music* are influential but to a slightly lesser extent.

**Per-class Feature Importance.** Next, we analyse the importance of individual attributes for each classification category, highlighting the factors that significantly contribute to household differentiation (see Fig. 6).

## 4 Machine Learning Experiments and Results

In this section, we apply state-of-the-art Machine Learning models to our dataset to infer household demographics, including Random Forest, K-Nearest Neighbour, and Gradient Boosting. We aim to address the following questions:

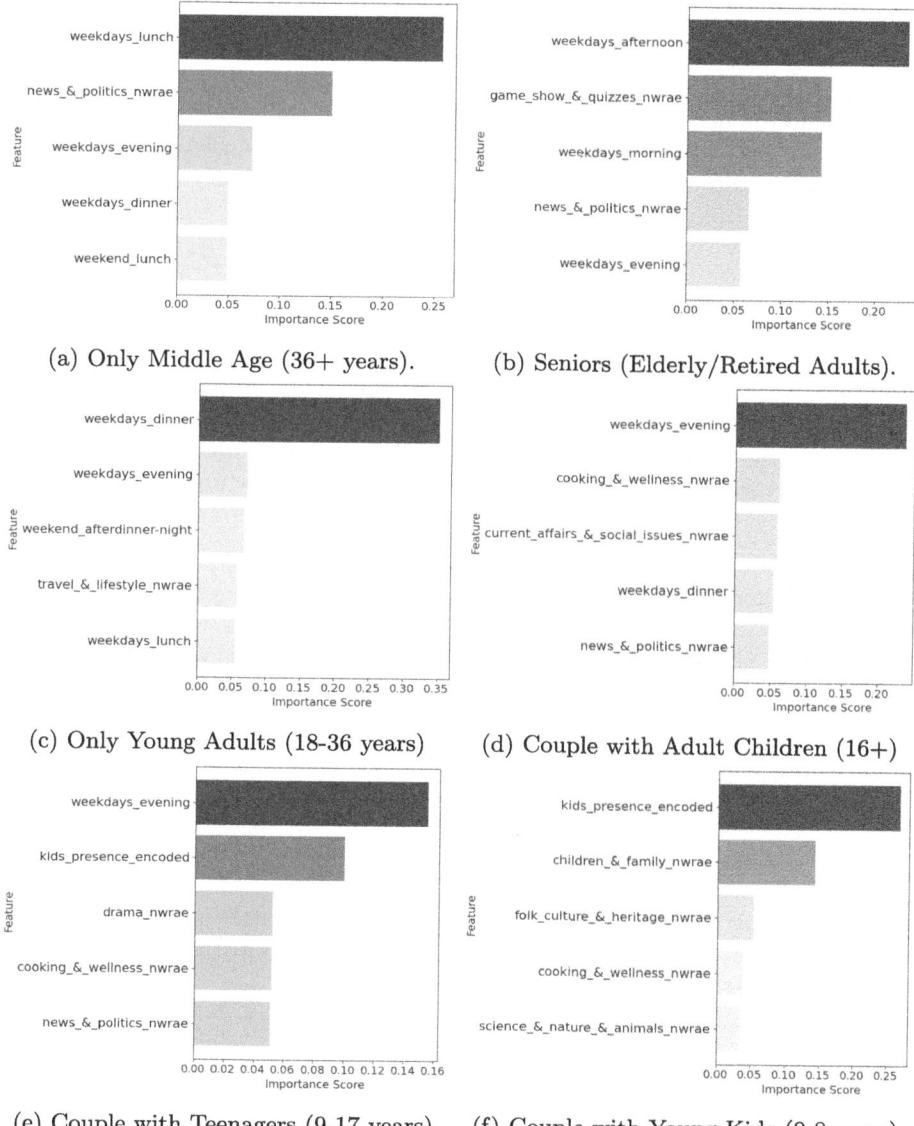

**Fig. 6.** Top features for each household classification.

- What are the accuracy in classifying household demographics?
- Which demographics are most challenging to classify?

### 4.1 Error Analysis: Confusion Matrices

In addition to the performance metrics previously discussed, the confusion matrices offers a more granular insight into the classification models' performance.

**Random Forest.** The model exhibited recurring misclassifications (see Fig. 7a), notably between *'Couple with adult children'* and *'Couple with teenagers'*, and *'Only middle age'*. Families with adult children or teenagers might share TV viewing habits, leading to classification classification based on similar content preferences (**similar content consumption patterns**). Similarly, middle age and young adults may have overlapping lifestyle and viewing preferences, posing challenges in distinguishing between them based solely on viewing behaviours (**age-based similarities**). *'Couple with young kids (0–8 years)'* faces frequent confusion, likely due to diverse content preferences within this demographic (**complex family dynamics**).

**K-Nearest Neigbour.** The KNN model exhibited similar confusion patterns to other models, especially in misclassifying *'Couple with adult children'* and related categories (see Fig. 7b). However, it demonstrated balanced performance across most classes. Unlike the other models, it encountered difficulties in accurately classifying *'Couple with teenagers'* and *'Couple with young kids'*, indicating distinctive challenges in capturing these specific categories accurately.

**Gradient Boosting.** The Gradient Boosting model showed similar confusion patterns to other models, particularly in distinguishing *'Couple with adult children'* accurately (see Fig. 7c). It performed moderately well with *'Couple with teenagers'* but aligned with other models in misclassification trends, indicating comparable behaviours in classifying different demographic groups.

### 4.2 Summary of Results

From the above results, **Random Forest** model emerged as the top choice due to its balanced performance across demographic categories (see Fig. 7). Despite **moderate confusion** between *'Couple with Adult Children'* and *'Couple with Teenagers'*, it consistently **performed well** across most demographic groups. Moreover, it demonstrated **good stability** and **reliability** during cross-validation (see Table 6).

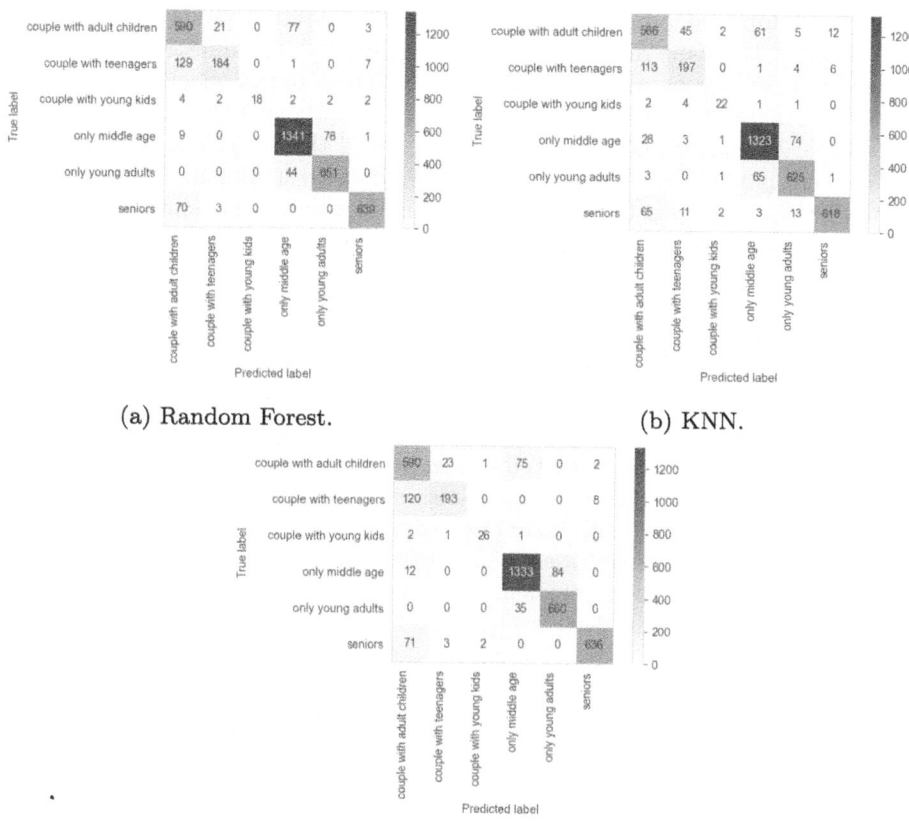

(a) Random Forest.      (b) KNN.

(c) Gradient Boosting.

**Fig. 7.** Confusion matrices of 3 Machine Learning models, illustrating their accuracy and misclassifications, distinguishing false positives from negatives.

**Table 6.** Machine Learning Model Comparison with Cross-Validation.

| Model | Fold Scores (Accuracy) | | | | | Mean | Precision | Recall | F1-Score |
|---|---|---|---|---|---|---|---|---|---|
| | Fold-1 | Fold-2 | Fold-3 | Fold-4 | Fold-5 | | | | |
| RF | 0.8889 | 0.8723 | 0.8788 | 0.8801 | 0.8873 | 0.8815 | **0.89** | 0.88 | 0.88 |
| KNN | 0.8896 | 0.8741 | **0.8816** | **0.8865** | 0.8811 | 0.8826 | 0.87 | 0.86 | 0.86 |
| GB | **0.8961** | **0.8806** | 0.8814 | 0.8842 | **0.8883** | **0.8861** | **0.89** | **0.89** | **0.89** |

## 5 Related Works

The traditional method of studying viewer behaviour in linear TV uses structured panels like the UK's 5,300-household panel, employing *Peoplemeters* to track viewership and programming. However, the limited panel size and concerns about participant reporting accuracy raise reliability questions.

Research often uses pay TV platforms for direct data collection, bypassing panel-based methods [9,11]. However, the high costs of pay TV systems introduce biases toward wealthier households that can afford these services.

Conventional audience measurement methods with small panel samples often lack the precision needed for precise ad-specific viewership measurement. Advertisers, prioritising commercial audience over programme content, struggle to accurately assess ad effectiveness [1].

Connected TVs and online devices are reshaping TV advertising by leveraging behavioural data for advanced analysis, aiding digital evolution and the adoption of AI and sophisticated algorithms [13].

Understanding **selective exposure** is key for precise audience segmentation, going beyond generic demographics and predicting behaviour accurately [12,14].

This study's **significant contribution** lies in its **dataset**, especially in ML and household classification tasks. It assesses the effectiveness and precision of classifying data into household taxonomy using diverse metrics, evaluation methods, and model performance assessments. Relevant literature offers insights into methodologies used to assess efficiency in comparable contexts [6,18].

## 6 Conclusions and Future Work

This paper proposed a novel ML approach using extensive first-party linear TV data to unveil viewership behaviour. Analysis of the dataset's demographic distribution revealed a significant prevalence in the '*Only middle age (36+)*' segment, surpassing '*Seniors*', '*Couple with adult children (18+)*', and '*Only young adults (18-35 years)*'. Preferences impact viewer engagement, with timing factors like *weekdays_dinner*, *weekdays_lunch*, *weekdays_evening*, and *weekdays_afternoon* were crucial in household categorisation. This representation contrasts sharply with notably lower numbers in '*Couple with teenagers (9-17 years)*' and particularly '*Couple with young kids (0-8 years)*', each accounting for 1% of recorded devices. These statistics underscore modern viewing trends, especially among younger demographics, highlighting a **sharp decline** in their engagement with linear TV platforms.

**Programme preferences** emerged as a crucial factor, indicating increased consumption in genres like *news & politics*, aligning with the interests of middle-aged and adult demographics. Despite the overall decline in television viewership, the enduring trust in TV as a dependable information source remains evident, consistently positioning TV as the preferred medium for advertisers [4,5].

Machine Learning performance varied in accuracy, showing recurring misclassifications, particularly between '*Couple with adult children (18+ years)*' and '*Couple with teenagers (9-17)*', suggesting shared content preferences. The Gradient Boosting model achieved the best result with an average accuracy of 88.7% across 5 data folds, demonstrating the potential of our approach in classifying household demographics with just first-party TV data.

This study explores TV viewership patterns, but future research could expand by incorporating children's programming from other channels for a comprehensive perspective. Adding viewer *surveys* could offer deeper insights beyond consumption patterns.

# References

1. Abernethy, A.M.: Television exposure: programs vs. advertising. Curr. Issues Res. Advertising **13**(1–2), 61–77 (1991)
2. Barwise, P., Ehrenberg, A.: Television and Its Audience, vol. 3. Sage (1988)
3. Bondad-Brown, B.A., Rice, R.E., Pearce, K.E.: Influences on tv viewing and online user-shared video use: demographics, generations, contextual age, media use, motivations, and audience activity. J. Broadcast. Electron. Media **56**(4), 471–493 (2012)
4. Bruce, N.I., Becker, M., Reinartz, W.: Communicating brands in television advertising. J. Mark. Res. **57**(2), 236–256 (2020)
5. Bulgrin, A.: Why knowledge gaps in measurement threaten the value of television advertising: the best available screen for brand building is at a crossroads. J. Advert. Res. **59**(1), 9–13 (2019)
6. Choi, J.A., Lim, K.: Identifying machine learning techniques for classification of target advertising. ICT Express **6**(3), 175–180 (2020)
7. Clark, J., Paiement, J.F., Provost, F.: Who's watching TV? Inf. Syst. Res. **34**(4), 1622–1640 (2023)
8. Cohen, P.N.: The family: diversity, inequality, and social change. (No Title) (2018)
9. Deng, Y., Mela, C.F.: Tv viewing and advertising targeting. J. Mark. Res. **55**(1), 99–118 (2018)
10. Fischer, W., Fischer, W.: Broadcast over internet, HbbTV, OTT, streaming. In: Digital Video and Audio Broadcasting Technology: A Practical Engineering Guide, pp. 903–913 (2020)
11. Fudurić, M., Malthouse, E.C., Lee, M.H.: Understanding the drivers of cable TV cord shaving with big data. J. Media Bus. Stud. **17**(2), 172–189 (2020)
12. Knobloch-Westerwick, S., Meng, J.: Looking the other way: selective exposure to attitude-consistent and counterattitudinal political information. Commun. Res. **36**(3), 426–448 (2009)
13. Malthouse, E.C., Maslowska, E., Franks, J.: The role of big data in programmatic TV advertising. In: Advances in Advertising Research IX: Power to Consumers, pp. 29–42 (2018)
14. Malthouse, E.C., Maslowska, E., Franks, J.U.: Understanding programmatic TV advertising. Int. J. Advertising **37**(5), 769–784 (2018)
15. Scott, J., Treas, J., Richards, M.: The Blackwell companion to the sociology of families. Wiley (2008)
16. Shutaywi, M., Kachouie, N.N.: Silhouette analysis for performance evaluation in machine learning with applications to clustering. Entropy **23**(6), 759 (2021)
17. Tagliaro, C., Hahn, F., Sepe, R., Aceti, A., Lindorfer, M.: I still know what you watched last sunday: privacy of the HbbTV protocol in the European smart TV landscape. In: 30th Annual Network and Distributed System Security, NDSS 2023 (2023)
18. Vaccari, I., Chiola, G., Aiello, M., Mongelli, M., Cambiaso, E.: MQTTset, a new dataset for machine learning techniques on MQTT. Sensors **20**(22), 6578 (2020)
19. Yeo, J.: The weekend effect in television viewership and prime-time scheduling. Rev. Ind. Organ. **51**(3), 315–341 (2017)

# Comparison of AI-Based Document Classification Platforms

Leon Görgen[1], Leon Griesch[1(✉)], and Kurt Sandkuhl[1,2]

[1] Rostock University, Rostock, Germany
{leon.goergen,leon.griesch,kurt.sandkuhl}@uni-rostock.de
[2] Jönköping University, Jönköping, Sweden

**Abstract.** Automatic text classification is an important area of study in natural language processing (NLP) and machine learning. Text classification has become essential for businesses and organizations to handle incoming documents effectively and efficiently. The main objective of this study is to introduce and evaluate a selection of Free Open Source Software approaches for document classification and compare them against each other regarding their prediction performance and efficiency to identify the best candidate for a specific use case. In addition, the study compares the selected approaches prediction performance, efficiency, and cost-effectiveness with commercial providers' proprietary software. This comparison provides insights into different approaches' relative strengths and weaknesses to help businesses decide on the best strategy for their needs.

**Keywords:** document classification · artificial intelligence · platform · Free Open Source Software · comparison

## 1 Introduction

Automatic text classification has been a subject of interest since the 1960s and continues to be an important area of study in natural language processing (NLP) and machine learning [21]. The process involves using algorithms to assign labels or categories to text documents based on their content, to minimize manual labour and reduce the likelihood of errors introduced by human factors such as fatigue, lack of expertise, and subjective biases [16]. In the era of big data analytics, where companies often deal with large volumes of data, manual classification of documents can be time-consuming and prone to errors. Therefore, text classification has become essential for businesses and organizations to handle incoming documents effectively and efficiently. This study is an extension of previous work [11] and focuses on document classification specifically, which involves assigning a label or category to a document based on its content. It is commonly used for tasks such as spam or fraud detection and organizing incoming documents into classes within a company [25].

The main objective of this study is to introduce and evaluate a selection of promising free open-source software (FOSS) approaches for document classification and compare them against each other regarding their prediction performance and efficiency to identify the best candidate for a specific use case. In addition, the study compares the selected approaches' prediction performance, efficiency, and cost-effectiveness with commercial providers' proprietary software (CPPS). This comparison can provide insights into different approaches' relative strengths and weaknesses to help businesses decide on the best strategy for their needs. As past projects on the use of artificial intelligence (AI) solutions in small and medium-sized enterprises (SMEs) [12] showed that SMEs hesitate to use AI [24], we aim to provide assistance for SMEs interested in AI-based document classification in particular. SMEs clearly prefer to select and apply software "ready for use" due to missing expert competence in the company. Thus, we use, if possible, the default parameterization of the models implemented in FOSS and CPPS without efforts to implement optimizations. Furthermore, it is essential to note that this study focuses solely on a specific use case, and therefore, the results presented may not be generalizable to other use cases.

To facilitate understanding of the study, Sect. 2 provides an overview of the field of document classification, including its fundamental concepts, various data preparation methods, and different FOSS approaches. Section 3 discusses the dataset used, the preprocessing steps taken, the implementation techniques for the FOSS, an overview of proprietary software, and the evaluation metrics used for comparison. Further, Sect. 4 presents the prediction performance and efficiency of the different FOSS approaches on the dataset, providing an analysis of the strengths and weaknesses of each method and how they compare to each other, followed by a comparison of the prediction performance, efficiency, and cost-effectiveness of the best FOSS approach with that of proprietary software solutions. Finally, Sect. 5 summarizes the study's main findings and suggests future research.

## 2 Overview of the Field of Document Classification

Document classification, a subfield of NLP, is the process of predicting group membership for data instances, meaning organizing documents into predefined categories or classes based on their content [23]. This prediction is often made using machine learning techniques, which involve training a model on a large dataset of labeled documents and then using the trained model to predict classes on new, unseen documents [22]. Document classification is used for various applications, including spam filtering, sentiment analysis, and topic modeling [25]. It is an active area of research with many open problems and opportunities for further study [22].

The most fundamental and crucial task in NLP is text classification [16], which evolves as new methods and techniques are created and improved. Many approaches, datasets, and evaluation criteria have been proposed in the literature over the past ten years due to the remarkable success in this sector [16]. Recent advances in machine learning and NLP have led to significant progress [25], such as deep learning techniques, which have shown promising results in improving the accuracy of document classification models [16]. In addition, transfer learning has emerged as a popular approach in document classification, in which pre-trained language models (PLM), such as bidirectional encoder representations from Transformers (BERT), are trained on a vast document corpus and fine-tuned on a specific document classification task [17]. This method has achieved state-of-the-art results on many benchmark datasets, such as the "IMDB movie review dataset", "Newsgroups dataset", and "Reuters-21578 dataset" [16,25].

Furthermore, research in document classification has focused on addressing some of the challenges in this field, such as the high dimensionality of document features, which can lead to computational complexity and overfitting [14,22]. To address this challenge, researchers have explored techniques such as dimensionality reduction, feature selection, and feature engineering [14]. Another challenge is the issue of class imbalance, where some categories have significantly fewer documents than others, leading to biased models [9]. Researchers have proposed various techniques to address this challenge, such as over-sampling, under-sampling, and class weighting [9]. Future research will likely address the remaining challenges in this field, such as the interpretability of models, the incorporation of external knowledge, and the development of models that can handle multiple languages and domains [16].

## 3 Comparison Methodology

### 3.1 Description of the Dataset Used for the Study

In the context of many businesses, the distinctions between different categories can be subtle, and the textual content may be intended for a specific, targeted audience rather than a general audience. For this reason, this study focuses on the Consumer Complaint Database[1] from the CFPB. This U.S. government agency collects consumer complaints through formal, textual exchanges between companies, public institutions, and private individuals. This dataset represents a scenario similar to how private individuals typically communicate with businesses and therefore provides a relevant and applicable context for the study of document classification.

The dataset comprises 3,218,032 consumer complaints sent to the CFPB with all required details and forwarded to the financial institution in question, giving the latter a chance to respond. Finally, CFPB makes a subset of the complaint data publicly available when fitting specific criteria (e.g., the absence of a lawsuit). Later the customer can file a review of the company's response [6]. The dataset under consideration includes a range of information for each complaint, including *Date received, Product, Sub-product, Issue, Sub-issue, Consumer complaint narrative, Company public response, Company, State, ZIP code, Tags, Consumer consent provided, Submitted via, Date sent to the company, Company*

---

[1] https://www.consumerfinance.gov/data-research/consumer-complaints/.

*response to consumer, Timely response, Consumer disputed, and Complaint ID*. However, for this study, the focus will be solely on the textual content provided in the *Consumer complaint narrative* and the class provided by the *Product* column. The CFPB divided the complaints into 18 distinct categories initially. The distribution of complaints across these categories is significantly imbalanced. Almost half of all complaints are in the credit reporting category, debt collection and mortgage account for 12 and 10 % respectively, and all other 15 categories are between 5 % and less than 0.1 %.

The dataset preparation involves the removal of redundant, noisy, or irrelevant data to improve the dataset's quality. Balancing the dataset ensures that each class is nearly equally represented to avoid creating bias. In addition, preprocessing techniques such as tokenization, stop word removal, and punctuation removal are applied to the text data to enhance the effectiveness of the machine learning algorithms used in the analysis. Overall, data preparation is essential in ensuring that the dataset used in this study is suitable for analysis and that the results obtained from the research are reliable and accurate.

### 3.2 Free Open Source Models Implementation

The document classification models were implemented using Python notebooks in Google Colab, which provided an efficient and convenient connection to Google Drive for loading and saving datasets, dumping the models, and comparing results. Google Colab also enabled linking the notebooks to this study for a comprehensive overview of the model implementation. This study explored three groups of models: traditional machine learning methods such as NBC, KNN classifiers, decision tree classifiers, logistic regression classifiers, and SVM; neural network-based models including LSTM, GRU, and CNN; and transformer-based models such as BERT, RoBERTa, XLNet, and GPT-2. Each model was trained on the same labeled dataset discussed in Sect. 3.1 after cleaning and balancing as described. In addition, the transformer-based models worked with raw text samples, while the other models used preprocessed text samples. While some common hyperparameters were set for each model, this study focuses on providing a general overview of each model rather than the most optimized implementation, meaning an adequate hyperparameter optimization could improve performance.

The traditional models were implemented using Scikit-learn [20], a popular open-source machine-learning library for Python that provides a range of supervised and unsupervised learning algorithms. It was chosen for its user-friendliness, efficiency, and consistent API, making switching between algorithms and models easy. The models were all trained with the BOW, TF-IDF, and LSA feature extraction methods, while the best prediction performance was chosen. The neural network-based models were implemented using Keras [7], a high-level open-source neural network library for Python that enables fast experimentation with deep learning models. It is built on top of lower-level deep learning frameworks, such as TensorFlow and Theano, which provide the computational backend for Keras. This study used the Keras standard layer for word embedding, i.e., the word embeddings were trained from scratch. Finally, the transformer-based models were implemented using Hugging Face Transformers [26], an open-source library built on top of PyTorch and TensorFlow that provides state-of-the-art NLP capabilities and offers a range of pre-trained models and tools that make it easy to develop and fine-tune models.

### 3.3 Overview of Proprietary Software

Several software providers offer tools to help businesses and researchers in document classification. This study will focus on several popular software providers and their products: Microsoft Azure, Amazon Comprehend, OpenAI GPT-3, Levity AI, Planet AI, and Vertex AI.

- **Microsoft Azure** [18] is a cloud-based platform that offers a range of AI and machine learning services, including Azure Cognitive Services for document classification. The service offers various features like text analytics, language detection, and sentiment analysis. Azure's Cognitive Services for text classification uses pre-built machine learning models and algorithms, making it a user-friendly option for those without extensive machine learning expertise. In addition, Azure offers a free trial for its "Cognitive Services", allowing users to experiment with the platform before committing to a paid subscription.
- **Amazon Comprehend** [4] is a machine learning-based tool that can analyze text data to extract relevant information and provides various services, including custom document classification, which this study utilized. Additionally, Amazon Comprehend supports multiple languages, including English, Spanish, French, German, Italian, and Portuguese.
- **OpenAI's GPT-3** [2] is a natural language processing tool using deep learning algorithms to generate text. The tool is handy for text generation tasks, such as language translation, chatbot, and content creation. Through its recently released product ChatGPT, OpenAI has gained massive attention. However, GPT-3 does not specialize in document classification but in text generation [8], so it suggests that this may not be the best choice for those explicitly seeking text classification capabilities. Despite the lack of specialization of the model, the findings in terms of accuracy as well as costs and training duration compared to the other models should be highlighted to what extent a generally trained model performs in comparison to the specialized models such as Levity, Google or Planet AI. OpenAI offers four models: Ada, Babbage, Curie, and Davinci (from weakest/cheapest to strongest/most costly). For this study, Baggage was chosen, due to the recommendation in OpenAI's documentation.
- **Levity AI** [15] is a machine learning-based document classification tool that offers a range of features, including text categorization, sentiment analysis, and document clustering. Levity's designed its platform to be very user-friendly, with an intuitive interface and drag-and-drop tools for data preparation. After arranging it with its sales team, Levity AI offered a free trial of its platform.

- **Planet AI** [3] is another machine learning-based tool for document classification that uses deep learning algorithms to analyze text data. The platform offers various features like entity recognition, sentiment analysis, and topic modeling. Planet AI also provided a free trial of its platform after arranging it with its sales team. However, it is to mention that Planet AI's primary focus is on visual-language modeling tasks, and the dataset used for the study only consists of text, which is why the strengths of the company are not being tested here.
- **Google Vertex AI** [1] is a cloud-based AI platform offering a range of machine learning and deep learning tools, including document classification. Vertex AI allows users to train and deploy models quickly and easily with built-in data preparation, training, and evaluation tools. In addition, Google offers a free trial for Vertex AI, allowing users to test the platform before committing to a paid subscription.

### 3.4 Evaluation Metrics and Methodology for Comparison

**Performance-Wise.** In assessing multi-class machine learning models, various metrics impart information on the model's effectiveness. The following section offers a succinct overview of the critical metrics employed. The discussion refers to [13] and [10]; the reader is encouraged to consult the original papers for a more comprehensive understanding. Initially, this section establishes an understanding of TP, TN, FP, and FN. In binary classification, the computation of these metrics is straightforward:

- **TP:** number of positive instances the model correctly classified as positive
- **TN:** number of negative instances the model correctly classified as negative
- **FP:** number of negative instances the model incorrectly classified as positive
- **FN:** number of positive instances the model incorrectly classified as negative.

A confusion matrix, a cross table that records the number of occurrences between two raters, visualizes these metrics, as shown in Fig. 1.

In multi-class classification, these metrics are extended by calculating each class's TP, TN, FP, and FN individually and then aggregating these values to get a single measure of the classifier's prediction performance. One standard method for doing so is to consider each class as a binary classification problem, with the instances of that class being positive and the instances of all other classes being negative. This approach allows calculating each class's TP, TN, FP, and FN and then averaging these values across all classes to measure the classifier's prediction performance. Based on these confusion matrix metrics, a wide range of prediction performance measures can be derived, which provide a comprehensive evaluation of the prediction performance of a classifier. This study uses several of these measures to evaluate the models. A brief overview of the binary measures is shown below:

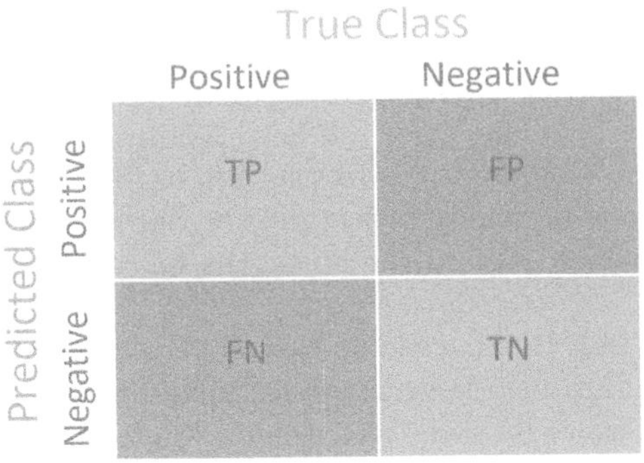

**Fig. 1.** Binary Confusion Matrix [19]

- **Accuracy:** Accuracy is one of the most popular metrics in multi-class classification and describes the probability that the model's prediction is correct:

$$Accuracy = \frac{TP + TN}{TP + TN + FP + FN} \quad (1)$$

- **Precision:** Precision tells how much the model can be trusted when it predicts an instance as positive:

$$Precision = \frac{TP}{TP + FP} \quad (2)$$

- **Recall:** Recall measures the model's predictive accuracy for the positive class: intuitively, it measures the ability of the model to find all the positive instances in the dataset:

$$Recall = \frac{TP}{TP + FN} \quad (3)$$

- **F1-Score:** The F1-Score can be considered a weighted average of precision and recall. The harmonic mean can be used to determine the optimal trade-off to balance the relative contributions of precision and recall to the F1 score:

$$F1\text{-}Score = 2 * \left( \frac{Precision * Recall}{Precision + Recall} \right) \quad (4)$$

Regarding multi-class classification, there are two different methods for calculating the overall measure for the classifier. The macro-average gives all classes the same weight, disregarding whether a class is densely or sparsely populated and instead using the average measurement score for each class. However, the micro-average considers the confusion matrix variables together, giving each sample the same weight rather than each class. As the dataset utilized for this study is reasonably balanced, this study solely presents the macro-average scores. Given that the F1-Score is the harmonic weight between precision and recall, this study solely displays the F1-Score within the evaluation table. In addition to the previously specified prediction performance metrics, the duration of model training and inference will be tracked in milliseconds and averaged for each document to gain insights into the computational efficiency.

**Cost-Wise.** This section provides a comprehensive outline of the comparison methodology used to evaluate the cost-effectiveness of various document classification products. The comparison process entails assessing three principal costs associated with the products, specifically training costs, hosting costs, and inference costs, which constitute the total pricing of the products in most cases. This study simulates a 30-day period, during which the classification model will be trained on the first day, hosted for the entire duration, and inference costs computed for varying document volumes. In addition, the hosting costs for the whole period will be added to the training costs at the outset to provide a clearer view of the costs. The primary objective of this comparison is to identify the most cost-effective product for document classification, considering varying document volumes for a month. The pricing for training, hosting, and inference was obtained from the respective providers' websites.

Furthermore, following the methodology introduced in Sect. 3, this study will evaluate the proprietary software against the best-performing FOSS model. However, this comparison presents some challenges as the pricing of the FOSS model is contingent on the implementation method. Therefore, this study focuses on a widely used variant, Amazon SageMaker. Amazon SageMaker is a fully managed machine learning service provided by AWS that facilitates the development, training, and deployment of machine learning models on a large scale. The service includes various pre-built algorithms and frameworks, making it a comprehensive platform for managing the entire machine-learning workflow. The FOSS model, previously trained on Google Colab, was uploaded and integrated into the SageMaker environment. It is essential to acknowledge that a cost comparison between different commercial providers for document classification systems may not be entirely equitable, as this comparison does not consider additional factors beyond the base cost of the service, such as pricing for ancillary services like cloud storage, the level of effort required by the user to train and adjust the model for their specific needs, and any API connection points that may be included in the pricing structure. These additional considerations may play a significant role in the total cost of ownership and the overall value proposition of a given provider. The same goes for the implementation of the FOSS model, which does not include additional charges for factors beyond the base cost of the service, such as local/cloud data storage, model maintenance, or human resource cost.

## 4 Results

This section presents a comprehensive analysis of the performance and cost comparison of different document classification models, providing valuable insights into the best models for document classification. The results obtained in this study may be specific to the dataset and use case considered in this study. Therefore, different datasets and use cases may produce different results, and it is essential to evaluate the models on the specific use case to determine the most suitable model.

### 4.1 Performance of Free Open Source Software

This section presents the performance metrics of various FOSS models used in the document classification task, categorized as traditional machine learning, neural network, and transformer-based models. Table 1 displays each model's accuracy and F1-Score, along with the average training and inference time in milliseconds per document.

Table 1. FOSS Results

| Modell | Accuracy | F1-Score | Training Time | Inference Time |
|---|---|---|---|---|
| NBC | 74.06 | 73.61 | **0.47** | 12.25 |
| KNN | 44.76 | 44.85 | 0.48 | 725.39 |
| Decision Tree | 61.84 | 61.77 | 11.41 | **1.55** |
| Logistic Regression | 76.49 | 76.25 | 38.06 | 17.99 |
| SVM | 76.69 | 76.57 | 316.13 | 106.52 |
| LSTM | 73.92 | 73.75 | 257.55 | 115.08 |
| Bi-LSTM | 72.96 | 72.82 | 264.59 | 127.37 |
| GRU | 74.67 | 74.09 | 68.54 | 71.55 |
| CNN | 71.03 | 70.97 | 4.16 | 49.24 |
| BERT | 79.57 | 79.41 | 78.65[a] | 20.49[b] |
| RoBERTa | **81.29** | **81.25** | 316.02 | 22.15 |
| XLNet | 80.20 | 80.20 | 168.97 | 36.95 |
| GPT-2 | 78.26 | 78.15 | 217.56 | 29.83 |

[a] Google Colab's premium GPU was used. [b] Google Colab's standard GPU was used.

The metrics for the traditional machine learning models show that the logistic regression and SVM models perform the best in accuracy and F1-Score. In contrast, KNN and decision tree models show the worst prediction performance. The unsatisfying results of the decision tree classifier might be due to the high dimensionality of the data and the significant number of relevant features. Additionally, the long inference time of KNN is due to its known computational intensity, mainly when dealing with large datasets. Finally, the poor prediction performance might be due to the wrong choice of the "k" nearest neighbors.

Among the neural network-based models, the best-performing models in terms of accuracy and F1-Score are GRU and LSTM; their prediction performance is still slightly lower than the best traditional machine learning models.

The Bi-LSTM model also performs well, while the CNN model performs the worst among the neural network-based models, potentially because CNN are mainly used for image and video processing tasks, where data has a grid-like structure, whereas RNN (LSTM, Bi-LSTM, and GRU) are used for processing sequential data, such as natural language text and speech.

Finally, transformer-based models perform better than traditional machine learning and neural network-based models in all prediction performance metrics. RoBERTa has the best prediction performance with an accuracy of 81.29% and a F1-Score of 81.25%. The other transformer-based models, BERT and XLNet, also perform very well. The slightly lower prediction performance of the GPT-2 model could be due to its primary design for tasks such as language translation, language generation, and language understanding rather than document classification. Notably, the transformer-based models had a very high training and inference time, which was reduced using a GPU. Nevertheless, as RoBERTa had the best prediction performance among all the models for this task, it will be the comparison model for evaluating the proprietary software.

## 4.2 Performance of Proprietary Software

This section presents the prediction performance metrics of the proprietary software, presented in Sect. 3.3, in the same way as Sect. 4.1. Table 2 displays each model's accuracy and F1-Score, together with the average training and inference time in milliseconds per document. RoBERTa, the best-performing FOSS model, can be found as a baseline at the bottom of the table.

**Table 2.** Performance of Proprietory Software

| Modell | Accuracy | F1-Score | Training Time | Inference Time |
|---|---|---|---|---|
| Microsoft Azure | 79.13 | 79.03 | 573.97 | 5439.81 |
| Amazon Comprehend | 78.04 | 78.01 | 260.68 | 14920.47 |
| OpenAI GPT-3 | **81.27** | **81.18** | 201.85 | 96.82 |
| Levity AI | 80.29 | 80.27 | 261.35 | 1491.67 |
| Planet AI | 79.04 | 79.01 | **132.21** | **27.24** |
| Google Vertex AI | 78.12 | 77.95 | 217.92 | 350.91 |
| *RoBERTa* | *81.29* | *81.25* | *316.02* | *22.15*[a] |

[a]Inference did not include an API.

Table 2 provides a comparative analysis of different commercial providers and the open-source baseline model, RoBERTa. The models' prediction performance is evaluated on accuracy and F1-Score. Additionally, the training and inference times of the models are also recorded. The results show that GPT-3 outperforms all other models in all prediction performance metrics, with an accuracy of 81.27% and a F1-Score of 81.18%. On the other hand, Amazon Comprehend scored the lowest in these metrics, with an accuracy of 78.04% and a F1-Score of 78.01%. Notably, all models show similar prediction performance, with the highest difference in accuracy being 3.23%.

However, there are significant variations in training and inference times. Planet AI demonstrates the shortest training time of 132.21ms on average per document and the shortest inference time of 27.24ms on average per document among all proprietary software. In contrast, Azure takes the longest training time of 573.97ms on average per document, approximately four times the training time of Planet AI. Aside from that, Amazon Comprehend has the longest inference time of 14920.47ms on average per document, which is approximately 548 times the inference time of Planet AI. Although GPT-3 outperforms all other models in prediction performance metrics, it falls short of the open-source baseline model, RoBERTa, which achieves an accuracy of 81.29% and a F1-Score of 81.25%. Despite its lower prediction performance metrics, Planet AI outperforms RoBERTa regarding training but not inference time. However, it should be noted that the inference of RoBERTa was made in-house and on a GPU, whereas Planet AI's inference was performed through an API and a single-core CPU, which slowed the process.

The findings shows that GPT-3 performs well in all performance metrics and achieves similar results as the FOSS baseline model, RoBERTa. Planet AI has the shortest training and inference times among all proprietary models, whereas Microsoft Azure and Amazon Comprehend demonstrate the longest training and inference times, respectively. If the inference time of RoBERTa was performed through an API and on a CPU, Planet AI could also outperform it regarding inference time. It should be noted that Levity AI, which is relatively less well-known in this comparison, achieved a highly competitive prediction performance compared to industry giants such as Google's Vertex AI, Microsoft's Azure, and Amazon Comprehend.

### 4.3 Cost Comparison

This section compares the various products offered by commercial providers against each other cost-wise. To do so, a 30-day time period was simulated. A new classification model was trained at the start of the period and hosted throughout the entire period. The costs were factorized for documents that needed to be classified within this period. For the whole period, there are three main cost components: training, hosting, and inference costs per document. The formulas for calculating the training, hosting, and interfering costs were accessed on the service providers' corresponding websites, found in references [18] to [1], on the 15th of December, 2023, and were applied to the dataset.

This section introduces several variables to enhance the clarity of the cost formulas shown in Table 3: $h$ represents an hour, $m$ represents a month, $b_t$ signifies the ratio of 1000-character text blocks rounded up to the nearest block, which is equal to 1.75, $b_h$ signifies the ratio of 100-character text blocks rounded up to the nearest block, which is equal to 12.74, and $t$ denotes the average number of tokens on each document, which is equal to 276.63. For clarification, a document containing 250 words and 1250 characters would equal two 1000-character text blocks, 13 100-character text blocks, and roughly 330 tokens. It is to mention, that GPT-3 counted four times more tokens (966) for the training data, so the billing is significantly higher. As some providers settle the training costs through the training time, the training time was measured, as shown in Table 2, and the costs were calculated. Finally, as Amazon bills per second of endpoint hosting for real-time inference, it was calculated how long it takes to classify one document based on the average number of characters per document. Amazon uses "Inference Units", which can process one 100-character text block per second. This study utilized one inference unit.

$$\frac{s}{document} = 1 \ \frac{100\text{-character-block}}{s} \cdot b_h = 12.74 \ \frac{s}{document} \qquad (5)$$

$$\frac{costs}{document} = 0.0005 \ \frac{\$}{s} \cdot 12.74 \ \frac{s}{document} = 0.00637 \ \frac{\$}{document} \qquad (6)$$

As stated in Sect. 3.4, RoBERTa was hosted via AWS SageMaker. AWS SageMaker includes a variety of costs which are listed below:

- **Model artifacts:** After training the RoBERTa model on Google Colab without any costs, the model artifacts must be uploaded into an Amazon S3 bucket to make it available for Amazon SageMaker. As the model is around 300 MB in size and needs to be stored for 30 days with up to 100,000 requests, the costs calculate as follows:

$$S3 \ costs = 0.3GB \cdot \$0.023/GB + 100,000 \cdot \$0.000005/request = \$0.51 \qquad (7)$$

- **ECR** container image The model needs to be contained in an ECR container image to make it available for Amazon SageMaker. The costs for this calculate as follows:

$$ECR \ costs = 0.3GB \cdot \$0.1 = \$0.03 \qquad (8)$$

Adding these costs to storing the model artifacts results in training costs of \$0.54.
- **Endpoint Hosting** For hosting the model, a "ml.m5.large" instance was chosen. The costs for hosting this instance 24 h a day for 30 days with one model and one endpoint calculate as follows:

$$hosting \ costs = 24h \cdot 30d \cdot \$0.115 = \$82.80 \qquad (9)$$

- **Inference** With the assumption that one document $x$ is 1MB in size, which is already very generous, the inference costs would calculate as follows:

$$inference \ costs = x \cdot 1MB \cdot \$0.000015625/MB \qquad (10)$$

**Levity AI** employs a monthly subscription plan that encompasses training, hosting, and processing a specified number of documents, hence the absence of this company from the pricing table. Furthermore, the inference numbers of

**Planet AI** typically exceed those of the simulation by a considerable margin, and owing to the complexity of its internal cost structure, it was not feasible to establish a comprehensive pricing scheme for the 30-day simulation, resulting in the exclusion of the company from the cost analysis. The costs for every other product offered by commercial providers and additionally for RoBERTa can be found in Table 3.

Table 3. Costs Formulas

| Service | Training | Hosting | Inference |
|---|---|---|---|
| Microsoft Azure | $3/h$ | $0.5/m$ | $0.005/b_t$ |
| Amazon Comprehend | $3/h$ | $0.5/m$ | $0.00637/document$ |
| GPT-3 (Babbage) | $0.0000006/t$ | $0 | $0.0000024/t$ |
| Vertex AI | $3.30/h$ | $0.05/h$ | $0.005/b_t$ |
| RoBERTa | $0.54 | $82.80 | $0.000015625/document$ |

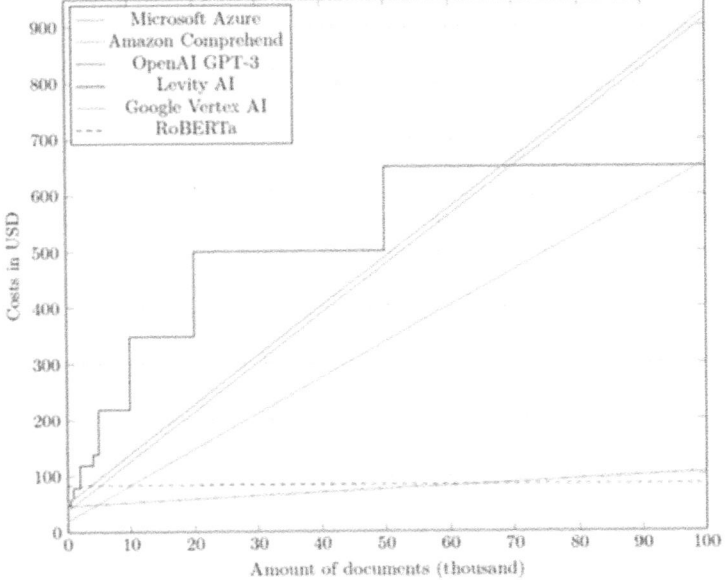

**Fig. 2.** Cost Comparison

A line graph has been constructed in Fig. 2 to facilitate the comparison of costs between different approaches. The chart displays the training costs accumulated with the hosting costs of each model at the beginning of the chart, as well as the costs incurred from processing different numbers of documents.

According to the findings, there are considerable differences in the total expenses between various suppliers. For example, the combined training and hosting expenses, further referred to as *upfront costs*, for Microsoft Azure are very moderate. However, its inference costs are comparatively high, making its overall prices the second-highest at 100,000 documents. The most expensive supplier is Google Vertex AI, which charges the same amount for inference as Microsoft Azure but has higher upfront costs. The second-lowest costs for practically all document volumes are achieved by Amazon Comprehend, which begins with the lowest upfront costs and retains comparable low inference costs. Levity AI initially appears to price comparatively higher for smaller document volumes, but it ultimately manages to overcome the costs of Microsoft Azure, Amazon Comprehend, and Google Vertex AI. Furthermore, despite having the highest upfront costs, the GPT-3 model from OpenAI is the most affordable among all proprietary models for practically all document quantities. Importantly, OpenAI's GPT-3 expenses at 100,000 documents are almost a ninth of Amazon Comprehend's. Finally, although RoBERTa has the highest upfront costs due to hosting the "ml.m5.large" instance, its negligible inference costs make it the cheapest option among all providers at higher document volumes. Again, however, GPT-3's costs are comparable.

## 5 Discussion, Conclusion and Limitations

Starting with the prediction performance of the FOSS, it can be observed that some models perform better than others in terms of accuracy and F1-Score. RoBERTa has the highest accuracy and F1-Score with 81.29% and 81.25%, respectively, while KNN has the lowest accuracy and F1-Score with 44.76% and 44.85%, respectively. In terms of training time, there are significant differences. SVM has the longest training time with 316.13ms on average per document, followed by RoBERTa and Bi-LSTM. On the other hand, the NBC has the shortest training time with 0.47ms on average per document, followed by KNN. Inference time also varies widely across the models. KNN has the longest inference time with 725.39ms on average per document, followed by Bi-LSTM and LSTM. The decision tree classifier has the shortest inference time, with 1.55ms on average per document, followed by NBC. Notably, the training and inference process of the PLM were accelerated with a GPU, which made them much faster.

However, it is essential to note that different models may have different strengths and weaknesses. The approaches can be optimised by analyzing these and applying techniques such as dimensionality reduction, which might drastically improve KNN's and decision tree's prediction performance, or different word embedding techniques, which might improve the prediction performance of CNN and RNN. Overall, the choice of the best model depends on the specific requirements of the problem, including the trade-off between accuracy, training time, and inference time. For example, if high accuracy is the most crucial factor, as it was for this study, RoBERTa may be the best choice, even though it has a long training time. On the other hand, if fast inference time is more important, decision tree or NBC may be a better choice, even though they may have lower accuracy than other models.

By comparing the performance of the proprietary software, it can be observed that the products perform similarly in prediction performance, with GPT-3 having the highest accuracy and F1-Score with 81.27% and 81.18%, respectively. However, there are significant differences between the models regarding time measurements. Planet AI performs best with 132.21ms training time on average per document and 27.24ms inference time on average per document. Still, no proprietary software achieved better prediction performance than the base comparison model RoBERTa, although GPT-3 came quite close. However, time-wise, Planet AI achieved a better training time and probably better inference time under the same conditions. It should be noted that we did perform parametric optimization of the different approaches, i.e., changes in parameters, such as training epochs or learning rate, might change the results.

Looking at the costs for the products, it is observable that GPT-3 also has the lowest cost for inferring with 100,000 documents among the proprietary software, followed by Amazon Comprehend, Levity AI, Microsoft Azure, and Google Vertex AI. In contrast, RoBERTa's implementation via AWS SageMaker is still the cheapest option. However, it is to mention that several providers offer different options, such as GPT-3 with models that are slower and more accurate but therefore more costly, or Amazon Comprehend, which offers a scalable number of "Inference Units" that accelerate inference but also increase pricing. Overall, the choice of the best service depends on the specific requirements of the problem, including the trade-off between accuracy, training time, and inference time, as well as the cost of the services and other external characteristics, such as availability, user-friendliness, scalability, data encryption, integration options or other services. Although the other external characteristics were not considered in this study, they would be interesting for further studies to investigate text classification and processing AI as a service solution in more detail.

Furthermore, it is to mention that as the dataset used for the study is publicly available, it can not be ruled out that one or more of the PLM used this specific dataset, or part of it, in their pre-training data, which would, of course, falsify the results. The same goes for some commercial providers, which might also use PLM. Moreover, as different models have different strengths and weaknesses, the results of using a different dataset may vary significantly.

Finally, for both FOSS and CPPS, we neither investigated how to optimize the different approaches using the available parameters nor if the results are similar for different datasets. Many investigations have shown (see, e.g. [5]) that the most suitable AI approach for a certain purpose often depends on the dataset. This is why we cannot assume that our results also are valid for other datasets. For the cost comparison, it has to be observed that the price lists of the commercial software providers and even their business models are subject to frequent change. Our evaluation was performed in December 2023.

# References

1. Google vertex ai. https://cloud.google.com/vertex-ai?hl=de. Accessed 28 Feb 2023
2. Openai. https://openai.com/. Accessed 28 Feb 2023
3. Planet ai. https://planet-ai.de/. Accessed 28 Feb 2023
4. AWS: Aws comprehend. https://aws.amazon.com/de/comprehend/. Accessed 28 Feb 2023
5. Bej, S., Davtyan, N., Wolfien, M., Nassar, M., Wolkenhauer, O.: LoRas: an oversampling approach for imbalanced datasets. Mach. Learn. **110**, 279–301 (2021)
6. Bureau, C.F.P.: Consumer complaints report 2021. https://files.consumerfinance.gov/f/documents/cfpb_2021-consumer-response-annual-report_2022-03.pdf. Accessed 09 Jan 2023
7. Chollet, F., et al.: Keras. https://keras.io (2015)
8. Dale, R.: GPT-3: what's it good for? Nat. Lang. Eng. **27**(1), 113–118 (2021)
9. Frye, M., Schmitt, R.H.: Structured data preparation pipeline for machine learning-applications in pro-duction. In: 17th IMEKO TC, vol. 10, pp. 241–246 (2020)
10. Grandini, M., Bagli, E., Visani, G.: Metrics for multi-class classification: an overview. arXiv preprint arXiv:2008.05756 (2020)
11. Griesch, L., Görgen, L., Sandkuhl, K.: Ki-als-service: Vergleich von plattformen zur dokumentenklassifikation. Lecture Notes on Informatics (LNI) (2024)
12. Griesch, L., Rittelmeyer, J., Sandkuhl, K.: Towards AI as a service for small and medium-sized enterprises (SME). In: IFIP Working Conference on The Practice of Enterprise Modeling, pp. 37–53. Springer, Cham (2023). https://doi.org/10.1007/978-3-031-48583-1_3
13. Hossin, M., Sulaiman, M.N.: A review on evaluation metrics for data classification evaluations. Int. J. Data Min. Knowl. Manage. Process **5**(2), 1 (2015)
14. Khan, A., Baharudin, B., Lee, L.H., Khan, K.: A review of machine learning algorithms for text-documents classification. J. Adv. Inform. Technol. **1**(1), 4–20 (2010)
15. LevitiyAI: Levity ai. https://levity.ai/. Accessed 28 Feb 2023
16. Li, Q., et al.: A survey on text classification: From shallow to deep learning. arXiv preprint arXiv:2008.00364 (2020)
17. Lin, T., Wang, Y., Liu, X., Qiu, X.: A survey of transformers. AI Open (2022)
18. Microsoft: Microsoft azure. https://language.cognitive.azure.com/. Accessed 28 Feb 2023
19. Mohajon, J.: confusion matrix. https://towardsdatascience.com/confusion-matrix-for-your-multi-class-machine-learning-model-ff9aa3bf7826. Accessed 07 Feb 2023
20. Pedregosa, F.: Scikit-learn: machine learning in Python. J. Mach. Learn. Res. **12**, 2825–2830 (2011)
21. Sebastiani, F.: Machine learning in automated text categorization. ACM Comput. Surv. **34**(1), 1-47 (2002). https://doi.org/10.1145/505282.505283
22. Sen, P.C., Hajra, M., Ghosh, M.: Supervised classification algorithms in machine learning: a survey and review. In: Mandal, J.K., Bhattacharya, D. (eds.) Emerging Technology in Modelling and Graphics. AISC, vol. 937, pp. 99–111. Springer, Singapore (2020). https://doi.org/10.1007/978-981-13-7403-6_11
23. Soofi, A.A., Awan, A.: Classification techniques in machine learning: applications and issues. J. Basic Appl. Sci. **13**, 459–465 (2017)
24. Vitera, J., et al.: On the importance of digital transformation for SME-results from a survey among German SME. In: BIR Workshops, pp. 56–69 (2022)

25. Wagh, V., Khandve, S., Joshi, I., Wani, A., Kale, G., Joshi, R.: Comparative study of long document classification. In: TENCON 2021 - 2021 IEEE Region 10 Conference (TENCON), pp. 732–737 (2021). https://doi.org/10.1109/TENCON54134.2021.9707465
26. Wolf, T., et al.: Transformers: state-of-the-art natural language processing. In: Proceedings of the 2020 Conference on Empirical Methods in Natural Language Processing: System Demonstrations, pp. 38–45 (2020)

# Towards Model-driven Enhancement of Safety in Healthcare Robot Interactions

Georgios Koutsopoulos[1] ✉ , Penelope Ioannidou[2] , George K. Matsopoulos[2] , and Dimitrios D. Koutsouris[2]

[1] Department of Computer and Systems Sciences, Stockholm University, Borgarfjordsgatan 12, Kista, 16407 Stockholm, Sweden
georgios@dsv.su.se

[2] Biomedical Engineering Laboratory, School of Electrical and Computer Engineering, National Technical University of Athens, Heroon Polytechneiou 9, Zografou, 15780 Athens, Greece
{pioannidou,gmatsopoulos,dkoutsou}@biomed.ntua.gr

**Abstract.** In the continuously evolving landscape of healthcare technology, the evolution of robotics has revolutionized a wide spectrum of services. This situation created a variety of opportunities and challenges. One of the main challenges concerns the interaction of robots with human users and other robots, along with the safety aspect of such interactions. The current paper introduces a project aiming to tackle this challenge, initially via a literature review aiming to explore and structure the domain of robotic interactions in healthcare. Subsequently, the results are conceptualized in a domain meta-model, aiming to establish the foundation for an information system, based on a multi-view modeling approach, with the capabilities to support by documenting and facilitating safer interactions between healthcare robots and external agents. The current study focuses on the safety viewpoint of robotic interaction. The developed model is suitable for initiating the development of the abovementioned system that will use multi-view modeling principles. It is demonstrated in a use case derived from the associated ENDORSE EU project.

**Keywords:** Healthcare robot · Multi-view modeling · Instantiation · Interaction · Communication · Collaboration · Safety

## 1 Introduction

The domain of healthcare is rapidly evolving as a result of the advent of robotics, which provides unique opportunities to researchers and scientists to transform a wide spectrum of healthcare services [1]. A few examples of operation areas that can potentially benefit from the use of healthcare robots include, but are not limited to, patient care, surgical procedures, and medical logistics.

One of the essential aspects that need to be taken into consideration regarding the efficiency of healthcare robotics is their interaction, not only with human users but also with other robots that operate within the same environment, and more so, the safety of such interactions [2]. The complexity of the healthcare domain is high, involving dynamic human behaviors, the potential for unpredicted scenarios and the constant critical requirement for error-free operations, due to the nature of the domain. This situation results in a need to govern healthcare robotics with robust safety mechanisms. The safety requirements in the medical domain cannot be considered eased, even though a variety of focal points have been used in approaches aiming to tackle this challenge [3], along with several protocols and standards like [4, 5] that provide guidelines for ensuring safety in healthcare robot interactions. This fact raises a significant challenge [6].

While conventional and contemporary approaches to robotic interaction design and support have contributed considerable advances to the domain, they are often relying on direct programming and rule-based systems [7], a fact which can be considered a disadvantage in terms of flexibility. The problem of flexibility can be addressed by employing conceptual modeling, and more specifically, a multi-view approach. Given the inherent complexity of the healthcare domain, a multi-view conceptual modeling approach can facilitate decomposing a complex model into specific viewpoints, layers, levels etc. [8]. The viewpoints can serve their own purpose, for example, the design and analysis of information systems that would otherwise have high complexity. Multi-view conceptual modeling can provide a structured, yet, flexible, solution to robotic interactions in healthcare, by decomposing the domain into perspectives focusing, for example on robot specification, operational context, interacting agents, collaboration, communication, safety. As a result, a research project has been initiated to employ multi-view conceptual modeling for the given domain.

The aim of the research project is to explore healthcare robotic interactions, in terms of communication, collaboration, and safety, and conceptualize the results using multi-view conceptual modeling, as a means to initiate the model-driven development of a system supporting and facilitating robotic interaction in healthcare. Due to the page limitations of this paper, we have opted for presenting and demonstrating a single viewpoint of the developed model, using safety as the focal point.

The objective of this specific paper is *to elicit a descriptive set of concepts for safety in healthcare robot interaction, and to elaborate on a detailed conceptualization of this aspect using the elicited concept set.*

The rest of the paper is structured as follows. Section 2 briefly describes the background of the study. Section 3 explains the involved methodological decisions, Sect. 4 presents the results regarding the safety aspect, Sects. 5 and 6 show the initial requirements and the developed conceptualization of the results, Sect. 7 presents an instantiation of the model, and Sects. 8 and 9 discuss the results and provide concluding remarks, respectively.

## 2 Background

This section provides a brief background on the topics that are relevant to the study.

### 2.1 Robots in Healthcare

With the introduction of robots, the healthcare industry is going through a major transition. Robots are showing significant potentials in a variety of medical and paramedical fields, from rehabilitation robots supporting the recovery of motor skills to surgical robots improving precision and less invasive operations [9]. Numerous opportunities exist to enhance surgical outcomes, patient care, and healthcare services in general as a result of this integration [10].

## 2.2 Robot Interaction

While human-robot interaction (HRI) offers numerous possibilities for collaboration and assistance, ensuring safety remains a paramount concern. The growing prevalence of robots in shared workspaces necessitates robust safety measures to protect both humans and robots [7]. Physical HRI (pHRI), where robots and humans coexist in close proximity, presents unique challenges due to the potential for collisions and injuries [11]. This underscores the need for thorough safety considerations across various applications in healthcare environments and everyday interactions for a variety of robots.

Effective and safe interaction between robots and humans is paramount for successful implementation in healthcare settings. This interaction encompasses diverse aspects, including (i) HRI: Principles of trust, transparency, and learnability are crucial for building trust and ensuring smooth collaboration and cooperation [12], (ii) Sensory modalities: Robots utilize various sensors (vision, touch, audio) to perceive the environment and interact with patients and healthcare professionals accurately [13], (iii) Natural language processing (NLP): Enables communication and collaboration by understanding and responding to natural language [14], and (iv) Adaptability and personalization: Robots should adapt their behavior based on individual needs and situations to enhance both safety and effectiveness [15].

Furthermore, traditional safety measures focused on limiting robot movement and minimizing physical interaction are insufficient for future HRI systems. Emerging research areas contributing to enhanced safety include (i) Reliable motion planning and control algorithms: These consider human presence and dynamics to ensure safe robot movement [16], (ii) Robust sensor fusion and perception: Integrating data from various sensors enables an accurate understanding of the environment and facilitates safer robot navigation [17], (iii) Human error anticipation and mitigation: Understanding and addressing potential human errors through design, training, and clear communication is crucial, and (iv) Collaborative safety protocols: Establishing protocols for safe and coordinated movement between humans and robots is essential for effective collaboration [4, 5]. Ensuring safe and effective HRI is crucial for integrating robots in healthcare. By addressing the unique challenges and continuously developing new safety concepts, HRI can play a significant role in improving healthcare delivery and patient outcomes.

## 2.3 Safety in Robot Interactions

Ensuring safe pHRI remains a complex and multifaceted challenge due to the inherent risks associated with close co-existence and communication between humans and robots. This complexity necessitates a thorough understanding of potential safety concerns, particularly in the realm of motion safety and collision avoidance.

Achieving safe cooperation between humans and robots across diverse environments, including industrial settings, healthcare, and everyday life, hinges on the fundamental principle of safety. Motion safety emerges as a critical concern, as collisions involving robots, humans, and surrounding structures can have severe consequences. Automated vehicles, humanoid robots, and mobile manipulators pose significant potential for harm during operation, highlighting the need for robust motion safety protocols before granting such systems complete autonomy in shared spaces [18].

Merely demonstrating a robot's functionality under controlled conditions is inadequate for guaranteeing real-world safety. A deeper understanding of achievable motion safety and the specific conditions under which it can be ensured is crucial for the widespread deployment of autonomous robots in human-populated environments.

### 2.4 Challenges and Shortcomings

The nature of safety in healthcare robots is multifaceted. It highlights that beyond preventing physical harm during HRI [19], ensuring safety encompasses (i) Data security and privacy: Safeguarding sensitive data exchanged between healthcare robots and other interconnected devices, (ii) Cybersecurity: Protecting robots from cyberattacks that could compromise patient data, privacy, and even physical safety.

Current robot safety frameworks, involving design, data exchange, and operation, address various aspects. Yet, concerns are raised about the adequacy of these frameworks, particularly regarding (i) Manufacturer priorities: Difficulty in building secure robots may lead manufacturers to prioritize functionality over robust cybersecurity and (ii) Legislative loopholes: Potential gaps are suggested in regulations for robots, especially in the healthcare sector. This necessitates a thorough evaluation by legislative authorities to establish clear responsibilities and address potential vulnerabilities [20].

By acknowledging the multifaceted nature of safety and the limitations of current frameworks, this study emphasizes the urgent need for robust cybersecurity measures and comprehensive legislation tailored to healthcare robots. These efforts are crucial to ensure the safe and responsible integration of robots into the healthcare environment.

### 2.5 Modeling

Conceptual modeling, as a discipline, is used to "apply abstraction to reduce complexity in a domain, for a specific purpose" [21]. Regardless of the field of application, the design of new systems or the analysis of existing ones can be substantially benefited from employing a conceptual viewpoint focused on capturing its significant structural, behavioral or semantic aspects, while in parallel ignoring the non-significant ones [22].

Conceptual modeling produces conceptualizations, which can be defined as set of concepts that consist of individual and relational concepts, the latter referring to properties and relationships of individual concepts [23]. When the modeling purpose concerns the development of modeling methods or languages, rules need to be defined, and this is achieved by several means like graph grammars and meta-models [24].

Defining a domain is often a complex activity, since specific patterns that establish the foundations for modeling a specific domain may be encountered in different domains too [22]. When the given domain is also characterized by high inherent complexity, like the domain of healthcare robot interactions, more elaborate approaches are required.

One such approach is multi-view modeling, and it specialization, slicing meta-models, aiming to decompose and split the original meta-model into smaller segments, called slices, where each segment is addressing a specific viewpoint [25]. Slicing meta-models may have exactly one or more than one common elements in different slices, referring to non-redundancy or redundancy, respectively. Other approaches include referencing meta-models which is a special case of slicing meta-models.

## 3 Methodology

The goal of this study is to explore the domain of robotic interactions in healthcare via a literature review and conceptualize the findings using safety as a focal point.

The data collection phase of the review was conducted in compliance with the PRISMA guidelines [26]. The databases used were Science Direct and PubMed, and the identification of papers has been conducted using the following set of keywords:

*(robots AND (medicine OR healthcare)) OR (communication/interaction protocols AND robots AND healthcare) OR (collaboration protocols AND robots AND healthcare) OR (safety AND robots AND healthcare)*

The initial search produced a set consisting of 1717 papers, to which the inclusion and exclusion criteria were applied. The criteria were (i) relevance to the research goal (i) provision of data analysis, (iii) English language, (iv) full-text availability, and (v) publication after 1990. Applying the criteria iteratively to the studies by screening the titles, abstracts, and main bodies resulted in a set of 97 incorporated studies (Fig. 1).

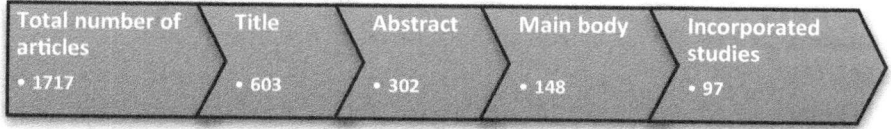

**Fig. 1.** The iterative procedure of paper selection.

After extracting data from the papers, the dataset was coded using descriptive coding [27], and deductive thematic analysis [28] was performed. Deductive thematic analysis is used when a pre-existing conceptual framework drives the analysis, in other words, the elicited findings are mapped to the framework. For the given research project, the framework was developed according to an initial exploration and mapping of the healthcare robot domain, which is in line with the research goal and includes a set of aspects that the research team has deemed as valuable for modeling the domain. In particular, the aspects of the domain are (i) Communication, (ii) Collaboration, (iii) Safety, (iv) Operational context, (v) Robot specification, and (vi) Interacting agent, as shown in the high-level meta-model in Fig. 2, which has been created using the principles of the Unified Modeling Language (UML) [29]. Every class in color will comprise a viewpoint in the complete meta-model of the domain. For reasons of feasibility, in terms of page limitations, in this paper, only the Safety aspect is reported.

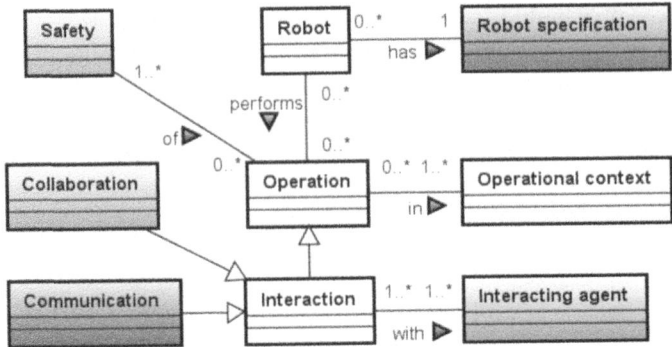

**Fig. 2.** The valuable aspects of healthcare robot interaction.

For the conceptualization phase of this study, UML has been employed [29], applying abstraction, classification and any other cognitive mechanism required during the modeling process. During the initial draft of the model, extensive size, complexity, and clutter was observed, therefore, decomposing the meta-model was deemed necessary, using the technique of redundancy slicing meta-models [25]. The safety viewpoint seems to be non-redundant, however, the other developed slices required more than one common element, leading to selecting a redundancy approach overall. The meta-model has been demonstrated using a use case from the completed EU project ENDORSE [30], which is described in more detail in Sect. 6.

## 4 Findings from the Literature Review

This section presents the main findings of the literature review.

### 4.1 Faults

*Fault* is a concept that bears a strong association to safety. Faults related to safety in robotic interaction in healthcare belong to four main categories [31], which are:

1. Hardware failures: Malfunctions in robotic components can lead to unpredictable movements and pose collision threats [32].
2. Software errors: Bugs or flaws in a robot's control software can result in unintended behaviors and deviations from planned trajectories, increasing collision risks [32].
3. Perceptual mistakes: Limitations in a robot's sensory system lead to inaccurate environmental understanding and misinterpretations, causing collisions [33, 34].
4. Logical or reasoning errors: Faulty decision-making by the robot's control system, resulting in incorrect movement commands, can contribute to collision risks [33, 34].

Addressing these diverse factors through robust engineering principles, rigorous testing procedures, and the implementation of safety measures such as sensor-based collision avoidance systems and safe robot design principles is paramount to ensuring safe and successful HRI in the future [3, 5, 35].

**Motion Safety**

Motion collision is confirmed as the most commonly encountered problem regarding safety in robotic interactions [36]. A motion collision incident may result in harm inflicted on interacting agents, like humans or other robots, or its surroundings. Motion safety refers to addressing the possibility of motion collision(s), and involves various monitoring and testing types [37], since the requirement for error-free operations before deploying an autonomous robot in a healthcare setting is critical.

**Fault Management**

A variety of approaches tackling the issue of fault management have been identified. Apart from a series of safety protocols and standards that have been developed to regulate robotic operations towards a higher level of safety, for instance [4, 5], there are other approaches too. The main categories of fault management approaches [38] are (i) Fault tolerance, (ii) Fault prevention, (iii) Fault removal, and (iv) Fault forecasting.

*Fault Removal.* The aim of these approaches is to find and correct faults in a given system. The task is hindered when it comes to autonomous systems due to the unpredictability of execution environments [39]. This involves static or dynamic verification. The former usually involves validation via comparison of system operations with system requirements, and is the most popular type of fault removal, while the latter involves identification of faults by testing to reveal shortcomings.

*Fault Prevention.* These approaches aim to avoid mistakes. Derived from best practices in system engineering, the majority of these approaches' focal point is on component-based frameworks and modularity [38], which also relate to hierarchical architectures associated to models and abstractions. Other prevention approaches focus on safety systems, algorithms, maintenance and training of interacting agents.

*Fault Tolerance.* Refers to approaches that aim to avoid operational disruption, despite of occurring faults. They result in reporting a tolerance level and are commonly classified in conjunction with the concept of *Decisional autonomy*. This concept bears augmented significance since it has been identified in relation to other aspects of healthcare robot interactions, i.e. the Collaboration aspect and modeling viewpoint. Autonomy has a layered architecture [38] that consists of the (i) Decisional, (ii) Executive, (iii) and Control/Functional layer, which are used to describe the tolerance approaches.

*Fault Forecasting.* These approaches have been highly popular for the development of industrial robots [40, 41]. Their goal is to estimate the causality behind an occurring fault. They are classified into two categories; bottom-up and top-down. The bottom-up approaches focus on the impact of a fault in terms of causality, likelihood and intensity, while the top-down ones focus on associating events that result in top-level faults.

## 4.2 Safety Dimensions

The literature review has resulted in identifying a set of *dimensions* that comprise the safety aspect. In particular, the dimensions of safety in healthcare robot interactions are (i) Cyber dimension, (ii) Societal dimension, (iii) Temporal dimension, (iv) Interaction dimension, and (v) Motion, which is also recognized as a dimension of safety and it has been described in relation to faults in a previous subsection.

The *cyber* dimension refers to the nature of robots as cyber-physical systems, which is challenged by the implementation of AI, and the increased interactions from a quantitative perspective, both with human agents and other devices and systems [42]. Offloading heavy computational tasks, like object recognition, to the cloud, improves robotic efficiency, yet, this increases the risk of vulnerabilities and attacks [43]. Thus, this dimension also involves potential external attacks, even though it is not limited to this part. It also involves transparency too, as in the case of ethical concerns derived from practices like collecting data on the employee performance [44].

Safety includes the potential for delayed harm, highlighting the importance of the *temporal* dimension, such as harm occurring outside standard work hours from technology use [42]. The use of machine learning algorithms in this case, presents new challenges for policymakers worldwide [45]. Safety standards must address risks from updates and enhancements via machine learning, including the risks posed by predictive analytics that could compromise user safety in case of inaccurate predictions [46].

The *societal* dimension of safety concerns the issues raised by the integration of robots in workplaces. Workers often fear that this integration leads to increased workload resulting in stress and burnout, as a result of lack of training. Employment insecurity and poor working conditions as a result of job oversupply [47], loss of essential skills [48], and limitations occurring due to the slow pace of adapting employment and social security policies [42] are a few points indicating the importance of this dimension.

The final dimension, *interaction*, has already been taken into consideration and described in Sect. 2, and the findings confirm its association to the aspect of safety.

### 4.3 Dependability

A noteworthy finding concerns *dependability*. Dependability can be defined as the capacity to operate and provide service(s) to a reasonably trustworthy degree [49], so, it has value in regard to safer robot interactions. What differentiates it from the previous findings is that dependability seems to be treated in the literature as a higher-level concept, in contrast to the other findings that are mapped to safety in a lower level and facilitated its description. In particular, dependability consists of the concepts of *maintainability* and *security* [49]. Security uses a set of concepts for its description. This set of concepts consists of (i) Availability, (ii) Reliability, (iii) Safety, (iv) Confidentiality, and (v) Integrity. The semantic relevance between dependability and security is clear, since they share five descriptive qualities, safety being one of them.

From a modeling perspective, this finding cannot be ignored, even if it does not directly facilitate the documentation and analysis of safety. These descriptive qualities need to be included as a means to capture safety via the higher-level concepts.

## 5 Elicited Requirements

Based on the findings that were derived from the literature review, an initial set of high-level requirements has been elicited for the envisioned artifact, as shown in Table 1. The requirements are specified semi-formally, which means that hey are expressed in a structured form of a natural language, using syntactic patterns [50].

**Table 1.** The initial set of high-level requirements for the safety perspective.

| No | Requirement |
|---|---|
| R01 | The artifact shall be able to document the types of errors encountered during robotic interactions in healthcare |
| R02 | The artifact shall be able to document employed fault management approaches |
| R03 | The artifact shall be able to document the tests that control motion safety and their types |
| R04 | The artifact shall establish theoretical demarcations between the reports about safety, security and dependability |
| R05 | The artifact shall document the safety protocols that regulate the safety aspect of robotic interactions in healthcare |
| R06 | The system shall document the decisional autonomy of robotic interactions in healthcare |
| R07 | The artifact shall be able to capture all the dimensions of safety in robotic interactions in healthcare |

From a modeling perspective, the requirements about the artifact concern the syntax and semantics. For the syntax perspective, the model needs to be built according to the principles of UML [29]. In the current iteration, the semantics are derived directly from the literature. The notation and modeling procedure are two aspects that are outside the scope of this paper, considering that only the first design iteration has been completed.

## 6 Safety as a Modeling Viewpoint

Figure 3 depicts the safety viewpoint of the healthcare robot interaction domain, as a UML domain meta-model. The high-level framework is included in the figure, even if it is not part of the viewpoint, to show its association to the view. A red frame has been used to distinguish the framework from the Safety viewpoint in the Figure.

According to the information derived from the literature findings, the meta-model has been developed as follows. Modeling-wise, Safety is associated to the class Level to capture the safety level of a robotic operation, and zero to many Safety protocols that regulate it. Safety protocol is a generalization of Safety standard, which in return is a generalization of ISO, which was deemed valuable to include in the model, since several ISO standards aim to regulate robotic operations. The higher-level concepts that are related to safety are also included, by modeling Safety as a specialization of Security aspect, which also generalizes Integrity, Confidentiality, Availability and Reliability. Security consists of these aspects and is also a specialization of Dependability aspect, and so is Maintainability. Dependability consists of Dependability aspects.

Safety is also associated to the superclass Safety dimension, which generalizes the Cyber, Temporal, Societal, and Motion safety dimensions. Motion safety is associated to zero or more Test(s), which has at least one Test type. Motion safety concerns zero to many Motion collisions, which is a Challenge. Motion collision is also the result of at least one Fault, which can be specialized as Software, Hardware, Perceptual or Logical fault. A Fault may be addressed by a Fault management approach, which has

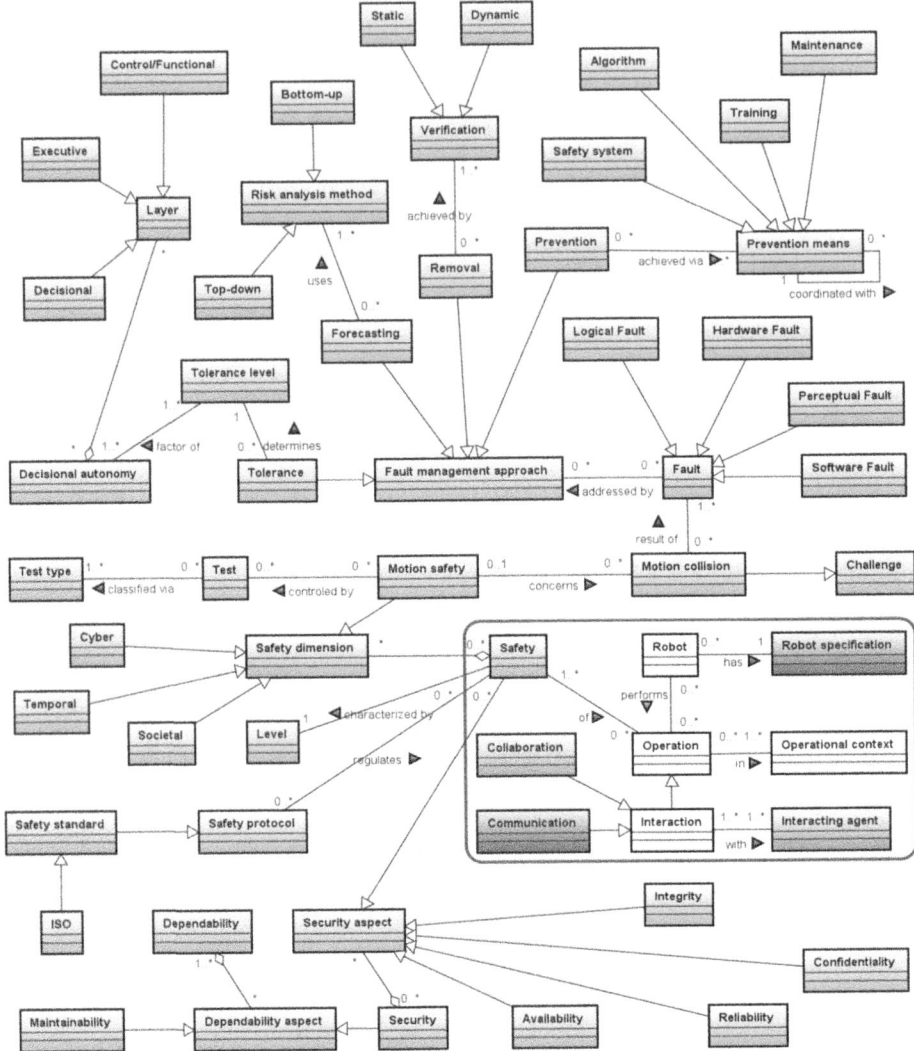

**Fig. 3.** Safety in healthcare robot interaction, shown as a UML meta-model.

been modeled as a superclass. Its specializations are Tolerance, Forecasting, Removal and Prevention. Tolerance is described by a Tolerance level, which is a factor of at least one instance of Decisional autonomy.

Decisional Autonomy consists of Layer(s), the specializations of which are Decisional, Executive and Control/Functional. Forecasting is associated to at least one Risk analysis method, which has two specializations, Bottom-up and Top-down. Removal involves at least one instance of Verification, which has two specialization classes, Static and Dynamic. Finally, Prevention in associated to at least one Prevention means, which is a superclass for Safety system, Algorithm, Training, and Maintenance.

## 7 Instantiation of the Meta-Model Slice for a Use Case

This section presents the instantiation of the meta-model for a specific use case, derived from the Horizon2020 EU project ENDORSE [30], to which two of the authors have been contributors. The project concerned the development and validation of a "safe, efficient and integrated indoor robotic fleet for logistic applications in healthcare and commercial space". The use case concerns the operation of the Fleet Management System (FMS), which involve the collaboration of healthcare robots for delivering materials like medicines and specimens within healthcare spaces. This fact makes the use case suitable for applying the entire meta-model, and the safety slice too (Fig. 4).

The Robot object involved in FMS is RB1-Base, collaborating with 2 other identical robots. The robots have their technical specification, which, on a high level, has been instantiated as a Robot specification object. These have been instantiated as Collaboration and Interacting Agent objects. The case takes place in Fundacio Ave Maria Healthcare center, which has been used to instantiate the Operational Context. The overall safety of the collaboration is associated to the FMS safety report, which is a Safety object. On a higher level of analysis, there are also case reports about the dependability, security and availability of the operation, and these are instantiated using the respective meta-model classes. The Mean Time to Recovery (MTTR) and Mean Time Between Failure (MTBF) are Maintainability objects and parts of Dependability.

The level of safety has been deemed as medium, and this is a (safety) Level object. The safety report is regulated by two ISO objects. The main safety aspect in the case is motion safety of the robot, since there are potential motion collisions involved. Motion safety is tested by assessing KPIs relevant to the operation. Thus, there are five tests involved, assessing the max number of missions per day, meters travelled per day, number of transported items, errors per mission, and number of missions before charging. These have been modeled as Test objects, all of KPI evaluation Test type.

Potential faults that cause motion collisions are Stop, Disorientation, Poor positioning, Erratic movement, and Lost connection, all modeled as objects of the Fault class and its specializations. The faults are addressed using different fault management approaches. The former three are addressed with the FMS System monitoring, which is a Tolerance object, and the latter two with FMS algorithms and analytics, which is a Prevention approach and object in the model. FMS System monitoring is associated to a low tolerance level for the specific operation, which, in return, is associated to the autonomy report of the robot, parts of which are the External party component use, and the Number of working minutes, modeled as object of the Decisional layer and Executive layer, respectively. Regarding the Prevention system, it is realized via a series of prevention means, in Particular, the Data Ingestion, Monitoring and alerting, and Status Management systems, modeled as Safety system objects, and Routing optimization, Routing analytics, and Routing prognostics, modeled as Algorithm objects.

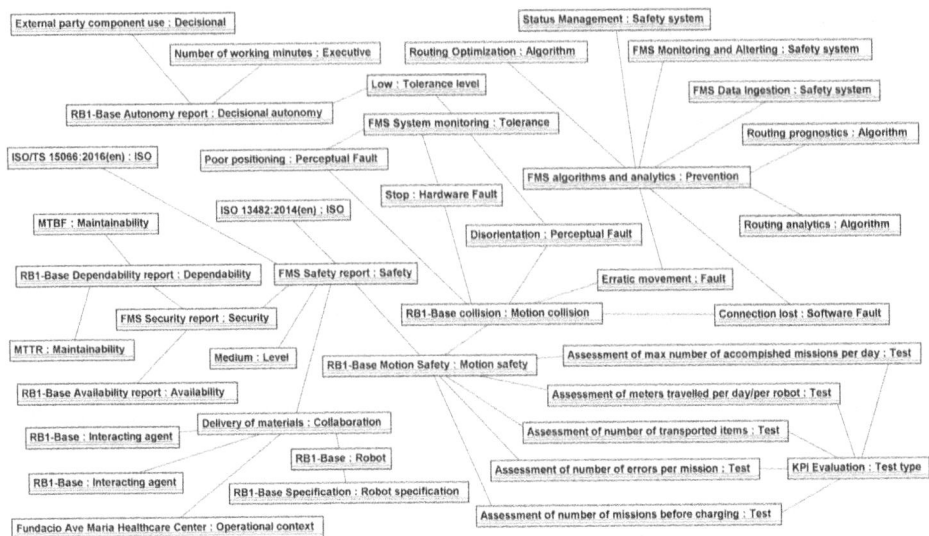

**Fig. 4.** The instantiation of the meta-model for the ENDORSE fleet management use case.

## 8 Discussion

The meta-model for the domain of robotic interactions in healthcare establishes the foundations for a modeling tool with attributes of a decision-support system (DSS). In practice, we aim for a modeling tool that will enable capturing the basic pieces of information of a robot or a robotic operation, and the system will assist in deciding which robots should be used to interact optimally with each other and with human users.

Even if the limited pages of this paper did not allow reporting more than one viewpoint, all the viewpoints have already been modeled. However, this is only the first iteration of the modeling activity, relying exclusively on literature sources. The literature findings provide an initial description and explanation of the reported meta-model slice, yet, we do not claim that they comprise a complete semantic elaboration of the model in this version. However, the instantiation of the meta-model in the FMS use case indicated that this version of the artifact is already valuable as a means to improve the documentation of cases that involve robotic interactions in the healthcare domain. The application shows that the meta-model can produce models that can be used in specific projects and used for documenting, analyzing, and communicating the interaction aspect of healthcare robots, before automating processes via a DSS system.

The current phase of the project is considered complete; however, there are more steps required towards the envisioned system. Initially, the requirements that have been elicited from the literature will be refined by including empirical sources complementing the literature search. Specifically, identifying and including stakeholders and domain experts from the healthcare domain via a systematic Requirements Engineering project will enable the validation, extension, or refinement of the current domain model.

The empirical step will also enable the clarification and potential decomposition of several concepts that have been modeled as high-level elements, such as Availability and

Reliability. These are planned to be implemented in the tool as a report, yet, technically, a report may require standardization, customization, or modularization, which means that only experts can provide adequate insight on how these concepts should be structured and decomposed in a valuable way. Technically, this may be performed by decomposing the high-level class or be enriching it with a set of attributes.

Another gain expected from the empirical validation is the clarification of terminology. In the literature, the boundaries among concepts like safety, security, and dependability are often obscured. So, another future step that has been motivated from this paper is a thorough exploration of the semantic consistency among the concepts of dependability, safety, and security. These concepts have often been used interchangeably, yet, this cannot be taken for granted, especially when it concerns the development of a structured information system that requires clear boundaries among its concepts.

Having presented a single perspective of the domain has value, in terms of structuring the aspect of safety in HRI and robot to robot interaction. Multi-view modeling, in its full extent, will have augmented benefits, confirming Aristotle's statement "the whole is greater than the sum of its parts", which is accurate when considering multi-view modeling. One technical question and decision that remains is whether a selective or projective multi-view approach will be employed [8]. That is, it has to be decided whether there will be real viewpoints coming from distinct meta-models, or if the viewpoints will be virtual, coming from selected concepts in a unified complex meta-model.

From a modeling analysis perspective, it was interesting observing the inclusion of many generalizations in the model, with a number significantly higher than that of the normal associations, a fact which attributes taxonomical/ontological characteristics to the current meta-model. It is worth exploring whether developing an exhaustive ontology of the domain of healthcare robots will provide additional benefits, in terms of improved structuring and descriptive power. In any case, the set of developed artifacts will serve as a basis for the creation of a modeling tool with DSS attributes.

## 9 Conclusions

The paper introduces a project aiming to improve the interactions of robots with humans and other robots in the healthcare domain. A multi-view modeling tool with DSS attributes is envisioned for development. Based on a literature review, a domain meta-model has been developed, and due to page limitations, only one viewpoint has been reported in this paper, the Safety viewpoint. The main aspects of safety that have been identified via the review and implemented in the meta-model concern faults and their management, the dimensions of safety, and the relation of safety with concepts like higher-level concepts like dependability. The meta-model has been applied and instantiated for a real case study derived from a EU project, to demonstrate the documentation potentials of the current version. The next steps will consist of an empirical validation and potential refinement of the meta-model, the ex ante application in real cases, and the evaluation of the model before developing the modeling tool with DSS attributes.

## References

1. Pradhan, B., et al.: Internet of things and robotics in transforming current-day healthcare services. J. Healthc. Eng. **2021**, 1–15 (2021). https://doi.org/10.1155/2021/9999504
2. Lestingi, L., Askarpour, M., Bersani, M.M., Rossi, M.: Formal verification of human-robot interaction in healthcare scenarios. In: De Boer, F., Cerone, A. (eds.) Software Engineering and Formal Methods, pp. 303–324. Springer, Cham (2020). https://doi.org/10.1007/978-3-642-24690-6
3. Olaronke, I., Oluwaseun, O., Rhoda, I.: State of the art: a study of human-robot interaction in healthcare. IJIEEB. **9**, 43–55 (2017). https://doi.org/10.5815/ijieeb.2017.03.06
4. International Organization for Standardization (ISO): ISO 13482:2014(en), Robots and robotic devices — Safety requirements for personal care robots. https://www.iso.org/obp/ui/#iso:std:iso:13482:ed-1:v1:en
5. International Organization for Standardization (ISO): ISO/TS 15066:2016(en), Robots and robotic devices — Collaborative robots
6. Haidegger, T., et al.: Industrial and medical cyber-physical systems: tackling user requirements and challenges in robotics. In: Kovács, L., Haidegger, T., Szakál, A. (eds.) Recent Advances in Intelligent Engineering, pp. 253–277. Springer International Publishing, Cham (2020). https://doi.org/10.1007/978-3-030-14350-3
7. Sheridan, T.B.: Human-robot interaction: status and challenges. Hum. Factors **58**, 525–532 (2016). https://doi.org/10.1177/0018720816644364
8. Bork, D.: Using conceptual modeling for designing multi-view modeling tools. In: Presented at the Twenty-first Americas Conference on Information Systems. Puerto Rico (2015)
9. Sadeghnejad, S., Abadi, V.S.E., Jafari, B.: Rehabilitation robotics: History, applications, and recent advances. In: Medical and Healthcare Robotics, pp. 63–85. Elsevier (2023)
10. Vallès-Peris, N., Barat-Auleda, O., Domènech, M.: Robots in healthcare? what patients say. IJERPH. **18**, 9933 (2021). https://doi.org/10.3390/ijerph18189933
11. Corke, P.: Introduction. In: Robotics. Vision and Control, pp. 1–19. Springer, Cham (2023)
12. Bartneck, C., Belpaeme, T., Eyssel, F., Kanda, T., Keijsers, M., Šabanović, S.: Human-Robot Interaction: An Introduction. Cambridge University Press (2020). https://doi.org/10.1017/9781108676649
13. Taylor, R.H., Stoianovici, D.: Medical robotics in computer-integrated surgery. IEEE Trans. Robot. Automat. **19**, 765–781 (2003). https://doi.org/10.1109/TRA.2003.817058
14. Zhou, B., Yang, G., Shi, Z., Ma, S.: Natural language processing for smart healthcare. arXiv: 2110.15803 (2021). https://doi.org/10.48550/ARXIV.2110.15803
15. Mukherjee, D., Gupta, K., Chang, L.H., Najjaran, H.: A survey of robot learning strategies for human-robot collaboration in industrial settings. Robot. Comput. Integr. Manuf. **73**, 102231 (2022). https://doi.org/10.1016/j.rcim.2021.102231
16. Braglia, G., Tagliavini, M., Pini, F., Biagiotti, L.: Online motion planning for safe human-robot cooperation using B-splines and hidden markov models. Robotics **12**, 118 (2023)
17. Sousa, S., Lamas, D., Dias, P.: A model for human-computer trust: contributions towards leveraging user engagement. In: Zaphiris, P., Ioannou, A. (eds.) Learning and Collaboration Technologies. Designing and Developing Novel Learning Experiences: First International Conference, LCT 2014, Held as Part of HCI International 2014, Heraklion, Crete, Greece, June 22-27, 2014, Proceedings, Part I, pp. 128–137. Springer International Publishing, Cham (2014). https://doi.org/10.1007/978-3-319-07482-5_13
18. Gualtieri, L., Rauch, E., Vidoni, R.: Development and validation of guidelines for safety in human-robot collaborative assembly systems. Comput. Ind. Eng. **163**, 107801 (2022). https://doi.org/10.1016/j.cie.2021.107801

19. Zacharaki, A., Kostavelis, I., Gasteratos, A., Dokas, I.: Safety bounds in human robot interaction: a survey. Saf. Sci. **127**, 104667 (2020)
20. European Parliament: Civil law rules on robotics | Legislative Train Schedule. https://www.europarl.europa.eu/legislative-train/theme-area-of-justice-and-fundamental-rights/file-civil-law-rules-on-robotics. Accessed 28 Feb 2024
21. Buchmann, R.A., Ghiran, A.-M., Döller, V., Karagiannis, D.: Conceptual modeling education as a "design problem". CSIMQ (21), 21–33 (2019). https://doi.org/10.7250/csimq.2019-21.02
22. Karagiannis, D., Buchmann, R.A., Burzynski, P., Reimer, U., Walch, M.: Fundamental conceptual modeling languages in OMiLAB. In: Karagiannis, D., Mayr, H.C., Mylopoulos, J. (eds.) Domain-Specific Conceptual Modeling, pp. 3–30. Springer, Cham (2016). https://doi.org/10.1007/978-3-319-39417-6_1
23. Guarino, N., Guizzardi, G., Mylopoulos, J.: On the philosophical foundations of conceptual models. In: Information Modelling and Knowledge Bases XXXI, pp. 1–15 (2019)
24. Karagiannis, D., Kühn, H.: Metamodelling Platforms. In: Kurt Bauknecht, A., Tjoa, M., Quirchmayr, G. (eds.) EC-Web 2002. LNCS, vol. 2455, pp. 182–182. Springer, Heidelberg (2002). https://doi.org/10.1007/3-540-45705-4_19
25. Bork, D., Karagiannis, D., Pittl, B.: How are metamodels specified in practice? Empirical insights and recommendations. In: Presented at the 24th Americas Conference on Information Systems, AMCIS 2018, New Orleans, LA, USA August 16 (2018)
26. Page, M.J., et al.: The PRISMA 2020 statement: an updated guideline for reporting systematic reviews. Int. J. Surg. **88**, 105906 (2021)
27. Saldaña, J.: The Coding Manual for Qualitative Researchers. Sage, Los Angeles, Calif (2009)
28. Braun, V., Clarke, V.: Using thematic analysis in psychology. Qual. Res. Psychol. **3**, 77–101 (2006). https://doi.org/10.1191/1478088706qp063oa
29. Object Management Group (OMG): OMG® Unified Modeling Language® (2017). https://www.omg.org/spec/UML/2.5.1/PDF
30. EU: Safe, efficient and integrated indoor robotic fleet for logistic applications in healthcare and commercial spaces | ENDORSE Project | Fact Sheet | H2020. https://cordis.europa.eu/project/id/823887. Accessed 05 May 2024
31. Fraichard, T., Kuffner, J.J.: Guaranteeing motion safety for robots. Auton. Robot. **32**, 173–175 (2012). https://doi.org/10.1007/s10514-012-9278-z
32. Genser, A.: Design-based safety and security of robotic systems. Ind. Autom. Asia 40–41 (2022)
33. David, D., Thérouanne, P., Milhabet, I.: The acceptability of social robots: a scoping review of the recent literature. Comput. Hum. Behav. **137**, 107419 (2022)
34. Islam, S.O.B., Lughmani, W.A.: A connective framework for safe human-robot collaboration in cyber-physical production systems. Arab. J. Sci. Eng. **48**, 11621–11644 (2023)
35. Rubagotti, M., Tusseyeva, I., Baltabayeva, S., Summers, D., Sandygulova, A.: Perceived safety in physical human–robot interaction—a survey. Robot. Auton. Syst. **151**, 104047 (2022). https://doi.org/10.1016/j.robot.2022.104047
36. Vasic, M., Billard, A.: Safety issues in human-robot interactions. In: 2013 IEEE International Conference on Robotics and Automation. pp. 197–204. IEEE, Germany (2013)
37. Haddadin, S., De Luca, A., Albu-Schaffer, A.: Robot collisions: a survey on detection, isolation, and identification. IEEE Trans. Robot. **33**, 1292–1312 (2017)
38. Guiochet, J., Machin, M., Waeselynck, H.: Safety-critical advanced robots: a survey. Robot. Auton. Syst. **94**, 43–52 (2017)
39. Menzies, T., Pecheur, C.: Verification and validation and artificial intelligence. In: Advances in Computers, pp. 153–201. Elsevier (2005). https://doi.org/10.1016/S0065-2458(05)65004-8
40. Dhillon, B.S., Fashandi, A.R.M.: Safety and reliability assessment techniques in robotics. Robotica **15**, 701–708 (1997). https://doi.org/10.1017/S0263574797000829

41. Visinsky, M.L., Cavallaro, J.R., Walker, I.D.: Robotic fault detection and fault tolerance: a survey. Reliab. Eng. Syst. Saf. **46**, 139–158 (1994)
42. Martinetti, A., Chemweno, P.K., Nizamis, K., Fosch-Villaronga, E.: Redefining safety in light of human-robot interaction: a critical review of current standards and regulations. Front. Chem. Eng. **3**, 666237 (2021). https://doi.org/10.3389/fceng.2021.666237
43. Michels, J.D., Walden, I.: How safe is safe enough? Improving cybersecurity in Europe's critical infrastructure under the NIS directive. (December 7, 2018). In: Queen Mary School of Law Legal Studies Research Paper (2018)
44. Bekir, T.A.V.A.S.: Artificial intelligence and robotics and their impact on business systems. J. Soc. Humanit. Adm. Sci. **6**(31), 1535–1546 (2020). https://doi.org/10.31589/JOSHAS.392
45. Center for Devices and Radiological Health: Artificial Intelligence and Machine Learning in Software as a Medical Device. FDA (2023)
46. Fosch-Villaronga, E., Mahler, T.: Cybersecurity, safety and robots: strengthening the link between cybersecurity and safety in the context of care robots. Comput. Law Secur. Rev. **41**, 105528 (2021). https://doi.org/10.1016/j.clsr.2021.105528
47. Stacey, N., Ellwood, P., Bradbrook, S., Reynolds, J., Williams, H.: Key trends and drivers of change in information and communication technologies and work location: foresight on new and emerging risks in OSH: Working report. In: European Agency for Safety and Health at Work, LU (2017)
48. Rinta-Kahila, T., Penttinen, E., Salovaara, A., Soliman, W.: Consequences of discontinuing knowledge work automation - surfacing of deskilling effects and methods of recovery. In: Presented at the Hawaii International Conference on System Sciences (2018)
49. Avizienis, A., Laprie, J.-C., Randell, B., Landwehr, C.: Basic concepts and taxonomy of dependable and secure computing. IEEE Trans. Depend. Sec. Comput. **1**, 11–33 (2004)
50. Pohl, K.: Requirements engineering. Springer Berlin Heidelberg, Berlin, Heidelberg (2010). https://doi.org/10.1007/978-3-642-12578-2

# Business Intelligence

# Modelling of Organisational Rules in Complex Adaptive Systems: a Systematic Mapping Study

Jöran Lindeberg[✉], Martin Henkel, and Eric-Oluf Svee

Department of Computer and Systems Sciences, Stockholm University,
7003, 16407 Kista, Sweden
{joran,martinh,eric-sve}@dsv.su.se

**Abstract.** Organisational rules, both created internally and externally mandated, are vital to an enterprise. Yet, understanding and managing these rules is problematic, as they are a part of a complex system. Thus, there is a need to view them in a complex setting of organisational actors and interactions. It has been suggested that enterprises, particularly in situations like collaboration in healthcare, should be analysed as complex adaptive systems (CAS). However, only some enterprise modelling contributions can represent perspectives of CAS theory. In this paper, we set out to examine how organisational rules in complex adaptive systems has been modelled. A systematic mapping study was conducted on modelling languages of organisational rules in collaborations, resulting in 22 identified languages. The constructs and modelling patterns of the identified languages were mapped against an analytical framework that included 15 concepts from CAS theory. Overall, even though most CAS concepts had yet to be addressed by the identified languages, potentially useful approaches were found, related to: abstraction of large organisational rule systems through power relations; interpretation and implementation of rules; feedback loops to rule-makers, including delays.

**Keywords:** Organisational Rule · Enterprise Modelling · Business Rule · Collaboration · Socio-technical System · Complex Adaptive System

## 1 Introduction

A crucial aspect of an enterprise is its organisational rules, either created internally or imposed by its environment. These rules guide and constrain the actions of the organisation's employees. Well-informed decisions on rule changes are also a vital aspect of organisational development [26]. However, interacting with organisational rules is far from trivial. Rules can be ambiguous and contradictory, as are the complex organisational realities they are designed to control. In for example Swedish healthcare, rules and regulations with regard to privacy and digital transformation are difficult even for experts to comprehend [12,28].

This leads to much uncertainty about the available legal space, conflicting interpretations between organisations, reduced interoperability, and ultimately lost opportunities for collaboration.

In this paper, we define an *organisational rule* as an element of guidance that constrains the action space of an organisational unit. It refers to the overall business rather than IT-systems. It is formalised, i.e., is written and has an official standing in the organisation it applies to. An organisational rule can be both of external and internal origin and can have any enforcement level, from rigid enforcement to mere guidelines.

Organisations, including their rules, are social-technical systems and can be understood through systems theory. As organisational life and the rest of the world become increasingly complex, many argue that enterprises should be viewed mainly through the lens of *complex adaptive systems* (CAS) theory [2,24]. A CAS is composed of two fundamental elements: agents and constraints. When agents interact according to these constraints, they produce results both at the local and the higher levels. Sometimes, emergent behaviour can stabilise into new agents of higher level [10]. Agents learn about the results through feedback loops and adapt accordingly. In short, CAS theory focus more on creating conditions on the ground for a desirable emergent behaviour, and less on defining exactly what that behaviour should look like. Moreover, since agents should expect the unexpected, CAS theory is also concerned with effective feedback loops with a minimum of delay. In Sect. 2, we will present CAS theory in more detail.

CAS theory is particularly strong in healthcare management [9,18,19,27], and even more so in organisational collaboration in healthcare [3]. Organisational collaboration is commonly seen to have great potential for improved outcomes, for example, in the healthcare sector [3]. Slightly adapting from Aunger et al., [3] *organisational collaboration* can be defined as a presumably mutually beneficial process by which stakeholders or organisations work together toward a common goal. However, "Much of what has been learnt about these collaborative efforts finds such interventions to be extremely complex, often resulting in a myriad of unforeseen consequences" [3, p. 2]. An important part of the problem can be found in organisational rules [4].

Organisational rules can, as other aspects of an organisation, be represented and understood through enterprise modelling (EM), which creates an overview and common understanding among different stakeholders in an organisation [22]. EM is done through different perspectives, such as rules and goals, or actors and roles [15]. EM is useful not only for designing IT-systems, but also for sense-making and design of sociotechnical systems, including the computational independent aspects of information systems, e.g. organisational rules. To create a model, a modelling language is needed. A modelling language, as defined by Karagiannis & Kuhn [13], is composed of notation, syntax, and semantics. A modelling language is also described with a metamodel [13].

The research aim of this study is to identify existing useful approaches for modelling organisational rules in a complex setting. The general research question (RQ) is the following: How have organisational rules in complex adaptive systems been modelled? The two specific research questions are:

1. What modelling languages have been used for modelling of organisational rules in organisational collaborations? (As explained above, organisational collaboration is characterised by its complexity.)
2. How can the identified modelling languages represent organisational rules in complex adaptive systems?

These research questions will be answered through a systematic mapping study. The remainder of this paper is structured as follows. In Sect. 2, CAS theory and the analysis framework for the study are introduced. This is followed by a methodological description in Sect. 3. The analysis is presented in two levels in Sect. 4 and Sect. 5. Finally, Sect. 6 summarises the findings.

## 2 Organisations as Complex Adaptive Systems

CAS theory has been proposed for understanding organisations in general [2], and in particular healthcare systems [18,19,23], both for the clinical encounter between the practitioner and the patient, and for the management of healthcare organisations and whole healthcare systems. As suggested by Stacey [21], CAS models can be used as analogies for the complex social world of organisations. This includes their organisational rules and the agents, such as organisational units, that interact with them.

CAS theory is intertwined with complexity sciences, which makes certain assumptions about organisational reality, including that it is characterised by messiness, fuzziness, nonlinearity, and nondeterminism [11,24].

*Messiness*, or messes, is defined by Ackoff as "large and complex sets of interacting problems, *dynamic systems of problems*" (italics in the original quote) [1, p. 22]. The many interrelations between different elements make it hard to start disentangling an issue without making it worse somewhere else. Messiness can be handled through abstraction, and one solution for abstraction is to model power relations, that is, what is superior to what. In legal systems, there is a principle of hierarchical superiority, e.g., that a business policy cannot violate the laws of the land or that a government regulation cannot contradict the same country's constitution. However, as previously observed by Krogstie [15], this aspect has not been common in the modelling of enterprise rules.

*Fuzziness* refers to a lack of neatly distinguishable boundaries and categories [18]. An agent can be part of several systems simultaneously, and is likely to interact not only with agents within the same CAS, but also with agents from other systems.

*Nonlinearity* occurs when alterations in an input variable do not result in proportional changes in an output variable [24]. For instance, a salary increase may initially have strong impact on employees motivation, but further increases could instead make unmotivated people unwilling to change employer. Nonlinearity can also refer to situations with strong threshold effects.

*Nondeterminism* refers to the phenomenon where repeated situations may lead to different outcomes each time [24]. For example, a rule can be interpreted differently between agents, and by the same agent at different occasions.

A CAS is composed of *agents* and *constraints*. Organisational rules are a type of constraint. Other types of constraints include, for example, personal objectives and company culture.

According to Snowden [20, Framework], constraints "shape a system by modifying its phase space (its range of possible actions) or the probability distribution (the likelihood) of events and movements within that space". Snowden views constraints as both enabling and governing; while some possibilities are limited, others are expanded. CAS theory emphasises enabling constraints over governing constraints, even if it also recognises that both types are needed. While *governing constraints* focus on limiting the range of possible actions, *enabling constraints* can be described as scaffolding: structures that allow interaction [20]. One type of structure for agents to gather around could be common evaluative rules, i.e., goals. Another type of structure opens up information flows, such as meeting routines that cross hierarchical divisions. A third type could be common standards that increase interoperability.

In a CAS, there is *interaction* [24] between agents according to constraints. The constraints of an agent can emanate, to different degrees, from the agent itself or be imposed by other agents. The latter also constitutes a type of indirect interaction, equal to rule creation in an organisational context. According to Burns [6], agents can interact with rules in three ways: creating, interpreting, and implementing. The interactions in a system will generate *events*, which in turn form dynamic patterns of *behaviour* [17]. The outputs, outcomes, results, and impact of an organisation are all examples of behaviour.

A CAS, like any open system, exists within an *environment* [8]. This environment can be constituted by other systems. A CAS is also likely to exist within a larger *multi-level* system [25]. While these concepts are basic notions in all systems thinking, recall that CAS theory emphasises fuzziness. It is not always clear to which system an agent primarily belongs, and a system will be part of many higher-level systems simultaneously.

Emergence, in short, is the existence of new properties that are more than the sum of parts. A distinction can be made between *structural emergence* [8] and *behavioural emergence* [7]. In the context of organisations, properties for structural emergence could, for example, be the degree of dependence through citations [26], if some rules are of constitutional character and set the boundaries for other rules, i.e. hierarchical superiority, and the ratio of rule makers compared to rule followers. Examples of emergent behaviour could be to what extent an organisational rules system is followed, or unexpected outcomes after a rule change. CAS theory underscores that complex emergent system behaviour can result from simple rules [18], which relates to self-organisation.

Agents will learn about the results of their interactions through *feedback loops* [11]. Feedback loops can be positive (reinforcing) or negative (balancing) [17]. They will always have a delay, which obfuscates cause-and-effect relationships and might lead to oscillations in a system if actors overreact to accumulated changes. Meadows [17] considers that deficient feedback loops are a primary cause of system malfunction. Feedback loops can be improved through consciously designed feedback channels. In an organisational context, this can e.g. take the form of weekly unit meetings, or performance reports. In the complex domain, characterised by unknown unknowns, there is particular need for feedback about the unexpected. This need can be addressed by what Beer [5], as part of the Viable Systems Model, calls *algedonic signals*, that quickly can travel from the lower levels of an organisation and its higher-level management.

Both individual agents and the system as a whole are *adaptive*. Agents learn from feedback loops and change constraints, both their own and those that affect others. This adaptation of an agent may be beneficial to the system, but not always [25]. In an organisational context, adaptation is close to the notions of learning and development.

In the above, 15 CAS concepts have been introduced. They were grouped into five themes, forming a framework, shown in Table 1, which was later used to analyse the modelling languages.

**Table 1.** Analytical framework with CAS concepts grouped into themes.

| Theme | Concept |
|---|---|
| Components | Agent [18], Constraint [20] |
| Part-of | Structural Emergence [8], Multi-level system [25], Environment [8] |
| Behaviour | Interaction [24], Event [17], Behaviour [17], Behavioural emergence [7] |
| Adaptation | Feedback loops [17], Adaptation [18] |
| Complexity | Messiness [1], Fuzziness, [11], Nonlinearity [24], Nondeterminism [24] |

## 3 Methodology

In our study, as the title conveys, we opted for a mapping study instead of a systematic literature review, since the research question was more about what modelling approaches exist than a profound evaluation of their quality. As explained by Kitchenham & Charters [14], a systematic mapping study differs from a systematic literature review insofar as the purpose is, for example, to classify and summarise rather than conducting a narrative synthesis.

The objective of the data collection was to identify the existing modelling languages that have been used to model organisational rules in the complex domain of organisational collaborations. The article search was conducted with the Scopus database on 25 March 2024 using the search string shown in Table 2, and yielded 554 records. Note that Scopus has some semantic capacity, which, e.g. makes the search term "modelling" equal to "(modelling OR modeling)". The results were stored and analysed in a spreadsheet. We concede that having used only one database is a limitation of the study. Including more databases would have yielded a more complete set of articles and modelling languages to analyse. On the other hand, Scopus indexes journals from a wide range of publishers, and its interdisciplinary focus aligns well with a mapping study.

Table 2. Search string in Scopus

| Concept | Query |
|---|---|
| modelling language | ("modelling language" OR "meta-model" OR "modelling method" OR "modelling notation" OR "enterprise model*" OR "conceptual model*" OR ontology OR "agent-based model*" OR "agent model*") |
| | AND |
| ... for rules | ("rule*" OR directive* OR polic* OR "constraint*" OR bureaucra* OR govern* OR control* OR "regulation*" OR law* OR legislation OR goal* OR objective*) |
| | AND |
| ... for organisations | (enterprise* OR organisation* OR compan*) |
| | AND |
| ... for collaboration | (collaboration* OR cooporation* OR exchang* OR interchang* OR sharing*) |

When selecting the articles, the inclusion criteria were the following:

- A diagrammatic modelling language has been used or is proposed. This includes extending or merging existing languages, such as UML class diagrams. The concept of modelling language is discussed in Sect. 1.
- The modelling language has been used to model organisational rules. Also this concept is discussed in Sect. 1. Concretely, the modelling language must have at least one construct designed to represent organisational rules. Note that concepts that the authors themselves do not label rules or similar, but that fit our definition of organisational rule, were included. In contrast, rules that are not on an organisational level, such as OR gateways in technical processes models, were excluded.
- The modelling language has been used in the context of organisational collaboration. Also this concept is defined in Sect. 1. Concretely, the modelling language must have constructs designed for representing that at least two organisations or organisational units interact.

After the abstract screening, 129 records were sought for retrieval, of which 113 could be accessed. The reports retrieved (full papers) were then screened using the same inclusion and exclusion criteria as during the abstract screening. After the full paper screening, 23 articles that had used 22 modelling languages were identified as eligible for analysis. A summary of the process is shown in Table 3.

**Table 3.** Identification of Studies

| Steps | Number |
|---|---|
| Records identified from Scopus | 554 |
| Records screened | 554 |
| Records sought for retrieval | 129 |
| Records assessed for eligibility | 113 |
| Records included in review | 23 |
| Modelling languages included in review | 22 |

Most of the included articles included a specification of the language used. However, five articles had used a language specified in another source. This concerned three languages: IDEF0, iStar, and Semantics of Business Vocabulary and Business Rules (SBVR). Also note that one of the articles had used two languages: iStar and CSRML4BI.

In Sect. 2, we explained CAS theory and presented an analytical framework. The framework was put in a spreadsheet and used for analysing the identified languages. Each language was mapped to each concept in the spreadsheet. If the concept was represented or otherwise addressed, the intersecting cell was marked with a "yes", otherwise a "no".

## 4 Results and Analysis

Table 4 shows the identified modelling languages (RQ1) and an overview of the mapping to the CAS concepts (RQ2), grouped into themes. The results are presented and analysed theme by theme in the following.

### 4.1 Components

This theme combined the fundamental building blocks of a CAS: agents and constraints.

A construct for *agent* or similar was found in all languages, which was expected considering the inclusion and exclusion criteria used. Some languages distinguish between an agent and the role the agent plays in a certain context. For example, iStar models both Agent and Role as subclasses to Actor.

Also in accordance with inclusion and exclusion criteria, all modelling languages had a construct for *constraint*, in one way or another. As discussed in Sect. 2, the constraints of most relevance for a CAS are enabling rather than governing. What we consider as enabling constraints was found in three forms in the languages: information flows (n = 4), interaction standards (n = 1), and flexible enforcement levels (n = 1).

We consider constraints for information flows as enabling, since information is a prerequisite for interaction. This includes constructs for indicators and

**Table 4.** Results overview of modelling languages and theme mapping. The concepts included in each theme are in turn shown in Table 1. The table shows, e.g., that IDEF0 addressed two out of three concepts included in the part-of theme. More granular results are available as an online supplement [16].

| Modelling Language | Components | Part-of | Behaviour | Adaptation | Complexity |
|---|---|---|---|---|---|
| Production and Innov. K. R. [46] | 2/2 | 2/3 | 3/4 | 1/2 | 0/4 |
| AMENITIES Conceptual F. [39] | 2/2 | 2/3 | 3/4 | 0/2 | 0/4 |
| EXTENDED Module [42] | 2/2 | 2/3 | 3/4 | 0/2 | 0/4 |
| VBE Value System Ontology [47] | 2/2 | 2/3 | 2/4 | 1/2 | 0/4 |
| Socio-technical System Model [38] | 2/2 | 2/3 | 2/4 | 2/2 | 2/4 |
| IDEF0 [33,48]. Specification in [29] | 2/2 | 2/3 | 2/4 | 0/2 | 0/4 |
| Strategic Planning Ont. [34] | 2/2 | 1/3 | 3/4 | 1/2 | 0/4 |
| Collaborative Network Ont. [32] | 2/2 | 1/3 | 2/4 | 0/2 | 1/4 |
| Generic Privacy Ontology [31] | 2/2 | 1/3 | 1/4 | 1/2 | 2/4 |
| ARDI Model [49] | 2/2 | 1/3 | 1/4 | 1/2 | 0/4 |
| SEMD meta-model [50] | 2/2 | 1/3 | 1/4 | 0/2 | 1/4 |
| SBVR [41]. Spec. in [30] | 2/2 | 1/3 | 1/4 | 0/2 | 1/4 |
| iStar [46,53]. Specification in [35] | 2/2 | 1/3 | 0/4 | 0/2 | 2/4 |
| myKinMatters [44] | 2/2 | 0/3 | 3/4 | 1/2 | 0/4 |
| Process Life Cycle Method. [43] | 2/2 | 0/3 | 3/4 | 0/2 | 0/4 |
| KiPPINOT-CORE [37] | 2/2 | 0/3 | 2/4 | 2/2 | 1/4 |
| Italian Business Network Ont. [54] | 2/2 | 0/3 | 1/4 | 1/2 | 0/4 |
| smashHitCore Ontology [52] | 2/2 | 0/3 | 1/4 | 1/2 | 0/4 |
| VE Architecture [45] | 2/2 | 0/3 | 1/4 | 2/2 | 0/4 |
| SDI Governance Model [51] | 2/2 | 0/3 | 1/4 | 0/2 | 0/4 |
| Collaboration Context Ont. [40] | 2/2 | 0/3 | 0/4 | 0/2 | 0/4 |
| CSRML4BI [53] | 2/2 | 0/3 | 0/4 | 0/2 | 0/4 |

measures, which were present in KiPPINOT-CORE, the Socio-technical System Model, the VBE Value System Ontology, and the Strategic Planning Ontology. Interaction standards was represented by the Interaction Protocol construct in the AMENITIES Conceptual Framework for Cooperative Systems. This construct represents how Groups and activities use Interaction Protocols, which would be organisational rules from its more enabling perspective, facilitating interoperability. Another example of enabling rules was found in SBVR's flexible Enforcement Levels. This construct recognises that rules should not always be implemented rigorously.

### 4.2 Part-of

The part-of theme consisted of the concepts structural emergence, multi-level system, and environment. The results from these three characteristics of CAS are presented together since they all concern how something larger is either created from parts or exists outside their boundaries.

The notion of *structural emergence* was observed in three ways: the first in the form of simply representing that parts form wholes (n = 6), the second using constructs to describe the wholes (n = 1) and the third using rules to define roles in wholes (n = 1). An example of the first variant was found e.g. in the SEMD meta-model and in the EXTENDED ontology. The second variant was observed in the Collaborative Network Ontology (CPO), which used the Topology construct to describe a Collaborative Network. The type of Topology can be Star, Peer-to-Peer, or Chain. The Topology is also characterised by its Power distribution, which can be Central, Equal, or Hierarchic, and by its Duration, which can be Continuous or Discontinuous. In particular, Power distribution relates to organisational rules. A third variant was that, as represented by AMENITIES, rules can create new roles and other organisational realities. Together, this shows the recursive nature of making rules and institutions: rules create institutional structures that stabilise into new actors, that create rules, and so on.

Among the languages analysed, two ways of representing *multi-level systems* were observed: fractal (n = 2) and non-fractal (n = 4). The first approach was found in IDEF0 and the EXTENDED Module. In IDEF0, every function of a model can be decomposed and modelled as its own system with its own functions. Going upward, a top-level IDEF0 diagram from one model can easily be inserted as a lower-level diagram in another model. The second approach was found in e.g. AMENITIES, which represents a Cooperative System as composed of both Organisations and Groups.

Some modelling languages (n = 5) represented boundaries and the notion of *environment*. SBVR (in combination with its sister standard Business Motivation Model), IDEF0, iStar, and the Strategic Planning Ontology, all could, in different forms, model the influence of an external environment. IDEF0 and iStar could also show how the modelled system affects its environment. SBVR and IDEF0 could, in addition, show that rules can come from outside of the system boundary. Moreover, SBVR could represent that, depending on the perspective, a particular rule can an internal Directive for one actor but an external Regulation for another.

### 4.3 Behaviour

This theme groups the concepts related to behaviour. Agent interaction, according to constraints, produces events that form pattern of behaviour. Moreover, some behaviour leads to emergent behaviour at the system level.

As explained in Sect. 2, agents *interact*, in other words, affect each other, both directly (e.g., sending an email) or, as mentioned in Sect. 2, indirectly through creating, interpreting, or implementing constraints that affect other agents. For example, one agent changes a company policy, a second agent interprets it and tells a third, who implements it. Since the creation of constraints is also crucial for adaptation, this aspect will mostly be discussed below, under the adaptation theme.

Three languages had to some extent addressed the interpretation and implementation of constraints. As for interpretation, SBVR distinguishes between two types of Directives: Business Rules, that are concrete enough to be enactable, and higher-level Policies that Business Rules are derived from. However, it does not represent who is doing the interpretations, nor who ensures that rules are implemented, e.g. through sanctioning capabilities. However, as mentioned, the ARDI model represents how Regulatory Actors can design Policy Instruments, who in turn control the conduct of Institutional Managers, which implies some kind of enforcement, which in turn implies interpretation and implementation. A similar representation was found in the Italian Business Network Contract ontology, which expresses that a Network Contract is associated to a Management Body. Another aspect of implementation, which was not reflected in any of the modelling languages, is how to capture deviations.

A simple modelling of *behaviour* is to recognise that *events* can occur (n = 7). This could be observed in e.g. the Process Life Cycle Information and Process Analysis Methodology and the myKinMatters ontology. Some languages (n = 4) had another approach and did not represent events, but instead modelled indicators and measurements of behaviour.

*Emergent behaviour*, i.e. behaviour of the system as a whole, was represented by some (n = 5) modelling languages. The Collaborative Network Ontology (CPO) represents emergent behaviour in the form of Abstract Service, which consists of Business Services. This Abstract Service is also the Common Goal of the network. Another example is IDEF0, in which outgoing flows from multiple Functions can join and cross the system boundary.

### 4.4 Adaptation

For adaptation to occur, two things are needed: a feedback loop to an agent, and the agent creating or changing constraints.

Although seven languages somehow addressed feedback, through e.g. measurements, only two could represent that the information reaches a specific agent. KiPPINOT-CORE represents that an Agent is informed about the measures of an indicator. Moreover, the Strategic Planning Ontology (SP Ontology) represents that an Analysis of an Objective is performed by an Analysis Agent, and that an Objective has an Objective Follow-up Agent.

As noted above, for *adaptation* to occur, an agent that receives feedback must be able to create or change constraints. Several models represented how agents create or control rules (n = 7). The ARDI model (Actors, Resources, Dynamics and Interactions) represents how Regulatory Actors can design Policy Instruments, who in turn control the conduct of Institutional Managers. While the former example was about rule creation based on a hierarchy defined in other rules, rules can also be created through equal partners establishing rules through a common contract. For example, the SmashHitCore ontology represents how a Contract has Contractors. A similar representation was found in the Italian Business Network Contract Ontology. Rules can also be created by adopting existing rule already put in place by an external agent, which SBVR's represents through its Authority construct.

## 4.5 Complexity

This theme included the concepts of messiness, fuzziness, nonlinearity, and nondeterminism, explained in Sect. 2. Nonlinearity and nondeterminism were not addressed in any of the analysed modelling languages; this observation will be discussed in Sect. 5.

Some (n = 5) of the languages analysed had addressed some aspect of *messiness*. The first approach was found in the iStar goal modelling language, which can hide the internal complexity of an organisation by collapsing actors that are not in focus, concealing their internal elements. The second approach was to embrace complexity employing a large number of constructs. It was found in KiPPINOT-CORE, an ontology for process performance indicators (PPIs), which has no less than nine classes labeled with a variant of "measure". While the complexity of such models allows for representing the intricacies of the domain, that same complexity also reduces its usability for sense-making. After all, modelling is about simplification. The third approach to complex models is to have classes that are prone to generate many instances. This design can be achieved through the use of recursive class relations. An example is the Generic Privacy Ontology, which had four recursive relations. Moreover, SBVR can represent situations in which any entity can play a role. This is a very flexible pattern, but also opens up for virtually infinitely complex instantiations. The fourth approach, also in the Generic Privacy Ontology, represents how lower-level, more specific, rules have precedence in case of conflict.

Regarding *fuzziness*, the Socio-technical System Model included a construct for vague relations between goals, meaning that it is unclear or depends on the situation if the relation is supporting or conflicting. This language also represents personal goals as a subclass of individual goals, thereby recognising that the organisational reality is shaped not only by formal structures, but also by the inherent properties of the agents themselves. A somewhat similar approach was found in SBVR's use of the entities' Viewpoint and Facet, which recognise that phenomena will be modelled differently depending on the point of view.

# 5 Discussion

This section amplifies the analysis on some of the observations in Sect. 4.

## 5.1 Abstraction and Power Relations

As discussed in Sect. 4.5, organisational rules form large sociotechnical systems with a high degree of messiness, and as mentioned is Sect. 2, messiness can be handled through abstraction and power relations, which according to Krogstie [15] is understudied in the modelling of enterprise rules. The closest finding in this direction was that SBVR represents that Business Rules are derived from Policies. Only one modelling language, the Generic Privacy Ontology, addressed rule precedence, by representing that in case of conflict between rules, the rule that according to its classification is more specific has precedence. For instance, if an organisation-wide rule contravenes a project rule, the project rule is what counts. This logic corresponds to another legal principle: *lex specialis* where the law that is more specific to the circumstances takes precedence over a more general one. These two principles can be conflicting in some situations.

## 5.2 Absence of Nonlinearity and Nondeterminism

As mentioned in Sect. 4.5, nonlinearity and nondeterminism were not found to have been addressed in any particular manner by the analysed modelling languages. This absence could indicate that there has been little need for modelling these characteristics. Still, in particular in process flow diagrams and other models with a functional perspective, it could be useful. One idea for nondeterminism could be, using IDEF0 as an example, to have two outgoing flows from a function and connect them with a symbol that conveys (a) that any token instance can go either way and (b) what is the likelihood for either option.

## 5.3 Social Interaction with Rules

As discussed in Sect. 4.3, while several modelling languages could represent rule creation, only a few could express other forms of interaction: rule interpretation and rule implementation, both of which are needed for rule enforcement. As mentioned in Sect. 1, differences in rule interpretation can be a barrier to interoperability and collaboration. To model this, a language must probably represent at least two things: a rule is interpreted by an actor, and a rule is interpreted for a certain situation. As mentioned in Sect. 4.5, SBVR has a pattern for modelling situations (but not for who interprets). As for rule implementation, SBVR's ordinal scale of Enforcement Levels could be reused, but to represent differences in actual enforcement instead of permitted enforcement.

## 5.4 Modelling Feedback Channels

It is critical that the actor behind a decision (such as rule making) is made aware of the consequences as soon as possible. As highlighted in Sect. 2, delays in feedback loops constitute a major factor in poorly functioning social systems [17]. Thus, an enterprise model should be able to express a complete feedback loop from an actor's decision, the detection of its consequences, and information back to the decision maker, including the delay. Some of these features were found in the analysed languages and discussed in Sect. 4.4, but not all. To detect the unknown unknowns that arise from emergent, systemic, behaviour, traditional indicators are not enough, since they focus on the expected. Instead, a CAS requires more of a surveillance process and algedonic signals, as discussed in Sect. 2

## 6 Conclusion

This study investigated how organisational rules in complex adaptive systems have been modelled. The method was a systematic mapping study of modelling languages that had been used to model organisational rules in organisational collaborations.

The first specific research question (RQ1) was: What modelling languages have been used for modelling of organisational rules in complex organisational collaborations? A total of 22 languages were identified in 23 articles, presented in Table 4.

The second specific research question (RQ2) was: How can the modelling languages identified in RQ1 represent organisational rules in complex adaptive systems? The languages were mapped according to 15 concepts from CAS theory, grouped into five themes. The analysis of the modelling languages yielded four main findings: First, to model large systems of organisational rules, abstraction is needed. However, abstraction in the form of representing hierarchical superiority relations between different rules was not found in the identified languages. Second, rules become alive through agent interaction. While several modelling languages could represent rule creation, only a few could express other forms of interaction —rule interpretation and rule implementation— both of which are needed for rule enforcement. Third, nonlinearity and nondeterminism was not found to have been addressed in any of the languages. Fourth, even if some models to some extent could represent feedback loops, there has been little focus on detecting unknown unknowns, modelling delays in feedback loops, and expressing how the information reaches the right actor.

## References

1. Ackoff, R.L.: The art and science of mess management. Interfaces **11**(1), 20–26 (1981). https://www.jstor.org/stable/25060027, publisher: INFORMS
2. Anderson, P.: Perspective: complexity theory and organization science. Organ. Sci. **10**(3), 216–232 (1999). https://doi.org/10.1287/orsc.10.3.216
3. Aunger, J.A., Millar, R., Greenhalgh, J., Mannion, R., Rafferty, A.M., McLeod, H.: Why do some inter-organisational collaborations in healthcare work when others do not? A realist review. Syst. Rev. **10**(1), 82 (2021). https://doi.org/10.1186/s13643-021-01630-8
4. Axelsson, R., Axelsson, S.B.: Integration and collaboration in public Health-A conceptual framework. Int. J. Health Plann. Manage. **21**(1), 75–88 (2006). https://doi.org/10.1002/hpm.826
5. Beer, S.: The viable system model: its provenance, development, methodology and pathology. J. Oper. Res. Soc. **35**(1), 7–25 (1984). https://doi.org/10.2307/2581927, https://www.jstor.org/stable/2581927, publisher: Palgrave Macmillan Journals
6. Burns, T.R., Flam, H.: The Shaping of Social Organization. Swedish Collegium for Advanced Study in the Social Sciences, SAGE Publications, London, England (1987)

7. Carmichael, T., Hadžikadić, M.: The fundamentals of complex adaptive systems. In: Carmichael, T., Collins, A.J., Hadžikadić, M. (eds.) Complex Adaptive Systems: Views from the Physical, Natural, and Social Sciences, pp. 1–16. Springer International Publishing, Cham, Understanding Complex Systems (2019)
8. Colchester, J.J.: Systems + Complexity An Overview. CreateSpace Independent Publishing Platform, 1st edn. (2016)
9. Ellis, B.: An overview of complexity theory: understanding primary care as a complex adaptive system. In: Handbook of Systems and Complexity in Health. Springer, New York (2013). https://doi.org/10.1007/978-1-4614-4998-0
10. Evans, W.H.: Constraints that Enable Innovation - Alicia Juarrero (2015). https://vimeo.com/128934608
11. Fraser, S.W., Greenhalgh, T.: Complexity science: coping with complexity: educating for capability. BMJ: British Med. J. **323**(7316), 799–803 (2001). https://www.jstor.org/stable/25468057, publisher: BMJ
12. Henkel, M., Perjons, E., Lappalainen, K.F., Fors, U., Sjöberg, C.M.: Digitalization of health and social care collaboration: identification of problems and solutions. In: Joint Proceedings of RCIS 2024 Workshops and Research Projects Track. CEUR Workshop Proceedings, Guimarães, Portugal (2024). https://ceur-ws.org/Vol-3674/RP-paper8.pdf
13. Karagiannis, D., Kuhn, H.: Metamodelling platforms. In: EC-web, vol. 2455, p. 182. Citeseer (2002)
14. Kitchenham, B., Charters, S., et al.: Guidelines for performing systematic literature reviews in software engineering (2007)
15. Krogstie, J.: Model-Based Development and Evolution of Information Systems. Springer, London (2012). https://doi.org/10.1007/978-1-4471-2936-3
16. Lindeberg, J., Henkel, M., Svee, E.: Modelling languages and CAS concepts for systematic mapping study (2024). https://github.com/JoranL/organisational-rules/raw/main/supplementbir2024lindebergetal.ods
17. Meadows, D.H.: Thinking in Systems: A Primer. Earthscan (2008)
18. Plsek, P.E., Greenhalgh, T.: Complexity science: the challenge of complexity in health care. BMJ: British Med. J. **323**(7313), 625–628 (2001). https://doi.org/10.1136/bmj.323.7313.625
19. Rouse, W.B.: Health care as a complex adaptive system: implications for design and management. Bridge-Washington-Nat. Acad. Eng. **38**(1), 17 (2008)
20. Snowden, D.: Constraints (2022). https://cynefin.io/wiki/Constraints
21. Stacey, R.: Tools and Techniques of Leadership and Management: Meeting the Challenge of Complexity. Routledge, London (2012). https://doi.org/10.4324/9780203115893
22. Stirna, J., Persson, A.: Enterprise Modeling: Facilitating the Process and the People. Springer International Publishing, Cham (2018). https://doi.org/10.1007/978-3-319-94857-7
23. Sturmberg, J.P., Miles, A.: The complex nature of knowledge. In: Handbook of Systems and Complexity in Health. Springer, New York (2013). https://doi.org/10.1007/978-1-4614-4998-0
24. Turner, J.R., Baker, R.M.: Complexity theory: an overview with potential applications for the social sciences. Systems **7**(1), 4 (2019). https://doi.org/10.3390/systems7010004
25. Wilson, D.S., Madhavan, G., Gelfand, M.J., Hayes, S.C., Atkins, P.W.B., Colwell, R.R.: Multilevel cultural evolution: from new theory to practical applications. Proc. Natl. Acad. Sci. **120**(16) (2023). https://doi.org/10.1073/pnas.2218222120

26. Zhu, K., Schulz, M.: The dynamics of embedded rules: how do rule networks affect knowledge uptake of rules in healthcare? J. Manag. Stud. **56**(8), 1683–1712 (2019). https://doi.org/10.1111/joms.12529
27. Zimmerman, B.: How complexity science is transforming healthcare. In: The SAGE Handbook of Complexity and Management, pp. 617–635. SAGE Publications Ltd. (2011). https://doi.org/10.4135/9781446201084
28. Ålenius, A., Saleh, B., Hedberg, K., Wolff, P.: Delbetänkande av Utredningen om infrastruktur för hälsodata som nationellt intresse (2023:83). Statens Offentliga Utredningar, Regeringskansliet (2023)
29. IDEF0 – Function modeling method – IDEF. https://www.idef.com/
30. Semantics of business vocabulary and business rules. Version 1.5. Tech. rep., Object Management Group (OMG) (2019). https://www.omg.org/spec/SBVR/1.5/Beta1/PDF
31. Allison, D.S., Kamoun, A., Capretz, M.A.M., Tazi, S., Drira, K., ElYamany, H.F.: An ontology driven privacy framework for collaborative working environments. Int. J. Auton. Adapt. Commun. Syst. **9**(3/4), 243–268 (2016). https://doi.org/10.1504/IJAACS.2016.079624
32. Benaben, F., et al.: Model-driven engineering of mediation information system for enterprise interoperability. Int. J. Comput. Integr. Manuf. **31**(1), 27–48 (2018). https://doi.org/10.1080/0951192X.2017.1379093
33. Cho, H., Kulvatunyou, B., Jeong, H., Jones, A.: Using business process specifications and agents to integrate a scenario-driven supply chain. Int. J. Comput. Integr. Manuf. **17**(6), 546–560 (2004). https://doi.org/10.1080/09511920420001936711
34. Dalmau-Espert, J., Llorens-Largo, F., Compa-Rosique, P., Satorre-Cuerda, R., Molina-Carmona, R.: Leveraging information for high level-of-abstraction organizational processes. Int. J. Des. Nat. Ecodyn. **11**(3), 416–427 (2016). https://doi.org/10.2495/DNE-V11-N3-416-427
35. Dalpiaz, F., Franch, X., Horkoff, J.: iStar 2.0 language guide (2016). https://doi.org/10.48550/arXiv.1605.07767
36. Diamantini, C., Potena, D., Proietti, M., Smith, F., Storti, E., Taglino, F.: A semantic framework for knowledge management in virtual innovation factories. Int. J. Inf. Syst. Model. Des. (IJISMD) **4**(4), 70–92 (2013). https://doi.org/10.4018/ijismd.2013100104
37. Estrada-Torres, B., et al.: Measuring performance in knowledge-intensive processes. ACM Trans. Internet Technol. **19**(1), 15:1–15:26 (2019). https://doi.org/10.1145/3289180
38. Fayoumi, A., Williams, R.: An integrated socio-technical enterprise modelling: a scenario of healthcare system analysis and design. J. Ind. Inf. Integr. **23**, 100221 (2021). https://doi.org/10.1016/j.jii.2021.100221
39. Garrido, J.L., Noguera, M., González, M., Hurtado, M.V., Rodríguez, M.L.: Definition and use of computation independent models in an MDA-based groupware development process. Sci. Comput. Program. **66**(1), 25–43 (2007). https://doi.org/10.1016/j.scico.2006.10.008
40. Gong, R., Ning, K., Li, Q., O'Sullivan, D., Chen, Y., Decker, S.: Context modeling and measuring for proactive resource recommendation in business collaboration. Comput. Ind. Eng. **57**(1), 27–36 (2009). https://doi.org/10.1016/j.cie.2008.07.003
41. Heintz, J., Belaud, J.P., Gerbaud, V.: Chemical enterprise model and decision-making framework for sustainable chemical product design. Comput. Ind. **65**(3), 505–520 (2014). https://doi.org/10.1016/j.compind.2014.01.010

42. Janowski, T., Lugo, G.G., Zheng, H.: Modelling an extended/virtual enterprise by the composition of enterprise models. J. Intell. Rob. Syst. **26**(3), 303–324 (1999). https://doi.org/10.1023/A:1008141227185
43. Kim, G.Y., Lee, J.Y., Park, Y.H., Noh, S.D.: Product life cycle information and process analysis methodology: integrated information and process analysis for product life cycle management. Concurr. Eng. **20**(4), 257–274 (2012). https://doi.org/10.1177/1063293X12460863
44. Konstantinidis, G., Chapman, A., Weal, M.J., Alzubaidi, A., Ballard, L.M., Lucassen, A.M.: The need for machine-processable agreements in health data management. Algorithms **13**(4), 87 (2020). https://doi.org/10.3390/a13040087
45. Narendra, N.C., Norta, A., Mahunnah, M., Ma, L., Maggi, F.M.: Sound conflict management and resolution for virtual-enterprise collaborations. SOCA **10**(3), 233–251 (2016). https://doi.org/10.1007/s11761-015-0183-0
46. Paja, E., Dalpiaz, F., Giorgini, P.: Modelling and reasoning about security requirements in socio-technical systems. Data Knowl. Eng. **98**, 123–143 (2015). https://doi.org/10.1016/j.datak.2015.07.007
47. Romero, D., Galeano, N., Molina, A.: Virtual organisation breeding environments value system and its elements. J. Intell. Manuf. **21**(3), 267–286 (2010). https://doi.org/10.1007/s10845-008-0179-0
48. Sadigh, B.L., Unver, H.O., Nikghadam, S., Dogdu, E., Ozbayoglu, A.M., Kilic, S.E.: An ontology-based multi-agent virtual enterprise system (OMAVE): part 1: domain modelling and rule management. Int. J. Comput. Integr. Manuf. **30**(2–3), 320–343 (2017). https://doi.org/10.1080/0951192X.2016.1145811
49. Sahraoui, Y., et al.: Integrating ecological networks modelling in a participatory approach for assessing impacts of planning scenarios on landscape connectivity. Landscape Urban Plann. **209**, 104039 (2021). https://doi.org/10.1016/j.landurbplan.2021.104039, https://www.sciencedirect.com/science/article/pii/S0169204621000025
50. da Silva Serapião Leal, G., Guédria, W., Panetto, H.: An ontology for interoperability assessment: a systemic approach. J. Ind. Inf. Integr. **16**, 100100 (2019). https://doi.org/10.1016/j.jii.2019.07.001
51. Sjoukema, J.W., Samia, J., Bregt, A.K., Crompvoets, J.: Governance interactions of spatial data infrastructures: an agent-based modelling approach. Int. J. Digit. Earth **14**(6), 696–713 (2021). publisher: Taylor & Francis _eprint: https://doi.org/10.1080/17538947.2020.1868585
52. Tauqeer, A., Kurteva, A., Chhetri, T.R., Ahmeti, A., Fensel, A.: Automated GDPR contract compliance verification using knowledge graphs. Information **13**(10), 447 (2022). https://doi.org/10.3390/info13100447
53. Teruel, M.A., Maté, A., Navarro, E., González, P., Trujillo, J.C.: The new era of business intelligence applications: building from a collaborative point of view. Bus. Inf. Syst. Eng. **61**(5), 615–634 (2019). https://doi.org/10.1007/s12599-019-00578-3
54. Villa, A., Bruno, G.: Promoting SME cooperative aggregations: main criteria and contractual models. Int. J. Prod. Res. **51**(23–24), 7439–7447 (2013). https://doi.org/10.1080/00207543.2013.831503

# Towards Method Support for Variability Modelling in Enterprise Architecture Management

Ahmed Dehne[1(✉)] and Kurt Sandkuhl[1,2]

[1] University of Rostock, Albert-Einstein-Street 22, 18059 Rostock, Germany
{ahmed.dehne,kurt.sandkuhl}@uni-rostock.de
[2] Jönköpng University, Gjuterigatan 5, 55111 Jönköping, Sweden

**Abstract.** Studies on the effects of digital transformation on enterprise architectures (EA) indicate that variability in the EA increases on different levels, such as the business and the data architecture. Dealing with variability becomes a common challenge in the daily operations of many enterprises and requires methodical and technological support. Methodical support for controlling variability in EA can help enterprises manage variability more efficiently. In this context, the conjecture motivating this paper is that building blocks integrating business and data architecture or allowing for data-aware business process building blocks can help to ensure a high level of flexibility and, at the same time, control complexity in variability management. The paper aims to contribute to a better understanding of the requirements, necessary activities and frame conditions of method support for variability management of EA. The paper's main contribution is an initial method for identifying building blocks in enterprise architecture models that integrate several architecture layers and a way to capture such building blocks as ArchiMate models.

**Keywords:** Variability · Enterprise Architecture · Enterprise Architecture Management · Enterprise Architecture building block

## 1 Introduction

Digital transformation, new business models and the introduction of cyber-physical systems or artificial intelligence solutions lead to increased variability in enterprises and require dealing with this variability on several levels of an enterprise at the same time, for example, several variants of business processes that cause variations in the underlying data architecture, or variants of smart connected products that create the need for variations in IT services supporting them. This has been the result of studies on the effects of digital transformation on enterprise architectures (e.g., [1–3]) and artificial intelligence on enterprises (see, e.g. [4, 5]). Thus, variability is a common challenge in the daily operations of many enterprises.

Different strategies can deal with variation with the extreme positions of allowing for no variability (rigid standardization) and full flexibility (no limitation for variability).

© The Author(s), under exclusive license to Springer Nature Switzerland AG 2024
V. Řepa et al. (Eds.): BIR 2024, LNBIP 529, pp. 119–134, 2024.
https://doi.org/10.1007/978-3-031-71333-0_8

Independently of the strategy selected, there is a need to understand better the effects of changes in enterprises to support strategy development for variability control. Enterprise architecture (EA) models are considered a suitable way to visualize and manage dependencies between different levels of an enterprise. Still, there is not much work on managing variability in enterprise architectures across different architecture layers.

Data engineering is gaining importance in many organizations due to the increasing number of data-driven products and services and the use of AI solutions [6]. From an EA perspective, data engineering should be based on and tightly coupled to an organization's data architecture to avoid incompatibilities or avoidable structural differences. However, business process management as part of the business architecture usually has a different focus on short execution times, efficient resource use or high process quality. This is not necessarily compatible with the aims of data engineering, which is to provide data prepared for use in data-driven applications or AI. Our conjecture is that building blocks integrating business and data architecture or allowing for data-aware business process building blocks could help to ensure a high level of flexibility and, at the same time, control complexity.

We argue that methodical support for controlling variability in EA can help enterprises manage variability more efficiently. In previous work, the state of research regarding variability in enterprise architecture models and enterprise architecture management (EAM) has been investigated, and variability challenges in a real-world case study have been investigated to understand the problems better [7]. Building on this previous work, this paper aims to contribute to a better understanding of what the constituents of method support for variability management of EA should be. This includes a first approach for identifying building blocks in enterprise architecture models that integrate several architecture layers.

The paper is structured as follows: Sect. 2 summarises our research approach. Section 3 briefly defines the background for our work from enterprise architecture management and method engineering. Furthermore, the section summarises related work on EAM building blocks. Section 4 describes the requirements for method support for controlling variability in EA. Section 5 contains details of the initial approach for developing building blocks. Section 6 gives an outlook on future work.

## 2 Research Approach

The main objective of this research is to contribute to a better understanding of variability management in enterprise architectures. The project follows the paradigm of design science research (DSR) [8]. DSR is a research paradigm aiming at problem-solving in organisational settings, focusing on developing valid and reliable knowledge for designing the required solutions. The envisioned solution, called "artefact" in DSR, in our research is methodical and technological support for managing variability based on enterprise architecture building blocks. DSR research projects typically consist of several phases and require the use of different research methods depending on the DSR phase and intended design solution. This paper concerns the second and third phases of a DSR project: requirements definition and initial design of the artefact. For this purpose, we consider an industrial case study to extract requirements for the envisioned method and tool support, and we develop a method prototype.

*Case Study*
Yin [9] differentiates various kinds of case studies: explanatory, exploratory and descriptive. The case study presented in Sect. 4 has to be considered descriptive, as it describes the phenomenon of enterprise architecture variability and the real-life context in which it occurs. Based on the case study results, we conclude that there is a need to develop methodical and technological support for variability management that applies the concept of building blocks. The research question for the case study is RQ-CS: "How to capture EA variability in industrial practice?".

*Prototyping*
Prototyping as a research method [10] is a way to better understand the envisioned artefact being designed. Based on early requirements, an initial design and implementation of the artefact is created and afterwards subject to rigorous evaluation. Prototyping in DSR is suitable for all kinds of artefacts that can be externalised, like software systems, conceptual models or methods.

## 3 Background and Related Work

This section describes the necessary theoretical information for this research approach, focusing on enterprise architecture management (Sect. 3.1) and method engineering (Sect. 3.3). Furthermore, Sect. 3.2 summarises related work on variability in EAM using the result of a literature analysis.

### 3.1 Enterprise Architecture Management

Many different stakeholder groups contribute to an enterprise's development, operations and management. Different stakeholder groups have different views on the enterprise and require different viewpoints on the established structures, processes and components. "Architecture thinking" [11] has been found to be a promising approach to support communication between stakeholder groups and the long-term development of an enterprise. The term architecture indicates in this context that the focus is on the main building blocks of an enterprise, the construction principles and relationships.

The field of enterprise architecture management (EAM) addresses modelling such architectures and their systematic management as a management function in an enterprise. In EAM, special techniques for coherently describing enterprise architectures (EA) and communicating them with all relevant stakeholders are used to create an integrated perspective of the enterprise. Enterprise Architecture Management (EAM) includes planning, transforming, monitoring, and improving the different architecture levels [12]. In this context, the Enterprise Architecture (EA) serves as a map with information of the current situation of its elements and dependencies. A coherent set of principles, methods, and models is used to design and realize the enterprise's organizational structure [13].

TOGAF [14] is considered by many enterprises and scholars as the industry standard and defines three different architectural levels that are also present in other EA frameworks: Business architecture defines business strategy, governance, organization, and core business processes. Information Architecture often is divided into two sub-layers: Data Architecture and Application Architecture. The Data Architecture describes the structure of an organization's logical and physical data units and data management resources. The Application Architecture provides a blueprint for the individual application systems to be deployed, for their interactions and relationships to an organization's core business processes. Technology Architecture describes the physical realization of an architectural solution. In addition to EAM frameworks, there are also different modelling languages to support different EAM activities. One such language is ArchiMate, which is widely used for these purposes. Table 1 shows a selected set of ArchiMate model elements. These elements are used in Sect. 5 for the illustrative example.

**Table 1.** Table of ArchiMate elements used in the method prototype

| Element name | Element picture | Element name | Element picture |
|---|---|---|---|
| Business role | Business role | Business activity | Business activity |
| Business process | Business process | Application service | Application service |
| Application interface | Application interface | Application Component | Application component |
| Data object | Data object | | |

### 3.2 Variability in EAM

Our previous work [7] focused on analyzing the current state of research in EAM and variability management across different architecture layers. In this context, we conducted a structured literature review (SLR) to identify existing work in the field. The research question was formulated as "What is the state of research on managing variability in enterprise architectures?". The SLR process followed the method defined by Kitchenham [15]. It involved identifying relevant literature, selecting papers based on inclusion criteria, collecting data from the selected papers, and analyzing the data to answer the research question. The analysis concluded with a summary of the research findings and suggestions for future work. Table 2 summarizes the results of the SLR by presenting the relevant research papers and with the architecture layer the individual papers have in focus.

The core result of the SLR is that existing research focuses on treating variability on one architecture level only without considering its impact on other levels. We have suggested that an architecture-spanning approach is needed to address this gap and facilitate complex changes in enterprises. We propose investigating the integration of reuse approaches at different scales. We also suggested that feature modelling could be a promising way to integrate these different research streams. Furthermore, we used the identified papers to derive some of the requirements presented in Sect. 4.

When preparing this paper, we repeated the literature analysis, concluding that the only additional publication addressing the above research question is our own paper ([7]). Thus, Table 2 still summarises the state of research.

**Table 2.** Relevant publications on managing variability in enterprise architectures

| Paper title | Architecture Layer |
|---|---|
| Rurua, N., Eshuis, R., Razavian, M. - *Representing Variability in Enterprise Architecture: A Case Study* [16] | Business Architecture |
| Allian, A.P., Sena, B., Nakagawa, E.Y.- *Evaluating variability at the software architecture level: An overview* [17] | Software Architecture |
| Wille, D., Wehling, K., Seidl, C., Pluchator, M., Schaefer, I.- *Variability mining of technical architectures* [18] | Technology Architecture |
| Langermeier, M., Rosina, P., Oberkampf, H., Driessen, T., Bauer, B.- *Management of variability in modular ontology development* [19] | Application Architecture |
| Wehling, K., Wille, D., Seidl, C., Schaefer, I.- *Decision support for reducing unnecessary IT complexity of application architectures* [20] | Technology Architecture |
| Nerome, T., Numao, M.- *A product domain model based software product line engineering for web application* [21] | Application Architecture |
| Mani, N., Helfert, M., Pahl, C.- *A Domain-specific Rule Generation Using Model-Driven Architecture in Controlled Variability Model* [22] | Business Architecture |
| Asadi, M., Mohabbati, B., Kaviani, N., Gašević, D., Bošković, M., Hatala, M.- *Model-driven development of families of service-oriented architectures* [12] | Business Architecture |
| Benavides, D., Galindo, J.A.- *Variability management in an unaware software product line company. An experience report* [13] | Business Architecture |
| Wehling, K., Wille, D., Seidl, C., Schaefer, I.- *Automated recommendations for reducing unnecessary variability of technology architectures* [14] | Technology Architecture |
| Adjoyan, S., Seriai, A.- *An architecture description language for dynamic service-oriented product lines* [15] | Information Architecture |

### 3.3 Method Engineering

Modelling methods and how to construct them have been the subject of research in method engineering for many years. Method engineering (ME) is defined by [23] as the engineering discipline of designing, constructing and adapting methods, techniques and tools for developing information systems. Situational Method Engineering (SME) [24] is an ME approach that allows for method adaptation, including the design of method parts supporting specific modelling tasks as well as tailoring them based on local situational factors (e.g. the business sector or size of the business). Each method part is represented according to the same template and adheres to a unique metamodel. Another practicable ME approach was proposed in [25]; it focuses on elaborating method parts such as meta-modelling procedures, i.e., choosing appropriate concepts for inclusion.

Since this paper aims to develop a new method, the core focus is to identify the main constituents of a method and their relevant relations. For this purpose, the approach described in [25] by Goldkuhl et al. has been chosen. It decomposes a method into different aspects:

- Method components: a modelling process consists of three parts: concepts, procedure, and notation. The concepts define what aspects of reality are important to capture in the model and should be named and explained as needed. The procedure describes how to identify these concepts and may include prerequisites and resources. The notation specifies how to document the results of the procedure, including defining symbols or expressions for each concept and its relationships.
- Framework: the method framework describes the relationships between the individual method components, i.e. which components are to be used and under what conditions, as well as the sequence of the method components.
- Forms of cooperation: many modelling tasks require a range of specialist skills or cooperation between different roles. These necessary skills and roles must be described, along with the division of responsibilities between the roles and the form of cooperation. The cooperation form also includes who will take responsibility for each task or method component and how the collaboration will be organized.
- Perspective: every method describes the procedure for the modelling process from a particular perspective, which influences what is considered important when developing a model. This perspective often is related to the aims and purpose of the method.

## 4 Requirements to Method Support

Using the result of the literature analysis mentioned in Sect. (3.2) and based on an industrial case study, we developed a list of initial requirements to method support. These requirements are divided into requirements from literature and requirements from case study. This section first briefly provides an overview of the industrial case study (4.1) followed by a list of initial requirements from the literature and the case study (4.2).

### 4.1 Industrial Case Study

The case study company is a leading provider of solutions for the energy and water industry is developing software that enables the design, optimisation, and scaling of business processes in the sector. The solution encompasses implementing business processes across multiple layers within a digital environment, including application, data, and technology. As business processes continuously evolve in response to regulatory changes and the need to adopt new technologies, it is crucial to find a method for rapidly capturing adaptations in the architecture.

The case study company captured all aspects of the solution in an enterprise architecture model documented using ArchiMate. The ArchiMate models serve as the foundation for defining and implementing development roadmaps for software products and defining customised solutions for clients.

The company's aim of creating future customer solutions by "simply combining building blocks" was a key motivator for investigating the decomposition of enterprise architecture with consideration of variability aspects. Another driver is the increasing use of artificial intelligence to detect anomalies in data, facilitate churn management, or support predictive analytics. With such AI applications in mind, the "data footprint" of the software must meet certain integrity constraints, which could lead to a more extensive data architecture than required for a specific combination of building blocks. The envisioned method must provide the capability to capture enterprise architecture in a modular manner. These modules should represent independent elements that perform specific tasks and form the building blocks for clients' operations. By identifying and structuring process modules, companies can systematically improve their processes and respond more nimbly to new requirements.

The core idea behind the company's ambition to form building blocks is straightforward: building blocks comprise sequences of activities that are part of processes, combined with the data required for these activities and the services or functions necessary to create or process them. Ideally, each building block should include only the minimum set of data required for activities. On the other hand, the data architecture should be kept consistent and not overly fragmented. Dependencies between building blocks on activity, data, and service levels must be visualised, for example, by using feature models.

### 4.2 Method Requirements

We have derived requirements for method support based on our literature analysis and the case study results. Table 3 provides an overview of these requirements, including an explanation of each requirement.

**Table 3.** Method support requirements

| No | Requirement | Category | Description |
|---|---|---|---|
| 1 | Approach has to address variability management in EAs at different architecture levels | Literature requirement | As we conducted a systematic literature review (SLR) on variability management in Enterprise Architectures (EAs). The review found a limited number of papers that addressed variability management at different levels of EAs, with various approaches mentioned, such as designing extended Metamodels, evaluating variability in software architecture, and using software product line techniques |
| 2 | Developing a Framework for Combining Approaches Across Enterprise Architectures | Literature requirement | Research is needed to understand how different approaches to managing variability in enterprise architectures can be combined and implemented. This involves exploring how different methods work together, creating guidelines for choosing the right methods, and developing tools for practical use |

(*continued*)

**Table 3.** (*continued*)

| No | Requirement | Category | Description |
|---|---|---|---|
| 3 | Finding an Integrated Architecture Modelling | Case study/ Literature requirement | Our literature review revealed that there is currently no established approach for integrated architecture modelling. Furthermore, the case study requires a modelling language that can effectively capture all architecture levels - business, application, and data - in a coherent and unified manner. This presents a significant challenge, as existing approaches often focus on specific domains or levels, leaving a gap in the market for a comprehensive solution |
| 4 | Defining Building Blocks in Standardized Modeling Languages | Case study requirement | The developed model's seamless exchange between individuals with diverse backgrounds and understanding is hindered by the use of non-standard modelling languages. This restricts its comprehension and further development, as different stakeholders may struggle to interpret and build upon the model. A standardized language is essential for effective communication and collaboration among experts, enabling the model's growth and improvement |
| 5 | Existing (commercial) tool support for modelling must be available | Case study requirement | The company will not invest resources in developing a custom tool for architectural modelling. Instead, it is crucial to identify and leverage existing, proven solutions that can effectively support this process, allowing the team to focus on core competencies and optimize resources |
| 6 | Visualization of dependencies and configuration options between building blocks has to exist | Case study requirement | The chosen modelling language and tool must enable visualization of dependencies and configuration options between building blocks, allowing for a clear understanding of the relationships between components. This facilitates the design, development, and maintenance of complex systems by providing a holistic view of the architecture, enabling better decision-making and minimizing errors |

## 5 Method Prototype

The main objective of this paper is to develop the core constituents of an initial method (i.e., a method prototype) to manage variability in EA that builds upon the concept of building blocks as reusable parts of EA. After defining the term building block in Sects.

5.1 and 5.2 proposes the steps included in our method proposal. Section 5.3 applies the steps for validation purposes in the industrial case study. With this systematic approach, we aim to set the foundation for a method prototype: the specific steps form the basis for method components, and the overall procedure corresponds to the method framework. As shown in Sect. 6, we propose to apply the ArchiMate EA modelling language with its defined concepts and existing tools.

### 5.1 Definition of Building Block

An essential element of the method support is to establish a defined and more formal understanding of the term building block as part of the conceptualisation for the method framework and the different method components. We define "Building Block" in the context of a defined application domain as solution elements for individual clients that can be represented as configurations, instantiations, and specialisations of parts of a comprehensive (reference) enterprise architecture. A building block is a self-contained solution unit designed for reuse, comprising:

- At least one business process or business activity, with all its related:
- Application and data architecture elements, ensuring seamless integration and functionality;
- An explicit interface definition for interactions with preceding and subsequent business activities or processes facilitating smooth workflow and data exchange.

Each building block is formally represented as an ArchiMate model, accompanied by a feature model that clearly defines its relationships with other building blocks.

### 5.2 Systematic Approach

Our proposal for a systematic approach derived from the requirements (Sect. 4) begins with an analysis of the enterprise architecture structure, focusing on the process. Examining the process allows for a comprehensive understanding of its complexity, as it often consists of multiple smaller processes with varying levels of variability. By identifying points of variation, we can streamline and simplify the process. This analysis also helps categorise the process into different types for further examination.

Another crucial step is determining the essential data needed for the process execution and integrating it into the architecture. As each process is unique, different types of data are required for each. This leads to the task of selecting the necessary data from a pool of available information.

Once the specific data is identified, the next step involves reassembling the process and defining it as a building block. In Goldkuhl's conceptualisation (see Sect. 3.3), the above forms the "framework" of the method, which is also depicted in the following figure.

Figure 1 gives an overview of the ME framework. This includes different method components visible in the framework that have to be described in more detail.

The components of the framework are meant to satisfy requirements 1 and 2 in Table 3. The steps (Development of feature mode and Definition of building blocks) are meant to satisfy requirements 3 and 4 in Table 3.

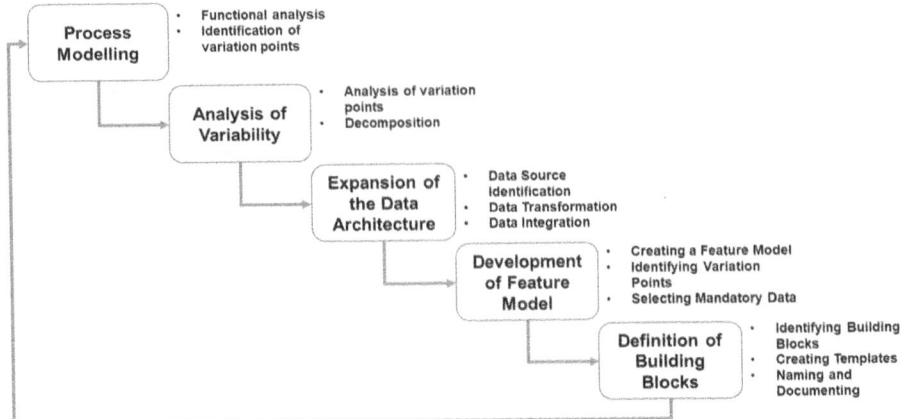

**Fig. 1.** Methodical approach and framework of the method prototype

In the following, we describe the different steps, each of which correspond to the procedure of a separate method component. The concepts and notation of the method components are, to a large extent, based on ArchiMate and tackled at the end of this section:

- Process modeling:
  - Using functional analysis is crucial for understanding business processes by identifying steps, actors, data flows, and resources. The main goal of process analysis is to achieve a comprehensive understanding of existing processes to enhance efficiency and effectiveness.
  - Next is the identification of variation points: involves identifying variation points in business processes, which are places where process variants can occur such as decision points, options, or deviations. Recognising these variation points is essential for designing processes that are flexible and adaptable to different requirements and changes.

- Analysis of variability:
  - Analysis of variation points: The variations found will be thoroughly examined to ascertain their nature, such as decision points, options, or deviations.
  - Decomposition: The process is segmented into sub-processes or modules based on identified variation points, with each module representing a different variant or sequence of activities.

- Expansion of the data architecture:
  - Data Source Identification: The objective is to pinpoint all pertinent data sources necessary for processes to guarantee access to the required data.
  - Data Transformation: The aim is to modify data from the identified sources to align with the specific requirements of the process variations.
  - Data Integration: The objective is to seamlessly incorporate the transformed data into the current process model to facilitate efficient use in the processes.

- Development of feature model
    - Creating a Feature Model: The initial step involves creating a feature diagram that showcases processes and data as features. This diagram provides a clear overview of the entire business architecture and its hierarchy.
    - Identifying Variation Points: Abstract features are incorporated into the model to represent variation points. Positioned at higher levels of the model, these abstract features act as decision points, offering different process variants. This approach makes all potential variants easily identifiable.
    - Selecting Mandatory Data: Within the feature diagram, the focus is on selecting mandatory data crucial for the process. These data are depicted as mandatory features in the diagram since they are indispensable for carrying out the process.
    - Tailoring the Process Model: Simultaneously, the process model is adjusted to include only the selected mandatory data. This ensures that unnecessary data is removed from the process model, guaranteeing that only essential data is integrated into the processes.
- Definition of building blocks
    - Identifying Building Blocks: Building blocks are identified through a detailed analysis of the comprehensive process model, which includes clearly defined sub-processes and essential data, as well as the feature model. Each building block represents a specific function or feature within the enterprise architecture.
    - Creating Templates: Building blocks are represented as templates that combine the process model and feature model. This involves creating a specific template within a modelling environment that seamlessly integrates both process components and features, illustrating the relationship between them clearly.
    - Naming and Documenting: Each building block is given a unique name and thoroughly documented to explain its function and role within the architecture. This ensures effective communication and management of the building blocks throughout the architecture model.

In our modelling, we used ArchiMate as a modelling language to describe the enterprise architecture as in the following section explained (5.2: Process modelling and Expansion of the data architecture) and once again to deliver an example of variation (Sect. 5.2: Definition of building blocks). The ArchiMate elements of the models are explained in Sect. 3.1, Table 1.

In addition, we used feature modelling to identify the different building blocks with their mandatory and optional components (Sect. 5.2: Development of feature model).

### 5.3 Application of the Method Prototype in the Case Study

This section aims to show how the method prototype can be applied. As the basis for this illustration, the case study presented in Sect. 4 is used. The case study applies the different architecture layers defined in TOGAF (see Sect. 3.1). The remainder of the section follows the steps defined in the method prototype.

- Process modeling:

We chose the process "Geräteeinbau" to implement our approach. This process, known as "Device installation" in English, details the steps for installing or uninstalling meters and other devices. The meter is primarily used to measure electricity and water consumption at a specific location. Figure 2 illustrates the current status of the "Device installation" process.

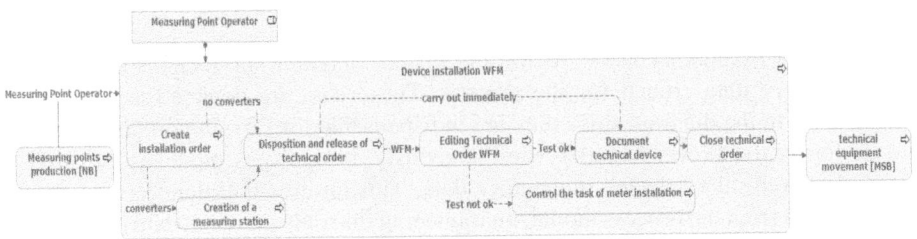

**Fig. 2.** Process of Device installation WFM

To explain the model more clearly, we outline its core components created with the ArchiMate framework. These key elements include:

The model illustrates that the Device installation WFM process is assigned to the Measuring Point Operator and can begin as a subsequent step to the Measuring Points production [NB] process.

- Analysis of variability:

    Within this process, there are several business activities that contain points of variation. For example, after the business activity of creating an installation order, a variation point occurs to determine if a converter exists or not. Another variation is found after the Sub-Business process of Editing Technical Order WFM [MSB/NB].

- Expansion of the data architecture:

    During our analysis of the model, we discovered that the current architecture lacks the data architecture model. Therefore, we have made the necessary addition, as presented in the following model. We used the ArchiMate element (Data object) to represent the data architecture layer. In some cases, we needed to add a higher-level category for the data objects. For instance, Device management acts as a parent category (data object) that includes both device type and device class as child data objects (Fig. 3).

- Development of feature model:

    Next, we created a feature model to visualize the activities of the Device Installation Process, identifying key building blocks and their data architecture requirements. This model in Fig. 4 illustrates dependencies between activities and potential combinations.

    For the Business Process of "Device Installation" (root of the example feature model) six activity sets are candidates for building blocks and shown on the second level. The relation type between business process and building block indicates if the building block

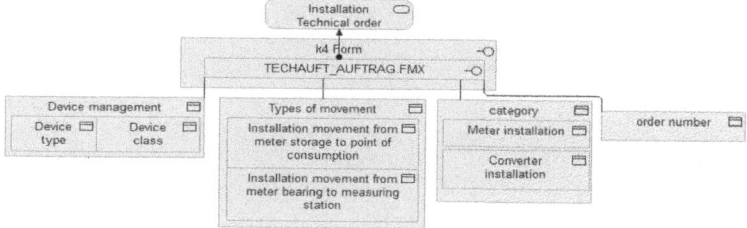

**Fig. 3.** Excerpt of the data architecture used in the Device installation WFM process

is mandatory for the process, optional, or has alternatives. All building blocks are mandatory with the exception of "document technical device installation" and "control meter installation", which are alternatives. For each building block, the required (mandatory or optional) data is shown on the third level, and their refinements on the fourth level. In our example, it becomes clear that some building blocks require the same data, i.e., there is a certain overlap which leads to dependencies on the data architecture layer although the building blocks seem to be independent from each other on business and application architecture level.

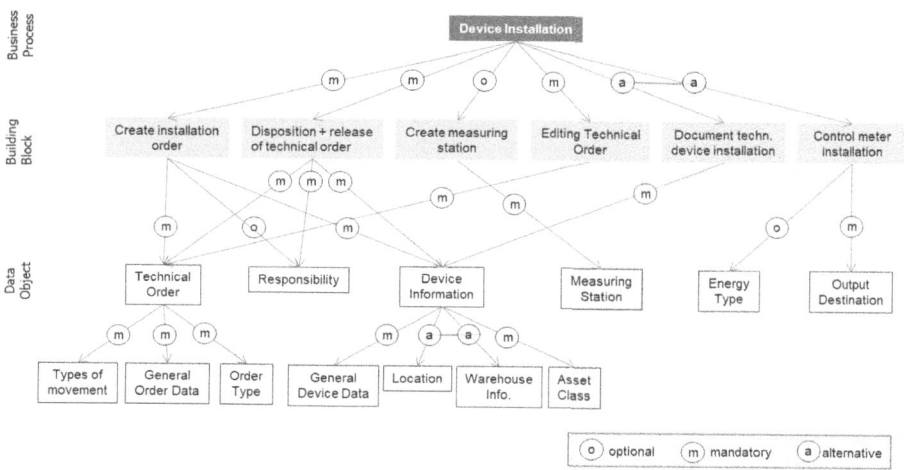

**Fig. 4.** Feature Model showing building blocks identified for the device installation process

- Definition of building blocks:

    By utilizing the feature model, we effectively defined distinct variants within the process and uncovered multiple potential building blocks. As a result, an example showcasing these building blocks will be presented in the following sections.

    In Fig. 5 we have the building block represented by the business activity "Create installation order" and the application service "Installation Technical order." This service is part of the application component "Technical order" and can be accessed through

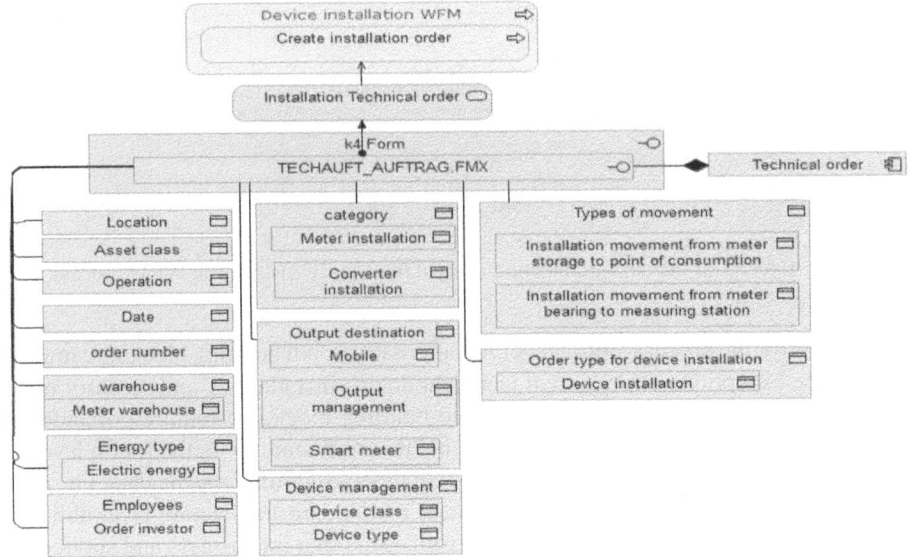

**Fig. 5.** Building Block (Create installation order)

the application interface "TECHAUFT_AUFTRAG.FMX." The application interface "TECHAUFT_AUFTRAG.FMX" is a software page used for editing the data objects.

## 6 Discussion and Conclusions

Starting from an industrial case study on industrial challenges of managing variability in industrial practice, the paper aimed at developing methodical support for identifying reusable EA building blocks. These building blocks are supposed to help reduce complexity in variability management by including required elements from both business and data architecture layers. With both layers included, the building blocks implicitly specify the permitted combinations between business and data architecture and discourage the use of any possible combination between the two layers when building customer solutions. To ease the use of the building blocks, their dependencies are visualized in feature models, which makes feature models part of our methodical approach. Section 5.2 included examples of the feature model and building blocks.

The method prototype was structured following Goldkuhl's method conceptualization with a focus on the method framework and method components. The future work has to include a more detailed description of the perspective, the cooperation principles and the tools supporting the method components. These three parts were not included in the method prototype in Sect. 5.

From a DSR perspective, our work so far included the analysis of business requirements, the existing body of knowledge and a first design and evaluate cycle. The design is presented in Sect. 5.1, the very basic evaluation in artificial setting for formative purposes is shown in Sect. 5.2. From the evaluation exercise, we conclude that a more detailed link between the feature model and building block and a more elaborated way of describing the building blocks have to be developed. Furthermore, identifying building blocks so far is done completely manually and could be accompanied by tool support. Including potential users of the method support would be another important aspect. All these findings form the input for the next design and evaluate cycle to perform in future work.

## References

1. Kaidalova, J., Sandkuhl, K., Seigerroth, U.: How digital transformation affects enterprise architecture management-a case study. Int. J. Inf. Syst. Proj. Manag. **6**, 5–18 (2018)
2. Zimmermann, A., Schmidt, R., Sandkuhl, K., Jugel, D., Bogner, J., Möhring, M.: Evolution of enterprise architecture for digital transformation. In: 2018 IEEE 22nd International Enterprise Distributed Object Computing Workshop (EDOCW), pp. 87–96 (2018)
3. Sandkuhl, K., Seigerroth, U.: Digital transformation of enterprises: case studies and transformation paths. In: PACIS, p. 35 (2021)
4. Rittelmeyer, J.D., Sandkuhl, K.: Effects of artificial intelligence on enterprise architectures-a structured literature review. In: 2021 IEEE 25th International Enterprise Distributed Object Computing Workshop (EDOCW), pp. 130–137 (2021)
5. Park, S., yoon Lee, J., Lee, J.: AI system architecture design methodology based on IMO (Input-AI Model-Output) structure for successful AI adoption in organizations. Data Knowl. Eng. **150**, 102264 (2024)
6. Fruhwirth, M., Ropposch, C., Pammer-Schindler, V.: Supporting data-driven business model innovations: a structured literature review on tools and methods. J. Bus. Models **8**, 7–25 (2020)
7. Dehne, A., Sandkuhl, K.: Variability modelling in enterprise architecture management-survey on existing approaches. In: 22nd International Conference on Perspectives in Business Informatics Research Workshops and Doctoral Consortium, BIR-WS 2023 Ascoli Piceno 13 September 2023 through 15 September 2023, vol. 3514, pp. 94–107 (2023)
8. Hevner, A., Chatterjee, S.: Design Research in Information Systems: Theory and Practice. Springer US, Boston, MA (2010). https://doi.org/10.1007/978-1-4419-5653-8
9. Yin, R.K.: Case Study Research: Design and Mthods. Sage (2009)
10. Wensveen, S., Matthews, B.: Prototypes and prototyping in design research. In: Rodgers, P.A., Yee, J. (eds.) The Routledge Companion to Design Research, pp. 262–276. Routledge (2014). https://doi.org/10.4324/9781315758466-25
11. Winter, R.: Architectural thinking. Wirtschaftsinformatik **56**, 395–398 (2014)
12. Simon, D., Fischbach, K., Schoder, D.: Enterprise architecture management and its role in corporate strategic management. IseB **12**, 5–42 (2014)
13. Ahlemann, F., Stettiner, E., Messerschmidt, M., Legner, C.: Strategic enterprise architecture management: challenges, best practices, and future developments. Springer Science & Business Media (2012)https://doi.org/10.1007/978-3-642-24223-6
14. The Open Group: The TOGAF® Standard, 10th edn. Van Haren Publishing, Architecture Development Method (2022)
15. Kitchenham, B., Brereton, O.P., Budgen, D., Turner, M., Bailey, J., Linkman, S.: Systematic literature reviews in software engineering-a systematic literature review. Inf. Softw. Technol. **51**, 7–15 (2009)
16. Rurua, N., Eshuis, R., Razavian, M.: Representing variability in enterprise architecture. Bus. Inf. Syst. Eng. **61**, 215–227 (2019). https://doi.org/10.1007/s12599-017-0511-3

17. Allian, A.P., Sena, B., Nakagawa, E.Y.: Evaluating variability at the software architecture level. In: Hung, C.-C., Papadopoulos, G.A. (eds.) Proceedings of the 34th ACM/SIGAPP Symposium on Applied Computing, pp. 2354–2361. ACM, New York, NY, USA (2019). https://doi.org/10.1145/3297280.3297511
18. Wille, D., Wehling, K., Seidl, C., Pluchator, M., Schaefer, I.: Variability mining of technical architectures. In: Cohen, M., et al. (eds.) Proceedings of the 21st International Systems and Software Product Line Conference - Volume A, pp. 39–48. ACM, New York, NY, USA (2017). https://doi.org/10.1145/3106195.3106202
19. Langermeier, M., Rosina, P., Oberkampf, H., Driessen, T., Bauer, B.: Management of variability in modular ontology development. In: Lomuscio, A.R., Nepal, S., Patrizi, F., Benatallah, B., Brandić, I. (eds.) Service-Oriented Computing – ICSOC 2013 Workshops: CCSA, CSB, PASCEB, SWESE, WESOA, and PhD Symposium, Berlin, Germany, December 2-5, 2013. Revised Selected Papers, pp. 225–239. Springer International Publishing, Cham (2014). https://doi.org/10.1007/978-3-319-06859-6_20
20. Wehling, K., Wille, D., Seidl, C., Schaefer, I.: Decision support for reducing unnecessary IT complexity of application architectures. In: 2017 IEEE International Conference on Software Architecture Workshops (ICSAW), pp. 161–168. IEEE (2017). https://doi.org/10.1109/ICSAW.2017.47
21. Nerome, T., Numao, M.: A product domain model based software product line engineering for web application. In: 2014 Second International Symposium on Computing and Networking, pp. 572–576. IEEE (2014). https://doi.org/10.1109/CANDAR.2014.105
22. Mani, N., Helfert, M., Pahl, C.: A domain-specific rule generation using model-driven architecture in controlled variability model. Procedia Comput. Sci. **112**, 2354–2362 (2017). https://doi.org/10.1016/j.procs.2017.08.206
23. Brinkkemper, S.: Method engineering: engineering of information systems development methods and tools. Inf. Softw. Technol. **38**, 275–280 (1996)
24. Henderson-Sellers, B., Ralyté, J., Ågerfalk, P.J., Rossi, M.: Situational Method Engineering. Springer Berlin Heidelberg, Berlin, Heidelberg (2014). https://doi.org/10.1007/978-3-642-41467-1
25. Goldkuhl, G., Lind, M., Seigerroth, U.: Method integration: the need for a learning perspective. IEE Proc. Softw. **145**, 113–118 (1998)

# Cross-section of Business Intelligence Projects: Information Systems Success Perspective

Dace Kvalberga[1](✉) and Jānis Grabis[2]

[1] flex.bi, Slokas iela 32-3, Rīga 1048, Latvia
`dace@flex.bi`
[2] Information Technology, Riga Technical University, Kalku 1, Riga 1658, Latvia
`grabis@rtu.lv`

**Abstract.** Business Intelligence systems have become one of the most widely used information systems yet their efficient and successful usage requires advanced digital skills of business users, implementation team and digital transformation of organization in general. These requirements are particularly profound in implementation of self-service business intelligence solutions. In order to evaluate factors influencing success or failure of implementation of self-service business intelligence solutions, this paper adopts a modified DeLone and McLean IS success model. The modified model emphasizes importance of organizational factors and correlates user intent and satisfaction with leading and lagging indicators characterizing the implementation. The model is applied to analyze more than a hundred business intelligence implementation projects in small and medium size companies. An in-depth analysis of one successful project and one failed project is performed. The model offers a tool for business intelligence project management teams to increase success rates, to get insights from ongoing projects, to understand past failures and to plan better work for future projects.

**Keywords:** Business intelligence · success model · self-service

## 1 Introduction

Business intelligence (BI) systems provide essential data analytical capabilities to companies. The recent wave of digitalization has opened many additional opportunities for using the BI systems. These systems have found new use cases and have been picked-up by new users. Self-service BI is one the approaches considered to service these additional needs [1]. It allows casual users to analyze data with a limited reliance on data analysts and IT support staff by providing easy to use and interactive data analytical functions. However, the users vary according to their needs and digital skills. While there are established methods and extensive experience on implementing fully-fledged BI solutions, implementation and governance of self-service BI systems is an ongoing research area [2].

Success of implementation of BI can be evaluated using theoretical frameworks like the DeLone and McLean model and the Technology Acceptance model [3]. The success is explained by such factors as system quality, information quality and service quality influencing intention of use and user satisfaction resulting in net benefits. In the case of self-service BI, organizational factors should be considered because organizations need to take ownership of the solution. That requires strategic alignment, digital maturity and involvement and preparedness of all stakeholders.

This paper incorporates the aforementioned consideration in the DeLone and McLean model based evaluation of the success or failure of BI implementation projects. It focuses on evaluation of individual projects and measurements of the constructs are defined and associated with business performance indicators.

The objective of the paper is to compare one successful and one failed BI implementation project according to the augmented DeLone and McLean information systems success model. The base success projects augmented with factors identified by analyzing a set of BI implementation projects. These projects are explored in the case studies and the investigation is performed from the perspective of the implementation company. The success model is interpreted as an operational project management tool not analyzing the project as something finished but rather continuously improving. The scientific contribution of the paper is in depth analysis of both successful and failed implementation projects of self-service BI solutions. It also highlights practical implementation challenges and shows that project management and organizational issues allow to predict success of the project in pre-implementation stages.

The rest of the paper is organized as follows. Section 2 briefly reviews the current literature on evaluation of BI implementation projects. The success evaluation model is discussed in Sect. 3. Two selected projects are analyzed in Sect. 4. Section 5 concludes.

## 2 Related Work

BI implementation is a complex information systems (IS) implementation project requiring significant emphasis on information value rather than just software development [4]. Data acquisition, quality, processing, analysis and interpretation accommodate every step of the implementation process. Krey et al. [5] identify specific implementation concerns to SME and propose the implementation process consisting of Readiness check, BIDevOps and Data Governance phases. Although the process provides a general framework, an implementation plan should be tailored to needs of individual companies with strong involvement of end-users.

The implementation projects have been studied both on individual basis (i.e., case studies) and at aggregated level (i.e., surveys). Case studies often focus on needs of specific industries, for example, manufacturing [6], healthcare [7] and utilities [8]. Companies need to optimize investment in development of BI artifacts [9]. That requires collaboration, cost accounting, model comprehensibility and strategic alignment according to the findings of action research project. Interviews conducted with employees from seven case companies show that the organizational dimension is one of the most important [10]. The cases also included experiences from failed projects. The review of 38 empirical studies reveals that most frequently considered implementation factors are management support, data sources systems (technical aspects) and organizational resources while user and project management factors are considered less frequently [11].

The surveys aim to identify a comprehensive set of success factors contributing to implementation of BI solutions. A survey of start-up companies shows that companies mainly use BI of data analysis in controlling while more advanced functions are used less frequently [12]. They emphasize information management and availability benefits, while development, application and employees' qualification problems are impediments. The literature review suggests that there are many implementation projects failing to reach their objectives [13]. The success factor taxonomy is elaborated to structure success factors and criteria in three perspectives - technical, organizational and process. The process perspective in particular concerns with project management and user-centric criteria. A Delphi study with 12 experts using AHP to weight importance of the success factors suggest that the most important factors are Top Management Support, Clearly Defined Business Needs and Goals, User Participation and Support, Identify User's Specific Issues and Requirement and Data Quality [14]. One can observe that these factors represent various dimensions related to management, process, people and data.

The DeLone and McLean model and the Technology Acceptance model are the most often used theoretical frameworks to analyze success of BI [3]. There are multiple variations of success models. Management support, project management, net benefit system quality and information quality are among success factors most often considered in literature [15]. Ergonomics, responsiveness, flexibility, integration and security are mentioned as BI specific adaptations of the IS success model [16]. It is suggested that project management also has a significant impact on BI success [17]. Change management and knowledge sharing are two particularly important aspects. It is also argued that IS Use is a consequence of IS success [18]. Popovic et al. [19] investigates the BI maturity as a key factor contributing to the implementation success.

Self-service BI solutions pose additional set of challenges [20]. These include user, education and technical challenges confirmed in interviews with users. The analysis of case studies indicates that many companies considering self-service BI lack a clear business strategy and a comprehensive change management plan [21]. Instead of that they rely on pilot projects. It is suggested that additional research on scaling-up BI usage is required.

The existing research suggests that project management and user related factors should be emphasized in evaluation of success of BI implementation. Additionally, implementation benefits should be measured using quantitative data and user's decision-making performance. The investigations also focus on aggregated behavior lacking insights about individual projects, their successes and failures.

## 3 Business Intelligence Implementation Success Model

Business Intelligence System Implementation Success Model (BISISM) for self-service BI systems is formulated on the basis of the Delone and McLone model [22] to account for the aforementioned considerations. Additional factors extending the base model are identified by analyzing BI implementation projects.

## 3.1 Foundation

The DeLone and McLean Success Factors Model is a framework to measure IS implementation success based on multiple factors. The model (Fig. 1) has three factors, namely, Service Quality, Information Quality and System Quality, influencing Intention to Use and User Satisfaction what in turn determine Net Benefits. The Information Quality stands for availability, readability, accuracy and ensures that data is complete, up to date and consistent. Compliance with only some of the established requirements may not be sufficient, as, for example, easily understandable but outdated information will not yield the desired results. The System Quality measures both the technical quality of the IS, including stability, frequency of updates, errors, and usability of the IS. Service Quality was added as an important factor and ensuring that users needs are met.

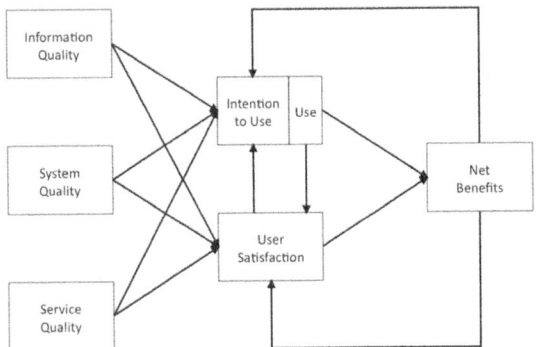

**Fig. 1.** DeLone and McLean Success Factors Model [22].

The "Intention to Use" characterizes users' attitude towards IS, while "Use" measures users' actual behavior. It should be noted that unlike "Use", which characterizes a static past state, in this model the new factor "Intention to Use" characterizes a future forecast, as high intention to use the system. The "User Satisfaction" represents users' opinion. The "Net Benefits" is proposed as the main result that all other factors lead to and reinforces the "Intention to Use" and the "User satisfaction".

Taking into consideration that model was developed 30 years ago with different market and practices and "Net Benefits" is an abstract concept, that requires long-term measuring and is not precisely described, research was performed to analyze DeLone factors in depth and possibly find new formula to measure and identify successful projects.

## 3.2 Implementation Factors

In order to identify factors contributing to success of implementation of self-service BI, empirical data from more than 100 implementation projects are gathered. Specifically, the implementations of flex.bi analytics platform[1] from 2016 to 2022 are analyzed. The data are extracted from the implementation reports gathered by the consulting company.

---

[1] https://flex.bi/.

## Survey Design

102 projects have been completed in six years including 72 projects in Latvia and 29 projects in other countries. The consulting company, i.e., service provider, classified 72% of the projects as successful what compares favorably with 43% rate reported in the literature [23]. Out of the projects, a set of 9 most successful projects that have been stable after 2 years from implementation and 8 failed projects were analyzed in depth. A questionnaire was created with the following factor groups (Table 1) with indicators for evaluation: **System, Service Provider, Organizational.**

Table 1. Questionnaire Factors and Indicators

| System | Service Provider | Organizational |
|---|---|---|
| ***Information Quality*** | ***Service Quality*** | ***Alignment with Strategy*** |
| S1 Dashboard Layout Readability | I1 Reaction Time | O1 KPI relevance |
| | I2 Proactivity | O2 Management Accept |
| S2 Data Quality and Calculations | I3 Conflicts & Empathy | O3 Clear purpose for BIS |
| ***System Quality*** | I4 Competence level | ***Readiness for BIS*** |
| S3 System Availability | ***Methodology*** | O4 Organization Lifecycle |
| S4 System Usability | I5 User Interaction level | O5 Human resources |
| S5 System Quality | I6 Change management | O6 Budget for BIS |
| S6 System Suitability | I7 Knowledge base | O7 Data Literacy |
| S7 Speed of data processing | I8 Trainings | ***Depth of Implementation*** |
| | | O8 Only BIS in organization |
| | | O9 Internal Consultant or analytics department |
| | | O10 BIS used in decision making |
| | | O11 Organization levels usage |

For each indicator, relevant questions were asked to project teams and historical records from the systems were gathered. For example, JIRA issues tracking records for service speed, conflicts and proactivity measuring, system error and report failure % records for usability and quality measuring, average report loading speed for data processing and usability. Organization life cycles were analyzed according to Adizes Methodology [24] and Data Literacy skills identified based on QlickView data Literacy Index description [25].

## Survey Results

As the result of this analysis, the importance of Organisational and Individual user factors were identified as highly meaningful in both project sets. Top 5 factors common for the successful projects where:

1. Organizational factor – Alignment with strategy,
2. Organizational factor – Depth of implementation,
3. Organizational factor – Readiness for BI System,
4. Service provider – Service quality,
5. System – System quality.

Top 3 factors all are from the Organizational factor group. The Alignment with Strategy represents that KPIs included in Dashboards were relevant and chosen according to strategy, organization management is supporting BIS usage in organization and there is a clear Purpose known for BIS. Second factor, the Depth of Implementation represents that BIS is the only or prioritized analytics system in organization, as according to latest research, on average companies now use 3.8 analytics platforms in the same time, 67% use more than one BI tool, and 55% of organizations confess that BI tools analyze the same data set [26]. This situation is new and creates unusual internal BIS competition situation that was not present some years ago. "Depth of Implementation" is also indicated by internal consultant/department that supports analytics process internally in organization and aligns solution with business needs, supports internal analytics processes, uses self-service BI possibilities. For the large organizations segment this is a very usual situation, but for SMEs it is very common that there is no one who has data analytics as primary duty. If such a person is present, chances of success are much higher. In those cases KPIs and dashboards are used in the decision making process and that more than one level of organization employees are using BI system. Third Factor The Readiness for BI system is represented by indicators of good Data Literacy skills as well as available human resources and funding that were present in all successful projects, not only for adding business knowledge but also for testing, internal support and maintenance, trainings.

From the opposite perspective analysis of the failed projects surprisingly showed that while implementation was satisfactory according to majority of the indicators, there was always a blocker indicator causing the failure. In many situations, the blocker indicator could not be affected by a service provider. The most often mentioned indicators for unsuccessful projects were:

1. Organizational – O4 Suitability of the organization's life cycle,
2. Organizational – O5 Availability of appropriate human resources,
3. Service Quality – I8 Volume of training,
4. Organizational – O6 Adequacy of financial resources for the organization,
5. System Quality – S6 System Suitability.

Most of these indicators can be related to organization size and maturity. For projects that failed many times, common was to implement BI system in a wrong stage of Organization lifecycle where too many changes in procedures, datasets and human resources are present. According to the Adizes methodology [24], this is a stage before the Infancy and after the Go-Go phase where many processes are re- defined and there is no stable basis for data analytics as well as "founders trap" might be present. Large organizations rarely experience these stages of their lifecycle, so this high risk indicator is typical to SMEs. This indicator can be diagnosed prior the implementation and should be defined as a blocker to start implementation as possibility to fail is very high.

The second indicator Availability of appropriate human resources is common for SMEs as many people serve multiple roles and are too busy to switch from main business focus to BI testing or discussing strategic goals. Situation identified in two projects was that BI was implemented by too technical person who was not validating result with business users, but that was the only employee available in the team. In this case this person is not considered to be "appropriate human resource" as BI system consists of Business and Technical intelligence parts, in these cases it was a blocker issue. I8 Indicator - The Volume of Training in theory can be affected by service provider, but could also be related to self- service BI in general, where users tend to decide in early project stages that they know enough and take over the implementation process, but fail to follow the best practices of BI implementation and as a result layouts of the dashboards that are build are hard to read, KPIs are not selected according to company strategy and user groups are not identified with their individual needs, dashboards are too basic and lack the intelligence part. In this situation organization does not get Net Benefits, but Service provider does not have much control over it.

Lack of Financial resources - O6, was identified as "blocker" in 2 cases where BI could not add enough value fast enough and management decided to return back to previous practices of data analytics with XLS reporting and manual work.

S6 - System suitability describes those situations where system was not able to handle the data processing technically. In current BI market where many data analytics platforms available and have similar functions, this indicator is crucial and must be specified by defining maximum report execution speed considered as "normal" or by describing desired technical possibilities of available data management tools in platform. For middle sized organizations this is critical point as they are too small for big segment tools like Tableau, QlickView or similar, and they want to save on project budget, but sometimes they have to sacrifice more advanced functions and choose small segment tools that can fail their expectations.

In both project groups the impact of Organisation factors and indicators was the most important one that confirmed our assumption that while implementing self-service BI systems in small and middle sized businesses they should be analyzed and observed prior and during the implementation process.

### 3.3 Augmented Success Model

Based on results described above, a new BISISM model is formulated that summarizes the causality perspective of the DeLone and McLean model and examines an additional group of Organizational factors that influence the project success and adds more specific factors to the System and Service factor groups (Fig. 2).

Changes are made to Service providers factor group and "Implementation methodology" is added as an important factor. Iterative, Agile and Spiral methodologies are commonly used for BI implementations in small and middle segment now [26] but in some cases customers request Waterfall implementations that is less suitable for self-service BI platforms like flex.bi or PowerBI, especially in SMEs, where project scope is very undefined at the beginning of the project. Wrong methodology can be in conflict with agile nature of self-service tools in that can lead to early project failure or crisis.

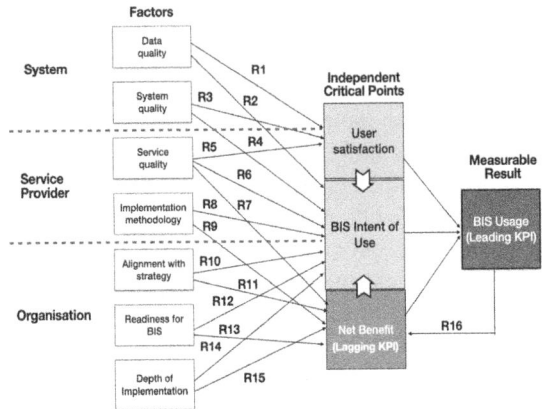

**Fig. 2.** BI System Implementation Success Model (BISISM)

In addition to factor changes, the new model offers different perspective and process of measuring project success in general, with main focus to user behaviour. Firstly, BISISM model offers to change focus from the lagging KPI Net benefits [27] to a directly measurable KPIs such as actual BIS Usage. This way the model is offered as an operational project management tool and it requires that result must be easy to measure at any given time moment of fast changing market. The Net Benefits still play an important role but for Service provider, who can impact the project pass, Usage statistics information is easier to access and control. Secondly, the model is more focused on the BI success management at any given project moment, not analyzing the project as something finished but continuously improving. It can be used to analyze a project in the starting phase as well as in retrospective analysis or future planning.

The most common relations (R1–R16) are defined to emphasize some important correlations. For example, Depth of implementation is closely related to Net benefits but will not affect User satisfaction that much. User satisfaction is more affected by System and Service provider factors like Service Quality, Data Quality or System Quality. For each project it is possible to draw most important relations figure that visually describes that a particular case and helps to understand the project result better (Fig. 5).

## 3.4 Project Success Evaluation

In this model relations are used to show co-dependency of factors and Independent Critical points – Net Benefits and User satisfaction that lead to Intent to use BIS as a consequence that ensures the most important Leading KPI to project success, i.e., BI System usage. In this visualization (Fig. 2), the Independent Critical points mean that if any of these conditions are not met, it directly affects the Usage of BIS. For example, if Users are not happy with Dashboard layouts it will lead to low User satisfaction rate and low Intent to use the system. As well as if Net benefits are not present in long term, for example, using BI system is more time consuming than manually calculations in an XLS sheet, this will also lead to low intent to use. Intent to use is a subjective and sensitive critical point as users could have irrational reasons to not use the system, even if technically sound. This aspect is based on Perceived Usefulness from the TAM model, i.e., the degree to which a person believes that using a particular system would enhance his/her job performance [17].

To assess the impact of individual factors, the success points of the $i$th factor are evaluated as:

$$R_i = N_j^{-1} \sum_{j=1}^{N_i} I_{ij}$$

where $I_{ij}$ is the expert evaluation of the $j$th indicator (Table 1) and $N_j$ is the number of indicators for the $i$th factor. The overall project success score is calculated as an average over all factors. The values of $I_{ij}$ vary from 0 to 1 where the former indicates a very unsatisfactory situation suggesting serious difficulties and the latter indicates an excellent situation with all conditions met.

Several KPIs can be used to measure main result - BIS Usage: Monthly Active users (MAU) is useful for projects where strategic KPIs are monitored, BIS usage will be rare, but still important. Weekly Active Users (WAU) is useful for projects with Operational dashboards, where dashboards should be used regularly. Daily Active Users (DAU) is more useful for projects where gamification is involved.

The overall project success points identified in research for the nine successful project varies between 79% and 86% while it is a range of 63% to 82% for the failed projects. However, just two failed projects have the score above 70%, and below 70% is chosen as a threshold to indicate high risk of failure is pre-implementation evaluation. This choice of borderline is also supported by customer satisfaction calculation method Net Promoter Score (NPS) (https://www.netpromoter.com/know/) where all values below 7 are identified as "bad" and require attention as they indicate that a problem situation is present.

## 4 Implementation Projects

### 4.1 Successful Project Evaluation

Kenfield Ltd is a company operating in the United Kingdom and engaging in wholesale trade of various types of doors required by different industries. It has been operating for 39 years. The company size is 50–100 employees. The projects was started November 2018 and continuous up to now. The project's main goal was to consolidate all relevant data for the company in one place and automate the generation of operational reports. The implementation of BIS in this company would provide time savings for the operational manager, as well as a holistic overview of the company's operations and possibility to create ad-hoc reports and save time in communicating the company's results to the board. The project was divided into two main phases: Basic Dashboard Creation and Integration of Data from Other Sources. Solution Prototype was delivered before the first specific requirements gathering period, so this project part is referred to as phase 0. The client uses the flex.bi Cloud version. Confluence and JIRA were used for configuration management and technical documentation.

The BIS is actively used in daily work and at various levels of the company, making it an indispensable system for daily operations (Fig. 3). Initially, only management was using dashboards, but step by step other user groups have been added as flex.bi users.

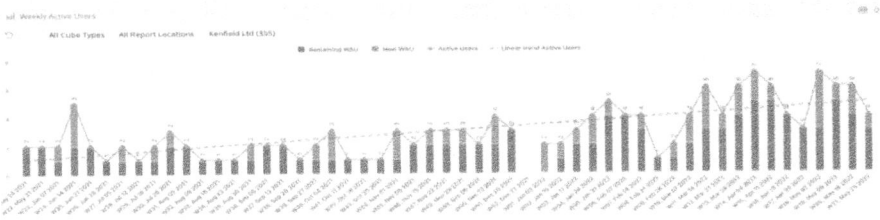

**Fig. 3.** Weekly active users and Usage statistics, 2021–2022

Evaluation of the project success factors shows that most of the ratings are positive on the evaluation scale (above 70%) indicating that the client is receiving a quality service and product that meets their organization's needs (Table 2).

Although the project is generally successful, there are also noticeable areas for improvement and shortcomings that need to be analyzed in more detail and addressed before they reach the critical threshold. None of the evaluation factors for this project have received a score lower than 70%, which does not indicate any critical issues that need to be addressed urgently. The highest risk factor in this project is the System Quality Factor, which has a 72% completion rate due to indicators S4 System Quality and S7 Data Processing speed. A reason for that are detected Report Execution errors in system (0.46%) that are higher than average for other accounts on the same server (0.23%). The average execution time is 3.8 s for the company and 1.05 s for other accounts. This topic needs investigation to understand if the user has built reports that are hard to process or heavy calculations.

**Table 2.** Evaluation of the Kenfield project with model and method

| Factor/Indicator | Points | % | Comments/Risks |
|---|---|---|---|
| **System** | 5.4/7 | 77% | |
| Data Quality | 1.8/2 | 90% | Could improve Layouts |
| System Quality | 3.6/5 | 72% | Report execution speed below the average, needs investigation (S4 & S7) |
| **Service Provider** | 7/8 | 88% | |
| Service Quality | 3.8/4 | 95% | |
| Methodology | 3.2/4 | 80% | Require more training |
| **Organizational** | 9/11 | 91% | |
| Alignment with Strategy | 2.4/3 | 80% | Could improve dashboard KPI choice |
| Readiness for BIS | 3.6/4 | 90% | |
| Implementation depth | 4/4 | 100% | BI tool used for management and sales representatives, used for decision making and motivation |
| TOTAL | 21.4/26 | 82% | |

Recommendations for Kenfield Ltd BIS project improvement and stabilization are 1) investigate slow report and measurement loading and improve algorithms, 2) investigate error notifications and address their root causes, and 3) strengthen data literacy skills within the customer team through training.

## 4.2 Failed Project Evaluation

The failed project is a project whose implementation has been stopped or BI system usage ends less than 2 years after the project implementation initiation. The analysis of unsuccessful projects is no different from the analysis of successful ones, except that the process is retrospective and there is no option to change the result. Still, it is very valuable for the project team to analyze mistakes to avoid them in future. The success model is used in a reverse mode – starting from analyzing usage statistics and then looking for critical points and events during the implementation that could have fostered the failure. Detailed analysis of all available records (e.g., conversations, emails, project team's and customer feedback) is conducted.

The company analysed is a Gas station chain having 8 stores at five locations. The project was implemented in 2021–2022. The main focus was on operational dashboards to monitor sales KPIs and stock management reports. To understand the project progression, Report Executions and Active users KPIs were analyzed (Fig. 4).

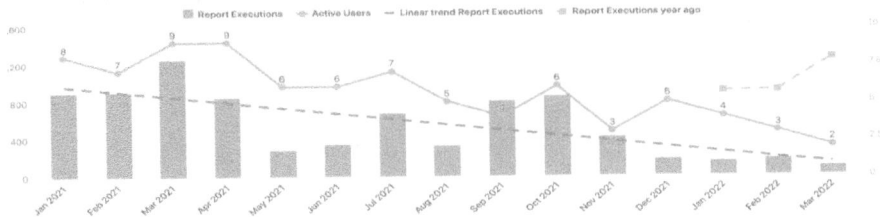

**Fig. 4.** Usage statistics with trend for Gas station Chain

From Usage statistics trend we can see that BIS usage decreased in Dec 2021 and until Mar 2022 there were only 2 users left who were running couple of reports. During the evaluation of this project according to the BISIS model, most critical indicators and relations were found that lead to BI project failure (Table 3 and Fig. 5). This project was the most affected by Organizational factors O2, O4, O8, but some System issues were also present. Two factors were identified as the most critical - S2 and O4. Net benefits could not be achieved due to incomplete data, that was technically not possible to display due to customer partially switching the ERP software and constant changes in project scope, due to fast growing company that was identified as organization "Go-go phase" in the Adizes methodology. In this particular situation Service provider was not able to affect the result in any way and no recommendations can be done to improve project success. Due to the reasons mentioned, there was no Intend to use the system.

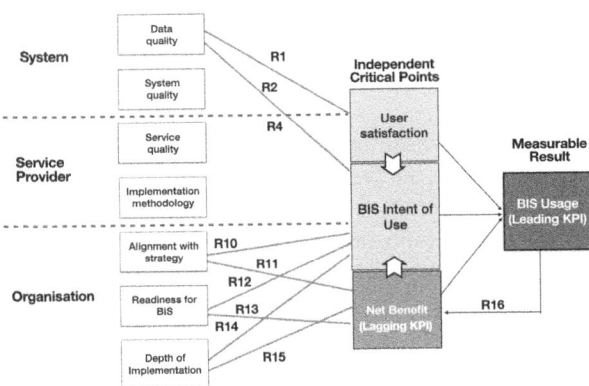

**Fig. 5.** Most important relations for unsuccessful Gas station chain project.

**Table 3.** Evaluation of Gas Station Chain project

| Factor/ Indicator | Points | % | Comments of Indicators |
|---|---|---|---|
| **System** | 4.4/7 | 62% | |
| Information Quality | 0.8/2 | 40% | S1 - long table layouts, hard to use<br>**S2 - received data is incomplete** |
| System Quality | 3.6/5 | 70% | S4 - Delay in bugfix deployment, S6 - not all desired features available in BIS. |
| **Service Provider** | 5.8/8 | 73% | |
| Service Quality | 3/4 | 75% | I4 - Delay in minor deployment |
| Methodology | 2.8/4 | 70% | I6 - Agile Iteration method not suitable for customer. Conflict of expectations<br>I8- Data literacy could be improved |
| **Organizational** | 5.4/11 | 49% | |
| Alignment with Strategy | 1.4/3 | 47% | O2 - No management Accept, used only for Operations team,<br>O3- Expectations about BIS tasks are not clear |
| Readiness for BIS | 1.4/4 | 35% | O4 - Critical Indicator, Constant Changes in data structures, requirements and company structure in general,<br>O6 - not enough budget for BIS project |
| Implementation depth | 2.6/4 | 65% | O8 - In parallel of BIS, reporting is done in XLS sheets, due to management requests |
| **TOTAL** | 15.6/ 26 | 60% | O11 - only for Operations team, Management not involved |

## 5 Conclusions

The information systems success model has been applied to study implementation of the self-service business intelligence solution. The model is proposed as a project management tool allowing to continuously monitor and improve the project implementation. The tangible KPIs are used to quantify net benefits achieved in the project. It is particularly important because the Service provider often is not involved in many activities and serves the role or a guide or observer. The service provider aims for at least 70% of the success points to consider the project successful. The two projects explored in detail show clear correlation among the usage KPI and the factors considered in the success model. The usage KPIs also should be considered in the organizational context depending on the way BI is used, e.g., either for strategic or operational purposes.

The findings confirm that strategic alignment and data quality are typical success factors for BI projects. Additionally, it is determined that user training and development of in-house expertise and sense of ownership is critical. However, one of the most critical aspects is organisation's maturity. If a company is not in a sufficiently stable mode of operation, BI implementation projects are prone to failure. That is a particular problem for many SMEs. In the analyzed project set, two companies were failing even 3 times in a row, meaning that they started to use BI tool, but could not stick to this habit again and again. THE Even those Net Benefits were reported as present, but their data literacy skills, company data policy and personal habits were not supportive for adopting the new tool.

One of the most important limitations of this work is that the observations are drawn from implementations of one specific self-service business intelligence tool.

## References

1. Alpar, P., Schulz, M.: Self-service business intelligence, business and information. Syst. Eng. **58**(2), 151–155 (2016)
2. Michalczyk, S. Nadj, M., Azarfar, D., Maedche, A., Gröger, C.: A state-of-the-art overview and future research avenues of self-service business intelligence and analytics. In: Proceedings of the 28th European Conference on Information Systems (ECIS), An Online AIS Conference, 15–17 June (2020)
3. Ain, N., Vaia, G., DeLone, W.H., Waheed, M.: Two decades of research on business intelligence system adoption, utilization and success – a systematic literature review. Decis. Supp. Syst. 125 (2019)
4. Larson, D., Chang, V.: A review and future direction of agile, business intelligence, analytics and data science. Int. J. Inf. Manage. **36**(5), 700–710 (2016)
5. Krey, M., Soriano Ramirez, M., Christen, M., Candreia, J.: Development of a model for the implementation of business intelligence in SMEs. In: ACM International Conference Proceeding Series, p. 61 (2022)
6. Bordeleau, F., Mosconi, E., de Santa-Eulalia, L.A.: Business intelligence and analytics value creation in Industry 4.0: a multiple case study in manufacturing medium enterprises. Prod. Plan. Control **31**(2–3), 173–185 (2020)
7. Spruit, M., Vroon, R., Batenburg, R.: Towards healthcare business intelligence in long-term care: an explorative case study in the Netherlands. Comput. Hum. Behav. **30**, 698–707 (2014)
8. Hawking, P., Sellitto, C.: Business intelligence strategy: a utilities company case study. Int. J. Enterp. Inf. Syst. **11**(1), 1–12 (2015)
9. Grytz, R., Krohn-Grimberghe, A., Müller, O.: Business intelligence, analytics cost accounting: an action design research approach. In: Proceedings of the 28th European Conference on Information Systems (ECIS), An Online AIS Conference, 15–17 June (2020)
10. Yeoh, W., Popovič, A.: Extending the understanding of critical success factors for implementing business intelligence systems. J. Am. Soc. Inf. Sci. **67**(1), 134–147 (2016)
11. El-Adaileh, N.A., Foster, S.: Successful business intelligence implementation: a systematic literature review. J. Work-Appl. Manag. **11**(2), 121–132 (2019)
12. Azeroual, O., Theel, H.: The effects of using business intelligence systems on an excellence management and decision-making process by start-up companies: a case study. Int. J. Manag. Sci. Bus. Admin. **4**(3), 30–40 (2018)
13. Williams, R.A., Sheikh, N.J., Duman, G.M., Kongar, E.: Critical success factors of business intelligence systems implementation. IEEE Eng. Manage. Rev. **50**(4), 88–97 (2022)
14. Shapouri, F., Najjar, L.: Critical success factors in implementing business intelligence systems. In: 26th Americas Conference on Information Systems, AMCIS (2020)

15. Gaardboe, R., Svarre, T.: Critical factors for business intelligence success. In: Proceedings of the 25th European Conference on Information Systems (ECIS 2017), vol. 471 (2017)
16. Dinter, B., Schieder, C., Gluchowski, P.: Towards a life cycle oriented business intelligence success model. In: 17th Americas Conference on Information Systems, AMCIS (2011)
17. Bach, M.P., Čeljo, A., Zoroja, J.: Technology acceptance model for business intelligence systems: preliminary research. In: Procedia Computer Science, p. 995 (2016)
18. Gonzales, R., Wareham, J.: Analysing the impact of a business intelligence system and new conceptualizations of system use. J. Econ. Financ. Admin. Sci. **24**(48), 345–368 (2019)
19. Popovič, A., Hackney, R., Coelho, P.S., Jaklič, J.: Towards business intelligence systems success: effects of maturity and culture on analytical decision making. Decis. Support Syst. **54**(1), 729–739 (2012)
20. Lennerholt, C., Van Laere, J., Söderström, E.: User-related challenges of self-service business intelligence. Inf. Syst. Manag. **38**(4), 309–323 (2021)
21. Berndtsson, M., Lennerholt, C., Svahn, T., Larsson, P.: 13 organizations' attempts to become data-driven. Int. J. Bus. Intell. Res. **11**(1), 1–21 (2020)
22. DeLone, W.H., McLean, E.R.: The DeLone and McLean model of information systems success: a ten-year update. J. Manag. Inf. Syst. **19**(4), 9–30 (2003)
23. Cartledge, A.: Business Intelligence Trends 2020 (2020). https://wiiisdom.com/ebook/business-intelligence-trends-2020/
24. Adiz, I.: The Pursuit of Prime: Maximize Your Company's Success with the Adizes Program. UNKNO (1996)
25. Capone, M. The Data Literacy Index (2018). https://www.qlik.com/us/-/media/files/resource-library/global-us/register/analyst-reports/ar-the-data-literacy-index-en.pdf
26. Muntean, M., Surcel, T.: Agile BI – the future of BI. Inform. Econ. **17**(3), 114–124 (2013)
27. Mihăiloaie, C.: KPIs. How Many Types Are There? (2021). https://www.performancemagazine.org/kpis-how-many-types-arethere/

# Business and Information Systems Development

# Incorporating Ethical Aspects in Information Systems Requirements Engineering

Olga Levina(✉)

Brandenburg University of Applied Sciences, Brandenburg an Der Havel, Germany
`levina@th-brandenburg.de`

**Abstract.** Ethical considerations in software requirements engineering are a critical but often overlooked aspect of the software development process. However, requests for transparency and autonomy in the way IT artefacts are designed, described, used, applied and integrated in the everyday life are getting more pressing within the society. In this research, the process of software engineering is taken as an illustrative model for the proactive incorporation of ethical principles in the system design within the design of a software artefact. Specifically, the phase of requirements elicitation and analysis are expanded with ethical aspects, since that is where the first steps of the software construction as an artefact are initiated and the first common ground of understanding is achieved. Being rooted in the security engineering, the SQUARE process is expanded to provide a basic structure for incorporating of ethical aspects into software design. By doing so, the social and moral values become central to the design and development of new technologies.

**Keywords:** System design · ethics · value-oriented design · requirements engineering

## 1 Introduction

The spread of information technology (IT) and its usage in the different and multiple realms of the everyday life, leads to the growing impact these technologies have on our society and behavior. Thus, ethical issues arise that put pressure on the values and highlight the responsibility of the actors in the IT domain. While ethical and value-oriented approaches for IT design have been emerging since decades, the call for the integration of the ethical values is getting louder [1–4]. While the public discussions are mostly focused on web technologies and applications, because of their widely visible privacy and copyright issues, focusing on information systems (IS) design allows a more general approach. In Information Systems Research (ISR) in general and specifically in computer science, the growth of design methods such as agile software development attempts a closer integration of different stakeholders—and their values—into developments of digital systems. At the same time, it seems that the gap between the presence of ethical issues in digital space and their incorporation into the IT artefacts is not yet receiving the attention that it deserves. To become part of the information systems in a meaningful way, the core ethical values such as the right to privacy need to be translated into the technical realm of the IT artefact, applied and specified at a concrete level in order to be used as functional requirements for the systems that are being constructed [5].

Therefore, this paper focuses on the phase of requirements engineering (RE) of the information system design. RE plays a vital role in IS design as a traditional software engineering process. Requirements are the ground stone of the system design and development since they describe what it is to be done. Therefore, they need to be complete, consistent and relevant. In this paper, it is suggested that ethical issues are part of the relevance and completeness dimension, since they define the acceptance and use of the artefact. It is also argued that the artefact usage needs to be considered at the requirements analysis stage, since ethical IT research points out that the ethical questions arise not necessarily from within the artefact, but as effects of its usage [6], as IT makes it easier to obtain "richer" information that might trigger unethical actions. Therefore, conducting a thorough RE focused on ethical issues might help to anticipate the potential negative effects and more on the practical side, additional costs. The goal of this paper is to present and discuss an approach for integrating ethical aspects in the first stages of the software or artefact development process, potentially proactively reducing the negative effects of its use and the follow up financial effect. By integrating ethics into the first stages of the design, we follow the call for more ethical consideration in ISR by [7]. After a brief introduction into the requirements engineering process, specifically into the elicitation and analysis phases, state of the art on the current research aimed to incorporate ethics and moral values into IS research is reviewed. The approach is discussed, while the conclusion also provides an outlook on future work finishing the paper.

## 2 Implementing Values into Requirements Engineering in Information Systems Context

In this section an overview of the state of the art in the ethical analysis and value-based requirements engineering techniques is presented. The insights provide the input for the development of the process for including ethical analysis in the process of requirements engineering for information system design in the following section.

### 2.1 Requirements Engineering

For IT artefact design, the process of RE is structured along the stages of: problem definition, system analysis, requirements engineering, development, deployment and evaluation (see e.g. [8]). The advantage of incorporating the analysis of ethical aspects in the RE phase is that the later in this process a problem or a mistake is spotted, the pricier it is to correct it [9]. Therefore, to reduce the potential for mistakes and to increase the satisfaction and acceptance of an artefact, the requirements engineering phase provides a suitable staring point. The requirements engineering process is divided in five main activities [10]: elicitation, analysis, negotiation, documentation, validation and management. An essential step before the elicitation of requirements is the identification of (future) stakeholders. This step is also crucial when defining values and ethical dilemmas, since the different stakeholders have different views on the use and nature of the artefact. The goal of requirements elicitation is to discover the requirements and system boundaries, i.e. the application domain, system constrains, application context, etc., by interacting with the stakeholders, e.g. potential users, clients, developers, etc. With the rise of the Internet technology, not only the software but also the generated and processed data came into the focus of IS design. Due to this fact, development approaches for the implementation of non-functional IS features such as security have been developed and implemented into the practice.

One of the popular approaches to consider security in the requirements elicitation and analysis is the Security Quality Requirements Engineering (SQUARE) [11] approach. It provides a means for eliciting, categorizing, and prioritizing security requirements for IT systems and applications. The focus of this methodology is to build security concepts into the early stages of the development lifecycle. This approach is chosen here as a foundation for further development, since security can be considered as an aspect of the ethical dimension of privacy, thus providing comparable characteristics that can be handled similarly during the elicitation and analysis phases. Based on these existing techniques, the approach to incorporate ethical aspects into the requirements analysis is set in the requirements elicitation and analysis phase, includes negotiation based on categorization, and applies use case models as a canvas for discussion.

## 2.2 Ethical Analysis in Information Systems Research

Ethical considerations in Software Engineering have also been raised by [12] with the argument that software process is a social process with the highest ethical concern that all the participants are treated fairly. The authors suggest applying this theory to determine fairness within the management of software process, from creation to daily use. The suggested reason is that software differs from other (tangible) products, as the errors may remain even after rigorous testing due to the structural complexity. Additionally, software is available to a large amount of people, thus influencing their behavior and providing a larger potential for risk spreading. Therefore, the authors suggest a number of moral obligations for software users, buyers and providers.

This considerations follow [13], who suggested four issues that pose a threat to human dignity in the IT context: privacy, i.e., what information can be asked for, accuracy (e.g., authenticity, fidelity and correctness of processed data), access (e.g., security, costs, changeability), and property. These issues have been picked up by other researchers and were extended to provide more detailed view on the ethical problem, e.g., [14, 15].

On the level of the IT artefact design, one approach stands out. Value- Sensitive Design (VSD) by [16] is one of the first and the more elaborated approaches that aim at integrating ethical considerations as value requirements into IS development. It has been defined as a theoretically grounded approach to the design of technology that accounts for human values in a principled and comprehensive manner throughout the design process. Three phases, called investigations, are part of the VSD process: conceptual, empirical and technical. While considering several aspects of the IT artefact and its context, VSD heavily relies on the identification of stakeholders and seeks to find empirical results on values, not only on functions. While stakeholders provide important insights on potential use and effects of the artefact, they also provide values that reflect their current views. Therefore, the elicited requirements might be prone to vast changes due to potential cultural or temporal value changes within a stakeholder group.

Value-Based Software Engineering [17] focuses on the inclusion of the people-orientation into software design. Using value-based requirements engineering it elicits values from success-critical stakeholders with respect to the system, resulting in prioritization as well as identification techniques. Therefore, the people-orientation is concentrated on a specific stakeholder group neglecting a broader view on the social and ethical context. [18] suggest how to meld existing software development methodologies with the ethical considerations. They demonstrate the potential on privacy sensitive topics such as UK health card. With the rise of the ubiquitous technology, specifically in the context of Internet of Things (IoT), questions about the generated data have become the topic of sociological dispute [19]. Here, the goal is to create devices that allow users to choose their own values as a matter of moral entitlement. [6] also suggest creating ethical designs as being built to empower and entitle users to frame their ethical choices. Meaning, that the final settings of the device communication and information exchange are decided by the user in turn requiring a good understanding of technology.

To address ethical issues, one technique is to conduct an ethical analysis. Ethical analysis is a tool that can be used to cut through the myriad of different aspects to get to the center of potential requirements, presenting it in a manner facilitating an overview. It is an instrument that would be used after the feasibility analysis, but before further analytic activities such as financial and temporal analysis. The concept of ethical analysis is used in different fields such as medical ethics [20] and business ethics, e.g. [21]. Ethical analysis can be performed as a method for seeking potential ethical issues in the construction or usage of the IT artefact as well as seeking the common ground in case a sustainable resolution of a dilemma is needed. Although, ethical analysis is conducted to solve ethical dilemmas, the method is often not expounded. The [21] process is one of the exception and is adapted here, since it also focuses on stakeholders and includes potential legal restrictions.

While engineers of business software have to take several decisions that concern business outcome and customer treatment, the values that are addressed originate from the business context. Nevertheless, the stakeholder that provide their requirements as well as the engineers that realize these requirements influence the values and decision outcomes that are involved in the realization of the software. To stress the importance of the role of software engineers in designing socially-aware information system [14], several ethical guidelines, especially in the context of ML-based software development, were issued on the policy level [6]. The emergence of the multiple guidelines for ML-based software development that originate in political institutions and firms position the reference for ethical decisions in the software development context onto the society. This development indicates that software products are increasingly being considered as being influential towards social behavior that can also be mapped onto the (non-ML-based) business software, evoking the stakeholder theory [22] for the businesses to not induce any harm to the individuals and organizations influenced by their actions.

Agile Worth-Oriented Systems Engineering (AWOSE) [23] is an approach to incorporating ethically relevant criteria during agile development processes of cyber-physical systems. It supports the assessment of society-level concerns related to public accountability. Nevertheless, it focuses on customer requirements, thus putting a less emphasis on the norms and values of other stakeholder groups.

For the inclusion of legal issues into the software requirements Aberkane et al. [24] identified possibilities for introducing natural language processing (NLP) techniques to automate manual requirements engineering tasks in the crossing of General Data Protection Regulation (GDPR) and engineering tasks, in addition to possibilities of using NLP-based machine learning techniques to achieve GDPR-compliance in engineering tasks. Nevertheless, automated solutions for this issue are yet to be developed.

Biable et al. [25] identified in their research an absence of industry practices, professional responsibility code of conduct standards, and other guidelines within companies when integrating ethical concerns of software during requirements engineering.

Following the implication of the reviewed related works, the suggested approach provides a pragmatic process to include values and ethical considerations into the existing software development process.

## 3 Towards Introducing Ethical Analysis into Requirements Engineering

The research cited above, takes different routes towards incorporating ethical or general values into an IT artefact through the engineering process. It shows that a thorough stakeholder analysis and user focus are essential in building an artefact that will consider general values. The approach suggested here is located in the phase of requirements elicitation, analysis and negotiation stages to serve as a proactive measure towards incorporating values into the design process from the beginning, and thus reducing the additional costs of potential inaccuracies. The suggested process of ethical requirements elicitation is shown in Fig. 1. Albeit the figure showing a linear process, feedback loops and iterations are expected to appear along the phases.

The suggested approach is based on the classic requirement analysis and prioritization processes, on the ethical analysis process as well as the SQUARE process. It is suggested to evaluate the use cases using the classical criteria but also applying the moral values of the actual features as well as of the potential effects of the future artefact use. Requirements are collected following the stakeholder analysis resulting in a list that is completed with use case diagrams and scenarios. For the requirements elicitation, stakeholders with knowledge of legal issues as well as corporate responsibility representatives should be present, aside from the internal, i.e., employee, and if applicable external, i.e., company's customer, users. It is suggested to consider the future information system as well as the context it will operate in as a starting point for the identification of potential ethical issues incorporated into the design. This might include the factors of integration into the present enterprise architecture as well as the integration potential with the application architecture. Therefore, the elicitation phase results in a set of requirements that were collected with a potentially broad scope not only on functionality but also on ethical implications and effects.

The first step of the analysis is to identify the requirements in terms of their importance to the actual result, i.e., functioning of the artefact, their importance to the stakeholders as well as their potential legal restrictions on the elicited functionality. The requirements that have been identified as important are then evaluated towards their feasibility in terms of technical realization. Before budget and scheduling constrains are

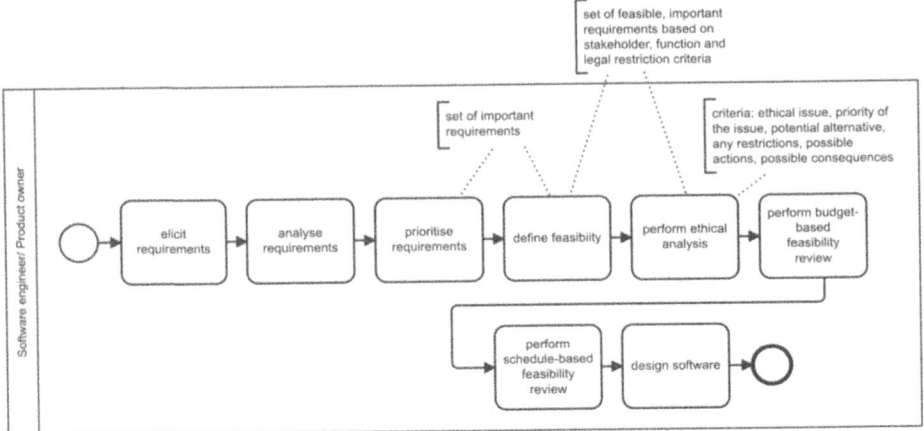

**Fig. 1.** Suggested requirement elicitation and analysis process

cited, it is suggested including ethical analysis of the most important feasible requirements that have been identified. The ethical analysis is performed in stages (see Fig. 2). First, the requirements are analyzed towards their potential reference to any of the ethical issue categories as defined by [13]: privacy, accuracy, access and property.

In corporate context these categories can be detailed with such aspects as accountability, liability (e.g., for data quality or system errors, reliability, etc.) and control.

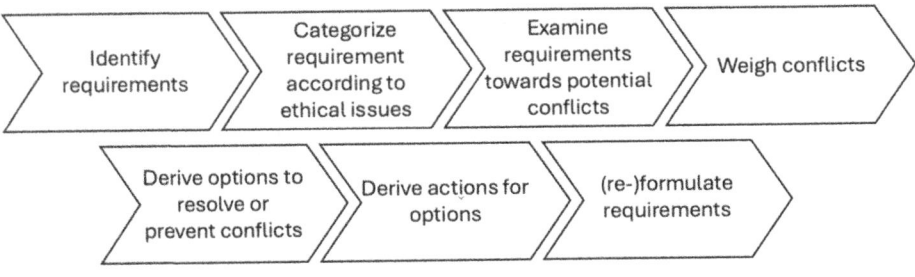

**Fig. 2.** Ethical analysis for the suggested approach

That is, potential ethical issues are identified for any of the stakeholder groups. Here, discussion groups or workshops can be used to perform the analysis and classification. A presence of a legal expert is very useful at this stage. Also, attention should be payed to the atmosphere in these groups. The open discussion methods bear the potential to disclose different or conflicting views on what is considered morally good or acceptable by different persons, potentially leading to a shift in communication patterns.

Each use case is now examined towards the ethical conflict that could be triggered by its deployment. These potential conflicts are then weighed according to their importance for the stakeholder group of the use case. The weighing of the conflict is conducted according to its consequence. For the evaluation of the conflicts, procedure inspired by the SQUARE process is adopted. The conflicts within the use cases are weighed using qualitative rankings: Pestilent (P), Conditional (C) and Minor (M). Conflicts are marked as "Pestilent" when the artefact becomes unacceptable in case this conflict is realized, resulting in e.g., in contradiction of the enterprise culture, general values or legal restrictions. "Conditional" conflict does not impair with functionality or legal aspects of the artefact, although its absence might reduce the acceptance of the artefact use or the effects of the use might be perceived as questionable by one or more stakeholder groups. "Minor" conflicts have clearly lower priority than "Pestilent" and "Conditional" conflicts. Potential options of how to contain the conflicts in ethically relevant use cases are discussed and negotiated. Then accordant actions are derived. According to the consequences of the actions, an option can be selected to address the ethical issue. In the case of where no acceptable option can be selected, the realization of the requirement needs to be negotiated, before being summarized as requirements. These are then discussed on the budgeting and scheduling level and transferred to the system development step.

## 4 Discussion and Outlook

This research in progress suggests that including the ethical values during the elicitation and prioritization process of the artefact requirements lays a cornerstone for further, sensitive design and use, as well as containing the effects of potential misuse. The approach presented here, builds upon known requirement analysis techniques, but enriches them with moral-oriented context. Taking a closer look at the ethical issues in IS designs via the requirements analysis reveals that the identified questions are not necessarily IS specific but keep going back to the general ethical issues such as personal rights (dignity, privacy, etc.) as well as legally established issues, such as using IS for performance evaluation, surveillance of digital activities during the working time. Nevertheless, these issues and their treatment should be carefully considered and realigned for the context of IS development. Ethical issues need to be considered in order to guide decision taking during requirements evaluation and requirements incorporation for a creation of a socially responsible artefact. It is important to identify the critical issues already in early stages of the artefact design. Their negligence can lead to ethical or at least ethically questionable behavior. Although, the legal restrictions are catching up with the pace of digitalization, the two domains still have significantly different velocities. Looking at the ethical issues identified by Mason, privacy has gotten a larger focus from the policy makers followed by the property issues so far. Accuracy and access, on the other hand are still to follow.

The obvious next step regarding future research will be to apply the analysis within an actual software or IT artefact development process, subsequently translate ethical issues into technical requirements as well as work towards a measure for its social performance. The application will be documented and evaluated to accommodate restrictions in enterprise software development projects.

## References

1. Harrison, M.I., Koppel, R., Bar-Lev, S.: Unintended consequences of information technologies in health care—an interactive sociotechnical analysis. J. Am. Med. Inform. Assoc. **14**(5), 542–549 (2007)
2. Majchrzak, A., Markus, M.L.: Methods for Policy Research: Taking Socially Responsible Action. SAGE Publications, Thousand Oaks, CA (2013)
3. Hein, A., Schreieck, M., Wiesche, M., Krcmar, H.: Multiple-case analysis on governance mechanisms of multi-sided platforms methods to master heterogeneity in IT service value networks. In: Mkwi, pp. 1613–1614 (2016)
4. Ann Majchrzak, M., Markus, L., Wareham, J.: Designing for digital transformation: Lessons for information systems research from the study of ICT and societal challenges. MIS Q. **40**(2), 267–277 (2016). https://doi.org/10.25300/MISQ/2016/40:2.03
5. Mahieu, R., van Eck, N.J., van Putten, D., van den Hoven, J.: From dignity to security protocols: a scientometric analysis of digital ethics. Ethics Inf. Technol. **20**(3), 175–187 (2018). https://doi.org/10.1007/s10676-018-9457-5
6. Baldini, G., Botterman, M., Neisse, R., Tallacchini, M.: Ethical design in the internet of things. Sci. Eng. Ethics **24**(3), 905–925 (2018). https://doi.org/10.1007/s11948-016-9754-5
7. Myers, M., Venable, J.R.: A set of ethical principles for design science research in information systems. Manag. Past Present Future **51**(6), 801–809 (2014). https://doi.org/10.1016/j.im.2014.01.002
8. Peffers, K., Tuunanen, T., Rothenberger, M.A., Chatterjee, S.: A design science research methodology for information systems research. J. Manag. Inf. Syst. **24**(3), 45–77 (2007). https://doi.org/10.2753/MIS0742-1222240302
9. Beck, K.: Extreme Programming Explained. Addison-Wesley Professional (1999)
10. Kotonya, G., Sommerville, I.: Requirements engineering with viewpoints. Softw. Eng. J. **11**(1), 5–18 (1996)
11. Mead, N.R.: System Quality Requirements Engineering (SQUARE) Process. Carnegie Mellon University (2013)
12. Collins, W.R., Miller, K.W., Spielman, B.J., Wherry, P.: How good is good enough?: an ethical analysis of software construction and use. Commun. ACM **37**(1), 81–91 (1994). https://doi.org/10.1145/175222.175229
13. Mason, R.O.: Four ethical issues of the information age. Comput. Ethics **10**, 41–48 (1986). https://doi.org/10.4324/9781315259697-8
14. Davis, M.: Part of: thinking like an engineer: the place of a code of ethics in the practice of a profession. Philos. Public Affair **20**(2), 150–167 (1991)
15. Floridi, L.: Information ethics- On the philosophical foundation of computer ethics. Ethics Inf. Technol. **1**, 37–56 (1999)
16. Friedman, A., Kahn, B., Borning, P.: Value Sensitive Design: Theory and Methods. University of Washington (2002)
17. Boehm, B.W.: Value-based software engineering: overview and agenda. In: Biffl, S., Aurum, A., Boehm, B., Erdogmus, H., Grünbacher, P. (eds.) Value-Based Software Engineering, pp. 3–14. Springer Berlin Heidelberg, Berlin, Heidelberg (2006). https://doi.org/10.1007/3-540-29263-2_1
18. Mingers, J., Walsham, G.: Towards ethical information systems: the contribution of discourse ethics. MIS Q. **34**(4), 833–854 (2010)
19. J. Happa, J. Nurse, M. Goldsmith, S. Creese, und R. Williams, „An Ethics Framework for Research into Heterogeneous Systems", 2018
20. Roberts, M.J., Reich, M.R.: Ethical analysis in public health. Lancet **359**, 1055–1059 (2002). https://doi.org/10.1016/j.forpol.2009.07.003

21. Hartman, L.P.: Perspectives in Business Ethics. McGraw Hill (2005)
22. Donaldson, T., Preston, L.E.: The stakeholder theory of the corporation: concepts, evidence, and implications. Acad. Manage. Rev. **20**(1), 65–91 (1995). https://doi.org/10.2307/258887
23. Strenge, B., Schack, T.: AWOSE - a process model for incorporating ethical analyses in agile systems engineering. Sci. Eng. Ethics **26**(2), 851–870 (2020). https://doi.org/10.1007/s11948-019-00133-z
24. Aberkane, A.-J., Poels, G., Broucke, S.V.: Exploring automated GDPR-compliance in requirements engineering: a systematic mapping study. IEEE Access **9**, 66542–66559 (2021). https://doi.org/10.1109/ACCESS.2021.3076921
25. Biable, S.E., Garcia, N.M., Midekso, D., Pombo, N.: Ethical issues in software requirements engineering. Software **1**(1), 31–52 (2022). https://doi.org/10.3390/software1010003

# Suitability of Business Process Modeling Methods for Requirements Elicitation

Liene Ieva Kraupša[✉] and Marite Kirikova[iD]

Institute of Applied Computer Systems, Riga Technical University, 6A Kipsalas Street, Riga 1048, Latvia
liene-ieva.kraupsa@edu.rtu.lv, marite.kirikova@rtu.lv

**Abstract.** Accurate identification and documentation of requirements for software development is fundamental to successful project implementation. Business process models help to clearly define and document the steps involved in a process, providing an opportunity to use the models for deriving system requirements. Thus, selecting appropriate business process modeling methods or languages for requirements identification can significantly impact the quality of the final software product. The purpose of this paper is to examine several business process modeling languages with the purpose of showing and comparing their potential to help derive functional and non-functional software requirements out of business process models.

**Keywords:** Business Process · Business Process Modeling Languages · BPMN · EPC · UML-AD

## 1 Introduction

Business process modeling is used for structuring, understanding, and improving processes in organizations. Business process models can also be used to derive system requirements for information systems supporting these business processes [1–4]. Using business process models efficiently may save time during requirements gathering and improve the quality of system requirements.

Business process models help clearly define and document the steps involved in the process [5–11], providing an opportunity to use these models for deriving system requirements. Deriving system requirements from business process models involves identifying the information, resources, and actions needed to support the process and specifying these requirements in a form that can be used to guide the development of supporting systems or applications [1].

This paper seeks the answer to the question what is the extent to which different business process modeling languages can be used to derive software requirements.

In the ever-evolving landscape of software development, precisely identifying requirements is a cornerstone of project success. To move toward the answer to the stated research question, the goal of this paper is to see whether the possibilities to derive the requirements depend on the type of business process modeling language. To achieve this goal, the following tasks are set:

- review existing literature on requirements engineering, business process modeling languages/methods, and best practices in method selection;
- compile a comprehensive list of business process modeling languages/methods commonly used in requirements engineering;
- analyze the suitability of identified business process modeling languages/methods for requirements identification.

The paper is structured as follows. The background of the research is discussed in Sect. 2. The analysis of business process modeling languages/methods is performed in Sect. 3. Section 4 provides a brief discussion, and Sect. 5 presents concluding remarks.

## 2 Background

In this section, we discuss the two basic areas that are analyzed further in the next section. These areas are (1) requirements engineering standards and (2) business process modeling approaches.

### 2.1 On Requirements Engineering Standards

To choose the criteria for analyzing the requirements elicitation potential of business process modeling languages, we first analyzed several professional standards such as ISO/IEC/IEEE 29148:2018, BABOK Guide, SWEBOK, and Volere Requirements Specification Template according to different criteria (see Table 1). The considered criteria are reflected in the rows of Table 1. The first criterion is coverage and scope concerning the software development lifecycle. The second criterion for analysis is clarity and understandability – whether the terminology and guidelines are clear and defined. The third criterion is applicability and flexibility – how practical and applicable the standard is for different types and sizes of projects. Further follow such criteria as applicability and flexibility, requirements classification availability, and standard availability.

After the review of the existing standards and guidelines for requirements elicitation, the Volere Requirements Specification Template was chosen as it provides a structured and systematic approach to requirements classification, offering clear guidelines for organizing and categorizing requirements according to various criteria such as functional vs. non-functional, user-centric vs. system-centric, and stakeholder perspectives. In addition, the Volere Requirements Specification Template is easy to use, provides clear guidance on the requirements elicitation process and documentation, and is focused on requirements discovery phase and communication with stakeholders.

The Volere functional requirements specification provides a structured approach for articulating, validating, and managing the detailed functional aspects of the product, ensuring alignment with stakeholder needs and project objectives throughout the development lifecycle [2].

According to the template, each atomic functional requirement outlined in the specification follows the structure provided in the requirements shell, ensuring consistency and completeness across all requirement types. To achieve clarity and testability, each functional requirement is accompanied by a fit criterion or test case, serving as a benchmark

**Table 1.** Comparison of professional standards for requirements elicitation.

| Criterion | ISO/IEC/IEEE 29148:2018 [16–18, 20] | BABOK Guide [13, 14, 19] | SWEBOK Guide [12, 15] | Volere Requirements Specification Template [2] |
|---|---|---|---|---|
| Coverage and Scope | Lists key engineering processes for system/software requirements across the life cycle | Guides Business Analysts for managing requirements; covers guidelines across the life cycle | Supports requirements elicitation across the software development life cycle | Designed for discovering and communicating the requirements |
| Clarity and Understandability | Provides guidelines both for the application and required format | Provides glossary and key terminology clarifications | Provides structure, terminology, and clarifications | Provides detailed guidance for each section, including content, motivation, considerations, examples, and form |
| Applicability and flexibility | Adaptable to various projects, irrespective of scope, size, or complexity | Adaptable to different contexts and projects | Adaptable to different contexts and projects | Adaptable to different contexts and projects |
| Requirements classification availability | Provides requirements classification | Provides requirements classification | Provides requirements classification guideline | Provides requirements classification |
| Accessibility | Accessible in IEEE Xplore Digital Library or by purchasing CHF 216 | Accessible with IIBA Membership; purchase USD 54.49 | Accessible for free for academic purposes in the IEEE Computer Society homepage | Accessible for free for academic purposes; purchase USD 55 |

for objective evaluation during testing. Considerations for deriving functional requirements include leveraging event/use case lists to trigger requirements and ensuring traceability by grouping requirements into related event/use case categories. The relevant aspects of functional requirements according to the Volere Requirements Specification Template are described in Fig. 1.

The Volere non-functional requirements categories are shown in Fig. 2.

Suitability of Business Process Modeling Methods     165

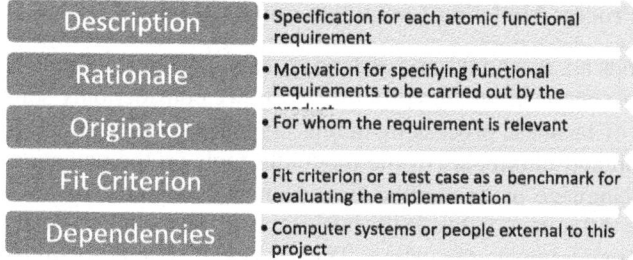

**Fig. 1.** Functional requirements aspects according to Volere Requirements Specification Template [2].

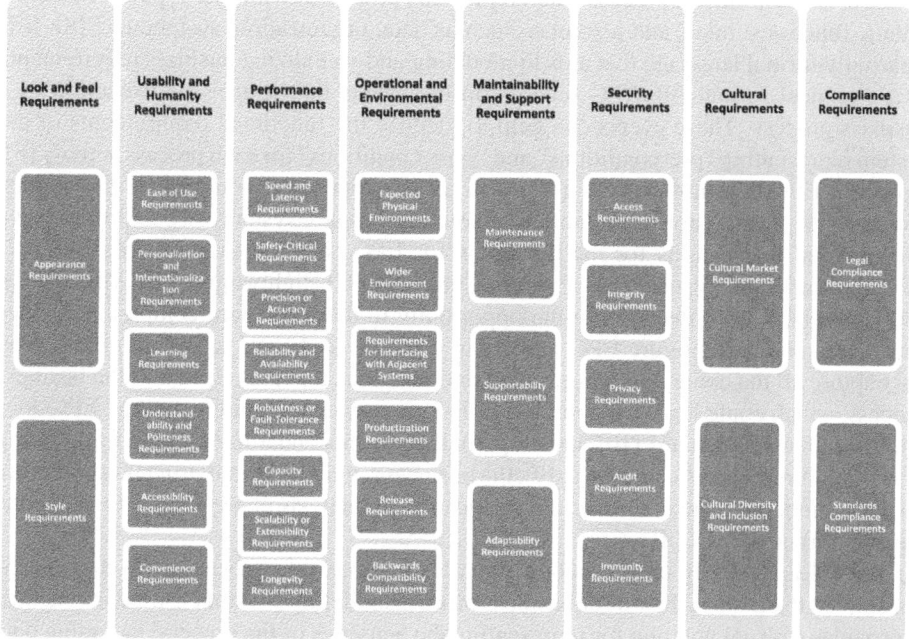

**Fig. 2.** Non-functional requirements categorization according to the Volere Requirements Specification Template [2].

The non-functional requirements listed by Volere encompass various aspects ensuring the usability, performance, operability, security, and compliance of a software system [2].

The elements from Fig. 1 and Fig. 2 will be further used to analyze different business process modeling languages.

## 2.2 Business Process Modeling Languages and Methods

Modeling methods are essential for visualizing, analyzing, and communicating requirements in software engineering [3, 4]. In this work, we consider only some of the most used variations of business process modeling languages, being aware of the vastness of their spectrum and the impact of the modeling tools on the potential or usefulness of a particular language or its modification. Our modest aim is to see whether there are considerable differences between the business process modeling languages/methods with respect to requirements elicitation. This knowledge would help to select further modeling methods for their analysis.

We consider the list of three languages/methods: BPMN, EPC, and UML-AD, as they are widely used and well-established business process modeling notations [5–7].

EPC or event-driven process chain represents processes with four types of objects – events, functions, rules, and resources such as data, organization, system, etc. [8]. It is a partially formal language that aids in modeling and visualizing business requirements in a graphical format [9]. EPC focuses on the events that trigger the execution of a business process. These events can help to identify the functional requirements of the system representing "pre-conditions" and "post-conditions" for each process activity [8]. However, EPC does not provide a lot of detail or support for modeling more complex processes, so it may not be suitable for large or complex systems [4], and there have been several suggestions for modifications for EPC, such as Configurable EPC (C-EPC), yet-another Event-driven Process Chain (yEPC), lightweight EPC (lightEPC), and CorrectEPC in order to have the opportunity to describe more complex processes and being able to configure EPC models in different tools [9]. In addition, EPC may not capture all the contextual information or constraints that are relevant to the business process, which could lead to incomplete or incorrect system requirements [9]. EPC does not have its own standard [10], creating challenges in standardized usage for eliciting system requirements. According to [9], the business requirement gathering is done before the EPC modeling, and after that, the verification or analysis phase is done to verify the business process itself [4].

BPMN is a widely used standard for modeling business processes [5] and can be considered the main standard for business process modeling [11] that is used in practice. It provides a visual notation for representing the activities of the process, including data involved in the process connecting the activities to objects and artifacts for additional information [7]. BPMN can be used to model processes at a high level of abstraction, making it suitable for eliciting system requirements. BPMN being a standard notation that is widely used, is supported by several business process modeling tools, which makes this language/method easy to use and facilitates collaboration and communication in its application. In addition, BPMN provides a rich set of symbols and constructs that can be used to model complex processes in detail, including activities, events, gateways, and data objects [5]. As one of the drawbacks of BPMN, we could mention that BPMN can be more complex than EPC or other simple notations, which may make it more difficult to learn and use [5].

UML is a general-purpose modeling language that can be used to represent a wide range of systems and processes [1]. UML consists of several different diagram types, including activity diagrams (AD), which can be applied to model business processes and elicit system requirements. UML-AD is widely used and well-known among software engineers [5]. UML-AD provides a rich set of symbols and constructs that can be applied to model complex processes in detail, including activities, events, and data objects [6]. Regarding the challenging aspects of UML-AD usage, it could be mentioned that it can be more complex than EPC or BPMN, which may make it more difficult to learn and use for some people who do not have a background in the IT domain [5].

## 3 The Analysis of the Languages/Methods

This section amalgamates the analysis results of the selected business process modeling languages/methods. As mentioned in the previous section, EPC, BPMN, and UML-AD were examined. .

The analysis was done using both the theoretical language/method descriptions and practical experiments. The experiments were done with ARIS modeling tool [21] for EPC and BPMN. For UML-AD, another business process modeling tool was used [22] as this language/method was not supported by the ARIS tool applied for EPC and BPMN. For each language/method, only one tool was used. The analysis of the impact of modeling tools on the suitability of business process modeling languages for software requirements elicitation is out of the scope of this paper. However, it must be acknowledged that slight differences in the suitability of business process modeling languages/methods might be observed when using different business process modeling tools even with the same set of available elements of notations.

The results of the analysis are amalgamated in several tables. For each business process modeling language/method, the functional requirements are first discussed, followed by the non-functional ones.

Table 2 provides an overview of the analysis of functional requirements' aspects that can be elicited from EPC model elements, as available in the ARIS [21] modeling tool.

Table 3 provides an overview of the possible use of EPC elements, as available in the ARIS [21] modeling tool, for retrieving non-functional requirements.

While EPC business process models provide valuable insights into functional requirements, their suitability for eliciting non-functional requirements is limited. However, these models can still offer some inputs for operational and environmental, security, and compliance requirements, particularly through the analysis of system interactions, organizational structures, and risk factors within the model.

Table 4 provides an overview of the analysis of functional requirements' aspects that can be elicited from BPMN elements as available in the ARIS modeling tool [21].

Table 5 provides an overview of the possible use of BPMN elements for retrieving non-functional requirements.

BPMN business process models can be a source for eliciting functional requirements for software systems. By analyzing tasks, gateways, events, lanes, and dependencies within the model, stakeholders can identify and define detailed functional requirements necessary for developing and implementing the software system. Additionally, understanding the rationale, origin, fit criteria, and dependencies associated with each requirement aids in ensuring the system meets the desired objectives and functions.

**Table 2.** Functional requirements' elicitation from EPC business process models.

| Functional requirement aspect | Possibility to elicit from an EPC model | Object(s) in EPC providing the information | Comments |
|---|---|---|---|
| Description | Yes | Function Connectors Cluster (together with entity type and attribute), Document | Functions in the EPC model represent the activities performed in the process, translating directly into functional requirements for the software system to support these activities. Connectors AND, OR, and XOR can be used as functional requirements' sources as they depict the process flow. The document can be functional requirements' input source |
| Rationale | Yes | Events, process interface | Events or process interfaces that trigger the function in EPC show the rationale for performing the specified function. Clusters can provide data-related requirements for functional requirements |
| Originator | Yes | Organizational unit, Position, Role, Internal person | Unit-related objects can indicate the origination of the functional requirement as they are the users |
| Fit criterion | Yes | Event | The event after the function indicates how the requirement shall be fulfilled |
| Dependencies | Yes | Function, events | Previously connected functions and events can show the existing dependencies for the specific function |

**Table 3.** Non-functional requirements' elicitation from EPC business process models.

| Non-functional requirement | Possibility to elicit from an EPC model | Object(s) in EPC providing the information | Comments |
|---|---|---|---|
| Look and Feel Requirements | No | – | |
| Usability and Humanity Requirements | No | – | |
| Performance Requirements | No | – | |
| Operational and Environmental Requirements | Yes | System Location | Having an interaction with several systems can provide requirements for Interfacing with Adjacent Systems. Potentially can provide Backward Compatibility requirements in case some legacy systems are used. Location objects can serve as an input for Expected Physical Environments |
| Maintainability and Support Requirements | No | – | |
| Security Requirements | Yes | Organizational unit, Position, Role, Internal person, Location | Organizational unit, Position, Role, as Internal person objects in EPC show the Access requirements. Location objects can be an input for physical access requirements |
| Cultural Requirements | No | – | |
| Compliance Requirements | Yes | Risk Location | If the risk defined in the EPC model is related to the compliance breach, then it contributes to Legal Compliance requirements. Location can serve as an input for Legal Compliance requirements, for instance, in case it is required by law to perform parts of the process in different locations |

**Table 4.** Functional requirements' elicitation from BPMN business process models.

| Functional requirement aspect | Possibility to elicit from a BPMN model | Object(s) in BPMN providing the information | Comments |
|---|---|---|---|
| Description | Yes | Task, Gateway, Subprocess, Call activity | Tasks and subprocesses in BPMN models represent specific functions to be performed, translating directly into functional requirements for the software system to support these actions. Gateways can be used as functional requirements' sources as they depict the process flow |
| Rationale | Yes | Start event, intermediate event, end event | Start, intermediate, and end events in BPMN show the rationale for performing the specified function |
| Originator | Yes | Lane | Lanes (e.g., in ARIS, Organizational unit lane, position, and role lanes) indicate the origination of the functional requirement as they depict the users |
| Fit criterion | Yes | Intermediate event, end event | Intermediate event and end event can indicate a fit criterion |
| Dependencies | Yes | Tasks, subprocess, call activity | Previously connected tasks, subprocess, and call activities before the specific task can show the existing dependencies for the specific task requirements |

**Table 5.** Non-functional requirements' elicitation from BPMN business process models.

| Non-functional requirement | Possibility to elicit from a BPMN model | Object(s) in BPMN providing the information | Comments |
|---|---|---|---|
| Look and Feel Requirements (Appearance, Style) | No | – | |
| Usability and Humanity Requirements | No | – | |
| Performance Requirements | Yes | Intermediate events with timers | Intermediate events with timers can specify the amount of time available to complete specified tasks, thus providing speed and latency requirements |
| Operational and Environmental Requirements | | Datastore, data object | Datastore and data objects' usage in the model provide requirements for Interfacing with Adjacent Systems. Potentially, we can provide backward compatibility requirements in case some legacy systems are used |
| Maintainability and Support Requirements | No | – | |
| Security Requirements | Yes | Lane | Lanes indicating involved roles in BPMN show the Access requirements |
| Cultural Requirements | No | – | |
| Compliance Requirements | No | – | |

While BPMN business process models are primarily focused on depicting the flow of business processes and activities, they can still offer some insights into certain non-functional requirements, particularly performance and security requirements. However, their suitability for eliciting other non-functional requirements such as usability, maintainability, cultural, and compliance requirements is more limited.

Table 6 provides an overview of the analysis of functional requirements' aspects that can be elicited from UML-AD elements as provided in the Sparx Systems tool Enterprise Architect [22].

UML-AD business process models can assist in eliciting functional requirements quite significantly. Even though UML-AD business process models are valuable for depicting the flow of activities within a process, they are not designed to capture or represent information related to non-functional requirements.

The features of the modeling languages discussed in this section were tested on the "handle bankruptcy process". The presentation of the test results is beyond the scope of this paper. The testing was done by Software AG ARIS Cloud tool [21] for EPC

**Table 6.** Functional requirements' elicitation from UML-AD business process models.

| Functional requirement aspect | Possibility to elicit from a UML-AD model | Object(s) in UML-AD providing the information | Comments |
|---|---|---|---|
| Description | Yes | Activity, action, decision node | Represents a specific task, operation, or action that is performed as part of the process and serves as a functional requirement |
| Rationale | Yes | Initial node, decision node | The initial node explains the rationale for performing the specified function |
| Originator | No | Lane | Lanes indicate the origination of the functional requirements as they depict the users |
| Fit criterion | Yes | Intermediate event, end event | Intermediate event and end event can indicate fit criterion |
| Dependencies | Yes | Activity, actions, decision nodes, Fork/Join Node | Previous activities, actions, and decision nodes before the specific task can show the existing dependencies for the specific task requirements |

and BPMN, and with Enterprise Architect 16.1 system trial version provided by Sparx Systems Pty Ltd. [22] for UML-AD as it was not available in ARIS Cloud tool.

## 4 Discussion

The findings of this paper suggest the following implications for both requirements engineering practitioners and researchers:

- *Selection of appropriate business process modeling languages* – practitioners should be knowledgeable regarding their choice of modeling languages based on the specific needs of their projects. For instance, BPMN's comprehensive set of symbols and constructs makes it a strong candidate for projects requiring detailed and complex process modeling. EPC's simplicity may be beneficial for high-level process documentation.
- *Consideration of requirements type (functional or non-functional)* – the paper highlights the strengths and limitations of different modeling languages/methods in capturing functional and non-functional requirements. Practitioners need to complement business process models with other techniques or tools to ensure non-functional requirements are adequately captured. For instance, EPC and BPMN can provide insights into certain non-functional requirements. However, additional methods are needed to address non-functional requirements more thoroughly.

Given the varying capabilities of different modeling tools, practitioners should select tools that best support the chosen modeling language and the specific requirements of their project. Integrating tools such as Software AG ARIS Cloud [21] or Sparx Systems Enterprise Architect [22] can enhance the accuracy and efficiency of requirements elicitation. In addition, researchers should investigate and compare different business process modeling tools to determine their relative strengths and weaknesses in supporting various modeling languages and requirements elicitation processes. This could lead to the development of tool-specific guidelines or best practices for requirements engineering practitioners.

## 5 Conclusion

This paper gives an answer to the question of how the choice of business process modeling languages impacts the possibility of retrieving functional and non-functional requirements for software that can be used to support these business processes. The literature analysis and experiments have led to the following conclusions:

- Each modeling language offers unique advantages in representing business processes. EPC provides a clear visualization of events, functions, and control flows, making it suitable for documenting high-level processes. BPMN offers a standardized notation with a wide range of symbols and elements, facilitating detailed process modeling and analysis. UML-AD provides a graphical representation of workflow logic, focusing on actions and control flow.
- EPC process models offer insights into functional requirements by analyzing functions, connectors, clusters, events, and organizational units. They can also contribute to operational, security, and compliance requirements.

- BPMN models are rich sources for functional requirements by analyzing tasks, gateways, events, lanes, and dependencies. They provide insights into performance and security requirements but have limitations in eliciting other non-functional requirements.
- UML-AD models significantly assist in eliciting functional requirements by depicting activity flows. While valuable for functional requirements, they are not designed for non-functional requirements capture, necessitating other techniques for their elicitation.

The authors admit the limitations of this research regarding the small number of business process modeling languages/methods considered in the analysis and the small variety of business process modeling tools applied. Consideration of more languages/methods and business process modeling tools would let the research evolve in the following further research directions:

- Comparison of different business process modeling tools to analyze additional objects and information attributes that can be modeled in certain systems.
- Analysis of alternative and non-standardized business process modeling approaches such as flowcharts in the context of requirements elicitation.
- Design the guidelines for business process modeling in the context of requirements elicitation.
- Design the recommendations for business process modeling tool vendors to enhance the suitability of tools for software requirements elicitation.

## References

1. Kluza, K., Wiśniewski, P., Jobczyk, K., Ligęza, A., Mroczek, S.: Comparison of selected modeling notations for process, decision and system modeling. In: Ganzha, M., Maciaszek L., Paprzycki M. (eds.) 2017 Federated Conference on Computer Science and Information Systems, FedCSIS, vol. 11, pp. 1095–1098. IEEE, Prague (2017)
2. Volere Requirements Specification Template. https://www.volere.org/templates/volere-requirements-specification-template/. Accessed 18 Sept 2023
3. Gregório, J.L., de Oliveira, H.C., Figueiredo, L.R., Prado, S.G.D.F.: Specification of software requirements with support of business process ontologies. In: Obaidat, M.S., Mi, Z., Hsiao, K., Nicopolitidis, P., Cascado-Caballero, D. (eds.) 2019 International Conference on Computer, Information and Telecommunication Systems, CITS, pp. 1–5. IEEE, Beijing (2019)
4. Amjad, A., Azam, F., Anwar, M.W., Butt, W.H., Rashid, M.: Event-driven process chain for modeling and verification of business requirements-a systematic literature review. IEEE Access **6**, 9027–9048 (2018)
5. Nizioł, M., Wiśniewski, P., Kluza, K., Ligęza, A.: Characteristic and comparison of UML, BPMN and EPC based on process models of a training company. In: Ganzha, M., Maciaszek L., Paprzycki M., Ślęzak, D. (eds.) Annals of Computer Science and Information Systems, ACSIS, vol. 26, pp. 193–200. Polskie Towarzystwo Informatyczne, Online (2021)
6. Gross, A., Doerr, J.: EPC vs. UML activity diagram - two experiments examining their usefulness for requirements engineering. In: Werner, B. (eds.) 17th IEEE International Requirements Engineering Conference, RE 2009, pp. 47–56. IEEE, Atlanta (2009)

7. Cruz, E., Machado, R., Santos, M.: From business process models to use case models: a systematic approach. In: Aveiro, D., Tribolet, J., Gouveia, D. (eds.) EEWC 2014, vol. 174, pp. 1–13. Springer, Cham (2014). https://doi.org/10.1007/978-3-319-06505-2_12
8. Davis, R., Brabänder, E.: ARIS Design Platform. Getting Started with BPM, 1st edn. Springer, London (2007)
9. Amjad, A., Azam, F., Anwar, M.W., Butt, W.H., Rashid, M., Naeem, A.: UMLPACE for modeling and verification of complex business requirements in event-driven process chain (EPC). IEEE Access **6**, 76198–76216 (2018)
10. Riehle, D.M., Jannaber, S., Karhof, A., Thomas, O., Delfmann, P., Becker, J.: On the de-facto standard of event-driven process chains: how EPC is defined in literature. In: Modellierung 2016, LNI, pp. 61–76. Gesellschaft für Informatik e.V, Bonn (2016)
11. Vega-Márquez, O.L., Chavarriaga, J., Linares-Vásquez, M., Sánchez, M.: Requirements comprehension using BPMN: an empirical study. In: Lübke, D., Pautasso, C. (eds.) Empirical Studies on the Development of Executable Business Processes, pp. 86–111. Springer, Cham (2019)
12. Software Engineering Body of Knowledge (SWEBOK). https://www.computer.org/education/bodies-of-knowledge/software-engineering. Accessed 23 Nov 2023
13. A Guide to the Business Analysis Body of Knowledge (BABOK Guide). https://www.iiba.org/career-resources/a-business-analysis-professionals-foundation-for-success/babok/. Accessed 23 Nov 2023
14. IIBA: International Institute of Business Analysis. BABOK v3 – ePub. Bookstore. https://my.iiba.org/CPBase__item?id=a131N000007iRX3QAM&_ga=2.251457734.1734995297.1714995969-1294981855.1714995969. Accessed 24 Nov 2023
15. ISO/IEC TR 19759:2015 Software Engineering Guide to the software engineering body of knowledge (SWEBOK). https://www.iso.org/standard/67604.html. Accessed 23 Nov 2023
16. ISO/IEC/IEEE 29148:2018. https://www.iso.org/obp/ui/en/#iso:std:iso-iec-ieee:29148:ed-2:v1:en. Accessed 24 Nov 2023
17. ISO/IEC/IEEE International Standard - Systems and software engineering – Life cycle processes – Requirements engineering. In: ISO/IEC/IEEE 29148:2018(E), pp. 1–104 (2018)
18. Online Browsing Platform (OBP). https://www.iso.org/obp/ui/en/#iso:std:iso-iec-ieee:29148:ed-2:v1:en. Accessed 20 Nov 2023
19. BABOK – A Guide to the Business Analysis Body of Knowledge. https://sfia-online.org/en/tools-and-resources/bodies-of-knowledge/babok-a-guide-to-the-business-analysis-body-of-knowledge. Accessed 18 Nov 2023
20. ISO/IEC/IEEE 29148:2018. https://www.iso.org/standard/72089.html. Accessed 24 Nov 2023
21. Software AG: ARIS Cloud Basic (trial version of the system). https://www.softwareag.com/en_corporate/platform/aris/aris-free-trial.html. Accessed 21 May 2024
22. Sparx Systems Enterprise Architect (trial version of the system). https://sparxsystems.com/products/ea/trial/request.html. Accessed 21 May 2024

# Software Architectures and the Use of Knowledge Graphs to Support Their Design

Ana-Maria Ghiran[✉][iD] and Sven-Alexander Gal

Faculty of Economics and Business Administration, Babeș-Bolyai University, Str. T. Mihali 58-60, 400591 Cluj-Napoca, Romania
`anamaria.ghiran@econ.ubbcluj.ro`

**Abstract.** Software architecture is concerned with identifying the essential components of a software system and the process of creating an abstract representation of the system. A representation encompasses software elements, their properties and relationships with other elements. Similar to the architecture of a physical building, it serves as a blueprint for both the system itself and the development process, delineating the tasks to be carried out by the development team. In e-business, a wide variety of such architectures can be found. These have evolved over time, and the emergence and subsequent developments of the Internet have been decisive factors in shaping applications and their associated software architectures. In the 1980s, the purpose of an application was to run on a single computer, but today, applications are increasingly interconnected and accessible from anywhere. Practitioners have realized that a sound architecture is critical for success in both design and development. In order to incorporate domain-specific semantics, knowledge graphs must become a key ingredient to architectural thinking and the codification of principles, methods, and practices has led to repeatable architectural design processes. However, despite these advancements, the field of software architecture remains relatively immature in its relation to knowledge graphs and how to leverage them for e-business – towards this goal, traditional architectural patterns such as MVCs will be revisited in this paper.

**Keywords:** Software Architectures · Knowledge Graphs · Client-Server Architecture · MVC Architecture

## 1 Introduction

The architecture of a system is critical for its development. A well-designed architecture considerably increases the chances of having a successful system, meeting crucial requirements like performance, reliability, portability, scalability and interoperability. Likewise, an inadequately designed architecture could result in disasters and cause significant harm to the system and the purpose it should accomplish. Therefore, software architecture discipline, as a field of software engineering, has received increasingly well-deserved attention and it proved to serve beyond its initial goal of guiding software development: it supports a better comprehension of the system, facilitates effective communication (not only between human stakeholders, but also between humans to machines and machines to machines), it enables analysis on the relationships and dependencies between different components setting the bases for informed decision making. A list with various aspects of software development that could benefit from software architecture was presented in [1]. Here is our adapted version:

**Understanding:** By presenting systems from a high-level abstraction, software architecture provides only the essential elements of the complex structure enabling a better understandability. Additionally, the architectural description can reveal constraints at system level and can explain the rationale for specific architectural choices. Knowledge graphs can contribute to this by capturing the architecting design decisions not only in diagrammatic forms but also in machine-readable forms describing the composition and dependency relationships to support semantic queries. This has been recently enabled for UML diagrams that are architecture-oriented (e.g. deployment diagram, component diagram) in the BEE-UP Tool [16].

**Reuse:** Architectural descriptions once created, have the main benefit of being reused. Component libraries, most of the time, were incorporating previous proven design patterns. Likewise, all architectural components could be reused in larger frameworks. Recent works explored domain specific software architecture (under the more general term domain specific modeling languages) suggesting a more flexible management of reuse. Knowledge graphs can repurpose its traditional function of master data management [17] over heterogeneous data sources to that of master component management over heterogeneous conglomerates of frameworks and software components.

**Construction:** Architectural descriptions must address various stakeholders' requirements with different knowledge and understanding capabilities. Most of the time, however, only a part of the architecture is required by each of them. A layered perspective in describing the system's architecture was adopted, where each layer addresses specific requirements. The abstraction documents elements within specific boundaries distinguishing interfaces between layers by establishing which parts of a system can rely on services provided by other parts. As granular coding patterns tend to be delegated to Generative AI taking on the role of coding assistants, the main focus of systems building shifts towards combinatorial engineering of architecture building-blocks – something that needs to be maintained by architecture representations that are both human and machine-readable, i.e. in technological knowledge graphs.

**Evolution:** Having a software architecture has the advantage that it can identify the elements that are anticipated to drive the evolution of a system. By explicitly defining the internal structure of a system, those responsible with the maintenance will get a better understanding of how the changes propagate and consequently, a more accurate estimate of the cost of these changes. Separately, architectural descriptions can describe functionality, and these could be connected with other architectural components. This segregation facilitates modifications to the connection mechanisms to manage any change in aspects regarding performance interoperability, prototyping and reuse. Knowledge graphs are tailored to manage traceability of components to design decisions and even project management tasks [18].

**Analysis:** A system can be evaluated for coherence or adherence to specific requirements as architectural descriptions enable a formal analysis. It means that the system's design can be subjected to a rigorous examination and examined based on clearly defined criteria or methodologies. As an example how knowledge graphs can be employed in analyzing the architectural descriptions, the paper of [19] showcases a technology-specific modeling method that exposes Node.js component dependencies to a knowledge graph treatment and semantic queries for tracing those dependencies.

**Management:** The success of software projects is highly dependent on viable software architectures. A thorough assessment of an architecture leads to enhanced comprehension regarding the requirements, implementation approaches and exposed risks. Software architectures are represented using languages meant to describe systems' structure like Architecture Description Language or standardized notations like UML. These languages provide constructs for describing components, connectors, interfaces, and their relationships. The ability to externalize these descriptions to semantic graphs is critical to ensuring that the granular details of an architecture description is exposed to machine-processing.

This paper communicates the vision of MVC (Model View Controller)-focused e-commerce projects treatment as knowledge graphs. Our proposal considers Laravel projects developed by bachelor students in the host institution, which are required to be documented through an MVC interpretation of the UML component diagrams. When created in Bee-Up, such diagrams can be turned into RDF graphs that enable the knowledge graph treatment on the architecture characteristics enumerated above. Once stored in a knowledge graph platform, they can be further linked to other knowledge – from tools offering similar treatment, e.g. the examples below will include links to Archimate diagrams for tracking the evolution of architectural plateaux.

## 2 Methodology

The proposal to treat MVC-e-commerce projects as knowledge graphs has strong potential for generalization to other software architecture patterns.

The paper contributes to the discipline of method engineering, by combining several *ingredients* to streamline a knowledge graph treatment (in design science terms) for architectural designs and subsequent systems engineering:

- The conversion of UML architectural diagrams to RDF graphs is possible in UML tools such as Bee-Up [16]; for exemplification we will use component diagrams, but the treatment is equally applicable to deployment diagrams (and other UML designs); UML is a widely used modeling language that is applicable to many software architectures patterns, not only MVC. Converting UML models into RDF facilities descriptions of various architectural components into a common representation, setting interlinking possibilities and identifying hidden relationships.
- The conversion of Archimate diagrams to knowledge graphs has been rather achieved via labelled property graphs, through the Archi-Neo4J integration [20]. To converge to a uniform RDF semantic graphs representation (i.e. to enable linking to the Bee-Up UML content), this can be achieved either by further applying LPG-to-RDF conversion [21] or directly, by using Archimate tools for which RDF exporting means are available – we took the second approach, by picking the OMILAB Archimate tool

TEAM [22, 23] which was developed on the ADOxx metamodeling platform, and applying to its content the ADOxx-to-GraphDB conversion that produces RDF graphs out of any ADOxx-based diagrams [24] – until Archimate and UML will be available in the same ADOxx-based tool this is a necessary workaround;
- Ontotext's GraphDB [25] is our preferred platform for accumulating the resulting hybrid knowledge base and experimenting with the semantic queries enabled by the knowledge graph treatment over software architecture concerns and design decisions.

Since our proposal deals with the current challenges in software engineering, we followed a systematic approach given by the Desing Science methodology [27], aiming to contribute to the advancement of knowledge in this domain. Therefore, we structured our research into phases recommended by the Design Science – problem identification, objectives definition, design and development, demonstration, evaluation and communication.

First, we investigated existing software engineering methods aiming to assess whether they are still suitable for the evolving requirements in the field. We *identified as problem* that software architecture domain had found numerous applications beyond the initial purpose as a software development guiding technology (e.g. to enable systems' analysis and simulations which require having the diagrammatic architectural representation translated into machine readable format). This is at the same time an opportunity and a demanding effort. However, advances in automatic serialization and machine processing as knowledge graphs are promising techniques to back up the visual representation of systems' architectures and enlarge their applicability to address not only human users but also so called "model aware systems".

Once we have identified the problem, we defined clear *research objectives* – to demonstrate how a sample software architectural pattern can be treated as a knowledge graph. This can lead to substantial insights on architecture modelling but also in reaching data outside the modeling environment. We will *exemplify* our approach on the MVC architectural pattern as documented for our student bachelor projects developed in the Laravel framework with e-payment integration provided by Stripe.

Using the Desing Science methodology principles, our proposal is designed and developed iteratively. This is the first iteration and the knowledge graph obtained in this phase is meant to work as a prof of concept, but future iterations will enrich it considering the input from reviewers and participants from scientific events as conferences.

To *evaluate* the developed method, we resorted on experts from our institution to set some competency questions [28] that were formulated as SPARQL [29] queries. Finally, this paper *communicates* the results.

## 3 Related Works

The work of [8] explored enterprise knowledge graphs (EKGs) and investigated to what extent exploratory search can be supported on EKGs of architectural knowledge. Their method for creating exploratory search systems using EKGs has been presented and showed how to utilize it within Siemens. This led to the creation of the STAR system, used by roughly 200–300 software architects [8].

Smajevic, Hacks and Bork used KGs to assess Enterprise Architecture (EA) Smells. They suggested adding EA scent detection capabilities to the extensible graph-based Enterprise Analysis platform by transforming ArchiMate models into knowledge graphs and offering a set of queries on the knowledge graph representation that may identify EA Smells [9].

Wan, Sun and Zhang [10] investigated the construction methods and current utilization of knowledge graphs within the software engineering domain, broadening the application area of knowledge graphs in this field and facilitating further investigations. Addressing software engineering challenges through knowledge graphs is paramount for the progress of both fields. The exploration of the knowledge graphs implementation in the software engineering domain, particularly, the integration of open-source community software and developer recommendations with knowledge driven microservice Operations and Maintenance (O&M), serves as a source of inspiration for academics to embrace knowledge graph technology in other scenarios.

De Boer [11] conducted an assessment about the application of architectural knowledge within public sector in Netherlands. The conclusion was that the semi-structure nature of the architecture knowledge has been effectively streamlined by incorporating it into semantic wikis.

Saham, Kamm and their team proposed knowledge graphs as enhancers of intelligent Digital Twins. Cyber-Physical Systems have numerous opportunities for industrial automation because of their networking capabilities and digital representations. Digital Twins enable failure diagnosis, simulations and managing heterogeneous data provided by various physical systems to which knowledge graphs can contribute with their semantic richness [12].

In describing architectures using knowledge graphs, Glaser et al. [13] focused on the enterprise level. They propose a model-based Enterprise Architecture Knowledge Graph construction method which starts from ArchiMate models and derives the knowledge graph enriched with Enterprise Architecture specific concepts. The new representation entails machine reasoning on the EA concepts.

Althar and Samanta focused on knowledge graphs application in software engineering. Their work provided us with some concrete examples of use cases where knowledge graphs can contribute – automation of test case creation, understanding the semantics of the architecture knowledge, building an intelligent development environment etc. [14].

Lin et al. put forward two key concepts: intelligent development environment (IntelliDE) and software knowledge graph. Software big data are gathered, mined, and analyzed within the IntelliDE ecosystem to offer intelligent support throughout the software development life cycle [15].

## 4 The Knowledge Structures of MVC

The variety of tools and frameworks to develop apps is constantly expanding, allowing software engineers to experiment with various platforms and design patterns [7]. Our current proposal of employing knowledge graphs as a method for architectural management and evolution will be exemplified with the MVC pattern, as implemented by our bachelor students in e-shops developed on the Laravel framework.

The MVC pattern is a software architectural pattern that separates the application into three main components: 1) the Model, that is in charge with the database connectivity and business logic, 2) the View that deals with the user interface and presentation and 3) the Controller which acts as an intermediary layer between the Model and the View, processing user input and managing the responses.

Using the UML language, the architect can use several diagram types to drill down architecture to any granularity level – we will exemplify the use of the component diagram for the MVC architectural pattern, but this can be further extrapolated (e.g. to deployment diagrams). In a UML component diagram, the system is broken down into functional subcomponents and typically includes as elements the components and the interfaces between those components. In these diagrams, the focus is on the high level view thus, the detail of the internal data structure or methods within the component are hidden (usually described in separate UML class diagrams). A port is used for cases when the interface is not provided directly by the component but by another internal encapsulated component. Component diagrams can also include references to third-party packages encouraging developers to apply a modular approach reusing components in other projects or complex systems.

To serve a project management perspective on the architectural evolution, we complement UML with the TOGAF's notion of "architecture migration" to depict the evolution in time of an expanding/changing software architecture – in terms of work packages and deliverable dependencies over several intermediate plateaux towards a targeted architecture. So, *multiple* UML component descriptions are created to represent the *temporal evolution* of the software architecture providing a systematic comparison of structural changes across different diagrams.

Through our approach we aim to bring together TOGAF and UML component diagrams that traditionally served distinct purposes for a better alignment of the IT applications and business strategies. To achieve this, we rely on conversion mechanisms of the UML diagrams into RDF structures. Once these diagrams are converted and stored in a knowledge graph, they enable connections among them and with other knowledge sources, thereby enriching contextual analysis and inference. For example, we can create connections with Archimate diagrams which can be used in monitoring and documenting the evolution of architectural plateaux over time.

In the UML diagram showcased in Fig. 1, the MVC components of a Laravel e-shop are explicitly detailed down to REST route level.

Realization relationships are used to indicate the HTML views and view fragments generated by controllers.

Dependency relationships are used to indicate when a view's functioning depends on the fulfilment of HTTP requests to the REST endpoints exposed by controllers; they also express how each controller depends on data entities exposed by Laravel models through its ORM (object-relational mapper) mechanism abstracting away the relational database.

Interfaces to external Stripe service for e-payments are also visible, as are other artifacts involved in the full deployment (e.g..css files). Each smaller rectangle on the border of a larger rectangle represents a port, abstracting an interface that hides how each interface is "related" to the respective module, i.e. a route providing access to a

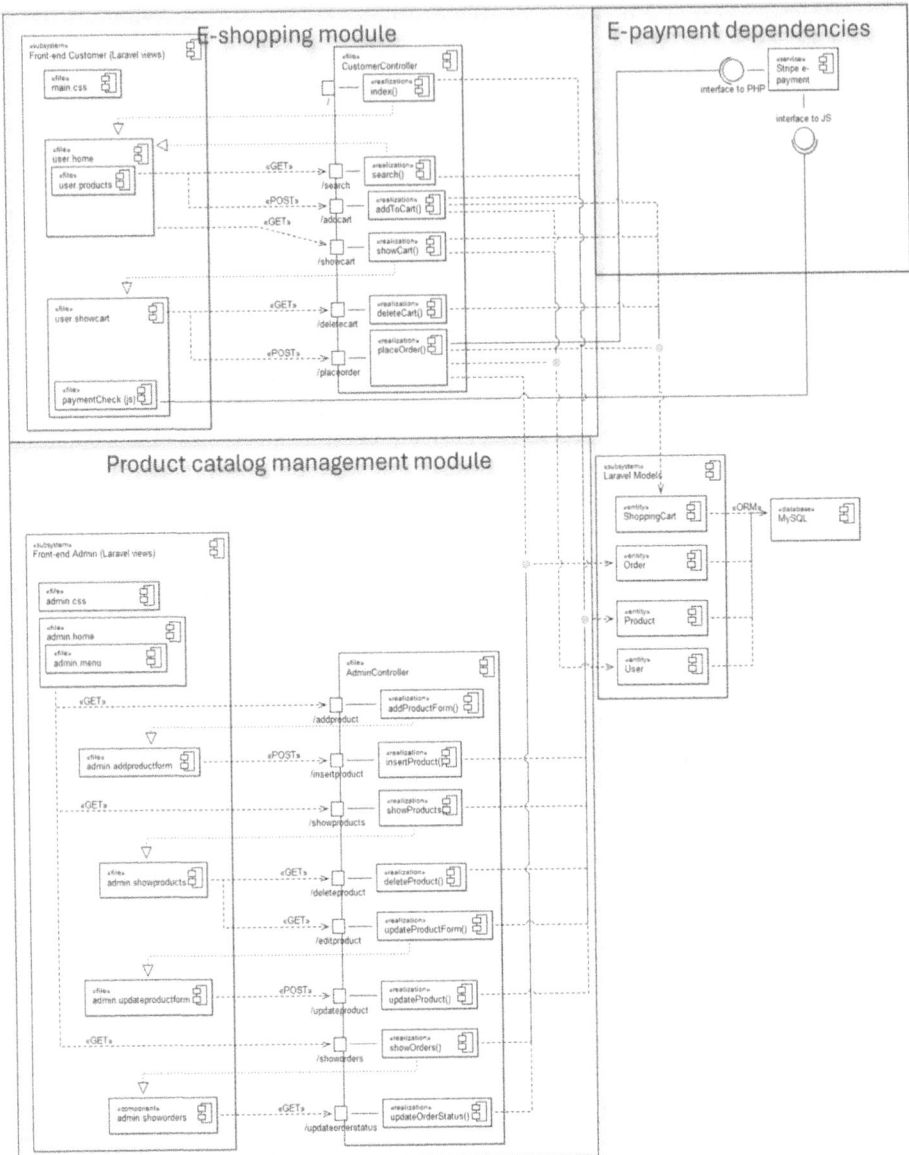

**Fig. 1.** UML component diagram of a Laravel MVC E-shop

controller function - it shows the schematic relationships between modules but does not provide details about the necessary and provided behaviors [5].

The diagrams, generally, capture only a small part or a facet of the necessary information - component structure, communication between components, use cases mapped on front-end components. The architectural description includes multiple "views" of the architecture.

They can also remain on a coarser granularity level of a reference architecture – e.g. the "industry de facto standard", such as J2EE for e-commerce, web-based applications. These reference architectures provide a high level of decomposition that establishes the basic structural design but leaves room for the architect to drill-down low-level decompositions to the level of granularity that should be traced – e.g. by the knowledge graph treatment hereby proposed.

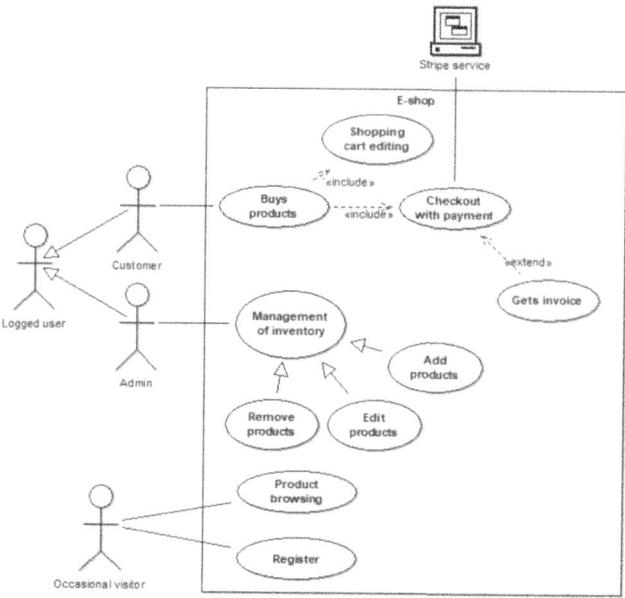

**Fig. 2.** Use-case diagram of the typical e-shop app

Furthermore, use cases captured in a use case diagram can be linked to the front-end components (MVC views) through which potential users will execute their use cases – an example aligned with the MVC components is provided in Fig. 2.

A current pragmatic scenario is also the development of a Single Page Web Application (SPA). In this case, the views are much richer in functionality, adding complexity to the modularization of the architecture – e.g. in Angular there is a tendency of fractalization of the MVC architecture: we have front-end services (similar to models, to obtain data from back-end controllers), components that prepare the data and render views. It communicates with the server acting as a general API (Application Programming Interface) and is hosted somewhere in a secure and opaque location for the user. The client components prioritize the optimal User Experience, presenting a usable service to the user and also retrieving data from the user. In this type of architecture, the disadvantage is that there needs to be an additional effort in terms of the number of interactions between components, which only strengthens the argument of capturing those dependencies in an architectural knowledge graph.

For an additional advantage brought by cohesion, the same fundamental programming language, JavaScript, can be used on both sides. Thanks to modern technologies, libraries, and frameworks have been developed, making it possible to create any type of software that can run platform-agnostically. Ultimately, all these changes add a new concern to the team, namely managing a complete client-side package, potentially reaching the same complexity level as the server-side [2].

## 5 Glueing Together UML Designs and TOGAF's Architecture Migration in a Knowledge Graph

Figure 3 introduces the main enabler of our proposal that acts as a unifying knowledge structure to support the work of the software architect with traceability regarding the architecture evolution.

The TOGAF framework for enterprise architecture (EA) has at its center the notion of iterative EA migration – e.g. it can be a digital transformation journey or something simpler that incrementally adds to the EA from one "plateau" to the next. Each plateau is a stable architecture that can be used with some limitations – those limitations are seen as a gap that must be overcome to advance to the next plateau.

This can be depicted by the TOGAF companion language Archimate, as shown in the lower part of Fig. 3, in terms of:

- Green plateaux and inter-plateau gaps showing the progress of a digital transformation journey – the example starts with a simple app for managing the inventory of a shop, continues with expanding it to an e-shop that also offers on-line selling with payment on delivery, and ends with an e-payment extension;
- Each of these plateaux can be mapped to a partial version of the UML diagrams in part 1 and part 2, showing the "delta" between different architectures during this evolution;
- Each plateau is also linked to the work packages and deliverables defined as part of a project management perspective on the digital transformation journey (pink elements in the lower part of the figure).

This can be further extended towards evolution in the cloud. A cloud-based MVC is based on the same fundamental structure as the traditional MVC architecture, but is adapted to work in a cloud environment:

1. Models intermediate access to services or Microservices: Data and business logic can be managed by separate services or microservices in the cloud paradigm. These are different parts that may be updated and scaled independently. Distributed databases are used to store data, offering scalability and redundancy as well as remote access and management.
2. Views are designed to be accessible from a distance and to adjust to various screen sizes and devices. These could be cloud-based web applications or cloud-accessible mobile apps. Front-ends can be distributed across multiple servers to handle a large number of requests and ensure high availability.
3. Controllers control the application logic and direct requests to the right services. In order to prevent single points of failure and guarantee quick response, these control services can also be distributed.

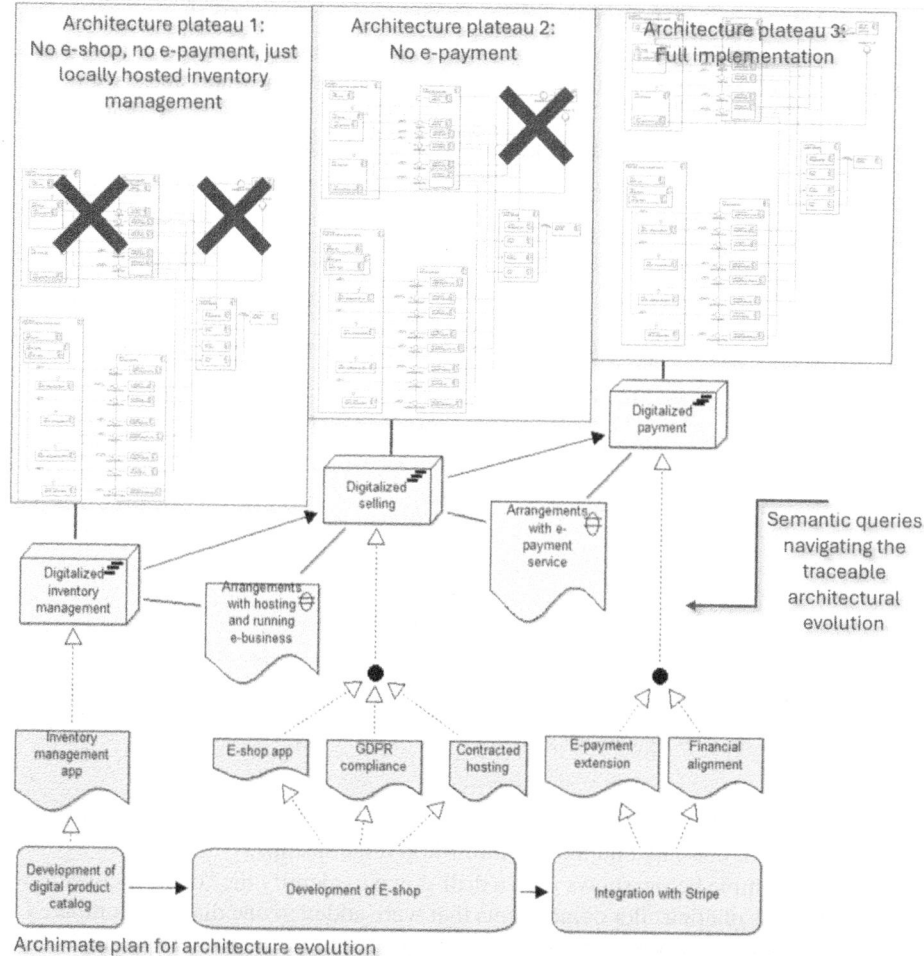

**Fig. 3.** Archimate migration+UML hybridization as knowledge graph

4. Cloud Infrastructure provides the application with the resources it needs by employing cloud infrastructure services including network, storage, and computation. Cloud MVC architecture can automatically scale resources to handle increased traffic and provide redundancy to minimize downtime.

The adaptation of MVC architecture for cloud environments focuses on scalability, availability and efficient resource management in a distributed and virtualized environment.

The knowledge graph for architecture management can be obtained with the technical means already summarized in Sect. 3. Named graphs will store the distinct diagrams, with explicit semantic links – not only from one diagram element to another (e.g. use case to component, crossing between different diagrams), but also from one diagram element to a full diagram (from Archimate plateau to component diagram).

Figure 4 shows a sample of the generated RDF content for the UML component diagrams describing the evolution of the e-commerce application from the initial plateau without e-shop and e-payment functionalities to another plateau where the e-shop functionality is added. We kept only the relevant statements, in Turtle format, that are used in the subsequent SPARL queries, omitting the prefix declarations:

```
:P1 a :Plateau;
    :hasComponents :ComponentDiagram1;
    rdfs:label "Digitalized inventory management".

:ComponentDiagram1 {
    :AdminComponent a :Component;
                    rdfs:label "Administrator Component";
                    :specificType :Controller.
    :CustomerComponent a :Component;
                    rdfs:label "Customer Component";
                    :specificType :Controller.
    ...
}
                                :P2 a :Plateau;
                                    :hasComponents :ComponentDiagram2;
                                    rdf:label "Digitalized selling".

                                :ComponentDiagram2 {
                                    :AdminComponent a :Component;
                                                    rdfs:label "Administrator Component";
                                                    :specificType :Controller.
                                    :CustomerComponent a :Component;
                                                    rdfs:label "Customer Component";
                                                    :specificType :Controller.
                                    :OrderComponent a :Component;
                                                    rdfs:label "Order Component";
                                                    :specificType :Controller.
                                    ...
                                }
```

**Fig. 4.** RDF statements generated from UML component diagrams

Semantic queries must take this into account to perform drill-down mechanisms during navigation, not only chaining in multi-hop relationships.

The first example below shows such a drill-down to identify the "delta" between two plateaux in terms of controller components that were added to one diagram compared to a previous one, further traced to the use cases for which those controllers where created.

*SELECT ?x*
*WHERE*
*{*
  *GRAPH :ArchimateGraph {:p1 a :Plateau; :hasComponents ?compDiag1.*
                        *:p2 a :Plateau; hasComponents ?compDiag2.}*
  *GRAPH ?compDiag2 {?x a :Component; :specificType :Controller;*
                   *:servesUseCase ?y.}*
  *FILTER NOT EXISTS*
    *{GRAPH ?compDiag1 {?x a :Component; :specificType :Controller }}*
*}*

The next example runs inside a diagram, to trace the dependencies on: AdminController – i.e. which views are connected to ports associated to its inner "realizations" (controller functions producing content for views).

```
SELECT ?x
WHERE
    {?x a :Component; :specificType :View; :dependsOn ?y.
    ?y a :Port; :specificType :Route; :associatedTo ?z.
    ?z a :Component; :specificType :Realization; :isInside :AdminController.}
```

The knowledge graph would also be sufficiently granular to act as a model interchange format or code generation base – e.g. to generate controller skeletons out of the relationships and elements depicted in Fig. 1, or to generate a basic Gantt chart out of the Archimate fragment in Fig. 3.

## 6 Discussion on Generalization Potential

Software development is a process that requires architectural planning and analysis as part of the project management concerns.

In early business analysis, where the team tries to understand the requirements - the most common techniques include document analysis, interviews, observation and workshopping. This inherently looks like a knowledge acquisition effort, covering domain-specific knowledge, procedural knowledge and business-IT alignment leading to a knowledge base that traditionally takes the form of unstructured documentation. Although useful, this unstructured documentation can be challenging to manage and utilize efficiently. Eventually, everything should be aggregated in a knowledge graph that links together visual modeling content – business processes, domain models, architecture models of gradually evolving granularity. In this way, the knowledge base can be easily navigated and queried throughout the software development lifecycle.

Planning itself, from a project management perspective (workpackages mapped on deliverables and plateaux) can be served by diagramming – see the migration diagram of Archimate already exemplified. These diagrams help in managing and communicating the project's progress and ensuring that all team members are aligned with the project's objectives and timelines, however if they are only available as visual models then they can only be used by humans. Capturing the knowledge beyond the visual representation enables support for higher quality software architectures backed by automated processing capabilities.

Design decisions are perhaps the most common knowledge captured in UML form and linkable across many different diagram types to enable traceability and deeper exploration – e.g. from stakeholders to use cases and further to UX components serving those use cases and their grounding in back-end or cloud services. Treating UML diagrams as RDF structures could enable further reasoning techniques ensuring that all design decisions are consistent and that the software architectures provide insightful analysis.

A knowledge graph treatment can fuse design with the actual development [26] by allowing front-end components to dynamically change their routing to back-end controllers or services based on queries run against the evolving design decisions in diagrams.

Treating software design artifacts as knowledge graphs can seamlessly integrate them, allowing architectural elements to be connected among them and with other relevant external data.

Finally, software testing could rely on semantic queries to generate test cases out of the design decisions. By using semantic queries to generate test cases directly from architectural descriptions, the testing process becomes easier and also aligned with the project's objectives. This ensures that all aspects of the project are thoroughly tested and validated against the design specifications, reducing the likelihood of defects and improving overall quality.

Leveraging knowledge graphs in software design process provides a structured and query-able way to aggregate and utilize various knowledge generated throughout the project.

## 7 Conclusions

A popular paradigm in today's IT landscape is that of knowledge graphs, but the dominant discussion around it has to do with AI and integration of large language models. We believe there is still untapped potential in applying it as a knowledge management enabler for software architecting and project management. The machine-readable format could leverage the automatic processing of models which might support more correct project descriptions and ultimately higher-quality software.

We believe that, as coding practices will be more and more delegated to GPT-like models for generative content, the attention of software engineers will switch to knowledge structures overarching many different code components and how to manipulate or analyze them from a knowledge management perspective, not only from a codebase perspective. Architecture is often neglected in outsourcing or open source projects and we hope that this paper highlights its importance beyond the function of visual documentation [4].

## References

1. Garlan, D.: Software architecture: a roadmap. In: Proceedings of the Conference on The Future of Software Engineering, Limerick, Ireland, pp. 91–101. ACM Press (2000)
2. Greif, S.: A Study Plan to Cure JavaScript Fatigue (2017). Retrieved from Medium: https://medium.com/free-code-camp/a-study-plan-to-cure-javascript-fatigue-8ad3a54f2eb1. Accessed 1 Mar 2024
3. Koroushfar, E.: A study on the role of software architecture in the evolution and quality of software. In: IEEE/ACM 12th Working Conference on Mining Software Repositories, pp. 246–257. IEEE (2015)
4. Sauer, S., Engels, G.: MVC-based modeling support for embedded real-time systems: position statement. In: Workshop on Object-Oriented Modeling of Embedded Realtime Systems, OMER Workshop, pp. 11–14 (1999)
5. Sesboue, M., Delestre, N., Katowicz, J.-P., Khudiyev, A., Zanni-Merk, C.: An operational architecture for knowledge graph-based systems. In: 26th International Conference on Knowledge-Based and Intelligent Information & Engineering Systems (KES 2022), pp. 1667–1676. Procedia Computer Science, Rouen (2022)
6. Stoyko, T.: How to Make an App Both for Android and IOS (2023). https://incora.software/insights/make-app-both-iOS-Android. Accessed 1 Mar 2024
7. Bhatt, T.: 7 Steps of the Software Development Process: From Idea to Reality (2023). https://www.intelivita.com/blog/software-development-process/. Accessed 1 Mar 2024

8. Sabou, M., et al.: Exploring enterprise knowledge graphs: a use case in software engineering. In: Gangemi, A., et al. (eds.) The Semantic Web. LNCS, vol. 10843, pp. 560–575. Springer, Cham (2018). https://doi.org/10.1007/978-3-319-93417-4_36
9. Smajevic, M., Hacks, S., Bork, D.: Using knowledge graphs to detect enterprise architecture smells. In: 14th IFIP Working Conference on the Practice of Enterprise Modeling (PoEM), pp. 48–63. HAL Open Science, Riga (2021)
10. Wang, L., Sun, C., Zhang, C., Nie, W., Huang, K.: Application of knowledge graph in software engineering field: a systematic literature review. Inf. Softw. Technol. **164**(C) (2023). https://dl.acm.org/doi/10.1016/j.infsof.2023.107327
11. De Boer, R.: Architecture knowledge graphs-a next step in architecture knowledge management. In: International Workshop New Trends in Software Architecture (SATrends 2024) (2024). https://www.researchgate.net/publication/378589025_Architecture_Knowledge_Graphs_-_a_Next_Step_in_Architecture_Knowledge_Management
12. Sahlab, N., Kamm, S., Müller, T., Jazdi, N., Weyrich, M.: Knowledge graphs as enhancers of intelligent digital twins. In: 4th IEEE International Conference on Industrial Cyber-Physical Systems (ICPS), Victoria, BC, Canada, pp. 19–24 (2021)
13. Glaser, P.L., Ali, S.J., Sallinger, E., Bork, D.: Model-based construction of enterprise architecture knowledge graphs. In: Almeida, J.P.A., Karastoyanova, D., Guizzardi, G., Montali, M., Maggi, F.M., Fonseca, C.M. (eds.) EDOC 2022. LNCS, vol. 13585, pp. 57–73. Springer, Cham (2022). https://doi.org/10.1007/978-3-031-17604-3_4
14. Althar, R., Samanta, D.: Application of machine intelligence-based knowledge graphs for software engineering. In: Advances in Systems Analysis, Software Engineering, and High Performance Computing, pp. 186–202 (2021)
15. Lin, Z., et al.: Intelligent development environment and software knowledge graph. J. Comput. Sci. Technol. **32**(2), 242–249 (2017)
16. OMILAB Bee-Up tool. https://bee-up.omilab.org/activities/bee-up/. Accessed 01 Mar 2024
17. Ramzy, N., Durst, S., Schreiber, M., Auer, S., Chamanara, J., Ehm, H.: KnowGraph-MDM: a methodology for knowledge-graph-based master data management. In: IEEE 24th Conference on Business Informatics (CBI), pp. 9–16. IEEE, Amsterdam (2022)
18. Floruț, C., Buchmann, R.A.: Semantic Bridging between Conceptual Modeling Standards and Agile Software Projects Conceptualizations. Published on Association for Information Systems (2022). https://aisel.aisnet.org/isd2014/proceedings2022/managingdevops/7/
19. Lixandru, B., Buchmann, R.A., Ghiran, A.M.: Conceptualizing Node.js projects: a graph-oriented technology-specific modeling method. In: Silaghi, G.C., et al. (eds.) ISD 2022. LNISO, vol. 63, pp. 53–72. Springer, Cham (2023). https://doi.org/10.1007/978-3-031-32418-5_4
20. Archimate Tool Database-Plugin. https://github.com/archi-contribs/database-plugin. Accessed 01 Mar 2024
21. NEO4J. https://neo4j.com/labs/neosemantics/4.0/export/. Accessed 01 Mar 2024
22. TOGAF based Enterprise Architecture Management. https://austria.omilab.org/psm/content/team/info?view=home. Accessed 01 Mar 2024
23. Bork, D., et al.: Requirements engineering for model-based enterprise architecture management with ArchiMate, In: 14th International Workshop on Enterprise & Organizational Modeling and Simulation (EOMAS 2018), Tallinn, Estonia, 11–12 June 2018, pp. 16–30 (2018)
24. Karagiannis, D., Buchmann, R.A.: A proposal for deploying hybrid knowledge bases: the ADOxx-to-GraphDB interoperability case. In: Proceedings of the HICSS 2018. Assoc. for Inf. Sys. (2018). https://aisel.aisnet.org/hicss-51/ks/ks_creation/4/
25. Graph DB. https://graphdb.ontotext.com/documentation/10.6/. Accessed 1 Mar 2024

26. Buchmann, R.A., Cinpoeru, M., Harkai, A., Karagiannis, D.: Model-aware software engineering - a knowledge-based approach to model-driven software engineering. In: Proceedings of ENASE 2018, pp. 233–240. Scitepress (2018)
27. Wieringa, R.J.: Design Science Research Methods. https://wwwhome.ewi.utwente.nl/~roelw/DSM90minutes.pdf. Accessed 1 Feb 2024
28. Bezerra, C., Freitas, F., Santana, F.: Evaluating ontologies with competency questions. In: 2013 IEEE/WIC/ACM International Joint Conferences on Web Intelligence (WI) and Intelligent Agent Technologies (IAT), vol. 3, pp. 284–285. IEEE (2013)
29. W3C, SPARQL 1.1 Query Language. https://www.w3.org/TR/sparql11-query/. Accessed 22 Feb 2024

# Technical Debt – Insights Into a Manufacturing SME Case Study

Katharina Greger[1] and Michael Möhring[2](✉)

[1] Department of Industrial Engineering and Health, OTH Amberg-Weiden, Hetzenrichter Weg 15, 92637 Weiden in der Oberpfalz, Germany
k.greger@oth-aw.de

[2] Reutlingen University, School of Informatics – HHZ, Alteburg Straße 150, 72762 Reutlingen, Germany
michael.moehring@reutlingen-university.de

**Abstract.** Due to data and its use being an upcoming source of value for all industries, the use of IT systems becomes increasingly important to the daily business of most companies. As digitalization efforts increase, some existing obstacles come into focus – such as technical debt (TD). TD is well-researched in the software industry, but not so much in other industries. This paper aims at answering the question of how clients of software vendors in other industries are confronted with TD by performing a case study in a manufacturing SME and using grounded theory to develop a theory model on how TD occurs on the client-side, considering the entire system landscape and its evolution.

**Keywords:** Technical Debt · Information Systems · Manufacturing Industry · System Change

## 1 Introduction

Digitalization is one of the megatrends of current times and in manufacturing titled as the fourth industrial revolution that influences and changes all areas of live worldwide significantly, including the industry [1]. One of the ways in which digitalization is expected to change industry and business is by creating value from the data generated by digital systems [2]. Demary et al. [2] developed a maturity model for the data economy, consisting of six stages from analog company up to data ecosystem, with three dimensions based on each other: data resource management, data valuation and data-driven activities, called data business.

Despite the emphasis put on digitalization and its general perception as a major driver of value in the future, according to the evaluation of Demary et al. [2], with a proportion of 84.0% most German companies are only in the beginning phases of the maturity model. They classify as analog or digitized companies, meaning their core business processes are either not, partly or fully supported by IT systems but without defined interfaces or further structured evaluation or use of the data collected by these systems [2]. Especially small to middle-sized enterprises (SMEs) are just beginning the digitalization and use of data for their business – not surprising as the main challenges of those companies are a lack of resources and competence regarding digitalization [2]. Other challenges include the introduction of IT systems to enable data-based processes in analog companies or, if they have existing IT systems, overcoming data discontinuities and implementing interfaces to connect the data. The latter is also an obstacle for enterprises in more advanced phases of the maturity model as there is often a variety of different IT systems in place. This is also described by Frey et al. [3] for large enterprises, and Kraus and Baumöl [4] for SMEs, who attribute the heterogeneous IT system landscape in most SMEs to their evolution over time. They stress the importance of an adequate IT management in enterprises to support the business objectives and development as IT gains importance in times of increasing digitalization. These differences in the degree of digitalization are not only the case for German but most European SMEs [5]. Brodny and Tutak [5] investigated the digital technologies related to Industry 4.0 (such as ERP systems, cloud computing services and big data analysis) implemented in European SMEs, as these organizations constitute the majority of European enterprises, and deduced the level of digital maturity for the countries of the European Union.

One risk that comes into focus during this digital transformation, is the technical debt (TD) incurred by past technical decisions [6]. TD has been a topic of research during the past years (e.g., [7–12]), mainly in the software industry. This may be attributed to the fact that the product and therefore the value creation of this industry is directly affected by TD, whereas in other industries IT and software are only used to support the process of value creation. However, due to data and its use being an upcoming source of value for all industries, the use of IT systems becomes increasingly important to the daily business of most companies. Oftentimes, a commercial-off-the-shelf system is obtained from a software company, hereafter referred to as vendor, and then customized rather than self-developed and -supported software. Additionally, the IT environment of many companies consists of multiple IT systems.

That raises the question whether there are differences regarding TD in other businesses, meaning on the client-side, compared to software companies, and if there are differences, what their cause is. Due to sparse research in the manufacturing sector as well as the importance of this sector, this paper will focus on the manufacturing industry, to answer the following research question (RQ): **How does technical debt occur in manufacturing businesses?** To answer this RQ, this paper first presents an overview of the background of TD including a definition of the essential terms used and the state of existing research regarding TD, followed by a description of the research method and data collection in Sect. 3. Section 4 consists of the results of the case study conducted and Sect. 5 closes with the conclusion and discussion of the results, providing implications for further research.

## 2 Background

### 2.1 Technical Debt

The term TD was first used by Cunningham in 1992 [13] relating to code that does not meet the standards of good coding, which can increase development speed, but will have negative effects in the long run if not resolved. TD is used as a metaphor for the impact and consequences of technical compromises, in particular for (potential) financial repercussions [14]. Similar to its financial equivalent, TD has a principal, which is the effort necessary to realize the ideal solution, and interest [14]. However, the interest comprises two elements, interest probability and interest amount, implicating the interest caused by TD may not necessarily need to be paid off [10]. The interest represents additional cost caused by the TD items over a given period of time. The concept of TD has evolved over time and there is no universal definition of TD, although there are several approaches of developing a classification. Most studies in this field propose dimensions (e.g., [8, 10, 11]), also referred to as types or levels of TD, describing where TD occurs. The most identified types according to Alves et al. [10], BenIdris et al. [11] and Li et al. [8] are architecture, build, code, defect, design, documentation, infrastructure, people, process, requirement, service, test, usability and versioning debt.

Fowler [15] proposed a different approach to classifying TD, differentiating whether the debt is incurred intentionally and the attitude towards it. In the dimension of intent, Fowler distinguishes the inadvertent and deliberate incurring of TD and regarding the attitude between reckless and prudent, resulting in four dimensions. McConell [16] also takes into account whether TD is incurred deliberately, but adds time horizon and purpose to his taxonomy. Tom et al. [7] develop a similar taxonomy with strategic, tactical, incremental and inadvertent TD. Strategic debt [7] is taken on to reach a strategic goal, while tactical debt intends to reach short-term goals and has a more reactive nature. Incremental debt consists of many intentional but small compromises, whereas inadvertent debt, similar to Fowler [15] and McConell [16], accrues without intent.

The broadening of the term TD, especially the aspect of incurring TD without being aware of it, sparked criticism. Kruchten et al. [17] propose to limit TD to invisible elements only, while Allspaw [18] requests to find another term for what Fowler [15], McConell [16] and Tom et al. [7] refer to as inadvertent debt. However, as TD is a term to describe the (possible) negative impact of technical decisions, it can be argued, that the concept of TD applies both to visible forms and debt accrued unintentionally.

The main consequence of TD according to Li et al. [8] is the impairment of system quality. Most frequently mentioned is the increase in the effort for and complexity of maintenance, although other aspects of compromised quality may include compatibility, performance efficiency, portability, reliability, and usability.

## 2.2 Literature Review

The term TD originates from software development and is mainly used and researched in this domain, as a brief literature review shows. Existing comprehensive systematic reviews in the field of TD include a study by Tom et al. [7] published in 2013, a mapping study by Li et al. [8] published in 2015, a literature review by Ampatzoglou et al. [9] from 2015, another mapping study by Alves et al. [10] from 2016 and one by BenIdris et al. [11] in 2018, and a tertiary study by Rios et al. [12] in 2018. The objectives of these studies were to gain an understanding of the state of research regarding TD, develop a classification or a common taxonomy for TD, understand how TD arises and its chances and risks, as well as identify methods applied for the detection, estimation or management of TD.

However, the objective of these papers was not to determine whether the concept of TD is studied in other industries than the software industry and thus they are not useful to answer the RQ. Therefore, another brief literature research is necessary to answer the question if existing TD research already expands into other industries, into other areas outside of software development, or not. For this purpose, a search strategy is developed as recommended in the scientific literature by Kitchenham [19], consisting of three phases: planning, conducting the review and then reporting the results.

Titles, abstracts and keywords are searched with the terms "technical debt" and "manufacturer", "manufacturing", "enterprise resource planning", "ERP", "enterprise system" or "system landscape" to find publications relating to TD studies in the manufacturing industry regarding the most frequently used types of systems, so the search string is as follows: ("technical debt") AND ("manufacturer" OR "manufacturing" OR "enterprise resource planning" OR "ERP" OR "enterprise system" OR "system landscape"). The time scope is limited to include January 2015 to December 2023. As resources for this search, the following major databases are chosen: IEEE Xplore, SpringerLink, ScienceDirect and ACM Digital Library. The inclusion and exclusion criteria are included in Table 1.

**Table 1.** Inclusion and exclusion criteria.

| Type | Criterion |
| --- | --- |
| Inclusion | Publication includes research of TD in other industries than the software industry |
| Inclusion | Publication includes research of TD outside of software development |
| Exclusion | Publication not available in English or German |
| Exclusion | Publications that are not conference papers or articles (e.g., books) |
| Exclusion | Duplicates of publications |

Then, the literature review [19] is conducted. The conduction begins with the stage of identifying research, using the search string in the resources defined above. The results are n = 4 matches in IEEE Xplore, n = 654 in SpringerLink, n = 4 in ScienceDirect, and n = 5 in ACM Digital Library. The number of results for SpringerLink is significantly higher compared to the other databases due to their full-text search; it is not possible to restrict the search to specific fields, such as abstract or keywords, but only an option to limit the search to the title. Therefore, as a second exclusion criterion it is determined to only consider publications of the types of conference paper or article, which are n = 66 conference papers and n = 62 articles in the SpringerLink database, totaling n = 128 matches. For the search in ACM Digital Library the option "The ACM Guide to Computing Literature" was selected as the more comprehensive search base. Next, the studies meeting the inclusion criteria but not any exclusion criteria are selected based on their abstracts, which leads to a total of n = 19 studies. Then, the full texts of the selected studies are read, and their quality is assessed, e.g., the research methods used. This results in two studies being excluded, one due to the inclusion of social media in the analysis process, another as it is an experience report of all authors working at the same firm. The overview of the results of each stage are shown in Table 2.

**Table 2.** Overview of literature review results.

| Review phase | IEEE Xplore | SpringerLink | ScienceDirect | ACM Digital Library |
|---|---|---|---|---|
| Identification of research | 4 | 128 | 4 | 6 |
| Removal of duplicates | 4 | 128 | 4 | 4 |
| Selection of studies | 1 | 14 | 3 | 1 |
| Qualified studies | 1 | 12 | 3 | 1 |

Afterwards, the data extraction and, finally, data synthesis are performed [19]. The results of the data extraction are as follows: Six of the 17 qualified studies examine TD outside of software development, but as part of the product or service of the company. Four papers study TD in software or software-based systems focusing on the client perspective, the term "client" referring to an organization using a system usually provided by another vendor. The examined systems comprise ERP systems, CRM systems, collaborative robots, and automated production systems. One study explores TD in contracting in the Netherlands, also focusing on the client perspective, noting that current contracts of the companies examined mostly do not protect clients from TD caused by vendors and state that TD "is predominantly not a service provider risk" [20]. The six other papers do not specifically examine TD but mention it in relation to the clients' point of view. The studies and their main extractions are listed in Table 3.

**Table 3.** Results of data extraction of the literature review.

| Finding | Source |
|---|---|
| Examination of TD as part of the product of a company outside of the software industry: in banking systems, embedded systems, mechatronics, automated production systems | [21–26] |
| Examination of TD in software or software-based systems focusing on the client perspective | [27–30] |
| Examination of TD in contracting focusing on the client perspective | [20] |
| Mention of TD relating to the client perspective: (near) invisibility of TD to clients, TD in context of digitalization or enterprise architecture, clients influencing or causing TD in software or software-based systems (e.g., by customization or postponing system updates) | [31–36] |

In summary, it can be observed that there are some TD studies related to companies that use software or software-based systems, also in the manufacturing industry, however these studies are restricted to one specific type of system. There is no general research regarding TD in companies of the manufacturing industry, e.g., regarding the system landscape in place and how TD arises in manufacturing businesses. Case studies in the field of TD, such as [37–40], are mainly performed in enterprises of the software industry or the software development department of a company. Therefore, this study aims at closing this gap in research as described in the following.

## 3 Research Method and Data Collection

To answer the RQ as well as due to the sparse research in this area, a qualitative research design is chosen [41]. The research design consists of qualitative research methods [41], as there is little knowledge about TD in the manufacturing industry and, in general, qualitative approaches allow for an exploration and comprehensive understanding of the subject. The research method chosen is a case study [42] combined with grounded theory [43] for the data analysis and theory development [44]. The data collection method selected are expert interviews, and for the data analysis coding techniques are used to generate theory on how TD occurs in manufacturing businesses. The coding procedure according to Corbin and Strauss [45] is applied, consisting of three modes of coding: open, axial and selective. Comparative analysis is applied during the coding process, following the suggestion of Glaser and Strauss [43], as well as after the theory development to compare the results of this research to TD in the software industry.

This paper contains an exploratory single case study according to Yin's classification of case study types [42]. The case selected is a German middle-sized metal processing company with approx. 100 to 150 employees of which the majority works in production or related departments. The supporting company wants to remain anonymous. The firm has one production site and does not use software as part of its products but as a mean to support its business processes. At the time of the research conduction of this study (the year 2023), the company is about to conduct a system change to exchange several legacy systems. As such a system change requires a thorough analysis of the current situation and needs of the business, this poses an ideal moment to analyse how TD occurs in the company. The company has a heterogeneous IT system landscape, typical for many enterprises of this size, due to the system landscape evolving and growing over time according to [2] and [4]. The system landscape consists of an ERP system, a document management system (DMS), a production planning system (PPS), a manufacturing execution system (MES) and a system for quality assurance. The latter two are less than five years old, the other software systems are significantly older and are to be replaced by a new ERP system with integrated DMS.

To collect data for the research, n = 11 expert interviews are conducted. The experts are from different departments, both business and technical, to gain different perspectives. A list of all interview partners (IPs) is included in Table 4. For the selection of interview participants, a combination of selective and theoretical sampling is used to provide a starting sample as well as keep the necessary flexibility as proposed by Coyne [46]. Initially, the sample includes candidates directly involved in the system change project, mainly key users (KUs). However, during the interviews, it becomes evident that both people new to the company as well as long-time employees provide a valuable source for additional information regarding a new perception towards the system landscape or how the system landscape developed over time. This leads to the inclusion of IP7 and IP9-IP11. All interviews are carried out in person or remote via video-call.

The interviews are conducted as semi-structured interviews using a previously developed interview guideline, consisting of nine questions. The questions include the structure and condition of the IT environment of the company, the assessment of the current situation, what is considered to be negative in or regarding the IT environment and the causes for these aspects. Furthermore, it is asked, how the IT environment developed over time, up to the last 15 years, if there is anything that has been postponed, whether the system change is regarded as necessary and why, as well as what can be accomplished with the system change. The purpose of the guideline is to establish comparability among the interviews for the data analysis stage. The interviews are recorded with the consent of the interviewees and manually transcribed afterwards to prevent information loss. The concept of TD is explained to the interview participants before the interview. To avoid confusion, the questions are phrased to be easily understandable instead of directly using the term TD as it is new for all interviewees.

**Table 4.** Overview of interview partners of the related case.

| IP | Job position | Function in system change project | Years of employment |
|---|---|---|---|
| IP1 | Employee procurement | KU procurement | 3 |
| IP2 | Employee sales | KU sales | <1 |
| IP3 | Head of IT | Project management | 4 |
| IP4 | Managing director | Project sponsor | 4 |
| IP5 | Head of commercial management | KU accounting | 20 |
| IP6 | Head of process engineering | Consultant MES-ERP interface | 9 |
| IP7 | Technical consultant | Indirect supporting role | 28 |
| IP8 | Head of production planning | KU production planning | 3 |
| IP9 | Head of production | Indirect supporting role | 16 |
| IP10 | Employee production planning | KU production planning | <1 |
| IP11 | Electrician, formerly responsible for hardware-bound IT systems | Indirect supporting role | 35 |

The transcripts are then analysed starting with the stage of open coding [45], where the data is broken down into codes, meaning key words or key phrases, using line-by-line analysis. Open coding [45] is performed for each question separately as the emerging codes are to be seen in context with the question. It is important to note, that the analysis of each question is not restricted to the direct answer of the participant to this question but rather to all responses related to the question due to the semi-structured conduction of the interviews. The number of mentions for each code is determined, but the occurrence of a specific code is only counted once per interview to prevent bias as some persons are more talkative or articulate than others. The investigation of other dimensions of the emerging codes as proposed by Corbin and Strauss in [45] is performed in transition to axial coding.

For axial coding [45], a threshold for the number of mentions is determined to eliminate likely less relevant codes and increase the conciseness of the data. The authors develop two approaches to do this: the weighted average and the calculation of the arithmetic mean, using the minimum above and maximum below a mention frequency of 50% of all questions, leading to a threshold of 47%. For the second approach, the number of mentions that meets this threshold or the next closest value above is set as the minimal code count classified as relevant for each question. For the weighted average approach, the weighted average for each question is rounded to the first integer and the result is the minimal code count classified as relevant. The results of both approaches are similar, but the weighted average excludes $n = 5$ codes with four mentions for one question while including $n = 2$ codes with two mentions for another, compared to the second threshold calculation. For this reason, the second approach is chosen. The determined relevant codes are assigned to one or more categories, which can include sub-categories, using the coding paradigm to ask open questions about the context, conditions, action or interaction, and consequences in which the code occurs. To ensure that the real meaning of the codes in their context is represented by the categories, the codes are compared with the question they belong to and with each other.

In the phase of selective coding [45], the developed categories are re-evaluated in different possible perspectives in relation to the phenomenon of TD, which is selected to be the core category. All categories and sub-categories [45] are classified according to the following modified dimensions of the coding paradigm: context, condition, phenomenon, consequence, moderator, action, result. To support the theory development and process documentation, a graphic coding structure is designed to visualize the connections and relationships between the codes, categories, and their classification. To develop a dense and comprehensive theory of TD in a manufacturing business based on the case studied, the coding structure and the developed graphic model of the theory are re-examined and compared to categories, codes, and the original text passages [44].

Glaser and Strauss [43] state the necessity to start without a preconceived theory and avoid theoretical bias. However, to develop a RQ, it is important to have at least a minimum of prior knowledge. For this purpose, the research design and industries of other studies are evaluated to establish the RQ, but the findings and conclusions are excluded to prevent bias. The literature review included in Sect. 2 is conducted after the study and results described in Sects. 3 and 4 are finalized. With the findings gained from the theory, a comparative analysis is conducted. The analysis examines TD in the manufacturing business case study compared to findings from the software industry, based on the theory model developed before.

# 4 Results

## 4.1 Technical Debt Model

Through the open coding analysis 286 codes are found (e.g., heavy reliance on user expertise, customized software, growing system scope, increasing interconnectedness, incomplete system change/implementation, system architecture based on/grew around an outdated system), which are reduced to 156 codes for axial coding. A total of 79 categories and sub-categories are developed (e.g., system knowledge, dependence on individual capabilities, interdependencies of processes/systems, complexity, isolated solutions, degree of integration of solution in IT environment and business).

Regarding this case, TD is caused by a set of conditions while its form depends on the given context in the company. The extent of TD can be augmented or reduced by moderator variables, hereafter called pre-moderator variables due to their presence before or parallel to the phenomenon of TD appearing [47]. The accrued TD leads to, often detrimental, consequences and to reduce or remediate the TD, action has to be taken. Whether action is taken and which action is chosen is influenced by the gravity of consequences and by post-moderator variables [47]. If action is taken, it leads to a result which, in turn, can lead to different context and pre-conditions in re-examination. Opposed to consequences, the post-moderator variables are not a direct effect of TD. The relations are depicted in the theory model in Fig. 1, an excerpt of the detailed findings of the theory elements elaborated in the next paragraphs are included in brackets.

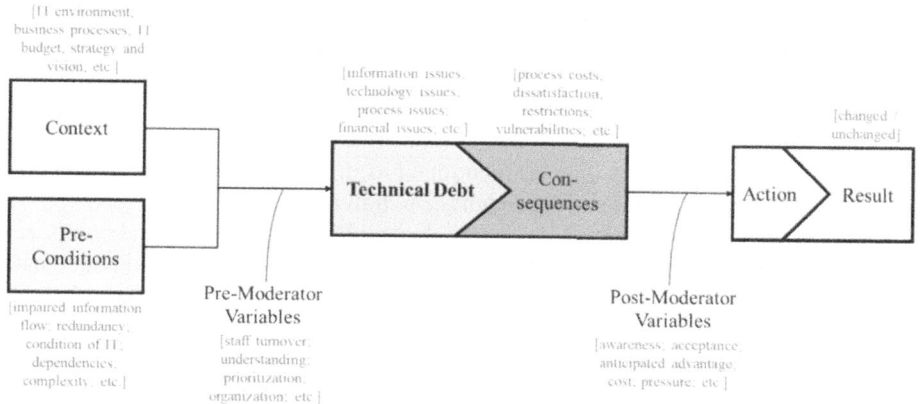

**Fig. 1.** Model of TD for manufacturing SMEs.

The first element, the context, does not hold or cause TD, it describes the circumstances and environment of a company. In the case studied, the context encompasses the IT environment including hardware and software, different business processes, machinery, IT budget, and strategy and vision for IT. Relating to the latter, IP3 states *"[the company] was very progressive [...], when this [PPS] was introduced. [...] But unfortunately, this strategy was no longer pursued."* It is important to stress that the main value chain is the physical production and selling of the products. The IT environment, similar to other SMEs, is heterogeneous and has grown over the years.

In contrast to the context, the conditions may separately or combined lead to TD. Most prominent to mention are the interruption of necessary information flows, redundancies, the degree to which the solution meets the actual business needs, and a low degree of integration of the solutions in the business and IT environment. The information flow may be impaired due to no or insufficient interfaces between systems. This is referred to by IP1, explaining *"We use different programs, [...] and none of them engage or are linked with one another. [...] So, you have [...] no flow within the system."* Other identified pre-conditions are the condition of the IT environment, the sustainability of the solutions, and dependencies on internal or external individual capabilities. Often, the system landscape is knowingly based on and built around legacy systems, as noted by IP7, *"Originally, [PPS] was the central system. [Later, the vendor disappeared from the market.] But then they kept it running and since they already had the system, they continued to build on it."* Another aspect is the complexity of processes or system infrastructure, including interdependencies of processes and systems, the number of systems, their scope, and customizations. This is outlined by IP5, *"[...] a lot of custom programming has been done for us [...] that is not part of the standard software. That's also a problem, because now that we've left our former [ERP] administrator, no one knows anything anymore."*

Pre-moderator variables that contribute to the extent of TD include staff turnover due to the loss of knowledge regarding IT systems and processes, the understanding of the function of IT or the influence of TD on the business in management, as well as the prioritization of TD and management decisions. This is reflected in the statements of IP3, *"[...] IT is always seen as a cost center or simply as a cost driver."* and IP4, *"[...] my predecessor as managing director had touched on these topics every now and then for a short time over the years, but then they were always more or less stopped and ended right at the beginning."* In addition to the aforementioned, the organization and management of processes is to be mentioned as this can either counterbalance or exacerbate conditions, such as the dependency on individuals.

The phenomenon of TD in the case study has multiple dimensions and comprises information, technology, process, and financial issues. Information issues include data discontinuities or inconsistencies, and correlate with process issues, for example inefficiencies such as the duplication of efforts due to repeatedly entering data, media or system discontinuities, or resolving errors. Relating to the latter, IP6 states, *"Well, the consequences are that I have different versions of data sets in different systems, or data records have been processed differently. Worst case, this is not noticed at all, or best case, it leads to an error that I can easily correct."* Some process issues are results of technology issues, these being impaired functionality or risks to IT security in system administration. The risk can be amplified by the system structure or postponed updates as mentioned in the interviews. The information, technology and process issues also manifest in the financial dimension as high accumulated investment needs.

Consequences of the TD in this case accrued are higher process costs due to the higher effort of processes or the introduction of non-value-adding processes. Other consequences are the restriction of productivity, of process evolution, of the ability to act due to an insufficient database for decisions or of the operating ability of the business. The latter is mentioned by IP3, *"So if we imagine that we now have to completely switch to a new office landscape, [...] unfortunately, we are so far behind that certain things may no longer work. So, in addition to the costs, it also has an impact on the general business or on the processes in the business, i.e., the workflows."* Errors can also impact the business and vulnerabilities can develop as reflected by IP4, *"It was only by luck that we didn't have major outages or major difficulties and problems."*

Whether action is taken is influenced by post-moderator variables. These include the assessment and the degree of acceptance of the current situation, the general willingness to act, as well as the anticipated advantage of action, its cost, and external or competitive pressure. Different perspectives are provided by IP11 and IP4, the former stating *"Many managers say, 'I'd rather use the money for something else, there's a fire in another corner, I'll wait a few more years, one or two more years', then they wait and as long as it still works, they don't do it."* In contrast, IP4 states *"After the introduction of this system, we have [...] the foundation to then work on further improvements in different areas, which today provide major deficits."* Especially the necessity to gain and use information to stay competitive is mentioned by several interviewees.

The action taken in the case studied is a system change to replace three legacy systems, and the implementation of adequate interfaces to the other remaining systems. In general, possible actions to remediate TD depend on the case and the possibilities a company has, and include refactoring, restructuring system architecture, or implementing interfaces between existing systems. The system change in this case is expected to result in a better integration of the IT environment, increased sustainability of the IT, improved information distribution and handling, and the evolution of business processes. Reasons for these positive changes are the reduction of system and data discontinuities, more transparency and better data availability due to the connection of the processes in the systems, as well as the streamlining of processes. This is expected to free up resources and be a long-term cost saving compared to the current situation, as noted by IP9 *"It's a cost saving for the company if it all works that way, longer term."* However, some issues will remain, including resource issues, initiative of staff, violations of system specifications, and information inaccuracy due to erroneous data or human-made mistakes. This is summarized concisely by a statement by IP5, *"[...] we must always keep in mind that there will still be problems in the processes and that data records will not be correct. We simply have to keep at it [...]. I think that is the greatest danger, that people simply believe in the system and say, 'new system, now everything will be fine'. But it's not always just the system, it's also the people."*

## 4.2 Comparison to Software Industry

Based on this theory model, the findings are compared to TD studies in or for the software industry. The comparison to studies of Tom et al. [7], Siebra et al. [48], Behutiye et al. [49], Verdecchia et al. [50], and Ramač et al. [51] shows that conditions, pre-moderator variables and consequences are similar in the manufacturing and software industry. Conditions include redundancies in form of code, dependencies on individual capabilities regarding the understanding of the system build or individual knowledge and experience or lack thereof, as well as the complexity of a project. Other conditions encompass the condition of software, relating to legacy systems or artifacts, sustainability as components may be discontinued, and the degree to which the solution meets the actual needs, negatively influenced by unsuitable decisions.

Pre-moderator variables in software development comprise organization, as communication and knowledge transfer are cross-industry challenges, and prioritization in general, which may include favouring quick delivery over proper development. The understanding of the influence of TD on the business in management, mentioned by Tom et al. [7] as ignorance or oversight in management, and staff turnover also influence the extent of TD. An additional software-specific pre-moderator variable is the visibility of TD to customers, proposed by Tom et al. [7], also mentioned by Ramač et al. [51] as the lack of transparency between client and development. This is an important aspect for both parties as the information asymmetry between system vendors and their clients can be a cross-industry variable facilitating TD as stated by Ramasubbu and Kemerer [27]. This also includes the invisibility of client-side TD to vendors. Despite the interdependencies of vendor and client, and vendor-customer situations being common for software systems in the manufacturing industry, the field of TD in vendor-client relationships is understudied with only two studies of Ramasubbu and Kemerer, [27] and [52], and one study of Banker et al. [53].

Consequences mentioned by [7, 48–51] include impaired functionality, increased costs, restrictions of maintainability, performance, and implementation possibilities of new functions, as well as the impact on the operating ability of the business. The latter may refer to reduced development velocity or, in some cases, short-term productivity boosts. The consequences are mainly of adverse nature, also incorporating dissatisfaction of employees and customers, vulnerabilities, and impact on business, which may manifest in the decrease of system quality, the loss of customers or users, and ultimately financial loss. In contrast to the other elements, only one post-moderator variable is found in these studies, namely the anticipated advantage of action regarding the remaining system lifetime [48]. Another difference is the competitive pressure regarding quick releases or regular release cycles as part of the context of many software companies [49].

## 5 Conclusion and Discussion

TD is an ongoing challenge in information systems research and practice as well [6]. Qualitative research insights based on this case study show that TD also occurs on the client-side through different pre-conditions and contexts, independently from or additionally to possible vendor-side TD and can manifest in adverse consequences, on which organizations must react in order to stay competitive. In conclusion, a congruity in most elements of TD can be found in this case study compared to existing research in the software field. The identified differences can mostly be attributed to the fact that the research in software development focuses on one system whereas this study examined the setting of several systems as part of an IT environment. Another cause for differences is the vendor-client relationship present in most SMEs that do not develop and use own software. Different implications for research and practice can be derived. This study extends previous literature on TD (e.g., [7, 8, 14, 17, 38, 39, 48–51]) by adding insights into a manufacturing case, which is a standard case for not software-intensive enterprises as well as a comparable case for many other similar SMEs in the European Union. Based on the findings of this paper, the issues regarding TD for SMEs as an important type of organization can now be better understood, evaluated and compared with other sectors. Enterprises can use the results to protect themselves from the issues occurring with TD, understanding the specific circumstances leading to TD, as well as save IT budget by preventing or controlling TD.

Due to the nature of research, several limitations and possibilities for future research can be found. First, this study investigated one specific case in detail. Although the case is comparable to many other similar manufacturing SMEs in the European Union, future research should discover more cases in different understudied fields and compare as well as extend these findings. Furthermore, the developed model and related factors are not examined in detail. Future studies should investigate the different components and factors in detail to explore and evaluate the strength of their influence. In addition, a practical guidance framework, derived from research in and for SMEs, and its evaluation in practice is important to research.

**Acknowledgments.** We thank all supporters from the company and from OTH Amberg-Weiden.

## References

1. Shang, Z., Zhang, L.: The sustainable digitalization in the manufacturing industry: a bibliometric analysis and research trend. Mobile Inf. Syst. **2022**, 1451705, 1–11 (2022). https://doi.org/10.1155/2022/1451705
2. Demary, V., Fritsch, M., Goecke, H., et al.: Readiness Data Economy. Cologne Institute for Economic Research (2019)
3. Frey, F.J., Hentrich, C., Zdun, U.: Capability-based service identification in service-oriented legacy modernization. In: Kohls, C. (ed.) Proceedings of the 18th European Conference on Pattern Languages of Program (EuroPLoP 2013), pp. 1–12. ACM, New York (2015). https://doi.org/10.1145/2739011.2739021
4. Kraus, P., Baumöl, U.: Erfahrungen im IT-Management für einen gewachsenen Mittelständler. Controlling **28**(12), 728–734 (2016). https://doi.org/10.15358/0935-0381-2016-12-728
5. Brodny, J., Tutak, M.: Digitalization of small and medium-sized enterprises and economic growth: evidence for the EU-27 countries. J. Open Innov.: Technol. Market Complex. **8**(2), 67, 1–31 (2022). https://doi.org/10.3390/joitmc8020067
6. Dalal, V., Krishnakanthan, K., Münstermann, B., et al.: Tech Debt: Reclaiming Tech Equity. https://www.mckinsey.com/capabilities/mckinsey-digital/our-insights/tech-debt-reclaiming-tech-equity/. Accessed 23 Mar 2024
7. Tom, E., Aurum, A., Vidgen, R.: An exploration of technical debt. J. Syst. Softw. **86**(6), 1498–1516 (2013). https://doi.org/10.1016/j.jss.2012.12.052
8. Li, Z., Avgeriou, P., Liang, P.: A systematic mapping study on technical debt and its management. J. Syst. Softw. **101**, 193–220 (2015). https://doi.org/10.1016/j.jss.2014.12.027
9. Ampatzoglou, A., Ampatzoglou, A., Chatzigeorgiou, A., et al.: The financial aspect of managing technical debt: a systematic literature review. Inf. Softw. Technol. **64**, 52–73 (2015). https://doi.org/10.1016/j.infsof.2015.04.001
10. Alves, N.S., Mendes, T.S., de Mendonça, M.G., et al.: Identification and management of technical debt: a systematic mapping study. Inf. Softw. Technol. **70**, 100–121 (2016). https://doi.org/10.1016/j.infsof.2015.10.008

11. BenIdris, M., Ammar, H., Dzielski, D.: Investigate, identify and estimate the technical debt: a systematic mapping study. Int. J. Softw. Eng. Appl. **9**(5), 1–14 (2018). https://doi.org/10.5121/ijsea.2018.9501
12. Rios, N., de Mendonça Neto, M.G., Oliveira Spínola, R.: A tertiary study on technical debt: types, management strategies, research trends, and base information for practitioners. Inf. Softw. Technol. **102**, 117–145 (2018). https://doi.org/10.1016/j.infsof.2018.05.010
13. Cunningham, W.: The WyCash portfolio management system. ACM SIGPLAN OOPS Messenger **4**(2), 29–30 (1993). https://doi.org/10.1145/157710.157715
14. Seaman, C., Guo, Y., Zazworka, N., et al.: Using technical debt data in decision making: potential decision approaches. In: Third International Workshop on Managing Technical Debt, pp. 45–48. IEEE, Zurich (2012). https://doi.org/10.1109/MTD.2012.6225999
15. Fowler, M.: Technical Debt Quadrant. https://www.martinfowler.com/bliki/TechnicalDebtQuadrant.html. Accessed 23 Mar 2024
16. McConnell, S.: Managing Technical Debt. http://www.construx.com/uploadedfiles/resources/whitepapers/Managing%20Technical%20Debt.pdf. Accessed 23 Mar 2024
17. Kruchten, P., Nord, R.L., Ozkaya, I.: Technical debt: from metaphor to theory and practice. IEEE Softw. **29**(6), 18–21 (2012). https://doi.org/10.1109/MS.2012.167
18. Stopford, B., Wallace, K., Allspaw, J.: Technical debt: challenges and perspectives. IEEE Softw. **34**(4), 79–81 (2017). https://doi.org/10.1109/MS.2017.99
19. Kitchenham, B.: Procedures for Performing Systematic Reviews. Technical Report, TR/SE-0401, pp. 1–26 (2004)
20. Beulen, E.: Implementing and contracting agile and DevOps: a survey in the Netherlands. In: Kotlarsky, J., Oshri, I., Willcocks, L. (eds.) Digital Services and Platforms. LNBIP, vol. 344, pp. 124–146. Springer, Cham (2018). https://doi.org/10.1007/978-3-030-15850-7_7
21. Ampatzoglou, A., Ampatzoglou, A., Chatzigeorgiou, A., et al.: The perception of technical debt in the embedded systems domain: an industrial case study. In: IEEE 8th International Workshop on Managing Technical Debt, pp. 9–16. IEEE, Piscataway (2016). https://doi.org/10.1109/MTD.2016.8
22. Hayretci, H.E., Aydemir, F.B.: A multi case study on legacy system migration in the banking industry. In: La Rosa, M., Sadiq, S., Teniente, E. (eds.) Advanced Information Systems Engineering. LNCS, vol. 12751, pp. 536–550. Springer, Cham (2021). https://doi.org/10.1007/978-3-030-79382-1_32
23. Block, L.: Managing software evolution in embedded automotive systems. In: Bargende, M., Reuss, H.-C., Wagner, A. (eds.) 20. Internationales Stuttgarter Symposium. PROCEE, pp. 557–571. Springer, Wiesbaden (2020). https://doi.org/10.1007/978-3-658-30995-4_48
24. Dong, Q.H., Ocker, F., Vogel-Heuser, B.: Technical debt as indicator for weaknesses in engineering of automated production systems. Prod. Eng. Res. Develop. **13**(3–4), 273–282 (2019). https://doi.org/10.1007/s11740-019-00897-0
25. Bi, F., Vogel-Heuser, B., Huang, Z., et al.: Characteristics, causes, and consequences of technical debt in the automation domain. J. Syst. Softw. **204**, 111725 (2023). https://doi.org/10.1016/j.jss.2023.111725
26. Vogel-Heuser, B., Bi, F.: Interdisciplinary effects of technical debt in companies with mechatronic products. J. Syst. Softw. **171**, 110809 (2021). https://doi.org/10.1016/j.jss.2020.110809
27. Ramasubbu, N., Kemerer, C.F.: Technical debt and the reliability of enterprise software systems: a competing risks analysis. Manage. Sci. **62**(5), 1487–1510 (2016). https://doi.org/10.1287/mnsc.2015.2196
28. Doğancı, Y., Özcan-Top, Ö., Koçyiğit, A.: Analyzing technical debt of a CRM application by categorizing ambiguous issue statements. In: Arabnia, H.R., Deligiannidis, L., Tinetti, F.G. et al. (eds.) Advances in Software Engineering, Education, and e-Learning. TRACOSCI, pp. 705–717. Springer, Cham (2021). https://doi.org/10.1007/978-3-030-70873-3_49

29. Ionescu, T.B., Schlund, S., Schmidbauer, C.: Epistemic debt: a concept and measure of technical ignorance in smart manufacturing. In: Nunes, I.L. (ed.) Advances in Human Factors and Systems Interaction. AISC, vol. 959, pp. 81–93. Springer, Cham (2020). https://doi.org/10.1007/978-3-030-20040-4_8
30. Dong, Q.H., Vogel-Heuser, B.: Cross-disciplinary and cross-life-cycle-phase technical debt in automated production systems. IFAC-PapersOnLine **51**(11), 1192–1199 (2018). https://doi.org/10.1016/j.ifacol.2018.08.428
31. Ivanov, I.I.: Chasing the crowd: digital transformations and the digital driven system design paradigm. In: Shishkov, B. (ed.) Business Modeling and Software Design. LNBIP, vol. 356, pp. 64–80. Springer, Cham (2019). https://doi.org/10.1007/978-3-030-24854-3_5
32. Kanin, O., Drews, P.: Enterprise architecture management support for digital transformation projects in very large enterprises. In: Almeida, J.P.A., Karastoyanova, D., Guizzardi, G., et al. (eds.) Enterprise Design, Operations, and Computing. LNCS, vol. 13585, pp. 74–90. Springer, Cham (2022). https://doi.org/10.1007/978-3-031-17604-3_5
33. Postolea, I.D., Bodea, C.-N.: Building resilience through digital transformation. In: Ciurea, C., Boja, C., Pocatilu, P., et al. (eds.) Education, Research and Business Technologies. SIST, vol. 276, pp. 371–381. Springer, Singapore (2022). https://doi.org/10.1007/978-981-16-8866-9_31
34. Sunyaev, A., Dehling, T., Strahringer, S., et al.: The future of enterprise information systems. Bus. Inf. Syst. Eng. **65**(6), 731–751 (2023). https://doi.org/10.1007/s12599-023-00839-2
35. Lampe, J.: Was Controller beim Einsatz von KI beachten müssen. Control. Manag. Rev. **65**(2), 24–31 (2021). https://doi.org/10.1007/s12176-020-0360-7
36. Ali, N., Baker, S., O'Crowley, R., et al.: Architecture consistency: state of the practice, challenges and requirements. Empir. Softw. Eng. **23**(1), 224–258 (2018). https://doi.org/10.1007/s10664-017-9515-3
37. Codabux, Z., Williams, B.: Managing technical debt: an industrial case study. In: Kruchten, P. (ed.) 4th International Workshop on Managing Technical Debt 2013, pp. 8–15. IEEE, Piscataway (2013). https://doi.org/10.1109/MTD.2013.6608672
38. Kazman, R., Cai, Y., Mo, R., et al.: A case study in locating the architectural roots of technical debt. In: IEEE/ACM 37th International Conference on Software Engineering, vol. 2, pp. 179–188. IEEE, Piscataway (2015). https://doi.org/10.1109/ICSE.2015.146
39. Martini, A., Bosch, J., Chaudron, M.: Investigating architectural technical debt accumulation and refactoring over time. Inf. Softw. Technol. **67**, 237–253 (2015). https://doi.org/10.1016/j.infsof.2015.07.005
40. Soliman, M., Avgeriou, P., Li, Y.: Architectural design decisions that incur technical debt — an industrial case study. Information and Software Technology **139**, 106669 (2021). https://doi.org/10.1016/j.infsof.2021.106669
41. Recker, J.: Scientific research in information systems: a beginner's guide. In: Progress in IS, 2nd edn. Springer, Cham (2021). https://doi.org/10.1007/978-3-030-85436-2
42. Yin, R.K.: Case Study Research and Applications: Design and Methods, 6th edn. SAGE Publications, Los Angeles (2018)
43. Glaser, B.G., Strauss, A.L.: The Discovery of Grounded Theory: Strategies for Qualitative Research. Aldine Transaction, New Brunswick (1967). https://doi.org/10.4324/9780203793206
44. Strauss, A., Corbin, J.: Grounded theory methodology: an overview. In: Denzin, N.K., Lincoln, Y.S. (eds.) Handbook of Qualitative Research, pp. 273–285. SAGE Publications, Thousand Oaks (1994)
45. Corbin, J., Strauss, A.: Grounded theory research: procedures, canons and evaluative criteria. Z. Soziol. **19**(6), 418–427 (1990). https://doi.org/10.1515/zfsoz-1990-0602

46. Coyne, I.T.: Sampling in qualitative research. Purposeful and theoretical sampling; merging or clear boundaries? J. Adv. Nurs. **26**(3), 623–630 (1997). https://doi.org/10.1046/j.1365-2648.1997.t01-25-00999.x
47. Fritz, M.S., Arthur, A.M.: Moderator variables. In: Braddick, O. (ed.) Oxford Research Encyclopedia of Psychology. Oxford University Press, Oxford (2017)
48. Siebra, C.A., Oliveira, R.G., Seaman, C.B., et al.: Theoretical conceptualization of TD: a practical perspective. J. Syst. Softw. **120**, 219–237 (2016). https://doi.org/10.1016/j.jss.2016.05.043
49. Behutiye, W.N., Rodríguez, P., Oivo, M., et al.: Analyzing the concept of technical debt in the context of agile software development: a systematic literature review. Inf. Softw. Technol. **82**, 139–158 (2017). https://doi.org/10.1016/j.infsof.2016.10.004
50. Verdecchia, R., Kruchten, P., Lago, P.: Architectural technical debt: a grounded theory. In: Jansen, A., Malavolta, I., Muccini, H., et al. (eds.) 4th European Conference on Software Architecture 2020. LNCS, vol. 12292, pp. 202–219. Springer, Cham (2020). https://doi.org/10.1007/978-3-030-58923-3_14
51. Ramač, R., Mandić, V., Taušan, N., et al.: Prevalence, common causes and effects of technical debt. J. Syst. Softw. **184**, 111114 (2022). https://doi.org/10.1016/j.jss.2021.111114
52. Ramasubbu, N., Kemerer, C.F.: Controlling technical debt remediation in outsourced enterprise systems maintenance. J. Manag. Inf. Syst. **38**(1), 4–28 (2021). https://doi.org/10.1080/07421222.2021.1870377
53. Banker, R., Liang, Y., Ramasubbu, N.: Technical debt and firm performance. Manage. Sci. **67**(5), 3174–3194 (2021). https://doi.org/10.1287/mnsc.2019.3542

# Knowledge and Traceability Management

# Discovery Rules for Depicting Tacit Knowledge Usage and Management in Fractal Enterprise Models

Ilia Bider[1,2](✉) and Erik Perjons[1]

[1] Stockholm University, Borgarfjordsgatan 12, 16455 Kista, Stockholm, Sweden
{ilia,perjons}@dsv.su.se
[2] University of Tartu, Ülikooli 18, 50090 Tartu, Estonia

**Abstract.** The paper introduces rules to help identify and depict in a model enterprise activities that engage tacit knowledge. This is done using a specific enterprise modeling technique called Fractal Enterprise Model (FEM). However, the result can be of interest to researchers and practitioners using other modeling techniques. Though representing tacit knowledge is more or less mandatory for research and practice of Knowledge Management (KM), it is very seldom depicted explicitly in enterprise models of any kind. The type of rules presented in this paper follows our suggestion to consider the so-called discovery power of enterprise modeling languages alongside its expressive power.

**Keywords:** tacit knowledge · discovery power · enterprise model · knowledge management · Fractal Enterprise Model · FEM

## 1 Introduction

This paper explores the concept of discovery power introduced in our previous paper [1]. The concept is informally defined as the "Degree of help provided by the structure of enterprise modeling language to expand a partly built model or fill gaps in it." What the enterprise modeling language helps to discover depends on the language, as the discovery power differs for different languages. For practical purposes, the discovery power of an enterprise modeling language can be represented as a set of rules that guide the modeler on what else can be found and depicted based on what is already depicted in the model[1].

In this paper, we investigate only one enterprise modeling language, the so-called Fractal Enterprise Model (FEM) [2, 3], and only in one aspect of discovery power -

---

[1] The term degree used in the informal definition does not imply that discovery power is a quantitative parameter. As the discovery power of different modeling languages lies in different areas, a quantitative description does not make much sense. The high discovery in the area that lies outside the current project goals will be irrelevant to the project. For example, a language with good discovery power related to tacit knowledge may not be useful for a project that is not intended to depict such knowledge.

adding to the model activities that are related to tacit knowledge. FEM was chosen because it is our invention; thus, we have enough knowledge about its structure, and we have experience of using it in enterprise modeling. Tacit knowledge was chosen because activities related to it are seldom depicted in enterprise models.

FEM has a form of a directed graph with two main types of nodes, *processes* and *assets*, where the arrows (edges) from assets to processes show which assets are used in which processes and arrows from processes to assets show which processes help to have specific assets in "healthy" and working order. The arrows are labeled with meta-tags that show how a given asset is used, e.g., workforce, reputation, infrastructure, etc., or how a given process helps to have the given assets "in order", i.e., acquire, maintain, or retire.

The term *tacit knowledge* was introduced by Michael Polanyi in several of his essays [4, 5] to differentiate the knowledge that a human being uses subconsciously from explicit knowledge that is depicted in human artifacts, like texts. The distinction between tacit and explicit knowledge is an established fact in the knowledge management discipline, which also considers various types of processes of converting one kind of knowledge into another. The most known type of conversions in the business world was presented in [6], which introduces the cycle of knowledge conversions that consists of the following elements: *socialization, externalization, combination*, and *internalization*.

The discovery rules presented in this paper guide the FEM modeler to add the usage of tacit knowledge to the model or to add processes that manage tacit knowledge, e.g., *socialization*, that may exist in the enterprise.

The rest of the paper is structured according to the following plan. In Sect. 2, we give a background to our research, i.e., knowledge base, research approach, and introduction to FEM. In Sect. 3, we introduced discovery rules related to the management of tacit knowledge inside an enterprise. In Sect. 4, we present some rules associated with the management of tacit knowledge outside an enterprise. In Sect. 5, we draw some conclusions and suggest future directions.

## 2 Research Background

### 2.1 Tacit Knowledge

The term *tacit knowledge* was introduced by Michael Polanyi to differentiate internal knowledge from explicit or codified knowledge in books, manuals, papers, etc. Moreover, he believed that actual knowledge was always personal and tacit [4], while explicit knowledge was used for transferring tacit knowledge. Now, the term tacit knowledge is central to the Knowledge Management (KM) discipline, which deals with the usage and management of knowledge in both tacit and explicit forms. One of the important achievements in KM is the SECI model of Nonaka [6], which explains how knowledge is created in organizations, where SECI stays for *Socialization – Externalization – Combination – Internalization*, see Fig. 1.

In Fig. 1, *socialization* refers to changing the knowledge while it remains in the tacit form without converting it to the explicit form; *externalization* refers to transforming the knowledge from the tacit to the explicit form; *internalization* refers to transforming knowledge from the explicit to the tacit form. In this paper, we will model three of

SECI's transformations, leaving the *combination* outside our consideration, as it does not include tacit knowledge.

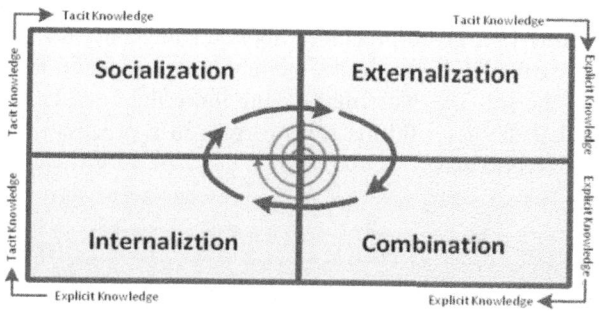

**Fig. 1.** Knowledge management in organizations

## 2.2 Introduction to Fractal Enterprise Model

As FEM is not a widely spread enterprise modeling technique, we will present the basic concepts and the relations between them used in this technique based on an example. The example concerns the model of internal IT support activities, and it was chosen because of its direct relationship to the usage and management of tacit knowledge. The model is presented in Fig. 2. The upper part of Fig. 2 presents a model, and the lower part gives some explanations.

The model represents a situation where people complete activities in a process or service supported by an IT system. When they do not understand how to use the system, they contact IT support, which helps them with advice on how to use the system in a particular situation. Sometimes, the support personnel discover that the system is not adjusted to handle the situation or that its manual does not cover what to do. In such cases, they ask the people who maintain the system to make the necessary changes.

The model in Fig. 2 uses two main FEM concepts for describing the internals of a company; a process – a repetitive behavior – represented as an oval, and an asset – a set of things or actors that are needed for the behavior to become repetitive – represented as a rectangle. A relation between a process and an asset is represented by an arrow. FEM differentiates two main types of relations between processes and assets. The first – *used-in* relation – is a relation of a process "using" an asset; in this case, the arrow points from the asset to the process and has a solid line. The second – *managed-by* relation – is a relation of a process managing the asset, e.g., adding elements; in this case, the arrow points from the process to the asset and has a dashed line.

Processes and assets have some properties, several of which are presented visually. For example, a dashed-dotted border of an asset (see Fig. 2) means that the asset is a tacit asset that resides in the heads of some agents. In which heads it resides is shown by a blue dashed arrow (a generic asymmetric association) with the label *Resides within*.

In FEM, a label inside an oval names the given process, and a label inside a rectangle names the given asset. Arrows are also labeled to show the meaning of relations between the processes and assets. A label on an arrow pointing from an asset to a process identifies the role the given asset plays in the process, for example, *Workforce* or *Infrastructure*. A label on an arrow pointing from a process to an asset identifies how the process manages (i.e., changes) the asset. In FEM, an asset is considered as a set of entities capable of playing a given role in a given process. Labels leading into assets from processes reflect how the set is affected; for example, the label *Acquire* identifies that the process can/should increase the set size. Note that having more than one label on an arrow is possible; it shows that the asset fulfills several roles in a process or that the process manages an asset in several ways.

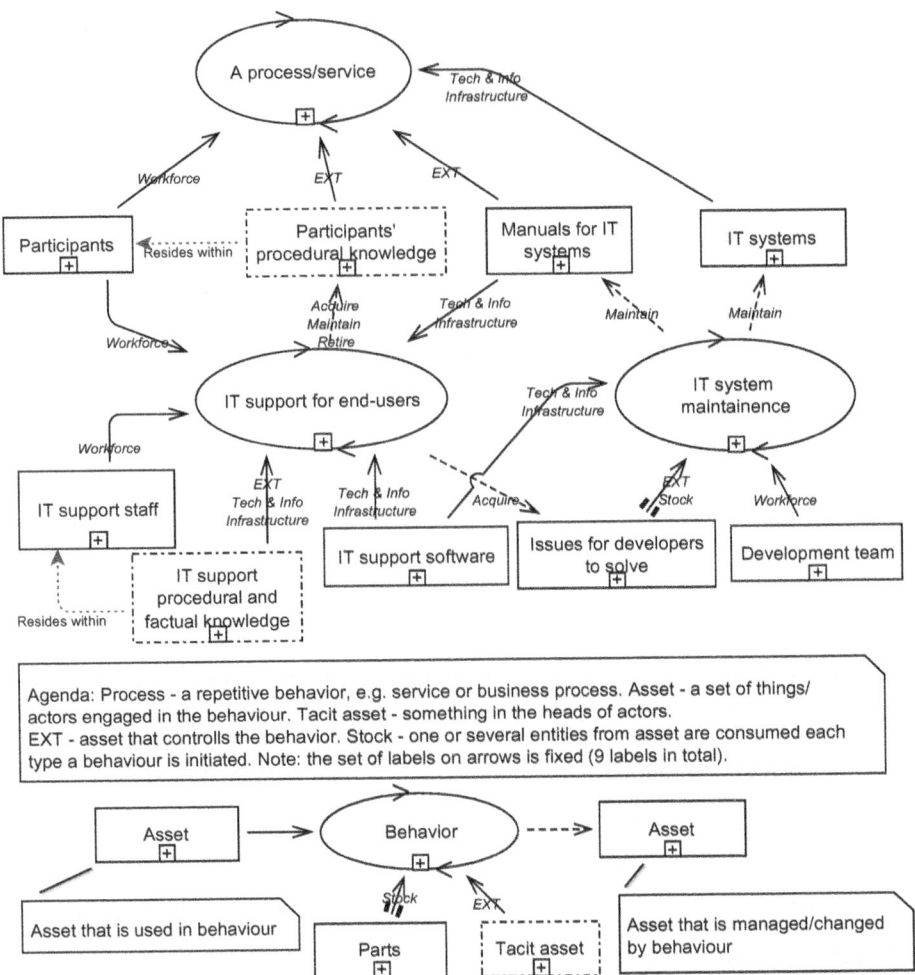

**Fig. 2.** FEM for internal IT support activities

Labels inside ovals (representing processes) and rectangles (representing assets) are not standardized. They can be set according to the terminology accepted in the given domain or be specific to a given organization. Labels on arrows (which represent the relations between processes and assets) are standardized. This is done using a relatively limited set of abstract relations, such as *Workforce* or *Acquire*, which are clarified by the domain- and context-specific labels inside ovals and rectangles.

Note that standard labels on relations are quite abstract, which forces the modeler to uncover the essence of the relations between the elements. This does not affect the readability of the models for the stakeholders, as they understand the models based on the labels inside the shapes. Standardization of the labels on the relations facilitates the formal analysis of the models and the usage of patterns based on the labels on relationships, which is essential for this work.

While several types of relations show how an asset is used in a process (see example in Fig. 1), only three types of relations describe how a process manages an asset – *Acquire*, *Maintain*, and *Retire*. *Acquire* means, as mentioned above, that new elements are added to the asset, *Retire* means that elements are removed from the asset, and *Maintain* means that elements are changed so that they can continue to be part of the asset engaged in the respective process.

The *Stock* label on used-in relation has a special meaning. It indicates that one or more of the asset elements are consumed in each run of the process. This means that the asset should be filled in constantly. The *Stock* label can be alone, which means that the asset has some consumable parts, or it can be accompanied by some other label that clarifies the essence of the elements of the asset. For example, the *Stock* label can be accompanied by the label *EXT* (EXecultable template), which means that the elements of the asset steer the execution of the process; see an example of such a case in Fig. 2. The *EXT* label can be used alone as well; in Fig. 2, *Manuals for IT systems* fulfills this function.

As we can see from Fig. 2, tacit knowledge can fulfill two roles:

- *EXT* – procedural tacit knowledge, that is, tacit knowledge on how to complete the activities
- *Tech & Info Infrastructure* – factual tacit knowledge, that is, tacit knowledge in the form of facts that might be needed for completing activities.

As we can see from the example, tacit knowledge is represented in FEM as assets that are used in activities in the same way as other assets in the model. Activities that use or affect tacit knowledge are shown in the same way as those that use or affect tangible elements like documents, IT systems, etc. Such activities are connected not only to elements that represent tacit knowledge but also to other kinds of elements. We also show in whose heads the tacit knowledge resides; this is done by using an association relation that connects a tacit asset with the asset that represents the actor(s) who possess this knowledge. This relation automatically gets the label *Resides within* if the modeler uses our *Fem toolkit* [3] for building the models.

The above introduction to FEM has concepts that are needed for understanding most of the rules presented in Sect. 3. Additional concepts are introduced as the needs arrive. Readers who are interested to know more about FEM and why it has the term *fractal* in the name are referred to papers [2, 3].

## 2.3 Research Approach

The goal of this research is to develop a set of rules that can help a FEM modeler to discover and depict activities that include tacit knowledge. Therefore, it is quite natural to choose the Design Science (DS) paradigm [7, 8] as a research approach. DS focuses on looking for generic solutions for problems, known and unknown. The result of a DS research project can be a "solution" to a problem in the terminology of [8] or an "artifact" in the terminology of [7]. Alternatively, the result can be in the form of "negative knowledge", stating that a particular approach is not appropriate for solving certain kinds of problems.

The artifact/solution that we want to develop – a set of rules – is a complement to FEM that allows a modeler that uses this modeling technique to find and add to the model new elements related to the usage and management of tacit knowledge.

The knowledge base that we use for this DS project was obtained during our engagement in the field of knowledge management; see, for example, [9–11], as well as in using FEM in various projects, e.g. [12]. The latter include the latest works, like [13], in which we have used elements that represent tacit knowledge.

Roughly speaking, a DS project can be represented as an iterative two-phase process, where in each iteration, the design phase is followed by the testing phase of the design in practice. The testing phase provides the basis for the design phase in the next iteration. The work presented in this paper covers the design phase of the first iteration.

## 2.4 Literature Review: Tacit Knowledge in Enterprise Models

Our search for literature on the topic used two different approaches. One was searching databases, like ResearchGate or Google Scholar, on *tacit knowledge* and *enterprise models*. Another was to send a request to email lists that are comprised of specialists in the domain; in particular, we used the AISworld list and the Ifip-wg81 list. The result was that we did not find any works that presented a holistic view on the issue, but we did find some work devoted to issues of presenting the usage and management of tacit knowledge. A typical example here is the paper [14] devoted to depicting tacit knowledge's externalization using the DEMO [15] language. In this section, we will overview some of these works to show which issues are taken into consideration.

In the paper [16], the authors suggested extending BPMN with knowledge objects that can be used and be affected by tasks included in the model. These suggestions are based on features in another modeling language called KMDL [17], which the authors consider the most advanced in presenting knowledge.

An extensive study of knowledge exploited in the system development process is presented in [18] using ArchiMate. It maps the skills needed and used in various parts of software systems development. However, elements representing skills in [18] are totally separated from elements representing business activities, like services and processes. The paper uses only the capabilities and roles/agents to present the ideas. Thus, this work does not realize our principle of having "normal" activities to show the usage and management of tacit knowledge.

An interesting example of a project related to knowledge management and modeling is presented in [19]. The paper describes the project aimed at creating a computerized assistant that helps in maintaining equipment. For this purpose, the authors created a more detailed version of Nonaka's SECI cycle [6] that includes more phases related to externalization and internalization. They use a conceptual model of an organization that maintains the equipment, which includes all active agents and their knowledge (presumably tacit) of particular parts of the equipment. This model is used by the computerized assistant to suggest who should be called when some part of the equipment has failed. The part that failed was established by sensors. The model used in [19] has elements that represent tacit knowledge and its connection to the agents that possess it and to the parts of the equipment it concerns. This allows to find the right experts when the equipment fails based on the signal of the sensor that determines which part of the equipment has failed.

The information on the knowledge included in the model used in [19] is aligned with the goals of the computerized assistant. It includes detailed information on who possesses the knowledge and where it should be used – in repairing a certain part of the equipment. The model does not include how this knowledge is obtained and maintained, as this information is not needed for the purpose.

To summarize this short section, we can state the following. Our focus is on a specific language for which no systematic effort has been made to understand how to represent the usage and management of tacit knowledge. Nevertheless, the result of our investigation might be of interest to researchers using other enterprise modeling languages. The challenges of integrating tacit knowledge representation within enterprise models depicted with the help of a modeling language remain largely unexplored.

## 2.5 Discovery Power of Enterprise Modeling Languages

Following [1], we informally define the concept of Discovery power of an enterprise modeling language as:

> *"Degree of help provided by the structure of enterprise modeling language to expand a partly built model or fill gaps in it."*

By the "structure of the enterprise modeling language", we mean not only syntax but a combination of syntax, semantics, and pragmatics of the language that facilitates looking for missing information. The discovery power is connected to specific means to express ideas in the given enterprise modeling language. In FEM, to such specific ideas belong the central concepts, such as *process* – repetitive behavior, *asset* – a set of things or actors that participate in the behavior, as well as specific labels on the relations, e.g., *EXT*, *Stock*, *Acquire*, etc. In addition, there are essential subclasses for the central concept, e.g., tacit asset that can increase the discovery power of FEM.

[1] suggest a way to operationalize the discovery power of a language so that it can be used in practice. It is done by having a set of rules that show what can be added to the model in case some specific elements already exist in it. In [1], each rule consists of two parts: the left part shows what should exist in the model, and the right part repeats the left part but has some new elements in it. In this paper, we simplify the rule by having only the right part from the previous suggestion but highlighting all elements that should be added. An example of such a rule that will be explained in the next section is presented

in Fig. 3. Concepts that should be added have the rose background, and relations that should be added are represented by thicker arrows.

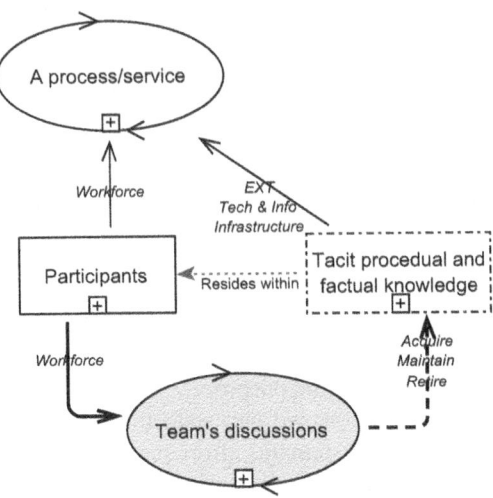

**Fig. 3.** Socialization within one team

## 3 Discovery Rules for Internal Tacit Assets Management

As has been mentioned in Sect. 1, according to [1], a discovery rule consists of two parts: (1) what should already be in the model and (2) what could be added based on it. The rule should be complemented by discussing how to find out whether the addition exists in reality. As the rules in this paper are related to the tacit, i.e., undocumented knowledge, the way to discover whether a new fragment should be added to the model is to ask the people who are supposed to possess this tacit knowledge. Typical methods for getting relevant information are interviews, surveys, and facilitating workshops.

### 3.1 Adding Tacit Asset

The rule *Adding Tacit Asset* concerns people's participation in a process (or service) and their use of tacit knowledge in that process. The rule is presented in Fig. 4a (left diagram). The tacit knowledge can be procedural knowledge – how to drive/participate in the process, which is marked by the *EXT* label, or factual knowledge that is used in completing activities; the latter is marked by the *Tech & Info Infrastructure* label. The modeler's task is to establish whether the tacit knowledge is used and of which type. For example, if the instructions of what to do are shown on the computer screen for each activity, and people read and complete instructions precisely as they are shown, the tacit procedural knowledge should not be added to the model.

### 3.2 Learning from Experience

The rule *Learning from experience* concerns changes in tacit knowledge that happen when people are engaged in repetitive behavior. The rule is presented in Fig. 4b (right diagram). It adds one relation to already existing ones, i.e., the relation that changes the tacit knowledge while people are participating in the repetitive behavior; this relation is highlighted by a thicker arrow in Fig. 4b. To establish whether such a relation exists, the modeler needs to talk to the participants.

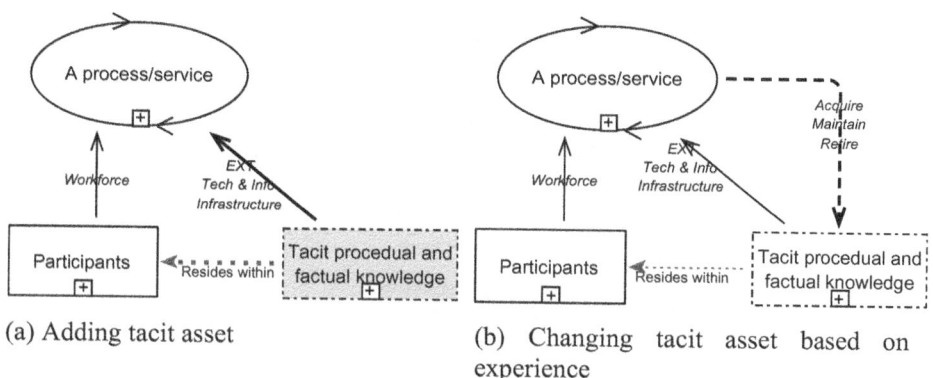

**Fig. 4.** Natural usage and management of tacit assets

### 3.3 Socialization

The rule of *Socialization within one team* is presented in Fig. 3. It adds a process/repetitive behavior (i.e., *Team's discussions*) that consists of team members periodically meeting to exchange their experiences related to the process. Such meetings do not need to be formalized; they can be held during lunches or breaks. To determine whether such meetings occur, the modeler needs to discuss it with the process participants.

Socialization between different teams happens in a larger enterprise where more than one team participates in the same kind of repetitive behavior. For example, a multinational company may have customer support centers in multiple locations. The rule of *Socialization between teams* is presented in Fig. 5. Whether such socialization exists needs to be established by talking to the team members in the different teams. It can be formally arranged as periodical conferences or be informal, e.g., be arranged through communication between the members of different teams via phone, email, etc.

### 3.4 Externalization

Externalization is related to converting tacit knowledge into an explicit form, e.g., in the form of text or a workflow diagram depicting the process in which people participate. Such explicit knowledge can be used to analyze the situation and decide on changes. Ultimately, it can result in new process maps or new manuals for the process in which people participate. When this happens, there will be a process of internalization, i.e., converting new explicit knowledge into the tacit form, see Fig. 1. Internalization is discussed in the next subsection.

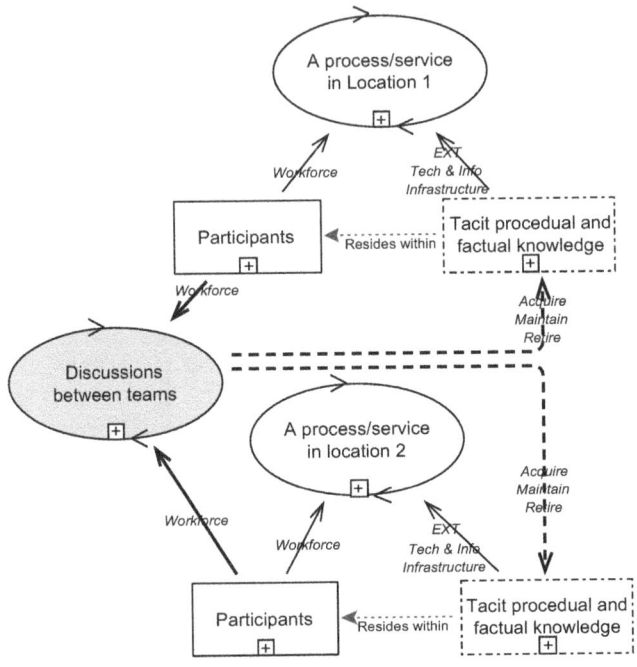

**Fig. 5.** Socialization between teams

In Fig. 6, we present two rules of externalization; diagram (a) represents *Externalization based on reflection*, while diagram (b) represents *Externalization with experts*, where an expert or group of experts are involved. In the second case, the investigation may include interviews, facilitating workshops, etc. Investigators can be people from the current enterprise (*Workforce*) or external consultants (*Partner*).

There is a new type of relations in these diagrams depicted as dashed-dotted blue arrows with a thick perpendicular line as a starting point. Such an arrow can be drawn between a process and any other concept of FEM. It means that the process monitors/investigates the reality behind the concept without an aim to change it. This relation is used in Fig. 6 to show that the aim of the added processes is to investigate the tacit knowledge, which cannot be done directly. It can only be done via the participation of people who possess this knowledge in the process, hence their role as *Workforce*.

### 3.5 Internalization

Internalization is a process of converting explicit knowledge into tacit. This is needed when some changes are introduced in the way a process/repetitive behavior should be carried out. The changes can be related to a new IT system or another kind of equipment that has been introduced, or when a new sequence of activities has been suggested. The rules for internalization are presented in Fig. 7. There are two rules: (a) *Self-studying* (on the left) when people read some documents, e.g., manuals, and (b) *Training* (on the right) - studying with a teacher or expert.

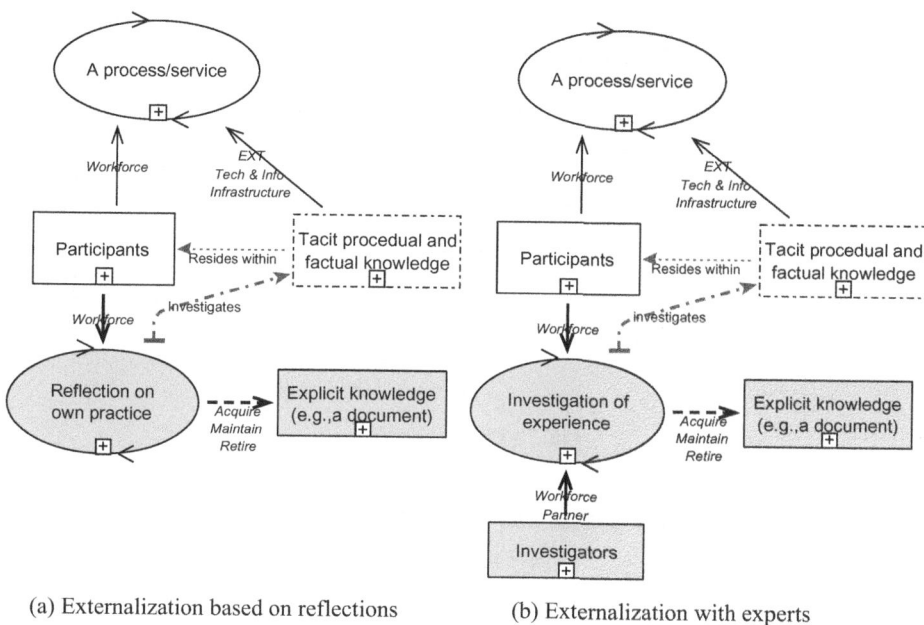

(a) Externalization based on reflections  (b) Externalization with experts

**Fig. 6.** Externalization

To find out whether one or both of the rules can be applied, the modeler needs to talk to the process participants.

### 3.6 An Example

Consider a situation depicted in Fig. 2. Let us start with a root node (*A process/service*) and three assets attached to it: (1) *Participants*, (2) *IT systems*, and (3) *Manuals for IT systems*. Then, we can try to apply the rule depicted on the left in Fig. 4. If we establish that tacit knowledge is used in the situation, we add one more asset to the root - tacit knowledge and its usage.

After that, we can try to apply the rule depicted on the right in Fig. 7. With the help of it we can add the process *IT support for end-users*, where *IT support staff* plays the role of *Teachers*. Note that the model in the example of Fig. 2 has more elements than what is depicted in the rule. These elements must be found separately; some can be found by using other type of discovery rules, the ones that have not been formulated yet.

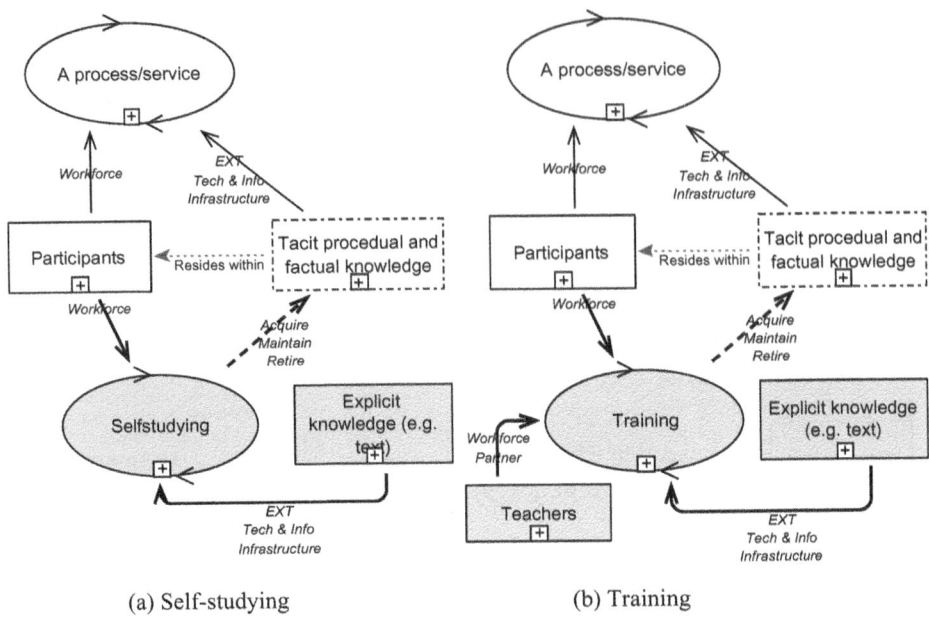

(a) Self-studying  (b) Training

**Fig. 7.** Internalization

## 4  Discovery Rules for External Tacit Assets Management

In this section, we will present examples of rules that are related to managing and using tacit knowledge that belongs to the agents outside the current enterprise. These rules are presented in Figs. 8, 9, and 10. The rule in Fig. 8, *Adding reputation*, shows the possibility of creating tacit knowledge (*Reputation of a good provider*) by providing customers with good products and services. To establish whether this rule applies, the modeler needs to investigate the customers; surveys or interviews are appropriate methods for this end.

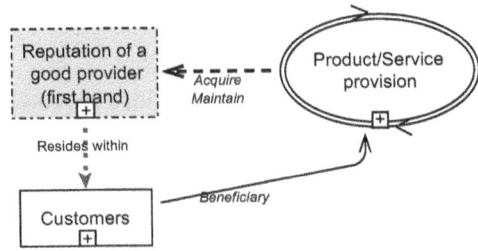

**Fig. 8.** Adding reputation

If customers have a favorable opinion of our products and services, the next step is to establish whether they spread this information to potential customers who do not know us. This, again, can be established by interviewing customers or having a survey.

If it is established that customers spread their opinions to people/organizations that do not know us, we can apply the rule presented in Fig. 9, *Adding reputation spreading*.

The rule in Fig. 9 has a new concept – *external pool* and new relations related to it – *draw from/add to*. An external pool is represented by a cloud shape, see Fig. 9; it depicts a set of things, active or passive, from which an organization can acquire some elements or to which it can add some elements. The label inside the external pool describes its content.

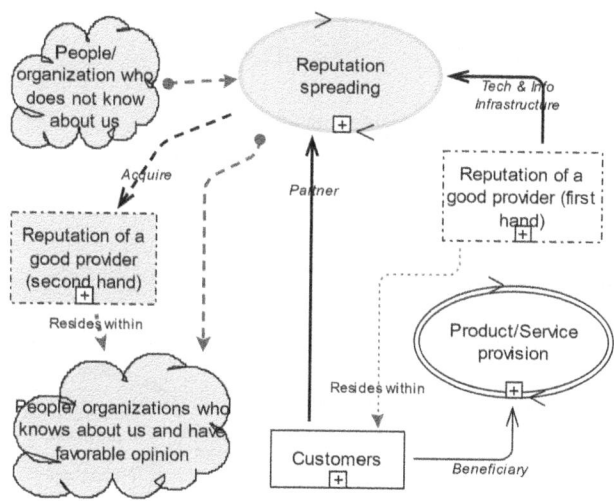

**Fig. 9.** Adding reputation spreading

The visual representation of the relations *draw from/add to* is an arrow with a dashed blue line and a rounded tail, see Fig. 9. If the arrow is pointing to a pool, the arrow tail shows who is adding elements to the pool. In the opposite direction, it shows who is drawing elements from the pool to convert them to assets or to add them to another pool. The labels on these relations are not standardized; a modeler can set any label to explain what the arrow represents.

Note that the yellow border for the *Reputation spreading* process in Fig. 9 means that this process is not under the control of the organization whose activities we depict.

The next step is to try to establish whether this fact is used by sales. The corresponding rule, *Using reputation spreading*, is presented in Fig. 10. If all three rules in Figs. 8, 9, and 10 can be applied, we will get a fragment of FEM that is presented in Fig. 11.

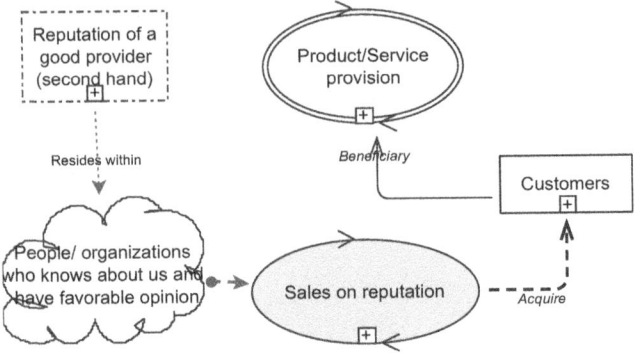

**Fig. 10.** Using reputation spreading

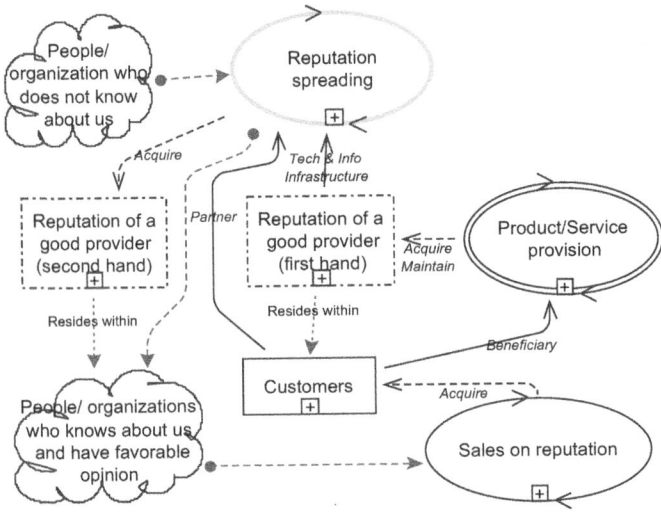

**Fig. 11.** A FEM fragment after applying all rules from Figs. 8, 9, and 10.

## 5 Conclusion and Plans for the Future

As stated in the introduction and Sect. 2.3, this paper aims to develop a set of discovery rules that concern the usage and management of tacit knowledge in an organization. The rules developed so far are presented in Sects. 3 and 4. We have chosen to depict only the rules that include tacit knowledge. Rules of transforming explicit knowledge, like *Combination* from Fig. 1, are left outside the scope of this paper.

The rules presented can be used to analyze how much attention a given organization pays to its tacit assets. If we find out that besides the natural usage and management covered by rules in Fig. 4, no other activities that include tacit assets exist, it means that the organization does not understand the importance of tacit knowledge. If applying all rules presented in this paper adds new elements to all processes depicted in FEM, it means that the organization understands and manages its tacit assets well. Pointing out the missing activities related to the management of tacit assets may help the organization to make some improvements.

Our plans for the future include several directions:

- The next step related to the set of rules presented in this paper is testing them in a project, which may lead to the extension of the set of rules or modifying some rules.
- Another direction is to adapt the rules presented in this paper to other enterprise modeling languages
- A more general direction is to continue work on discovery rules for FEM related to other areas

We also plan to create computerized support to facilitate the work of adding new elements to the model. The basic idea has already been discussed in [1]:

*"One can envision an algorithm that scans a partly built model against the formal rules and suggests which elements must be found. The modeler then uses available sources of information to find these elements and add them to the model, after which the scan is repeated. The cycle stops when the algorithm can no longer find which new elements could be added."*

There are several approaches to building such computerized support. One is to build it from scratch as a special function for an existing FEM toolkit [3] that has been built using the ADOxx environment [20]. Another possibility is using already existing knowledge graph capabilities. This will require the translation of a partially built FEM into a knowledge graph and converting each discovery rule into a query to find possible places in the model to apply it. An example of this sort of using knowledge graphs is presented in [21].

**Acknowledgment.** The work of the first author was partly supported by the Estonian Research Council (grant PRG1226). The authors are also grateful to the anonymous reviewers whose comments helped improve the text.

# References

1. Bider, I., Perjons, E.: On the concept of discovery power of enterprise modeling languages and its relation to their expressive power. In Malinova Mandelburger, M., Guerreiro, S. (eds.) Advances in Enterprise Engineering XVII. EDEWC 2023, LNBIP, vol. 510, pp. 92–106 (2024)
2. Bider, I., Perjons, E., Elias, M., Johannesson, P.: A fractal enterprise model and its application for business development. SoSyM **16**(3), 663–689 (2017)
3. Bider, I., Perjons, E., Klyukina, V.: Tool support for fractal enterprise modeling. In: Domain-Specific Conceptual Modeling, pp. 205–229. Springer, Heidelberg (2022)
4. Polanyi, M.S.: Knowing and Being. University of Chicago, Chicago (1969)
5. Polanyi, M.: The Structure of Consciousness. Brain LXXXVIII, pp. 799–810 (1965)
6. Nonaka, I.: A dynamic theory of organizational knowledge creation. Organ. Sci. **5**(1), 14–37 (1994)

7. Hevner, A., March, S.T., Park, J.: Design science in information systems research. MIS Q. **28**(1), 75–105 (2004)
8. Bider, I., Johannesson, P., Perjons, E.: Design science research as movement between individual and generic situation-problem-solution spaces. In: Organizational Systems. An Interdisciplinary Discourse, pp. 35–61. Springer, Cham (2013)
9. Andersson, B., Bider, I., Perjons, E.: Business process support as a basis for computerized knowledge management. In: Althoff, K., Dengel, A., Bergmann, R., Nick, M., Roth-Berghofer, T. (eds.) Professional Knowledge Management (WM 2005). LNAI, vol. 3782, pp. 542–553. Springer, Heidelberg (2005). https://doi.org/10.1007/11590019_61
10. Bider, I.: Analysis of agile software development from the knowledge transformation perspective. In: Perspectives in Business Informatics Research. LNBIP, vol. 194, pp. 143–157. Springer, Cham (2014). https://doi.org/10.1007/978-3-319-11370-8_11
11. Bider, I.: Can the systems perspective help in attaining success in software engineering projects? Inquiry into the area of applicability for agile software development. In: Jacobson, J., Lawson, H. (eds.) Software Engineering in the Systems Context: addressing frontiers, practice and education, pp. 423–466. College Publications, London (2015)
12. Bider, I., Perjons, E.: Identity management in an institution of higher education: a case study using structural coupling and fractal enterprise model. CSIMQ (27), 60–86 (2021)
13. Bider, I.: Integrating models of observing and observed activities based on an example of empirical research in information systems discipline. CSIMQ, Forthcoming (2023)
14. Rao, S., Nayak, A.: Enterprise ontology model for tacit knowledge externalization in sociotechnical enterprises. Interdiscip. J. Inf. Knowl. Manag. **12**, 99–124 (2017)
15. Dietz, J.L.G.: Understanding and modelling business processes with DEMO. In: 18th International Conference on Conceptual Modelling (ER 1999), pp. 188–202 (1999)
16. Supulniece, I., Businska, L., Kirikova, M.: Towards extending BPMN with the knowledge dimension. In: BPMDS 2010 and EMMSAD 2010. LNBIP, vol. 50, pp. 69–81. Springer, Heidelberg (2010). https://doi.org/10.1007/978-3-642-13051-9_7
17. Gronau, N., Korf, R., Müller, C.: KMDL-capturing, analysing and improving knowledge-intensive business processes. J. Comput. Sci. **4**, 452–472 (2005)
18. Calhau, R.F., Almeida, J.P.A., Kokkula, S., Guizzardi, G.: Modeling competencies in enterprise architecture: from knowledge, skills, and attitudes to organizational capabilities. Softw. Syst. Model. (2024)
19. Karagiannis, D., Buchmann, R., Walch, M.: How can diagrammatic conceptual modelling support knowledge management? In: Proceedings of the 25th European Conference on Information Systems (ECIS), Guimarães, 5–10 June 2017, pp. 1568–1583 (2017)
20. ADOxx.org: ADOxx. https://www.adoxx.org. Accessed January 2024
21. Smajevic, M., Hacks, S., Bork, D.: Using knowledge graphs to detect enterprise architecture smells. In: Serral, E., Stirna, J., Ralyté, J., Grabis, J., (eds.) The Practice of Enterprise Modeling. PoEM 2021. LNBIP, vol. 432, pp. 48–63. Springer, Heidelberg (2021). https://doi.org/10.1007/978-3-030-91279-6_4

# DDIs-Graph: an Approach to Identify Drug-Drug Interactions and Recommend Alternative Drugs

Amin Jalali[✉], Paul Johannesson, and Erik Perjons

Department of Computer and Systems Sciences, Stockholm University, Stockholm, Sweden
{aj,pajo,perjons}@dsv.su.se

**Abstract.** Drug-drug interactions (DDIs) pose significant risks to patients, ranging from adverse effects to fatal outcomes. Preventing these issues depends on providing caregivers with timely information on DDIs and offering viable alternative options. Currently, there is a gap in the formal specifications of systems designed to alert caregivers about potential DDIs. This gap hinders the development of further support, such as algorithms that can recommend alternative drugs. This study adopts the Design Science approach, defining a formal knowledge graph to capture DDIs. Then, algorithms are defined to identify drug interactions and suggest alternative medications with less severe consequences. As a proof of concept, we implemented our approach using Neo4j and Python, transforming data from the Swedish DDIs database. The implementation was applied to real care session data in the healthcare region of Stockholm for a randomly selected day, focusing on instances where caregivers prescribed drugs with severe DDIs. Validation occurred through expert interviews, discussing the correctness and utility of the approach. Results indicate that our graph-based model effectively supports the development of systems that alert caregivers to potential DDIs and recommend alternative drugs with reduced interactions. To the best of our knowledge, this paper introduces the first graph-based model serving as a blueprint for developing DDI systems. This model enables systems to i) warn caregivers about the presence of DDIs in prescribed drugs and ii) assess the availability of alternative drugs with less severe interactions, providing recommendations.

**Keywords:** knowledge graphs · recommendation systems · drug-drug interactions

## 1 Introduction

Drug-drug interactions (DDIs) are defined as a change in the effect of a drug due to the presence of another drug, and they are identified as a significant proportion of Adverse Drug Reactions (ADRs) [15]. ADR is a noxious and unintended injury resulting from taking one or multiple medicines [6]. ADRs can result in the hospitalization of patients and, in most severe cases, death. Indeed, they are reported as between the fourth and sixth leading cause of death [14]. They can also prolong the service time of care processes at hospitals [6], which is also an extra burden on healthcare services. DDIs are often preventable if caregivers know about *the presence of an interaction* and *available alternative options* [1].

To alert caregivers about *presence of interaction*(s), DDI systems are developed and integrated with Electronic Health Record (EHR) systems, e.g., the DDI system Janusinfo in Sweden [1]. These systems categorize alerts to avoid alert fatigue problems [1], which was one of the reasons for caregivers to ignore such systems beforehand - due to the existence of too much information [1]. The evaluation result of Janusinfo shows that 98% of participants would recommend the system to their colleagues. It also shows that 74% of caregivers have changed the prescription by receiving information using the system [1].

Despite the effort in developing systems to alert caregivers about the existence of possible interactions, there is a need to acquire the knowledge of *available alternative options*. Several systems include information about alternatives for a few well-known interactions [17], yet there is a lack of a systematic way to find alternatives for all possible interactions. The study on DDI systems shows that 86.9% of participants thought that there is a lack of suggestions for non-interacting alternative drugs [3]. Thus, the objective of this paper is to contribute to the development of systems that can recommend non-interacting alternative drugs to caregivers.

To assist caregivers in knowing about *the presence of an interaction* and *available alternative options*, this paper defines a graph-based approach for storing DDIs, called *DDIs-Graph*. We formally define the semantics of DDIs-Graph, and subsequently, we defined algorithms to alert caregivers about *the presence of an interaction* among drugs and recommending *available alternative drugs*.

As a proof of concept, we implemented the *DDIs-Graph* using Neo4j and Python by leveraging data from the Swedish DDIs database. The implementation is used on real care session data in the healthcare region of Stockholm for one randomly selected day, where caregivers prescribed drugs with severe DDIs. The results indicate that in 12% of cases, the recommendation algorithm identified alternative drugs with reduced interaction potential, thereby addressing the risk of negative drug interactions. The result was validated using an interview with experts, where the correctness and usefulness of the approach were discussed.

The remainder of this paper is organized as follows. Section 2 gives a short summary of related background. Section 3 elaborates on the method. Section 4 formalizes DDIs-Graph and defines algorithms to alert DDIs and recommend available alternative drugs with less severity. Section 5 elaborates on the validation result. Section 6 concludes the paper.

## 2 Background

There are many studies investigating how drugs interact with each other; however, there are fewer that focus on how information systems shall assist prescribers in knowing about *the presence of an interaction* or *available alternative options* [1].

Some information systems have been developed to alert prescribers about *the presence of an interaction*. Nabovati et al. reviewed these systems systematically [17]. They conclude that IT-based systems improved surrogate outcomes (i.e., indirect measures used as substitutes for direct clinical endpoints) and compliance. They defined the main characteristics of different systems by including 19 studies. Among these, 4 studies were identified that mentioned recommendation support for alternative therapy as a feature to consider when checking DDIs, i.e., [2,16,18,19]. We review these studies below.

Armstrong et al. conducted a study where prescribers get the list of interacting DDIs and recommended clinical management strategies through fax [2]. Unlike computer-supported systems, this study relied on fax communication to alert prescribers. The result does not show any static difference, and the approach is evaluated as not effective.

In another study, Polidori et al. [18] explored how adding an acknowledgment feature could influence prescribers' practices. The acknowledgment feature asks prescribers to confirm their awareness of existing interactions, potentially improving the situation when alternative options are available. However, the system does not provide any assistance in recommending available alternative options.

In their study, Strom et al. [19] investigated the impact of suggesting acetaminophen as an alternative option when ordering warfarin and nonsteroidal anti-inflammatory drugs. The study focuses only on one pair of known drug-drug interactions, and the recommendation was not made for every potential DDI.

Addressing gaps in DDI warnings, McMullin et al. devised a web-based system to supplement the alerts provided by their commercial tool. The study focuses on covering cisapride drug, and it results in a significant reduction of i) potentially dangerous drug combinations, ii) the duration of overlapping drug orders, and iii) the number of patients being discharged under treatment with a dangerous drug combination [16].

These studies show the impact of systems to support caregivers to know *the presence of an interaction* or *available alternative options* [1]. However, there is no specification stating how such a system can be developed to the best of our knowledge.

Recent studies show the effectiveness of knowledge graphs in analyzing adverse drug reactions in the healthcare prescription process [9,10]. Indeed, the data for the prescription process can be stored in knowledge-graphs [7] - enabling the processing of vast volumes of data due to the scalability of the approach. Such data usually contains different objects (e.g., caregiver, patient, care session, etc.), which requires analyzing the process and considering several objects simultaneously. Such analysis is recently enabled by introducing event logs where events are related to several objects [4,5,12]. Therefore, defining an approach to identify *the presence of an interaction* or identifying *available alternative drugs* can elevate the level of analyzing healthcare data.

## 3 Material and Methods

This paper follows the design science approach [11], which is a scientific approach aiming to create novel artifacts for improving practices. Figure 1 shows the steps followed in this study as well as artifacts that are developed to address the objective. We explain this research process by its steps, i.e.:

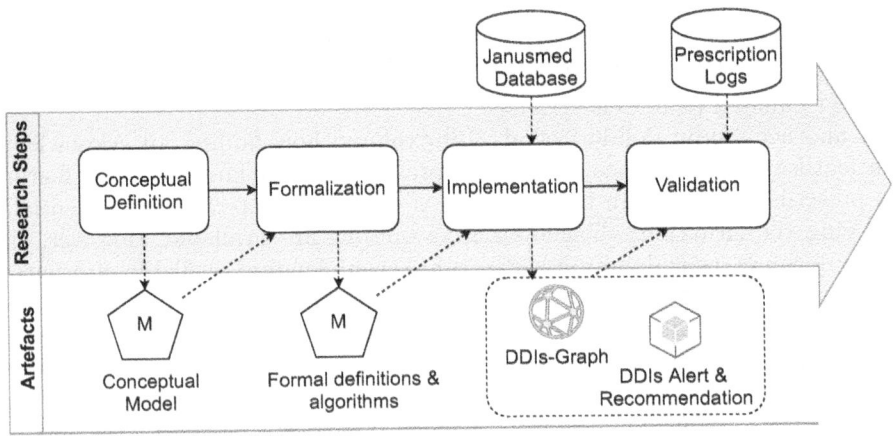

**Fig. 1.** The research steps followed in this study.

- "Conceptual Definition": The first step of our research process was to design the concepts by interviewing caregivers and drug-drug interactions experts and studying the supporting systems. The output of this step is the conceptual model (represented by a pentagon annotated by M - which stands for Model) that defines the elements and their relations.
- "Formalization": The second step was i) formalizing a graph-based model that can support storing information about drugs and their interactions based on the conceptual model and ii) defining the algorithms that warn the existence of interactions among a set of drugs as well as recommending alternative drugs with less severe interaction. The output of this step is the formal definitions and two algorithms.
- "Implementation": The third step was to implement the graph model using a graph database as well as implementing algorithms as a service to identify interactions and recommend suggestions. The DDIs were loaded from the Swedish DDIs database, i.e., Janusinfo, taken from the Janusmed Database.

– "Validation": The final step was to validate the approach by using the implementation to check the existence of less severe alternative drugs for care sessions when caregivers prescribed drugs with highly severe interactions. The data were anonymous and contained all prescribed medicine in patients' EHR for one randomly selected day in Stockholm. The result is validated by interviewing experts and checking the correctness and usefulness of the approach.

## 4 Approach

This section introduces the conceptual model for the DDIs and provides a running example through which we will explain concepts and definitions later. It also formalizes the syntax and semantics of the DDIs-Graph based on which two algorithms are defined to i) discover the interactions among several drugs in the DDIs-Graph and ii) investigate the existence of alternative drugs with less severity to suggest to caregivers.

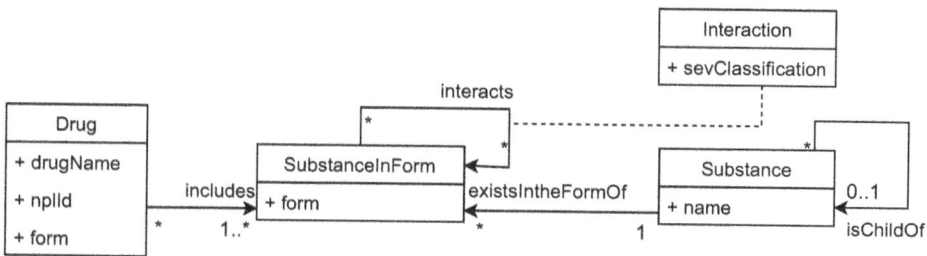

**Fig. 2.** The conceptual model for DDIs

**Conceptual Model.** Figure 2 illustrates the conceptual model for DDIs using a UML class diagram. It has three main classes, i.e., *Drug*, *Substance*, and *SubstanceInForm*, where each class can have different attributes - only a few are mentioned in this diagram. A *drug* is a physical medicine that one can buy from a drugstore, and each drug has a name, a unique identifier (nplid), and a form (representing the physical form, e.g., solid as exists in tablets, or liquid as exists in oral suspensions). A *substance* is a chemical compound or molecule that produces a pharmacological effect when introduced into the body, which has a name. A *"substance in form"* is a substance that exists in a form which, if used in a drug, will have the same form as the drug.

A drug can include one or more "substance in forms", and each "substance in form" can be used in different drugs. A substance can be a child of another substance, meaning that the parent substance will be an active ingredient in the child's substance. A "substance in form" can have interaction with other "substance in forms", and these interactions can have different levels of severe drug effects, represented by an attribute named sevClassfication.

As an example, Alvedon®, with the nplid of 19750613000031, is a drug in the form of solid (tablet), and Alvedon®, with the nplid of 19590713000018, is a drug in the form of liquid (Oral suspension) - both contain the paracetamol substance but in different forms. There are huge numbers of substances and "substance in forms", and the interactions among "substance in forms" are discovered through different sorts of studies. However, some of the interactions can be inferred from reported ones, explained below using a running example.

**Motivating Example.** Figure 3 shows a running example that is defined based on concepts introduced in the conceptual model. In this figure, we have three instances of the Drug class, named $d1$, $d2$, and $d3$, where $d1$ and $d2$ are in solid form (e.g., tablet), while $d3$ is in liquid form (e.g., oral suspension). Also, we have three substances, i.e., $s1$, $s2$ and $s3$. $S1$ exists in the form of solid ($sf11$) and liquid ($sf12$), while $s2$ and $s3$ only exist in the form of solid, i.e., $sf2$ and $sf3$. As illustrated, there is a severe interaction between $sf11$ and $sf3$.

Despite not being explicitly reported, we can infer another interaction between $sf2$ and $sf11$ from this graph. The reason is that $s2$ is a child of $s3$, and we know there is an interaction between $sf3$ and $sf11$. Thus, $sf2$ will also interact with $sf11$ as it indirectly represents the existence of $s3$ in solid form (the same form for which the interaction is reported).

This means that if a doctor prescribes $d2$ with $d1$, they can cause severe problems for the patient if taken simultaneously - as they include $sf2$ and $sf11$, respectively. However, it is safe to prescribe $d2$ and $d3$, because there is no interaction between i) the substances that they include considering their form (i.e., $sf2$ and $sf12$), and ii) the *substance in forms* of all parent substances with the same form as selected drugs (i.e., $sf3$ and $sf12$). It is worth mentioning that the definitions of drug, substance, "substance in form" and interaction are defined by interviewing domain experts, which is how they have described the domain. Also, the interaction rules are how the interactions are currently persisted and reported to doctors in Region Stockholm in the Janusmed system, which is integrated with EHR - serving as a service to assist caregivers in prescribing drugs for millions of patients in Sweden.

**Formal Definitions.** The relations between drugs, substances, forms, and substances in forms can be very complex. Such complexity is hard to deal with without any formal definition of the model. Such a formal definition can also assist us in analyzing the network and defining algorithms to identify problems. Thus, we specify the formal definition of the DDIs-Graph notation in this section.

**Definition 1.** *(Drug Interaction Graph) A Drug Interaction Graph is a tuple $G = (N = D \cup S \cup F \cup SF, R, W)$, where:*

– *N is the set of nodes with the following disjoint subsets:*

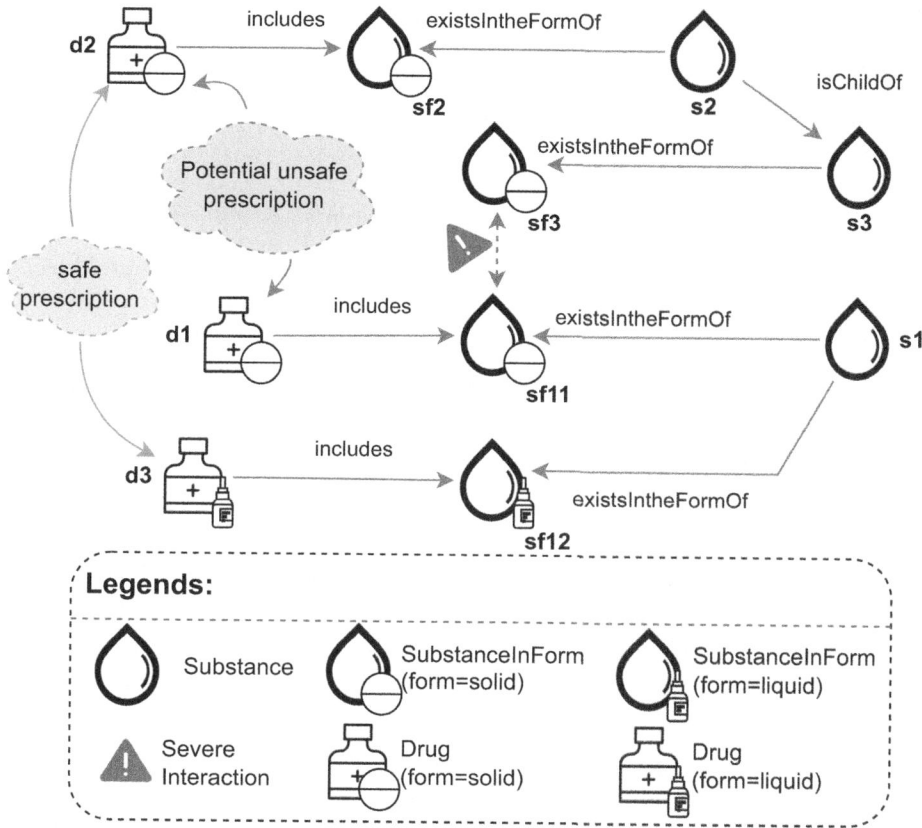

**Fig. 3.** The running example used to explain the conceptual model, the formalizations, and interaction rules.

- $D$ represents the set of Drugs,
- $S$ represents the set of Substances,
- $F$ represents the set of Forms,
- $SF$ represents the set of Substance in Forms.
- $R = N \times N$ is the set of directed edges that connect one node to another one based on connectivity rules that are defined using these two operations:
  - $\overset{S}{\bullet} n$ represents the operator that retrieves the set of nodes belonging to set $S$ from which there are relations to node $n$, i.e., $\overset{S}{\bullet} n = \{\forall n' \in S | (n', n) \in R\}$.
  - $n \overset{S}{\bullet}$ represents the operator that retrieves the set of nodes belonging to set $S$ to which there are relations from node $n$, i.e., $n \overset{S}{\bullet} = \{\forall n' \in S | (n, n') \in R\}$.

  The connectivity rules are:
- $\forall d \in D : (\overset{N}{\bullet} d = \emptyset) \land (d \overset{N}{\bullet} = d \overset{SF \cup F}{\bullet}) \land (|d \overset{F}{\bullet}| = 1)$,
- $\forall sf \in SF : (\overset{N}{\bullet} sf = \overset{D \cup SF/sf}{\bullet} sf) \land (sf \overset{N}{\bullet} = sf \overset{F \cup S \cup SF/sf}{\bullet}) \land (|sf \overset{S}{\bullet}| = 1) \land (|sf \overset{F}{\bullet}| = 1)$,

- $\forall s \in S : (s\overset{N}{\bullet} = s\overset{S}{\bullet}) \wedge (\overset{N}{\bullet}s = \overset{S \cup SF}{\bullet}) \wedge (|s\overset{S}{\bullet}| = 1),$
- $\forall f \in F : (f\overset{N}{\bullet} = \emptyset) \wedge (\overset{N}{\bullet}f = \overset{D \cup SF}{\bullet}f)$
- $W : SF \times SF \mapsto \mathbb{N}$ is a function that assigns a natural number, representing the severity of interactions as weight, to the relation between two $SF$s, where $W(sf_1, sf_2) = W(sf_2, sf_1)$.

Let's also define an operator to retrieve all parents' substances:

- $n\circlearrowleft$ represents the operator that retrieves the set of substances that are directly related to a node in addition to all the substance's parents, i.e.:

$$n\circlearrowleft = \begin{cases} \emptyset, & \text{if } (n\overset{S}{\bullet} \in \{\{n\}\}) \\ (\{n\} \cap S) \bigcup_{n' \in (n\overset{S}{\bullet})} n'\circlearrowleft, & \text{otherwise} \end{cases} \quad (1)$$

- $I$ is a function that retrieves the interaction severity between two substances in form, where it retrieves zero if there are no interactions between the given substance in forms, i.e.:

$$I(sf_1, sf_2) = \begin{cases} W(sf_1, sf_2) & \text{if } (sf_1, sf_2) \in R \\ 0 & \text{otherwise} \end{cases} \quad (2)$$

Let's see all these definitions using our running example, represented in Fig. 3. The graph for our running example is $G = (N = D \cup S \cup F \cup SF, R, W)$, where:

- $D = \{d1, d2, d3\}$
- $S = \{s1, s2, s3\}$
- $F = \{f1, f2, f3\}$
- $SF = \{sf1_1, sf1_2, sf2, sf3\}$
- $R = \{(d1, sf1_1), (d1, f2), (sf1_1, s1), (s1, s1), (d2, sf2), (d2, f2), (sf2, f2),$
  $(sf2, s2), (s2, s3), (s3, s3), (sf3, s3), (sf3, f2), (sf1_1, sf3), (sf3, sf1_1),$
  $(d3, f3), (d3, sf1_2), (sf1_2, s1), (sf1_2, f3)\}$
- $W = \begin{pmatrix} (sf1_1, sf3) & (sf3, sf1_1) \\ 1 & 1 \end{pmatrix}$

The defined operations enable us to query information about each node in this graph. For example, $d2\overset{SF}{\bullet}$ retrieves all substance in forms of drug $d2$, i.e., $\{sf2\}$. $sf2\circlearrowleft$ retrieves the substance and all parent substances of $sf2$, i.e., $\{s2, s3\}$. $I(sf1_1, sf3)$ retrieves the severity of interactions between $sf1_1$ and $sf3$, i.e., 1.

**Discovering DDIs Interactions.** Two drugs can have an interaction if there is an interaction between one of their substance in forms or any of their parent substance in form with the same form as the drug. It is possible that a drug has multiple substances in forms, so it is possible that two drugs have multiple interactions.

Algorithm 1 specifies how interactions among two drugs can be discovered. This algorithm gets the set of drugs ($\mathfrak{D}$) and the DDIs-Graph, and it retrieves the set of interactions that exists between these drugs. Let's look at this algorithm using our running example, where we aim to discover interactions among $d1$ and $d2$, i.e., $getDrugsInteractions(\mathfrak{D} = \{d1, d2\}, G = (N = D \cup S \cup F \cup SF, R, W))$.

---

**Algorithm 1:** algorithm for retrieving drug interactions

1  **Algorithm** getDrugsInteractions($\mathfrak{D}, G = (N = D \cup S \cup F \cup SF, R, W)$)
2  $\quad DSF \leftarrow \bigcup_{d \in \mathfrak{D}} \bigcup_{sf \in d_\bullet^{SF}} \bigcup_{s \in sf\circlearrowleft} \bigcup_{sf' \in s_\bullet^{SF}} \{(d, sf') | sf_\bullet^F = sf'_\bullet^F\}$;
3  $\quad \chi \leftarrow \emptyset$;
4  $\quad$ **foreach** $(d_1, sf_1), (d_2, sf_2) \in DSF$ **do**
5  $\quad\quad | \quad \chi \leftarrow \chi \cup \{(d_1, sf_1, d_2, sf_2, I(sf_1, sf_2))\}$;
6  **return** $\chi$;

---

The $2^{nd}$ line retrieves the set of substances in forms that have the same form as the given drugs based on the drugs substances or any parent substances. In our example, $DSF$ is equal to $\{(d1, sf1_1), (d2, sf2), (d2, sf3)\}$. The loop in $4^{th}$ line retrieves the interaction lists that exist between any tuple in $DSF$. The result is $\{(d1, sf1_1, d2, sf3, 1), (d2, sf3, d1, sf1_1, 1)\}$, which shows that there is an interaction with the severity of 1 between a substance in form $sf1_1$ from $d1$ to substance in form $sf3$ from $d2$. As the interaction is bidirectional, we have two tuples in the list.

**Drug Recommendations.** Algorithm 2 specifies how alternative drugs with less severe interactions can be discovered for a set of drugs while they have the same substance. Please note that it is not possible to recommend drugs with other substances as the prescription process is very knowledge-intensive, and we are relying on caregivers' knowledge of the usefulness of substances for a particular disease.

This algorithm gets the same input as the Algorithm 1. Such discovery is possible because there are different substances in forms for a substance, and it is possible that one of the substances in form interacts with another, while there is a substance in form with another form for a given substance that does not interact. Let's look at this algorithm using our running example, i.e., $getAlternativeDrugs(\mathfrak{D} = \{d1, d2\}, G = (N = D \cup S \cup F \cup SF, R, W))$.

The $4^{th}$ line of this algorithm assigns all substances based on which the given drugs are made. In our example, $V_s$ will be equal to $\{s1, s2\}$. The $5^{th}$ line of this algorithm retrieves all potential substances in the forms of the identified substances, so $P_{sf}$ will be equal to $\{sf1_1, sf1_2, sf2\}$. The $6^{th}$ line of this algorithm has a loop that identifies the maximum severity of interactions by going through all interactions that it retrieves from Algorithm 1. It assigns this severity to variable $i$, so it will be equal to 1 in our example.

**Algorithm 2:** algorithm for getting drug replacements

```
 1  Algorithm getAlternativeDrugs(𝔇, G = (N = D ∪ S ∪ F ∪ SF, R, W))
 2    i ← 0;
 3    χ, χ_s, R ← ∅;
 4    V_s ← ⋃_{d∈𝔇} ⋃_{sf∈d^{SF}•} s ∈ sf^S•;
 5    P_{sf} ← ⋃_{s∈V_s} ^{SF}•s;
 6    foreach (d_1, sf_1, d_2, sf_2, n) ∈ getDrugsInteractions(𝔇, G) do
 7      if i < n then
 8        i ← n;
 9    foreach sf, sf' ∈ P_{sf} do
10      if (sf ≠ sf') ∧ (I(sf, sf') < i) then
11        χ ← χ ∪ (sf, sf', I(sf, sf'));
12        χ_s ← χ_s ∪ {sf^S•, sf'^S•};
13    if V_s = χ_s then
14      foreach (sf, sf', n) ∈ χ do
15        R ← R ∪ ^D•sf × ^D•sf' × n;
16  return R;
```

The $9^{th}$ line of this algorithm has a loop that collects the pair of all potential substances in forms where their interaction's severity is less than the maximum interaction. It collects all of these pairs in $\chi$, and it collects their substances in $\chi_s$. In our example, $\chi$ and $\chi_s$ are equal to $\{(sf1_2, sf2, 1)\}$ and $\{s1, s2\}$, respectively.

The $13^{th}$ line of this algorithm checks if the identified set of substances is equal to $V_s$. If yes, it means that there is a set of alternative drugs with less severity on our list. In this case, it retrieves the drugs of those substances in forms with their interactions. In our example, $V_s$ is equal to $\chi_s$. Thus, the result ($R$) is $\{(d3, d2, 0), (d2, d3, 0)\}$. The result includes all alternative drugs that can be recommended to caregivers, which are $d3$ and $d2$, which is an alternative recommendation for currently selected drugs, i.e., $d1$ and $d2$.

## 5 Validation

We have implemented DDIs-Graph using Neo4j and Python as proof of concept, and we have used it on real prescription data in one day in the healthcare region of Stockholm. To validate our approach, we have transferred the Swedish DDIs database into DDIs-Graph. We implemented the DDIs-Graph in Neo4j, which is a graph database. The generated graph includes 26,517 nodes, which contain 17,591 drugs, 2,912 substances, 6,010 substances in forms, and 4 forms. It also has 641,900 interactions between substance in forms.

Neo4j supports querying the graph using a language called Cypher. We implemented Algorithm 1 using cypher and Algorithm 2 in python. We also implemented a query to visualize interactions among elements that are involved in drugs' substances and substance in forms. By comparing the result with the current DDIs systems, we could validate the correctness of our DDIs-Graph and its capability to discover DDIs.

We applied the implementation to real care session data in Stockholm for one randomly selected day, where caregivers prescribed drugs with severe DDIs. For the selected day, there were 51,211 care sessions, of which 3,947 sessions ended with the most severe interactions. Our Algorithm 2 could propose alternative drugs with less severe interactions for 323 sessions. Thus, the result shows that the recommendation algorithm could propose less interactive alternative drugs for 12% of cases.

To demonstrate a case, we selected the interactions among the drugs at the end of one of the care sessions where a caregiver selected some drugs with severe interactions for a patient. Th caregiver would see the warning showed in Fig. 4, where (s)he could see the existence of very severe interactions between Ciprofloxacin Arrow (Filmdragerad tablett) and Solvezink (Brustablett).

Reducing the interactions is not easy as the current system does not recommend any solution. There are many different drugs on the market, so it is difficult for a caregiver to come up with a replacement without any prior experience or knowledge about possible replacement drugs. Please note that sometimes, the

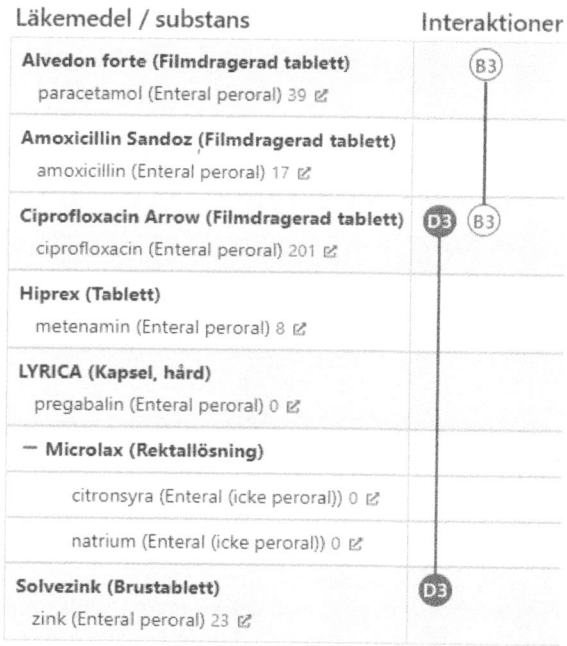

**Fig. 4.** The warning received by a caregiver when selecting a set of drugs for a patient (based on real data) showing the existence of a very high severe interaction level (D) between Ciprofloxacin Arrow (Filmdragerad tablet) and Solvezink (Brustablett).

interactions can be handled by taking drugs at different times. It is also possible that a patient stops taking a drug for a while and starts it when the period of another drug is over. Our aim is not to investigate how the treatment has been done in this particular care session, as we do not have such data. Rather, we aim to investigate how our recommendation algorithm can help caregiver to resolve this problem.

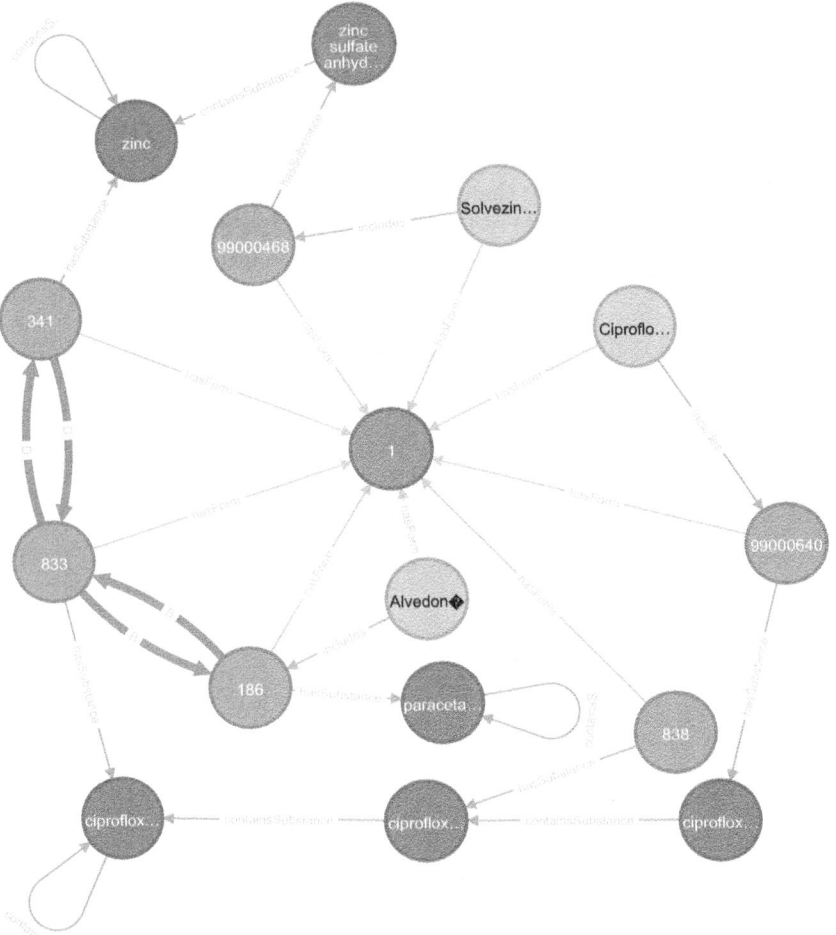

**Fig. 5.** The graph representation of selected drugs for a patient in neo4j, where thick red arrows show the drug-drug interactions; yellow, blue, purple, and red nodes represent drugs, substances, drugs-in-substances, and drug forms, respectively. (Color figure online)

Figure 5 shows how the selected drugs look in our graph. In this graph, *Drugs*, *Substances*, *Forms*, and *Substance in Forms* are visualized using yellow, blue, red, and purple nodes, respectively. *Drug* and *Substance* nodes are labeled by their names. *Form* nodes are labeled by their ids. *Substance in form* nodes are labeled by their substance ids. All edges are labeled with their types of relations except interaction edges, which are labeled with their *sevClassification* to show the severity of their interaction. The interaction edges are visualized as thick edges to make them more visible.

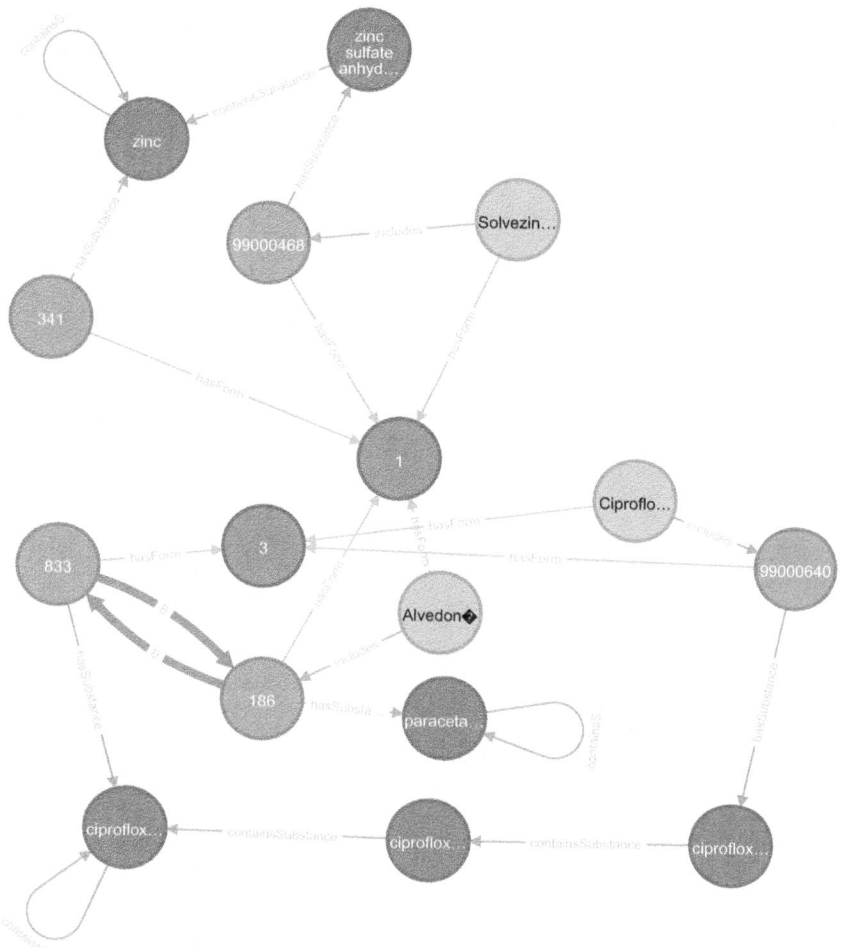

**Fig. 6.** The graph representation of drugs after changing the form of "Ciprofloxacin" drug from *tablett* (tablet in EN) to *lösning* (liquid in EN) showing the severe interactions is reduced from very high severe level (D) to low severe level (B).

As it can be seen, the most severe interaction is between *Substance in forms* with substance ids of 833 and 341. The *Substance in form* labeled by 833 is related to *ciprofloxacin Substance*. This substance is the parent substance of *ciprofloxacin hydrochloride*, which is the parent substance of *ciprofloxacin hydrochloride monohydrate*. The latter substance exists in the *Substance in form* of *Ciprofloxacin Arrow* drug. The *Substance in form* labeled by 341 is related to *zinc Substance*. This substance is the parent substance of *zinc sulfate anhydrous*, which exists in the *Substance in form* of *Solvezink* drug.

We could identify 14 alternative drugs to remove interaction D in this case using the implementation of Algorithm 2. One alternative is to replace *Ciprofloxacin Arrow* with *Ciprofloxacin Sandoz*. The graph representation of the replacement can be seen in Fig. 6. As can be seen, we have the same substances but with less severe interactions. Note that both of these drugs have *ciprofloxacin hydrochloride* substance but in different forms.

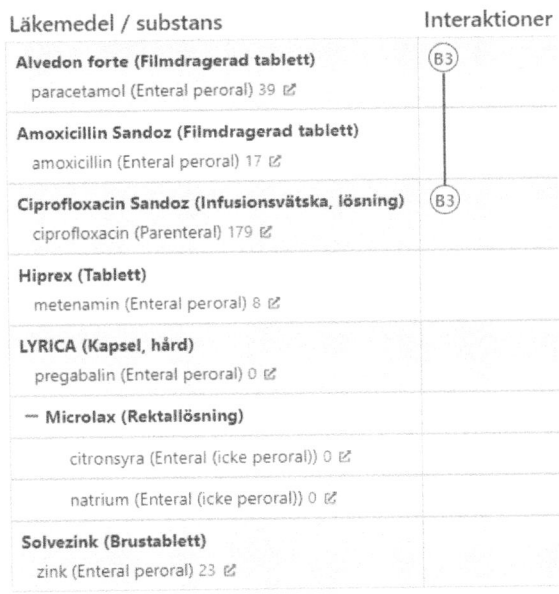

**Fig. 7.** The result of drug-drug interaction warning after replacing the form of "Ciprofloxacin" drug when caregiver would select the recommendation.

Figure 7 shows the result of drug-drug interaction warning after replacing the form of "Ciprofloxacin" drug when caregiver would select the recommendation.

**Discussion.** To evaluate the usefulness of the recommendations, we consulted experts responsible for the Janusinfo drug-drug interaction database, which is integrated with the Electronic Health Records (EHR) used by caregivers in Sweden. They found the approach beneficial when applied as a recommendation system. However, they noted that some alternatives might not be preferred due to practical issues. For example, drugs in the form of injections require additional support, so caregivers might prefer increasing the interval between drug intakes rather than replacing them. Nonetheless, suggesting alternative drugs remains valuable as it provides caregivers with more options based on their specific circumstances.

We also used the DDIs-Graph to examine how caregivers have utilized built-in drug-drug interaction systems in Stockholm [9,10]. This investigation demonstrated the model's utility in facilitating further research on caregivers' use of DDIs systems in practice.

**Limitations and Future Work.** The recommendation service in the prescription process encompasses more than just drug-drug interactions. It also includes other services that were not covered in our study, representing a limitation and suggesting directions for future research. For instance, caregivers receive recommendations for drugs and their dosages based on the patient's sex and gender. Specific recommendations are also provided when the patient is pregnant or breastfeeding. Additionally, recommendations are personalized based on the patient's kidney function. Recently, caregivers have started receiving warnings about interactions between drugs and certain foods. These factors are crucial and should be incorporated in future research.

Expert feedback highlighted practical issues, such as the form of medication (e.g., injection vs. oral), which can influence the feasibility of alternative recommendations. Adjusting the recommendation algorithms to account for these practicalities may enhance the utility and acceptance of DDIs-Graph in clinical settings. Providing caregivers with flexible options, such as altering drug intake intervals, can further increase the system's practical benefits.

The approach introduced in this paper opens numerous future directions for enhancing healthcare processes through various research opportunities, enabling different types of data analytics, such as descriptive, diagnostic, predictive, and prescriptive.

DDIs-Graph supports descriptive, diagnostic, and predictive healthcare data analysis by enabling data augmentation or enrichment. Typically, EHRs contain lists of prescribed drugs but not the potential adverse drug reactions they might cause. Our approach can enable descriptive analytics by enriching the dataset with insights into potential ADRs, allowing researchers to identify what has happened or is currently happening within their study domain. Additionally, DDIs-Graph facilitates diagnostic analytics by uncovering correlations between prescribed drugs and potential ADRs and future reactions registered for patients in the EHR. Furthermore, DDIs-Graph supports predictive analytics by developing machine learning algorithms to predict the outcomes of prescribing a particular drug to a patient.

As a future work, we are interested in transforming the prescription events data to a temporal Event Knowledge Graph [13] to capture the changes in prescriptions of drugs for patients over time. Such log file enables applying different clustering algorithms, e.g., [8], to identify common patterns in the prescription process causing the most severe interactions for patients.

## 6   Conclusion

This paper presents a novel graph-based approach, DDIs-Graph, for identifying drug-drug interactions and recommending potential alternative drugs with less severe interaction. Our graph-based model and associated algorithms were validated using real-world data from the Stockholm healthcare region, proposing less interactive alternative drugs for 12% of cases, demonstrating the potential to significantly enhance patient safety and support caregivers in making informed prescription decisions. The expert validation further underscores the practical utility of our approach in a clinical setting.

The DDIs-Graph approach can potentially improve DDI management in healthcare by offering a tool for improving medication safety. The implementation and validation of the DDIs-Graph are promising, paving the way for future innovations in this critical area. The findings from the DDIs-Graph approach also underscore the importance of ongoing research and development in this area, ensuring that healthcare providers have access to the most advanced tools for managing drug interactions.

The findings highlight the need for continued research and development in this area to address the limitations and expand the capabilities of the DDIs-Graph model. Future work will focus on integrating advanced data analytics techniques and expanding the scope of recommendations to further improve the system's effectiveness and usability in diverse healthcare environments.

**Acknowledgements.** This research was funded by Region Stockholm with ethical approval no. 2018/968-31/5 granted by the Stockholm Regional Ethical Review Board.

## References

1. Andersson, M.L., Böttiger, Y., Bastholm-Rahmner, P., Ovesjö, M.-L., Veg, A., Eiermann, B.: Evaluation of usage patterns and user perception of the drug-drug interaction database SFINX. Int. J. Med. Informatics **84**(5), 327–333 (2015)
2. Armstrong, E.P., Wang, S.M., Hines, L.E., Gao, S., Patel, B.V., Malone, D.C.: Evaluation of a drug-drug interaction: fax alert intervention program. BMC Med. Inform. Decis. Mak. **13**(1), 1–9 (2013)
3. Bergk, V., Gasse, C., Schnell, R., Haefeli, W.E.: Requirements for a successful implementation of drug interaction information systems in general practice: results of a questionnaire survey in Germany. Eur. J. Clin. Pharmacol. **60**(8), 595–602 (2004)
4. Berti, A., et al.: OCEL (Object-Centric Event Log) 2.0 Specification (2024)
5. Esser, S., Fahland, D.: Multi-dimensional event data in graph databases. J. Data Semant. **10**(1), 109–141 (2021)
6. Giardina, C., et al.: Adverse drug reactions in hospitalized patients: results of the forward (facilitation of reporting in hospital ward) study. Front. Pharmacol. **9**, 350 (2018)
7. Jalali, A.: Graph-based process mining. In: Leemans, S., Leopold, H. (eds.) ICPM 2020. LNBIP, vol. 406, pp. 273–285. Springer, Cham (2021). https://doi.org/10.1007/978-3-030-72693-5_21

8. Jalali, A.: Object type clustering using Markov directly-follow multigraph in object-centric process mining. IEEE Access **10**, 126569–126579 (2022)
9. Jalali, A., et al.: Evaluating a clinical decision support system for drug-drug interactions. In: MEDINFO 2019, pp. 1500–1501. IOS Press (2019)
10. Jalali, A., et al.: dfgcompare: a library to support process variant analysis through Markov models. BMC Med. Inform. Decis. Making **21**(1), 1–13 (2021). https://doi.org/10.1186/s12911-021-01715-3
11. Johannesson, P., Perjons, E.: An Introduction to Design Science. Springer, Cham (2021). https://doi.org/10.1007/978-3-030-78132-3
12. Khayatbashi, S., Hartig, O., Jalali, A.: Transforming event knowledge graph to object-centric event logs: a comparative study for multi-dimensional process analysis. In: Almeida, J.P.A., Borbinha, J., Guizzardi, G., Link, S., Zdravkovic, J. (eds.) International Conference on Conceptual Modeling, vol. 14320, pp. 220–238. Springer, Cham (2023). https://doi.org/10.1007/978-3-031-47262-6_12
13. Khayatbashi, S., Hartig, O., Jalali, A.: Transforming object-centric event logs to temporal event knowledge graphs. In: International Workshop on Business Process Management (accepted) (2024)
14. Lazarou, J., Pomeranz, B.H., Corey, P.N.: Incidence of adverse drug reactions in hospitalized patients: a meta-analysis of prospective studies. JAMA **279**(15), 1200–1205 (1998)
15. Magro, L., Moretti, U., Leone, R.: Epidemiology and characteristics of adverse drug reactions caused by drug-drug interactions. Expert Opin. Drug Saf. **11**(1), 83–94 (2012)
16. McMullin, S.T., Reichley, R.M., Watson, L.A., Steib, S.A., Frisse, M.E., Bailey, T.C.: Impact of a web-based clinical information system on cisapride drug interactions and patient safety. Arch. Intern. Med. **159**(17), 2077–2082 (1999)
17. Nabovati, E., et al.: Information technology-based interventions to improve drug-drug interaction outcomes: a systematic review on features and effects. J. Med. Syst. **41**(1), 1–17 (2017)
18. Polidori, P., Di Giorgio, C., Provenzani, A.: Incidence of potential drug interactions in a transplant centre setting and relevance of electronic alerts for clinical practice support. J. Innov. Health Inform. **20**(4), 257–262 (2013)
19. Strom, B.L., Schinnar, R., Bilker, W., Hennessy, S., Leonard, C.E., Pifer, E.: Randomized clinical trial of a customized electronic alert requiring an affirmative response compared to a control group receiving a commercial passive CPOE alert: NSAID-warfarin co-prescribing as a test case. J. Am. Med. Inform. Assoc. **17**(4), 411–415 (2010)

# Exploring the Information Flow and the Grounding of Digital Product Passports Using the Work-Oriented Approach, an Industrial Case Study

Anders W. Tell

Department of Computer and Systems Sciences, Stockholm University, Stockholm, Sweden
anderswt@dsv.su.se

**Abstract.** Product information flows internally between stakeholders and their practices, externally between partners and across supply chains. Upcoming EU regulations mandate that all physical goods placed on the EU market or put into service must be linked to a digital product passport (DPP). A DPP provides digital information about a product's entire lifecycle, materials utilised, environmental footprint, disposals, warranty and other data. This poses significant challenges for all organisations regarding understanding and designing their information systems and flows, feeding accurate public and restricted product information into their DPPs. The Work-Oriented Approach to Information Products (WOA) has been designed to address challenges with multi-stakeholders and multi-practice information flows involving information products, including DPP. This paper presents an industrial case study that aims to demonstrate the application of the WOA method and constructs in a knowledge development project by a global manufacturer of premium metal-cutting tools that aims to gain insights into future production and flow of product (lifecycle) information to their DPP.

**Keywords:** Digital Product Passport · Work-Oriented Approach · Information Management · Product Information · Case Study · Demonstration

## 1 Introduction

Access to relevant and usable information is significant for organisations and individuals engaged in collaboration. The design, production, consumption, and sharing of information internally or with partners, possibly due to regulations, is an important topic not only for the IT department but for many internal stakeholders.

The European Green Deal is a comprehensive set of policy initiatives and strategies to make the European Union (EU) more sustainable and climate-neutral by 2050, including the digital product passport (DPP) legislation. A DPP is publicly available digital information linked to all physical goods placed on the EU market or put into service. It is an enabler for sustainable products, the new norm in the EU, by making them last longer, using energy more efficiently, making them more accessible to repair and recycle, and containing fewer substances of concern and more recycled content [11].

The function and purpose of a DPP are simple to understand, yet the regulations, standardisation, and implementations provide many challenges for small and large companies. The production of a DPP will be based on many disparate (internal and external) data sources and flows inside an organisation. The publication of a DPP opens up challenges across sustainable supply chains, both upstream and downstream, where the new transparency of product information influences data sharing, sourcing, procurement, sales, recycling, and monitoring of regulatory compliance.

The Work-Oriented Approach to Information Products (WOA) is a novel artefact designed to address identified challenges with the representation, design, use, evolution and evaluation of information products (IP), such as the DPP, across information flows and networks of collaborating stakeholders in their practices [4, 5, 31].

The WOA provides a method and concepts that enrich the description and analysis of IP production, offers, fit, needs, and IP consumption in multi-stakeholder networks by incorporating practices and relationships in addition to the use of information. WOA, therefore, extends traditional methods based on use cases and information flows.

WOA specifically addresses challenges a) when a single information product does not suit different stakeholders in their practices when stakeholders collaborate, b) when stakeholders are not engaged in using IPs, and c) when there is a lack of detailed knowledge about practices and relationships between stakeholders that limits the understanding of collaborating stakeholders with diverse and specialised perspectives, interests, work, responsibilities, access to people and data, practices, information needs, use of IPs, goals and definitions of success. Furthermore, WOA strengthens and clarifies the evaluation of the co-use of IPs and the aggregated utility of collaborations.

This paper presents an industrial case study that empirically demonstrates the feasibility and applicability of applying the WOA in a challenging situation where product (lifecycle) information flows towards inclusion in Digital Product Passports.

The structure of the paper is. The background of DPP is described in Sect. 2.1, and WOA in Sect. 2.2. The Research and Case Method is described in Sect. 3, and the Case study in Sect. 4. Sections 5 and 6 conclude with discussions and conclusions.

## 2 Background

### 2.1 Digital Product Passport

A Digital Product Passport (DPP) is digital information attached to all physical goods placed on the EU market or put into service, including components and intermediate products [11]. It provides digital information that offers insights into a product's entire lifecycle. This encompasses details such as the materials utilised during its creation, the product's environmental footprint, ownership information, guidelines for responsible disposal, and essential warranty and maintenance data.

The regulations covering DPP are 2024 addressed by EU institutions [11] and EU standardisation organisations to establish a regulatory framework for a DPP system and DPP data. The *DPP System* is the IT standards and protocols required to ensure the interoperability of digital product passports, and *DPP data* is the information included in a DPP and accessible to different users based on their own respective access rights.

Delegated acts and action plans for 2027 and onwards are expected to cover different product categories, such as textiles, batteries and steel, with different DPP data [11].

The digital product passport-related research is new, with few peer-reviewed papers. A SCOPUS search in May 2024, with "digital product passport" in the title, abstract or keywords, resulted in 9 papers. Adding "information system" OR "information flow" OR "information management" OR "information stream" resulted in 1 paper [35].

The research focus is diverse, as exemplified by proposing a research agenda [35], identifying requirements [1], technical enablement for Industry 4.0 infrastructures and the rise of Industry 5.0 [36], and actors and value chains [7]. The spread in focus is expected due to the possible far-reaching consequences through the transparency of the product information across sustainable supply chains, both upstream and downstream.

The limited research covering both DPP and information management methods suggests there are knowledge gaps that the WOA can address. Within WOA and this paper, a Digital Product Passport is considered an Information Product (see Sect. 2.2).

### 2.2 Work-Oriented Approach to Information Products (WOA)

The Work-Oriented Approach to Information Products (WOA) offers a method and constructs to improve the analysis, explanation and evaluation of stakeholders' (possibly diverging) interests and co-use of information products (IP) [31]. This is done by emphasising that stakeholders' practices and relationships are major contributors to the aggregated utility of the co-use of information products [4, 5].

**WOA Constructs.** WOA provides three key groups of concepts, as illustrated in Fig. 1. *Firstly*, stakeholders' work in organisational settings is considered a practice. A practice is a way of doing something that involves stakeholders and information products in specific roles and can be used to represent the use of IP and other entities, responsibility, information needs, offerings of IPs, and other information needed to understand the use of IPs. The practices address the "what is in it for me" for stakeholders and their intention to use and actual use of IP in their daily work. The concept of practices can be seen as an enrichment of use cases by enabling the representation of all the knowledge that is needed to understand the use of IP. *Secondly*, relationships organise stakeholders' practices to represent collaborations in constellations where stakeholders produce, exchange, consume, and co-use knowledge and IPs for mutual benefits. The relationships provide a foundation for representing, analysing and evaluating how stakeholders' different perspectives fit each, practically and theoretically, the co-use of IPs and the aggregated utility of collaborations. *Thirdly*, the practices and relationships constitute parts of a situation to focus on within contexts, interpreted through one or more frames.

The WOA concepts enable the identification of important questions to be asked and addressed, improve the understanding of the nature of information products and their production and consumption, and the governance, management and control of the flow (production and consumption) of information (product) between people and/or machines within or between networks of organisations.

## Practice

- A *Stakeholder* is a type of *agent* that can bring about a change in the world. Agents can have their own points of view, responsibilities, interests, needs, goals, and access to people and data, which may lead to disagreement and conflicts.
- An *Information Product* represents a) a separately identifiable body of information that is produced, stored, and delivered for human and machine use, b) a participation in practices as a work product, and c) an offer to someone for a potential reward.
- A *Practice* represents a customary, habitual, or expected procedure or way of doing something [4, 8, 9, 24, 32]. A practice represents more than activities, such as responsibilities, questions that should be answered, access to data, Jobs to be done [34], experienced problems or pains [26], information needs [21], and the use of IP.
- Agents and information products *Participate* [30] in a practice in (thematic) roles.
- Agents, information parts/products, practices, and relationships are *specified* at the desired level of detail by *statements* representing concepts, propositions, and facts from one or more controlled languages [25].
- Each statement can be associated with the agent that has *stated* the statement.

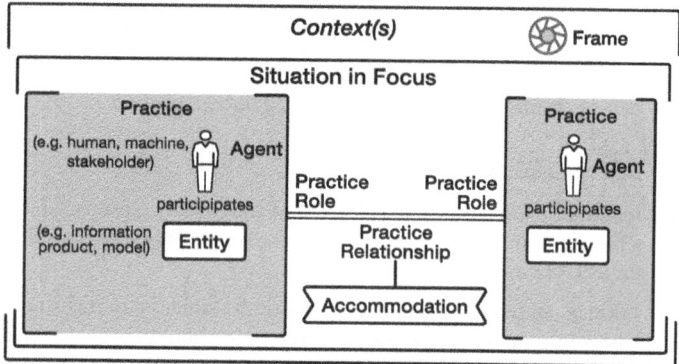

**Fig. 1.** Illustration of key WOA constructs and concepts

## Relationship and Role

- *Practice Relationship* represents the way in which two or more practices with their participating agents and entities are connected, interact or involve each other.
- *Practice Role* represents how a practice plays a part or assumes a function in a practice relationship.
- *Co-Use* represents the use of an information product in more than one practice.
- *Practice Accommodation* represents how practices in a relationship fit or are suitable or congruous, in agreement, or in harmony with each other [3]. The accommodation characterises a relationship with respect to a) (fit) which entities fit each other, b)

(mechanism) the specific ways a cause leads to some effect, a means leads to some ends, or how a feature satisfies a requirement [13, 15], or well as how a pain reliever satisfies a pain [26] and c) (effectuation) how the fit is (dynamically) achieved through actions over time.

**Situation, Context and Frame**

- A *Situation in focus* represents a situation that is the focus of attention and involves allocating effort and resources, such as a study, analysis, or design.
- A *Context* represents the facts or circumstances surrounding a situation. Two kinds are important to separate: contexts surrounding the project vs. the studied situation.
- A *Frame* represents the selection, emphasis and presentation of some facets or theories of events or issues with connections among them to promote a particular interpretation, evaluation and/or solution.

**WOA Method.** The WOA method consists of method chunks defined in the "A Situating Method for Improving the Utility of Information Products" [31] developed based on situational method engineering principles [20] and experiences from situating information products [33]. The WOA method chunks are designed to be included in methods constructed to suit specific projects and/or situations to focus on [31]. Table 1 summarises descriptions of relevant methods chunks and wireframe activities, and Sect. 4.1 describes the approach and method applied in this case study.

**Table 1.** Summary of WOA Method Chunks

| Method Chunk | Description |
| --- | --- |
| **Starting Point** (wireframe) | Identifies and clarifies the background and the key reasons behind the start of a project to inform, guide and direct the intended execution and to outline the project's relevance to the organisation |
| **Locate** | Locates, and establishes the contexts of the situation to focus on in the project where information (products) is invented, produced, exchanged and/or consumed within surrounding contexts [14, 17, 22] |
| **Frame** | Identifies factors and frames that influence the projects and the understanding, interpretation and addressing of the project and situation in focus. The method chunk supports active work with frames [14, 29] and enables a situational and constructionist approach with the notion that reality is not objective but rather socially constructed |
| **Characterise** | Characterises, analyses and represents the situation-in-focus with relevant work practices, with participating agents and information products, roles, and relationships between the work practices |
| **Ground** (new) | Identifies and represents the knowledge that the parts of the situation in focus depend on for their definitions or existence |
| **Retrospect** (wireframe) | Offers a space where participants in a project can discuss the project, results, the approach, document lessons learned, and (un-)learn |

The **WOA Ground** has been added after the definitions of the method chunks [31]. The seed for adding *grounding* came from applying WOA in other cases and the insight that IPs and practice are not typically defined separately but dependently on underlying knowledge clusters in larger contexts such as an organisation. In the WOA Ground, knowledge about underlying structures, concepts, facts, processes, material and information flows, rules, etcetera is identified that *influence the definitions and existence of information (products), practices, agents, and relationships in a situation in focus.*

## 3 Research and Case Method

This paper presents an industrial case study that aims to empirically demonstrate the feasibility and applicability of applying the WOA method and constructs. This research effort uses a design science research methodology, which is carried out to change the state of affairs by designing innovative artefacts. The applied research method by Peffers [27] follows the steps: 1. Problem identification and motivation, 2. Objectives of a solution, 3. Design and development, *4. Demonstration,* and 5. Evaluation.

The research addresses overall problems relating *to differences in perception and use across practices that may hamper the utility of information products over time.*

This includes challenges that appear in multi-stakeholder environments with networks of users of information products, where stakeholders may have different volitions or purposes, divergent interests, practices, goals, information needs, access to people and data, and can disagree, leading to potential conflicts, misalignment and diverging views of the aggregated utility of information products.

The Work-Oriented Approach [31] has been developed as a response to challenges [4, 5, 32] in the use of information products by collaborative stakeholders.

In the Peffers Demonstrate activity, artefacts are considered as expository instantiation [18] used to solve one or more instances of problems [27], thereby enabling an in-depth inquiry into an event within a real-life context.

### 3.1 Case Study Design

A case study is a methodology for design science research within the context of information system science since it studies a phenomenon in its natural setting [27, 28]. The case study design follows the guidelines of Runeson [28] and Benbasat et al [6].

The case study is descriptive and serves to improve the phenomenon studied [26], that is, the application and feasibility of the Work-Oriented Approach as a precursor to upcoming quantitative studies.

**Unit of Analysis.** A single case was purposefully selected: a large-scale organisation with multi-stakeholder challenges in its information flows and management. The study object was the application of WOA by a core team in a situation-in-focus where product information flows towards inclusion in a Digital Product Passport.

**Ethical Considerations.** The case study was performed according to the European Code of Conduct for Research Integrity [2]. A formal ethical review [12] was not deemed necessary. During the case study, no ethically significant situations occurred [19].

The principle of informed consent [10, 12] was applied, and the participants were informed about secrecy, professional secrecy, and confidentiality [12]. They consented to the purpose of the case study, the method used, how the results were expected to be used, that participation was confidential, anonymous, and voluntary, and that personal and study information would be kept in a secure location.

**Data Collection Method.** Multiple data collection methods were used in the case study, as described in Benbasat et al [6]. The data were circulated back to the participants to ensure the quality of the answers, and the results were used and synthesised in subsequent steps.

- **Direct Observation.** During workshops with the core team, observations were made on their work, their deliberations and questions, as well as their reflections on the workshop method. One of the participants kept a diary of the participants' feedback and raised questions and interesting topics for future discussions.
- **Interviews.** Interviews were performed with organisational stakeholders. A core team member participated in the interviews to listen in, gain insights into interviewees' responses, and act as a carrier of knowledge for the core team. The interviews lasted around 60 minutes, and the answers were made visible to all participants to ensure that the answers were correctly documented.

**Data Analysis.** After each workshop and interview, the written protocols with observations and answers were collected, qualitatively analysed and thematically coded [23].

**Reporting.** The results from workshops and interviews were collected, analysed and formative presented at the following workshops. At the end of the case study, in the WOA method chunk Retrospect, summative results, reflective discussions, and lessons learned were discussed by the core team. Finally, a seminar was conducted where summative results were presented to stakeholders outside the core team.

## 4 Industrial Case Study

The industrial case study was conducted at Sandvik Coromant, a global manufacturer of premium metal-cutting tools since 1942 that provides high-end services and machining technology in 150 countries with about 8000 employees worldwide, from January to March 2024. The company produces various metal-cutting tools for different application areas: Turning, Milling, Drilling, Boring, Tool holding, and Digital machining.

Sandvik Coromant manages over 1 million products and introduces thousands of new products to the market yearly. The production is mature and ISO 9001, ISO 14001 and ISO 45001 certified, supported by product, quality, environment, health and safety management systems, as well as by product management and ERP software systems.

Sandvik Coromant strives to take a leading position in sustainable business by reducing the impact of climate change, increasing resource efficiency through circularity, and using innovation and knowledge, leading to the interest in DPP.

At the centre of the case is the core Business Information Modelling Team (BIM), established in August 2023 as part of the line organisation. The BIM comprises information and product management experts tasked to harmonise and standardise product information related to business solutions. The vision is to enable corporate efficiency by establishing common usage and understanding of product-related business terms. The BIM team has been assigned to review the EU regulations regarding digital product passports. The project was an initial knowledge development project in preparation for larger organisational projects and prototyping.

Therefore, the case study provides a relevant context and challenges that an application of WOA addresses.

### 4.1 Case Study Approach

The case study was conducted by applying the WOA method chunks. At the start of the projects, an *approach* [16] with an intended method for the case study was constructed based on the available method chunks and wireframe activities [31].

The intended method instantiates, in order of execution, Starting Point, Locate, Characterise, Ground and Retrospect as activities as illustrated in Fig. 2. The Situate and Evaluate were omitted since the studied case is a knowledge development project.

The first three activities were conducted with the BIM team leader to start, scope and frame the project, and the last three were held in workshops with the whole BIM team. The workshops and interviews were conducted online using the MS Team and Miro software, which enables graphical discussions in participatory workshops. WOA provided canvases containing themes and talking points used as backdrops for structured discussion in Miro and as documentation of workshops. The OmniGraffle software was used after the workshops to create informative, structured diagrams and infographics, which had explanatory qualities that were not possible to achieve with Miro.

### 4.2 WOA Starting Point

The Starting Point activity focused on answering structured questions relating to the start of the project. At the centre was, what is the *situation to focus* on?

- What is the Seed and trigger for the change?
- What is the situation, and what are the questions to focus on?
- Where are you Now? Where have you Been? Where do you Want to Be?
- How do you Get There? What needs to be true? What hinders you?
- How do you know if you got there or not?
- What are the key Success and Failure Criteria? Key Stakeholder Values? Key Outcomes and Impacts? Key Assumptions and Risks?

The answers revolved around BIM's challenges with getting and reaching out with the information about their deliverables, i.e., common definitions and reference information models. The BIM team was working to establish a value proposition for their planned deliverables, such as the *COR Common Product Life Cycle*. Sustainability was a high priority for management, and the *Digital Product Passport* is part of an upcoming EU regulation. This opened questions about the information flows for the production and consumption of their planned information product COR Common Product Life Cycle and the flow to the production of Digital Product Passports.

The workshop resulted in an understanding of the reasons and expectations for the project and that WOA is suitable to address the situation in focus and raised questions.

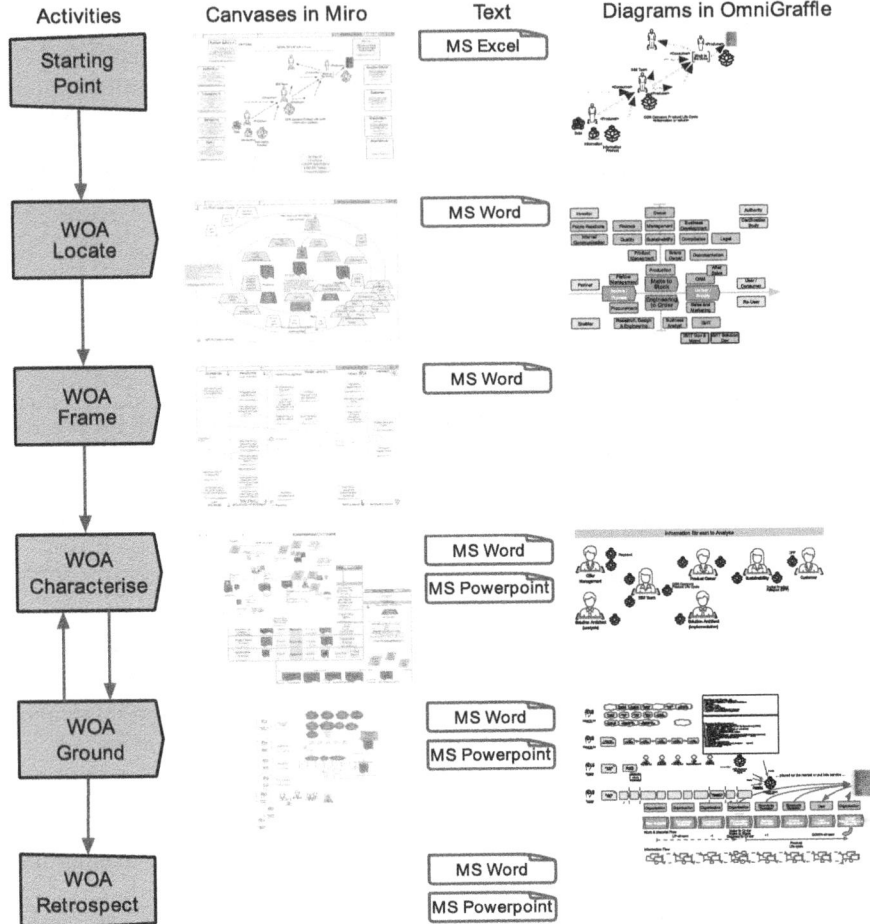

**Fig. 2.** Illustration of the applied process, tools and results from workshops and interviews.

### 4.3 WOA Locate Context

In this activity, key contexts of the situation in focus were located, the situation-in-focus from the starting point step was elaborated, and the stakeholders that could potentially be affected by the information products were identified.

For the project, 13 stakeholders were identified, of which 6 participated in the project in focus. For the overall situation to study, 22 stakeholders were identified, of which 6 participated directly in the situation in focus. An additional 24 internal and 7 external stakeholders that could potentially be affected by the DPP were identified.

## 4.4 WOA Frame

In this activity, the factors, premises and frames that influence the understanding, interpretation, and addressing of the project and the situation in focus were identified. Table 2 provides a description of key identified factors.

At the end of the workshop, the factors and themes were synthesised into two (2) frames, *Information Logistics* and *Business*, that provide lenses for the project.

**Table 2.** Identified key factors influencing the project and situation in focus.

| Categories of factors | Key Identified Factors |
| --- | --- |
| Project in focus | Use of the product-oriented terms but with different definitions |
| Project Context | All organisation units shall publish developed PlayBooks<br>Ongoing LCA and SAP implementation projects both use and influence product information definitions |
| Situation in focus | Many use the same terms but with different definitions |
| Situation Context | Loose collaborations with BIM teams<br>High focus on sustainability<br>More than 1 million products in product management systems |
| Premises | Products Lifecycles are important |
| Ways and Means | Wiki, Sparx Enterprise Modelling Tool |
| Themes | Information Logistics. Business (value proposition, pain, gain)<br>Organisational Information Management |

## 4.5 WOA Characterise

In this activity, the situation-in-focus was characterised and analysed based on the identified starting point, contexts, factors and frames. The activity was conducted two times, before the interviews and after the Ground activity. The starting situation in focus was narrowed down to a study with 6 internal stakeholders and their practices and a customer (not interviewed) forming an information flow as illustrated in Fig. 3.

Four (4) interviews were conducted with representatives of a select set of organisational stakeholders collaborating in the studied situation-in-focus to gather information about the stakeholders' views and their practices.

The interviews were guided by a structured questionnaire following key WOA concepts and the '*star*' *pattern*' used to visualise and analyse information logistics, with a single stakeholders' practice in the middle, surrounded by producers to the left and consumers to the right.

The Interviewees were asked about their *practices* (understanding of product (life cycle) information and DPP, what they do with this information, the utility of using the information, and their responsibilities relating to the information), *consumption* (who is providing this information, the features and utilities of this information, and if the

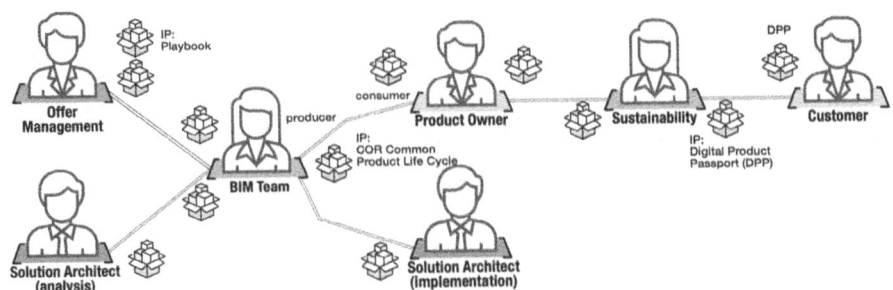

**Fig. 3.** OmniGraffle illustration of the information flow at the centre of the situation in focus.

qualities match their needs), *production* (for whom do they produce this information, what do the consumers do with the information, what features and utilities are offered to the consumers, does the information match the consumer's needs), and the *potential offering of the information product: "COR Common Product Life Cycle" model* (what features and utilities can it offer them, and from whom do they prefer to receive it).

The workshops and interviews generated discussions and questions that were anchored in the information flow and WOA concepts, as exemplified in the following list.

- How are product information terms and definitions shared?
- Who is responsible for standardising product information within Coromant?
- What kinds of product information are needed (concept type, category article, operational, batch, lot, items, lifecycle, lifecycle state, etc)?
- How do implementation in SAP and product management systems define information about products and their lifecycles?
- When is a product born, and when is the end of life (ala Coromant and EU)?
- How does life cycle assessment (LCA) treat product information about life cycles?
- Who works with what product (lifecycle) information?
- Where does the information about products come from (input)?
- Who is responsible for producing information about products (output)?
- Does the information produced fit the needs of the consumers?
- Do the consuming stakeholders understand and agree to use the information the BIM team currently offers or plans to offer?
- What are the value propositions and benefits of packaging information as IP?
- Have BIM team deliverables been packaged and offered as IP?
- What information is potentially restricted/public/required/optional in a DPP?
- What would an internal workflow that produces DPP look like?
- How does Coromant handle the value stream (upstream, downstream) with regard to the flow of product information outside of the organisation?
- How does Coromant handle downstream and circular information about products (end of life, reconfigure, repair, repurpose, etc)?

The step resulted in an improved understanding of and insights into the BIM team's vision, mission and value propositions regarding their current and planned production of information and the internal flow of the product information towards future DPPs.

## 4.6 WOA Ground

In this activity, the grounding knowledge that the elements of the situation in focus depend on for their definitions or existence was identified. A wide range of grounding concepts and flows was identified and organised into themes. The following list and Fig. 4 exemplify grounding knowledge themes.

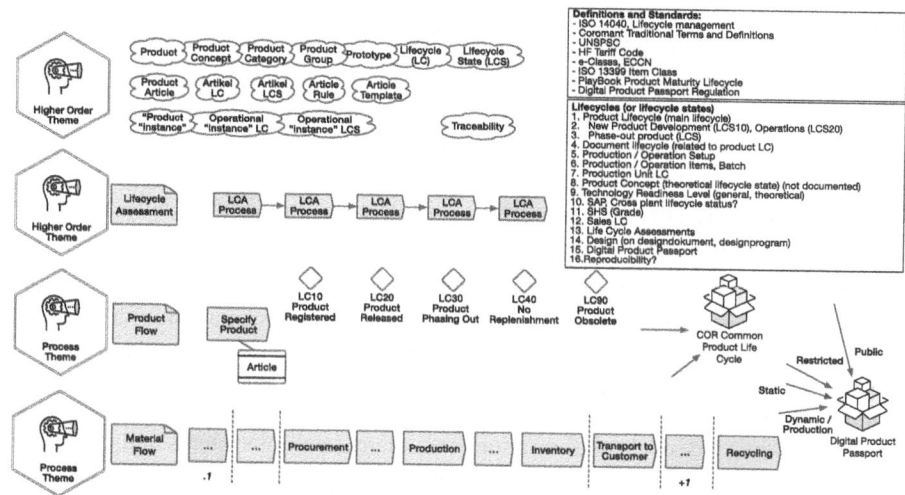

**Fig. 4.** OmniGraffle illustration of grounding knowledge.

- Existing product(lifecycle) concepts, definitions and standards.
- Traceability between definitions and across information flows.
- Lifecycle assessments of production processes, cradle to cradle.
- Product development and management lifecycles and lifecycle states that are or should be covered by the COR Common Product Life Cycle information product.
- Material and information flow supporting the production across value chains.
- Potential content of Digital Products Passports.
- Sources of public, restricted, static, and dynamic parts of Digital Products Passports.

The step resulted in an improved understanding of and gained insights into grounding knowledge that influences the definitions of product (lifecycle) information.

## 4.7 WOA Retrospect

In this activity, the project, its results, the application of the WOA, and learning points were summed up, discussed and documented.

The step resulted in an improved understanding of and insights into the project, application of WOA, situation in focus, and the influences of the project results on the BIM Team, Coromant, and the production of Digital Product Passports.

## 5 Discussions and Lessons Learned

This section presents thematically coded observations, diary and interview answers, lessons learned from applying WOA organised per WOA step, and general themes.

The **Starting Point, Locate,** and **Frame** steps were conducted with the BIM team leader, who perceived them as beneficial in understanding the project start, influencing factors, key stakeholders and focus. While the Frame step was a new kind of activity for the BIM team leader, it generated actionable insights into the situation in focus. The BIM team appreciated the Retrospect as an opportunity to summarise and look forward.

**Characterise:** The workshops and the interviews were considered to create awareness of the BIM team's internal workings, deliverables, potential information products, and the information flow feeding into DPP. The BIM team highly appreciated the structured interviews, based on WOA, with stakeholders about their views of the BIM team and its deliverables, the DPP. The interviews were considered neutral and friendly and a good tool for discussing complicated organisational dynamics and collaborations.

**Ground:** The grounding activity was considered an important activity that generated valuable discussions and questions that connected product information with lifecycles, product, and material flows in a visible and agreeable format, as outlined in Sect. 4.6.

While the step was a new kind of activity for the BIM team, it generated an understanding of the wide range of information that feeds into a DPP, static, dynamic, restricted and public product (lifecycle) information from many internal systems and definitions, and that a DPP is an extension of the Coromant view of product (lifecycle) information. The grounding brought to the surface 15 additional lifecycles and lifecycle states that were considered relevant in addition to the initial common product lifecycle.

*Theme:* **Raised questions:** The consensus among the BIM team was that the application of WOA raised valuable questions (as reported in Sects. 4.5 and 4.6) and generated insights that were relevant to their work and the integration with DPP.

*Theme:* **Discussion of information definitions vs. usage**: The Characterise and Ground steps generated considerable discussions about different kinds of product (lifecycle) information and its definitions. The focus was mostly on terms and definitions and less on what the information would be used for. The interviews and the WOA practices raised awareness that knowledge about who used what information for what needs is important to consider when producing useful information (products) for others. The interviews brought to the surface the usefulness of understanding stakeholders' potentially different views of the same kind of information.

*Theme:* **Productisation of Information**: The idea that key information could be produced and offered as an information product to consumers with information needs was difficult to incorporate into the BIM team's thinking and way of working. Their thinking and discussions were initially focused on the need for common terms and definitions. Also, the BIM team deliverable COR Common Product Life Cycle was not packaged or offered as an information product. Later, the interviews changed the teams' views and understanding of the differences between production and consumption, how product (lifecycle) information is perceived, received and used by others, and how packaging of information can improve discussions about terms and definitions.

**Lessons Learned on the Application of WOA.** The experienced BIM team was unfamiliar with a structured method that addresses information logistics similarly to WOA, which covered aspects beyond their normal work. The WOA was thus initially considered theoretical, but this view changed when WOA was practised in the workshops. This suggests that the enactment process of WOA into internal and existing ways of working or projects can be improved, partly for teams unfamiliar with thinking about practices, relationships between practices, differences between production and consumption, diverging points of view and delivery of information as products.

The experience using canvases was novel for the BIM team in their daily work but considered valuable tools for organising and visualising complex topics and questions.

The 'star pattern' used to organise the interview questions was considered a useful tool to visualise and analyse information flows from a single stakeholder's point of view, generate questions, and create positive climates in the interviews.

## 6 Conclusions

This paper presents an industrial case study that aims to empirically demonstrate the feasibility and applicability of applying the WOA method and constructs.

The purpose of the application of WOA was to develop knowledge for the BIM team about their situation where they work with the standardisation of product information and how this information can feed into future digital product passports.

The BIM team deemed the application successful and intends to incorporate WOA into their upcoming ways of working and for the definition of their value propositions.

Key results are that WOA a) generates valuable discussions and questions relating to information flows and information products, b) improves the awareness of the importance of discussing information in co-use by stakeholders in addition to discussing terms and definitions, and c) can add value by supporting the systematic formulation of information products which are offered to consumers to satisfy their information needs.

Therefore, it is deemed feasible to apply WOA to address challenging situations that involve information products and information flows between stakeholders.

In this project, the time allocated did not allow for a detailed study of the situation in focus, practices, relationships, accommodations and information products. However, it was considered sufficient for the project's purpose of knowledge development. Further case studies are planned to study aspects of WOA not covered by this study.

The idea of adding a method chunk where WOA is used to demonstrate and simulate stakeholders' practices, IPs, and networks was discussed as an addition to and improvement to WOA. Also, the question, "If you find spaghetti in the relationships and flow of information, what do you do?" suggests future work to identify patterns of larger relationships, practices, and information flows that can be used to simplify analysis.

## References

1. Adisorn, T., Tholen, L., Götz, T.: Towards a digital product passport fit for contributing to a circular economy. Energies **14**(8), 2289 (2021)
2. ALLEA. The European Code of Conduct for Research Integrity. Berlin (2023)
3. Tell, A.W., Perons, E., Henkel, M.: Using the Concept of Accommodation to Facilitate Problem-Solution Analysis. Baltic DB&IS 2024 (2024)
4. Tell, A.W., Henkel, M.: Enriching enterprise architecture stakeholder analysis with relationships. In: 22nd International Conference on Perspective in Business Informatics Research (BIR2023). Springer (2023)
5. Tell, A.W., Henkel, M.: Review of evaluations of enterprise architecture. In: Proceedings of the 19th International Conference on Evaluation of Novel Approaches to Software Engineering (ENASE 2024) (2024)
6. Benbasat, I., Goldstein, D.K., Mead, M: The case research strategy in studies of information systems. MIS Q. **11**(3), 369 (1987)
7. Berger, K., Baumgartner, R.J., Weinzerl, M., Bachler, J., Preston, K., Schöggl, J.-P.: Data requirements and availabilities for a digital battery passport - a value chain actor perspective. Clean. Prod. Lett. **4** 100032 (2023)
8. Bueger, C., Gadinger, F.: International Practice Theory: New Perspectives. Palgrave Macmillan (2014)
9. Clark, A.E., Friese, C., Washburn, R.S.: Situational Analysis: Grounded Theory After the Interpretive Turn. Sage Publications (2018)
10. Cohen, L., Manion, L., Morrison, K.: Research Methods in Education. Routledge, London (2018)
11. Union Council of the European. Proposal for a Regulation of the European Parliament and of the Council Establishing a Framework for Setting Eco-design Requirements for Sustainable Products and Repealing Directive 2009/125/EC (2024)
12. Council SR. Good Research Practice (2017)
13. Dorst, K.: The core of ,design thinking, and its application. Design Stud. **32**(6) (2011)
14. Dorst, K.: Frame Innovation: Create New Thinking by Design. MIT Press (2015)
15. Drechsler, A., Hevner, A.: Knowledge Paths in Design Science Research. Found. Trends Inf. Syst. **6**(3), 171–243 (2022)
16. European C, Directorate-General FDS. PM2 Project Management Methodology - Guide 3.1. Publications Office of the European Union (2023)
17. Friedman, A.L., Miles, S.: Developing stakeholder theory. J. Manag. Stud. **39**(1), 1–2 (2002)
18. Gregor, D.J., Shirley: The Anatomy of a Design Theory (2007)
19. Guillemin, M., Gillam, L.: Ethics, reflexivity, and ,"ethically important moments", in research. Qualit. Inquiry **10**(2) (2004)
20. Henderson-Sellers, B., Ralyte, J., Ågerfalk, P., Rossi, M.: Situational Method Engineering. Springer, Heidelberg (2014). https://doi.org/10.1007/978-3-642-41467-1
21. INCOSE. (2023). https://www.sebokwiki.org
22. Missonier, S., Loufrani-Fedida, S.: Stakeholder analysis and engagement in projects: from stakeholder relational perspective to stakeholder relational ontology. Int. J. Project Manag. **32**(7), 1108–1122 (2014)
23. Myers, M.D.: Qualitative Research in Business & Management. Sage Publications Ltd. (2009).
24. Nicolini, D.: Practice Theory, Work, and Organization: An Introduction. Oxford University Press (2012)
25. Group, O.M.: Semantics of Business Vocabulary and Business Rules (SBVR) v1.5. (2019)

26. Osterwalder, A., Pigneur, Y., Bernarda, G., Smith, A.: Value Proposition Design: How to Create Products and Services Customers Want. Wiley (2015)
27. Peffers, K., Tuunanen, T., Rothenberger, M.A., Chatterjee, S.: A design science research methodology for information systems research. J. Manag. Inf. Syst. **24**(3), 45–77 (2007)
28. Runeson, P., Höst, M.: Guidelines for conducting and reporting case study research in software engineering. Empiric. Softw. Eng. **14**(2), 131–164 (2009)
29. Schon, D.A., DeSanctis, V.: The reflective practitioner: how professionals think in action. J. Cont. High. Educ. **34**(3), 29–30 (1986)
30. Smith, B., Grenon, P.: Basic Formal Ontology (BFO) 2.0 (2019)
31. Tell, A.: A situating method for improving the utility of information products. In: 25th International Conference on Enterprise Information Systems (ICEIS), pp. 589–599. SciTePress (2023)
32. Tell, A.W., Henkel, M.: Capabilities and work practices - a case study of the practical use and utility. In: World Conference on Information Systems and Technologies, pp. 1152–1162. Springer, Cham (2018). https://doi.org/10.1007/978-3-319-77703-0_112
33. Tell, A.W., Henkel, M., Perjons, E.: A method for situating capability viewpoints. In: Řepa, V., Bruckner, T. (eds.) BIR 2016. LNBIP, vol. 261, pp. 278–293. Springer, Cham (2016). https://doi.org/10.1007/978-3-319-45321-7_20
34. Ulwick, A.W.: Jobs To Be Done: Theory To Practice. Idea Bite Press (2016)
35. Van Engelenburg, S., Rukanova, B., Ubacht, J., Tan, S.L., Tan, Y.-H., Janssen, M.: From requirements to a research agenda for governments governing reuse of critical raw materials in the circular economy. In: DG O 2022: The 23rd Annual International Conference on Digital Government Research, pp. 62–67 (2022)
36. Voulgaridis, K., Lagkas, T., Angelopoulos, C.M., Boulogeorgos, A.-A.A., Argyriou, V., Sarigiannidis, P.: Digital product passports as enablers of digital circular economy: a framework based on technological perspective. Telecommun. Syst. **85**(4), 699–715 (2024)

# Author Index

**A**
An Nguyen, Khuong  53

**B**
Bider, Ilia  209
Brunnbauer, Matthias  3
Buchmann, Robert Andrei  19

**C**
Carreno, Javier  53

**D**
Dehne, Ahmed  119
Dolha, Damaris Naomi  19

**F**
Fish, Andrew  53

**G**
Gal, Sven-Alexander  176
Ghiran, Ana-Maria  176
Görgen, Leon  68
Grabis, Jānis  135
Greger, Katharina  191
Griesch, Leon  68

**H**
Henkel, Martin  103

**I**
Ioannidou, Penelope  85

**J**
Jalali, Amin  225
Johannesson, Paul  225

**K**
Kirikova, Marite  162
Koutsopoulos, Georgios  85
Koutsouris, Dimitrios D.  85
Kraupša, Liene Ieva  162
Kvalberga, Dace  135

**L**
Levina, Olga  153
Lindeberg, Jöran  103
Luo, Zhiyuan  53

**M**
Matsopoulos, George K.  85
Möhring, Michael  191

**P**
Perjons, Erik  209, 225

**S**
Sandkuhl, Kurt  36, 68, 119
Svee, Eric-Oluf  103

**T**
Tell, Anders W.  242

**SPRINGER NATURE**

## GPSR Compliance

The European Union's (EU) General Product Safety Regulation (GPSR) is a set of rules that requires consumer products to be safe and our obligations to ensure this.

If you have any concerns about our products, you can contact us on ProductSafety@springernature.com

In case Publisher is established outside the EU, the EU authorized representative is:

Springer Nature Customer Service Center GmbH
Europaplatz 3
69115 Heidelberg, Germany

The manufacturer's authorised representative in the EU is Springer Nature Customer Service Centre GmbH, Europaplatz 3, 69115 Heidelberg, Germany. If you have any concerns regarding our products, please contact ProductSafety@springernature.com

Printed and bound by CPI Group (UK) Ltd, Croydon, CR0 4YY

25/03/2026

02078187-0013